Concept and Form

VOLUME 1, SELECTIONS FROM THE *CAHIERS POUR L'ANALYSE*

Edited by Peter Hallward and Knox Peden

VERSO

London • New York

First published by Verso 2012
In the Collection © Verso 2012
Chapters 1, 3 translation © Cécile Malaspina and Peter Hallward
Chapters 2, 5 translation © Christian Kerslake, revised by Peter Hallward
Chapter 4 translation © Jacqueline Rose
Chapters 6, 8 translation © Christian Kerslake, revised by Knox Peden
Chapters 7, 11 translation © Peter Hallward and Knox Peden
Chapter 9 translation © Zachary Luke Fraser with Ray Brassier
Chapter 10 translation © Robin Mackay with Ray Brassier
Chapter 12 translation © Christian Kerslake, revised by Steven Corcoran
Chapters 2 and 4 were reprinted in Jacques-Alain Miller, *Un Début
dans la vie* (Paris: Gallimard, 2002), and are translated with kind
permission of Gallimard.

Introduction © Peter Hallward 2012
Preface and editorial notes © Peter Hallward and Knox Peden

3 5 7 9 10 8 6 4 2

Verso
UK: 6 Meard Street, London W1F 0EG
US: 20 Jay Street, Suite 1010, Brooklyn, NY 11201
www.versobooks.com

Verso is the imprint of New Left Books

ISBN-13: 978-1-84467-872-3

British Library Cataloguing in Publication Data
A catalogue record for this book is available from the British Library

Library of Congress Cataloging-in-Publication Data
A catalog record for this book is available from the Library of Congress

Typeset in Minion by Hewer UK Ltd, Edinburgh
Printed in the USA

Contents

Preface

Concept and Form is a two-volume work dealing with the 1960s French philosophy journal the *Cahiers pour l'Analyse*. Volume One is made up of English translations of some of the most important texts published in the journal. The introduction to Volume One tries to reconstruct the general context in which the journal was produced, and sketches the main intellectual and political influences that shaped its work. Volume Two collects newly commissioned essays on the journal and interviews with people who were either members of the editorial board or associated with its broader theoretical project. The introduction to Volume Two situates the journal in the context of twentieth-century French rationalism and considers how its commitment to conceptual analysis shaped its distinctive approach to Marxism and psychoanalysis.

These two printed books are complemented by an open-access electronic edition of the *Cahiers*, produced by the Centre for Research in Modern European Philosophy (CRMEP) and hosted by Kingston University London, at cahiers.kingston.ac.uk. The Concept and Form website provides the original French texts in both html and facsimile pdf versions, substantial synopses of each article, discussions of the most significant concepts at issue in the journal, and brief entries on the main people involved with it, as well as full-length French versions of the interviews abbreviated and translated in Volume Two. The materials in these two printed volumes are also included on the website, and posted as pdfs on the Verso website. The website's search box and lists of concepts and names may serve to some extent as a substitute index for the books.

All the articles published in the *Cahiers* receive fairly thorough consideration in the Concept and Form website, but here space constraints have obliged us to include only those articles that seem to carry the most far-reaching theoretical implications (which serves to favour pieces by Miller, Badiou, Regnault and Milner) and that, at least in most cases, have not already been translated and published elsewhere (which serves to exclude articles by Lacan, Althusser, Foucault, Derrida, Irigaray, Leclaire, and Pêcheux). As anyone familiar with the original French texts can attest, these articles pose some formidable translation problems, and our attempts to solve them have drawn on a good deal of prolonged collaborative work; we are very grateful to the translators and to some of our bilingual friends for their help, in particular Patrice Maniglier, Alberto Toscano, Craig Moyes, Sinéad Rushe, Sebastian Budgen, Leslie Barnes, Peter Cryle, and Eric Hazan. Needless to say we assume responsibility for any errors that remain.

This project was made possible by a research grant awarded by the Arts and

Humanities Research Council (2006–2009). We would like to thank Christian Kerslake for all the work he did on the website and for preparing some of the translations, Ray Brassier for helping to revise material for the website and the book, and all the colleagues at the CRMEP who helped with various aspects of the project. We're especially grateful to Nick Balstone, Karl Inglis and Ali Kazemi for their technical work on the website, and to all those readers of the site who have helped to improve it.

Peter Hallward and Knox Peden

Abbreviations

CF1, CF2   *Concept and Form*, Volume 1 or 2.

CpA   *Cahiers pour l'Analyse*. A reference of the form 'CpA 6.2:36' is to page 36 of the second article in the sixth volume of the *Cahiers*, as listed in its table of contents (online at cahiers.kingston.ac.uk, and appended to this volume). Where an English translation for an article is available, inclusion of the English page number follows the French, after a forward slash. Numbers inside square brackets, set in bold type, refer to the original French pagination.

tm   Translation modified.

TN   Translator's note.

WORKS BY LOUIS ALTHUSSER

ESC   *Essays in Self-Criticism*, trans. Grahame Lock. London: New Left Books, 1976.

FM   *For Marx*, trans. Ben Brewster. London: New Left Books, 1969.

HC   *The Humanist Controversy and Other Writings 1966–67*, trans. G.M. Goshgarian. London: Verso, 2003.

LP   *Lenin and Philosophy and Other Essays*, trans. Ben Brewster. London: New Left Books, 1971.

PSPS   *Philosophy and the Spontaneous Philosophy of the Scientists*, ed. Gregory Elliott, trans. Warren Montag et al. London: Verso, 1990.

RC   [with Étienne Balibar] *Reading Capital* [1968 ed.], trans. Ben Brewster. London: New Left Books, 1970.

WORKS BY SIGMUND FREUD

SE   *The Standard Edition of the Complete Psychological Works of Sigmund Freud,* ed. James Strachey et al. London: Hogarth Press, 1953–1974, in 24 volumes. A reference of the form 'SE14:148' is to page 148 of volume 14.

WORKS BY JACQUES LACAN

E   *Écrits*. Paris: Seuil, 1966. *Ecrits*, trans. Bruce Fink, in collaboration with Héloïse Fink and Russell Grigg. New York: W.W. Norton, 2006.

References in the form 'E, 803/680' refer to the French/English pagination.

S   *Seminars* (1954–1980), in 27 volumes. A reference in the form 'S11, 278' is to page 278 of volume 11. References are to English translations where available. The published volumes have been edited by Jacques-Alain Miller; Cormac Gallagher has made available some draft English translations.

THE MAIN VOLUMES CITED INCLUDE:

- *Seminar I: Freud's Papers on Technique* [1953–54], trans. John Forrester. New York: W.W. Norton, 1988.
- *Seminar II: The Ego in Freud's Theory and Technique of Psychoanalysis* [1954–55], trans. Sylvana Tomaselli. New York: W.W. Norton, 1991.
- *Seminar III: The Psychoses* [1955–56], trans. Russell Grigg. New York: W.W. Norton, 1993.
- *Seminar V: The Formations of the Unconscious* [1957–58], trans. Cormac Gallagher, unpublished manuscript.
- Seminar *VII: The Ethics of Psychoanalysis* [1959–60], trans. Dennis Porter. London: Routledge, 1988.
- *Seminar VIII: Transference* [1960–61], trans. Cormac Gallagher, unpublished manuscript.
- *Seminar XI: The Four Fundamental Concepts of Psychoanalysis* [1963–64], trans. Alan Sheridan. London: Penguin, 1977.
- *Seminar XII: Crucial Problems for Psychoanalysis* [1964–65], trans. Cormac Gallagher, unpublished manuscript.
- *Seminar XIII: The Object of Psychoanalysis* [1965–66], trans. Cormac Gallagher, unpublished manuscript.
- *Seminar XIV: The Logic of Fantasy* [1966–67], trans. Cormac Gallagher, unpublished manuscript.

Peter Hallward
Introduction: Theoretical Training

'Do you think that our movement cannot produce heroes like those of the seventies? But why? Because we lack training? But we are training ourselves, we will go on training ourselves, and we will be trained!'[1]

The *Cahiers pour l'Analyse* was a journal edited by a small group of philosophy students at the École Normale Supérieure (ENS) in Paris. Ten issues of the journal appeared between 1966 and 1969, arguably the most fertile and productive years in French philosophy during the whole of the twentieth century. The *Cahiers* published major articles by many of the most significant thinkers of the period, including Louis Althusser, Jacques Derrida, Michel Foucault, Luce Irigaray, and Jacques Lacan, and many of the young ENS students and graduates involved in the production of the journal (notably Jacques-Alain Miller, Jean-Claude Milner, Alain Badiou, François Regnault, Yves Duroux and Jacques Bouveresse) were soon to become major figures in French intellectual life. The *Cahiers* was a 'youthful' and precocious venture in more ways than one, and no collective project did more to express the vaulting ambition and almost oracular quality of 'structuralist theory' in the run-up to the events of May 1968. Althusser himself was confounded by his students' brilliance, and considered people like Badiou and Duroux to be among the most promising thinkers of their generation; after listening to one of Miller's 'sensational exposés' of Lacanian theory, in January 1964, Althusser concluded that 'at just twenty-one years old, this kid is already smarter than most of the philosophers in France.'[2]

Oriented by a concern for scientific rigour and guided in particular by the teachings of Lacan and Althusser, the *Cahiers* privileged the analysis of formal structures and concepts in opposition to theories based on the categories of lived experience or on the conscious subjects of such experience. Although the label remains notoriously vague and contested, the *Cahiers'* project can be called 'structuralist' in the familiar sense of the term insofar as it attributes unilateral causal power to the relations that structure configurations of

---

1   V. I. Lenin (as 'N. Lenin'), *What Is to Be Done?*, in Lenin, *Collected Works* vol. 5 (Moscow: Progress Publishers, 1960), 447.
2   Louis Althusser, letter to Franca Madonia, 21 January 1964, in Althusser, *Lettres à Franca (1961–1973)* (Paris: Stock/IMEC, 1998), 505; cf. 472, 576. See also Althusser, letter to Hélène Rytman, spring 1966, in Althusser, *Lettres à Hélène (1947–1980)* (Paris: Grasset/IMEC, 2011), 472; Althusser, *The Future Lasts Forever*, trans. Richard Veasey (New York: New Press, 1993), 209.

elements, in whatever domain (mathematical, linguistic, psychological, economic, literary . . .), rather than accord primacy to the presumed nature or essence of these elements themselves, which are 'given' instead as effects of the structure.[3] Alongside and in partial rivalry with a more openly political editorial project at the ENS (the *Cahiers Marxistes-Léninistes*), the *Cahiers pour l'Analyse* were conceived as a contribution to the 'theoretical formation or training'[4] required for an adequate grasp of such 'structural causality'. This theoretical training was intended to provide its trainees with the tools required for the analysis of 'discourse' in the broadest sense, so as to enable, negatively, a critique of the various obstacles that might block such analysis (e.g. ideological illusions, humanist reflexes, empiricist temptations and other un-scientific presumptions), and positively, a clear understanding of the operations that structure complex social, psychological or epistemological configurations (e.g. the structuring operations that govern an economic mode of production or shape a configuration of class relations, a neurotic disposition or the organization of a domain of scientific inquiry). Making no concessions to the norms that might prevail within a given structured domain, the goal is to achieve a lucid command of these structuring operations so as to isolate their weakest and most vulnerable point, and thus to prepare the way for their transformation or re-structuration.[5]

If 'structuralism' is best understood along these conceptualizing and anti-humanist lines, then the *Cahiers* deserve to be recognized not only as 'the single most symptomatic, most ambitious and most radical manifestation of

---

3   As Gilles Deleuze observes, a structuralist approach assumes that 'the elements of a structure have neither extrinsic designation nor intrinsic signification', and that 'places in a purely structural space are primary in relation to the things and real beings which come to occupy them' (Deleuze, 'How Do We Recognise Structuralism?', in *Desert Islands and Other Texts*, ed. David Lapoujade, trans. Michael Taormina [Cambridge, Mass.: Semiotext(e), 2004], 173–174). By a 'system', Foucault explains along similar lines, 'we should understand a set of relations that maintain and transform themselves independently of the things they relate' (Michel Foucault, 'Entretien avec Madeleine Chapsal', *La Quinzaine Littéraire* 16 May 1966, in Foucault, *Dits et écrits*, vol. 1 [Paris: Gallimard, 1994], 514). One of the most influential accounts of structural linguistics, for instance, characterises its method in terms of 'four basic operations. First, structural linguistics shifts from the study of *conscious linguistic* phenomena to the study of their *unconscious* infrastructure; second, it does not treat *terms* as independent entities, taking instead as its basis of analysis the *relations* between terms; third, it introduces the concept of *system* – "modern phonemics does not merely proclaim that phonemes are always part of a system; it *shows* concrete phonemic systems and elucidates their structure"; finally, structural linguistics aims at discovering *general laws*' (Claude Lévi-Strauss, *Structural Anthropology*, trans. Claire Jacobson and Brooke Grundfest Schoepf [NY: Basic Books, 1963], 33, citing Nikolai Trubetzkoy). For Saussure and Trubetzkoy as for Lévi-Strauss, Barthes or Althusser, the priority is to understand the rules that govern synchronic combinations of elements in a structured system, rather than the historical genesis or derivation of these elements (see for instance Lévi-Strauss, *Structural Anthropology*, 279ff; RC, 68, 225, 247; François Wahl, *Qu'est-ce que le structuralisme?* [Paris: Seuil, 1968], 361; Jean-Claude Milner, *Le Périple structural* [Paris: Seuil, 2002], 122, 154–155, 195ff.).

4   The French word *formation* carries both connotations.

5   Cf. Wahl, *Qu'est-ce que le structuralisme?*, 12–13.

the structuralist project of the 1960s',[6] but also as the most significant collective anticipation of some of the themes that would soon be associated with 'post-structuralism' – an emphasis on precisely those aspects of a situation that remain un- or under-structured, on absence, lack, displacement, exception, indetermination, and so on.[7] Several of the themes explored in the journal, moreover, have in recent years gained new significance in ongoing debates in philosophy, psychoanalysis and political theory. While the theoretical priorities of the *Cahiers* were eclipsed in the practical aftermath of May 1968 and then dismissed in the late 1970s backlash against anti-humanism and *la pensée 68*, new developments in French philosophy and recent critical theory (signalled for instance by interest in the work of Alain Badiou and Slavoj Žižek) have restored some of the issues explored in the journal to the top of today's philosophical agenda. At the same time, as we will see in a moment, it is impossible to forget that the *Cahiers* was very much a creation of its place and time – the creation of a specific conjunction of students and teachers working in a unique academic institution, at a moment when student political mobilization was rapidly approaching an explosive threshold.

The *Cahiers* have so far been largely ignored in intellectual histories of the period,[8] and a general reconsideration of the journal and its legacy is long overdue. For reasons that are as much political as philosophical, after decades of retreat from revolutionary ambitions in both theory and practice, the time is ripe for a re-appraisal of the less compromised theoretical project of the mid 1960s – the project that would eventually combine Lacanianism with Maoism in the wake of May 68. Omission of the *Cahiers* and its legacy from the critical reception of recent French philosophy has also led to significant distortions in the reception of this philosophy abroad, including an exaggeration of the influence of neo-Nietzschean and neo-Heideggerian tendencies. This omission has

---

6   'The *Cahiers pour l'Analyse* in the sacred ENS on the rue d'Ulm was the most symptomatic emanation of the structuralist fervour of the sixties, in its unbounded ambitions, in its most radical scientistic experiments, in its most elitist appearance as an avant-garde/popular dialectic that claimed to speak in the name of the world proletariat, and which it used to legitimate the most terrorist and terrifying of theoretical practices. [. . .] It was this unharmonious mixture that inspired an entire generation of philosophers' (François Dosse, *History of Structuralism* vol. 1, trans. Deborah Glassman [Minneapolis: University of Minnesota Press, 1997], 283). Dosse describes the broad Althusserian project as enabling a 'paradoxical combination of an often mad political voluntarism – a desperate activism – and the notion of a subjectless process that resembled a mystical commitment' (299tm).

7   Cf. Wahl, *Qu'est-ce que le structuralisme?*, 189; Étienne Balibar, 'Structuralism: A Destitution of the Subject? *differences* 14:1 (2003), 10–11. In 1980, Vincent Descombes described the general 'effect' of structuralism concisely: 'deconstructions have taken the place of descriptions' (Descombes, *Modern French Philosophy* [Cambridge: Cambridge University Press, 1980], 77).

8   Whereas suitably detailed work has been done on journals like *Tel Quel* and *Les Temps Modernes*, the *Cahiers* are not even mentioned in the most substantial book-length histories of French philosophy in the twentieth century (Eric Matthews, *Twentieth-Century French Philosophy* [Oxford: Oxford University Press, 1996]; Gary Gutting, *French Philosophy in the Twentieth Century* [Cambridge: Cambridge University Press, 2001].

contributed to the lasting impression of an uncrossable gap between the analytic concerns of Anglo-American philosophy and a supposedly obscurantist continental tradition. A superficial glance at the contents of the *Cahiers* (included as an appendix to this volume) is enough to demonstrate that this divide is at least partly an illusion: its first article is entitled 'Science and Truth', and new articles on psychoanalysis, linguistics, logic and mathematics appear alongside translations of texts by thinkers like Cantor, Gödel and Russell, together with substantial commentaries of canonical figures like Aristotle, Galileo and Hume.

As even the most sceptical readers of 'French theory' will have to admit, what is first and foremost at stake here is the status of science, and in particular the capacity of science to penetrate the imaginary or ideological illusions that normally govern human experience. The best way to approach the *Cahiers*, I think, is as the most determined effort of its day to pursue the implications of Althusser's argument that 'from Plato to Lenin [. . .], by way of Cartesian philosophy, eighteenth-century rationalist philosophy, Kant, Hegel and Marx, the philosophy of science is much more than one part of philosophy among others: it is philosophy's *essential* part.'[9] And the best way to introduce the *Cahiers*' project, accordingly, is with a brief overview of the conception of science and epistemology that they came to defend and explore.

I THE SCIENTIFIC TURN

On balance, French philosophy in the 1940s and 50s was dominated by various combinations of phenomenology and existentialism, and thus by a broadly shared appreciation for the 'concrete' or 'lived' dimensions of experience. In this context, science *per se* could only figure as a secondary concern. Husserl and Heidegger remained primary points of reference in academic circles, humanist writers like Sartre, Merleau-Ponty and Camus shaped the broader philosophical discussion, and in their different contexts figures like Georges Politzer, Simone de Beauvoir, Henri Lefebvre, Frantz Fanon and Roger Garaudy shared a common emphasis on the experiential dimensions of human alienation, oppression and struggle. What was at stake, in a world ravaged by war and imperialism, was the 'realization of man'[10], the 'total realization of man'.[11] In line with the Soviet Party's partial turn away from Stalinism in 1956, and reflecting the apparent dissipation in affluent post-war Europe of the proletariat's revolutionary

---

9   Althusser, presentation of Pierre Macherey, 'Georges Canguilhem's Philosophy of Science: Epistemology and History of Science', in Macherey, *In a Materialist Way* (London: Verso, 1998), 161–162.

10   Maurice Merleau-Ponty, *Humanism and Terror* [1947], trans. John O'Neill (Boston: Beacon Press, 1969), 101–102.

11   Henri Lefebvre, *Dialectical Materialism* [1940], trans. John Sturrock (Minneapolis: University of Minnesota Press, 2009), 155.

vocation, French Marxist theory also tended to embrace a version of the human-ist priorities that dominated philosophical reflection more generally.[12]

Sartre was the most influential thinker of this period. His point of depar-ture, early and late, remained the self-illuminating clarity of consciousness and freedom, reworked in the 1950s on the basis of 'the translucidity of praxis to itself' (which is to say on the basis of 'nothing other than my real life').[13] Marxism remained the 'untranscendable philosophy of our time,'[14] Sartre acknowledged, but it had been too quick to slap pre-fabricated concepts onto the living drama of individual existence. 'Marxism ought to study real men in depth', he argued in his *Search for a Method* (1957), 'not dissolve them in a bath of sulphuric acid.'[15] His *Critique of Dialectical Reason*, published in the autumn of 1960, went to elaborate lengths to ground the 'intelligibility of history' on the basis of concrete human praxis, i.e. to account for social structures, revolutionary agency and bureaucratic degeneration in terms of freely chosen projects and the inertia of their consequences, such that 'structures are created by an activity which has no structure, but suffers its results as a structure.'[16]

But when Sartre came to the École Normale to discuss his *Critique* in April 1961, Jacques Rancière and other students in the audience were not impressed – 'it was more like a burial than a celebration.'[17] As Alain Badiou remembers, Sartre persisted with a 'genetic' approach to social complexity, 'he wanted to engender structures on the basis of praxis', but the attempt fell flat.[18] It was no longer plausible, at this stage of post-war history, to present social or economic structure (e.g. the class relations operative in a mode of production) as effect rather than cause. Sartre's presumption of an originary freedom and his uncom-promising insistence on the primacy of engagement and responsibility had struck a powerful chord during the period of resistance to Nazism and to French wars in Vietnam and Algeria; it was less convincing as a way of understanding the social constraints operative in a complex economy or the epistemological

---

12   Cf. Roger Garaudy, *Humanisme marxiste* (Paris: Editions sociales, 1957); Garaudy, *Perspectives de l'homme* (Paris: PUF, 1959); Mark Poster, *Existential Marxism in Postwar France* (Princeton: Princeton University Press, 1975), 27, 50–51, 126–127, 243; William Lewis, *Louis Althusser and the Traditions of French Marxism* (Lanham: Lexington Books, 2005), 161ff; Robert Geerlandt, Roger Garaudy and Louis Althusser, *Le Débat sur l'humanisme dans le Parti commu-niste français et son enjeu* (Paris: Presses Universitaires de France, 1978).

13   Jean-Paul Sartre, *Critique of Dialectical Reason* vol. 1 [1960], trans. Alan Sheridan-Smith (London: Verso, 1976), 74.

14   Sartre, *Critique of Dialectical Reason*, 822.

15   Sartre, *Search for a Method*, trans. Hazel Barnes (New York: Knopf, 1963), 43–44.

16   Sartre, 'Itinerary of a Thought' (1969), in *Between Existentialism and Marxism* (London: NLB, 1974), 55.

17   Jacques Rancière, 'Only in the Form of Rupture', CF2, 263.

18   Badiou, 'Theory from Structure to Subject', CF2, 278; cf. Althusser and Balibar, RC, 172–173, 253. As Althusser put it in a lecture at the ENS in 1966, 'Sartre is alive and kicking, combative and generous, but he does not teach us anything about anything' and 'will not have any posterity whatsoever: he is already philosophically dead' (HC, 8).

constraints operative in intricate fields of scientific inquiry. Soviet communism had degenerated into a form of bureaucratic inertia, and bourgeois Europe appeared more or less impervious to radical social change. The experience of the solitary individual began to appear trivial in relation to forces operating at 'deeper' levels, be they geographical, unconscious, economic, anthropological . . . We admire Sartre's courage, Foucault explained in the spring of 1966, but 'our present task is to liberate ourselves definitively from humanism' and to embrace our *own* passion, 'the passion of the concept.'[19] Althusser made the point more vigorously: 'it is impossible to *know* anything about men except on the absolute precondition that the philosophical myth of man is reduced to ashes' (FM, 230). More and more, people who – like most of the future editors of the *Cahiers* – shared Sartre's radical political objectives turned away from his philosophical approach, away from an emphasis on freedom and the subject and towards analyses of social and cultural complexity, analyses that required more elaborate conceptual resources and thus more systematic reference to science and the history of the sciences.

Claude Lévi-Strauss anticipated the broader shift in priorities when he rejected the 'continuity between experience and reality' assumed by phenomenology, concluding that 'to reach reality we must first repudiate experience.'[20] His assault on Sartre's *Critique* also marked a watershed. 'I believe the ultimate goal of the human sciences to be not to constitute but to dissolve man,' he argued, so as to clear a space for a more adequate account of the way fundamental structuring and ordering principles (e.g. the configuration of kinship relations, the projection of meaningful patterns onto social differences or elements in the environment, etc.) that shape human behaviour.[21] Althusser, Foucault, Deleuze and Lacan were already making versions of a similar argument. Militant determination and class consciousness no longer seemed adequate to the task of changing a complex mode of production 'structured in dominance'; introspective or reflexive awareness was not an adequate approach to understanding the shifting boundaries of sanity and insanity, or for expressing the 'will to power' at work in hierarchical social and psychological configurations; only suitably detached analysis appeared to offer any genuine understanding of the

---

19   Foucault, 'Entretien avec Madeleine Chapsal', 514. 'The breaking point came when Lévi-Strauss, in the case of societies, and Lacan, in the case of the unconscious, showed us that "meaning" was probably no more than a superficial impression, a shimmer, a foam, and that what was really affecting us deep down inside, what existed before us, and what was supporting us in time and space, was *system*. [. . .] The "I" has exploded', in favour of the impersonal pronoun 'one [*on*]'. 'In a certain sense we thus go back to the viewpoint of the seventeenth century, but with this difference: it is not man we set in the place of God, but anonymous thinking, knowledge without subject, theory without identity' (514–515).

20   Lévi-Strauss, *Tristes Tropiques*, trans. John Russell (London: Hutchinson, 1961), 62.

21   Lévi-Strauss, 'History and Dialectic', in *The Savage Mind* (Chicago: University of Chicago Press, 1966), 246–247.

unconscious drives at work in the psyche. Radical change was only viable if it went to the roots of what must be changed, to the structures that govern a mode of producing, speaking or thinking. On all fronts, in short, the priority was now less to explore the dimensions of lived experience than to analyse the causal mechanisms that generate such experience, and the subjects of such experience, as their effect.

By the time this project took hold in the ENS, in the early 1960s, many of the theoretical pieces required for a more general turn to science were already in place.[22] The founding texts of structural linguistics (Saussure, Trubetzkoy and Jakobson) were published between the wars, as were fundamental developments in set theory and mathematical logic; although their careers were cut short by the war, Jean Cavaillès and Albert Lautman distilled some of the implications of these developments for French audiences, before the Bourbaki group undertook a more systematic formalization of mathematics as a whole. In the 1920s, Georges Dumézil began working on his 'trifunctional' (sacral, martial, economic) account of early Indo-European societies. In the 1930s, Bachelard and Koyré demonstrated the discontinuous and relatively autonomous logic of scientific discovery, reconstructing the abrupt reconfigurations of knowledge associated with names like Galileo, Lavoisier or Einstein; in the 1940s, Canguilhem began similar research in the life sciences and psychology. Lévi-Strauss's *Elementary Structures of Kinship* appeared in 1948. The following year, Fernand Braudel – marked, like Althusser, by his experience of defeat and isolation as a German prisoner of war – published his seminal account of the early modern Mediterranean world, one shaped primarily by geographic and social forces operating on a scale and at a pace incompatible with any sort of 'experience' at all.[23] By the mid 1950s, Lévi-Strauss had distilled the broader principles of a 'structural study of myth', and Roland Barthes had begun a parallel investigation of the 'mythologies' guiding the contemporary world of spectacle and consumption.

A year before his execution by a German firing squad, Cavaillès anticipated the conclusion that would become a commonplace of his structuralist admirers in the 1960s: since 'consciousness' is no clearer a notion than is the vague representation of a 'thing', 'it is not a philosophy of consciousness but only a philosophy of the concept that can yield a true doctrine of science.'[24]

The general principle at stake in this appeal to science was at least as old as the one that motivated Plato's 'second voyage', the self-reliant voyage of true

---

22   Cf. Badiou, 'Theory from Structure to Subject', CF2; Milner, *Le Périple structural*, 37 and passim.

23   Fernand Braudel, *The Mediterranean and the Mediterranean World in the Age of Philip II* [1949], trans. Siân Reynolds (New York: Harper & Row, 1972).

24   Jean Cavaillès, *Sur la logique et la théorie de la science* [1946] (Paris: Vrin, 1997), 90.

understanding: since what is initially given through experience and the senses proves unreliable, genuine knowledge must set out to establish itself on strictly intelligible principles, liberated from deceptive appearances and partial approximations.[25] The dominant phrase at the ENS in the early 60s, as Yves Duroux remembers, became the '*detour*' of science, on the assumption that any attempt at a direct or immediate engagement with the 'hard reality' of the world is doomed to futility.[26] The alternative to this detour, as much from a Platonist as from an Althusserian perspective, was to settle for ignorant immersion in 'the false obviousness of everyday practice' (RC, 96), 'the obvious facts of everyday life, which are given and imbued with the self-evidence of ideology' (HC, 276). As Althusser argues in his own essay on 'Theoretical Training' (of April 1965), 'far from reflecting the immediate givens of everyday experience and practice, [a science] is constituted only on the condition of calling them into question, and breaking with them.'[27]

At the École Normale, Althusser taught the history of philosophy in terms of this emancipatory detour away from the given and towards truth. After Plato, after Galileo and the scientific revolution, Spinoza anticipated the essential step that would later be consolidated by the structuralist reading of Marx: Spinoza recognized the 'opacity of the immediate' (RC, 16), and thus the essential difference between the merely given, experienced object (the object of unreliable opinion and imagination) and the *constructed* 'object of knowledge or essence' (the object of true insight).[28] An adequate idea is not one that corresponds to what appears as given, but rather one that – like the idea of a circle or triangle – constructs the object that it thinks. Scientific truth thus establishes itself by its own standard, *sui generis*, independently of mere 'verification' in the domain of experience.[29]

In keeping with the thrust of Spinoza's geometric approach, the great mathematical innovations of the nineteenth century were paradigmatic of the sort of epistemological independence at issue here, i.e. the independence

---

25   Plato, *Phaedo*, 99d; cf. Seth Benardete, *Socrates' Second Sailing: On Plato's Republic* (Chicago: University of Chicago Press, 1989), 2, 31.

26   Yves Duroux, 'Strong Structuralism, Weak Subject', CF2, 198.

27   Althusser, 'Theory, Theoretical Practice and Theoretical Formation [*formation*]', PSPS, 14–15tm; cf. RC, 41, 172, 194–195.

28   RC, 40. As Gaston Bachelard puts it, what is at issue in science is an 'object without a direct realist value in ordinary experience, or an object which has to be designated as a secondary object, an object preceded by theories' (Bachelard, *Le Matérialisme rationnel* [Paris: PUF, 1953], 142). According to Roland Barthes, 'the goal of all structuralist activity, whether reflexive or poetic, is to reconstruct an "object" [through 'dissection' and 'articulation'] in such a way as to manifest thereby the rules of functioning (the "functions") of this object'; in this general sense, 'the object of structuralism is not man endowed with meanings, but man fabricating meanings' (Barthes, 'The Structuralist Activity', in *Critical Essays*, trans. Richard Howard [Evanston: Northwestern University Press, 1972], 214, 218).

29   RC, 59, 102; cf. FM, 78n.40; ESC, 122, 132–141.

central to the accounts of science defended by Bachelard and Cavaillès and then embraced as an article of faith by Althusser and his students. From Euclid through to Descartes and Newton, the science of geometry had been based on the 'naïve' presumption that what it described in its idealized terms of points, lines, planes and so on was the actual reality of three-dimensional space and physical extension themselves. The non-Euclidean geometries developed by Lobachevsky and Riemann in the mid-nineteenth century, however, presented a multitude of coherent but thoroughly counter-intuitive spaces comprising any number of dimensions, such that geometric axioms had to be recognized to be irreducibly relative to a particular *model* of space, rather than a formal description of 'actual' or intuitable space. The broader formalist or anti-intuitionist revolution in mathematics spurred by Georg Cantor in the 1870s and then consolidated by Hilbert in Germany and by Cavaillès in France proceeded along comparable lines: where Frege, for instance, had wanted to define geometric objects like points or lines in terms that correspond to a given property or entity, Hilbert insisted on the sufficiency of axiomatic principles applied to terms whose own 'reality' is of no consequence for the application of the principles.[30] The Bourbaki group went on to define a 'mathematical structure' on this basis, as the rigorous application of axiomatic consequences to 'unspecified' elements, 'forbidding oneself any other hypothesis concerning the elements under consideration (and especially any hypothesis with regard to their particular "nature")'.[31] Althusser subsequently adopted the implications of this point as the organizing principle of his whole pedagogical project:

> No mathematician in the world waits until physics has *verified* a theorem to declare it proved, although whole areas of mathematics are applied in physics: the truth of his theorem is a hundred per cent provided by criteria purely *internal* to the practice of mathematical proof [. . .]. We can say the same for the results of every science: at least for the most developed of them, and in the areas of

---

30   According to Hilbert, any attempt to define a point, for instance, in terms of an actual entity that has no parts or that has the property of being extensionless, say, invites extra-mathematical confusion: 'one is looking for something one can never find because there is nothing there; and everything gets lost and becomes vague and tangled and degenerates into a game of hide and seek.' Any genuine 'theory is only a scaffolding or schema of concepts together with their necessary relations to one another, and the basic elements can be thought of in any way one likes. If in speaking of my points, I think of some system of things, e.g., the system love, law, chimney-sweep . . . and then assume all my axioms as relations between these things, then my propositions, e.g., Pythagoras' theorem, are also valid for these things' (Hilbert, letters to Frege, 27 and 29 December 1899, in Gottlob Frege, *Philosophical and Mathematical Correspondence*, ed. Brian McGuinness, trans. Hans Kaal [Oxford: Blackwell, 1980], 39–40).

31   Nicolas Bourbaki, 'The Architecture of Mathematics' [1948], *The American Mathematical Monthly* 57:4 (April 1950), 226tm.

knowledge which they have sufficiently mastered, they themselves provide the criterion of validity of their knowledges.[32]

Between Hilbert and Althusser, two of the most important steps along the detour through theory that was to shape the trajectory of the *Cahiers pour l'Analyse* were taken by Bachelard and Canguilhem. In the summer of 1966, Althusser applauded their work in particular as an essential contribution to the defence of rationalism and science against a 'profoundly reactionary' spiritualist tradition stretching from Maine de Biran to Bergson and his followers; Foucault and then Badiou later proposed versions of a similar antagonism as the structuring principle of contemporary French philosophy in general.[33]

Before Althusser, Gaston Bachelard offered the most trenchant refutation of the view that science proceeds as some sort of gradual, cumulative clarification of ordinary experience or 'common knowledge', coloured as these are by all sorts of prejudice, affective association and unconscious investment. Whereas the connoisseur of common knowledge tries to 'live' tangible 'quality in its essence, as one tastes a fine wine',[34] in his first major work Bachelard condemned any presumption of 'adequation between thought and experience' as an 'epistemological monstrosity'.[35] Experience is 'opinionated' and deluded by definition,

---

32   RC, 59–60; cf. Balibar, 'From Bachelard to Althusser: The Concept of "Epistemological Break"', *Economy and Society* 7:3 (August 1978), 211.

33   Althusser, 'The Philosophical Conjuncture and Marxist Research' [26 June 1966], HC, 5. Foucault likewise sees a general 'dividing line' running through the various other oppositions that shape the field of modern French philosophy, 'one that separates a philosophy of experience, of meaning, of the subject, and a philosophy of knowledge, of rationality, and of the concept. On one side, a filiation which is that of Jean-Paul Sartre and Maurice Merleau-Ponty; and then another, which is that of Jean Cavaillès, Gaston Bachelard, Alexandre Koyré, and Canguilhem.' Foucault also considers the political dimension of this distinction, in terms that shed light on the *Cahiers*' relation to May 68. 'On the surface, the second [filiation] remained the most theoretical, the most geared to speculative tasks, and the farthest removed from immediate political inquiries. And yet, it was this one that during the [second world] war participated, in a very direct way, in the combat, as if the question of the basis of rationality could not be dissociated from an interrogation concerning the current conditions of its existence. It was this one, too, that in the sixties played a crucial part in a crisis that was not just that of the university, but also that of the status and role of knowledge. One of the main reasons [for this] appears to lie in this: the history of the sciences owes its philosophical standing to the fact that it employs one of the themes that entered, somewhat surreptitiously and as if by accident, the philosophy of the seventeenth century. During that era, rational thought was questioned for the first time not only as to its nature, its basis, its powers and its rights, but as to its history and its geography, its immediate past and its conditions of exercise, its time, its place, and its current status' (Michel Foucault, 'Life: Experience and Science', trans. Robert Hurley, in *The Essential Works*, vol. 1: *Aesthetics, Method, and Epistemology*, ed. James D. Faubion [London: Penguin, 1998], 466–469). Cf. Badiou, *Gilles Deleuze: The Clamor of Being*, trans. Louise Burchill (Minneapolis: University of Minnesota Press, 2000), 98–99; Elisabeth Roudinesco, 'Canguilhem: A Philosophy of Heroism', *Philosophy in Turbulent Times*, trans. William McCuaig (NY: Columbia University Press, 2008), 1–32.

34   Bachelard, *Le Matérialisme rationnel*, 62.

35   Bachelard, *Essai sur la connaissance approchée* (Paris: Vrin, 1928), 43.

and science cannot proceed as the refinement of delusion or non-knowledge as such. Science can only begin with a principled *break* with experience and 'sensory knowledge', a *rupture épistémologique* that enables a rational, self-recti-fying explanation of problems that are not given in or even accessible to lived experience, however 'intimate' or 'authentic' its phenomenological elucidation might be.[36] Once we abandon 'unthinking' opinion and move over to the scientific side of this epistemological break, 'nothing is self-evident, nothing is given, everything is constructed,' on the model of that mathematical knowledge that founds all 'physical explanation.'[37] Because science can only begin through rejection of the self-perpetuating illusions of pre-scientific experience, the 'formation' or *training* of the scientific mind requires nothing less than a 'conversion', a denial or 'destruction' of non-scientific habits and a replacement of the 'interests of life' with the exclusive 'interests of the mind.'[38]

On the basis of the break that initiates it, science can then assert its objectivity as an inaugural 'fact', and it's only on the basis of this assertion, Bachelard argues, that science can begin to grasp its own development and history.[39] Having broken with lived experience, this history is itself punctuated by the breaks ('mutations', 'recastings', 'revolutions', etc.) that separate one scientific mindset [*esprit*] from another, e.g. Galileo from Aristotle, Einstein from Newton or Lavoisier from Priestley.[40] 'Scientific progress always reveals a rupture, constant ruptures, between common knowledge and scientific knowledge', and 'all knowledge at the moment of its construction is a polemical knowledge; it

---

36   Bachelard, *The Formation of the Scientific Mind: A Contribution to a Psychoanalysis of Objective Knowledge* [1938], trans. Mary McAllester Jones (Manchester: Clinamen, 2002), 111, 237; Bachelard, *L'Activité rationaliste de la physique contemporaine* (Paris: PUF, 1951), 10. 'Scientific objectivity is possible only if one has broken first with the immediate object [. . .]. Any objective examination, when duly verified, refutes the results of the first contact with the object. To start with, everything must be called into question [. . .]. Far from marvelling at the object, objective thought must treat it ironically' (Bachelard, *The Psychoanalysis of Fire* [1938], trans. Alan Ross [Boston: Beacon Press, 1964], 1–2).

37   Bachelard, *The Formation of the Scientific Mind*, 25tm, 229; cf. 237–238.

38   Bachelard, *The Philosophy of No: A Philosophy of the New Scientific Mind* [1940], trans. G. C. Waterston (New York: Orion Press, 1968), 8–9; *The Formation of the Scientific Mind*, 248. Cf. Bachelard, 'Rationalism and Corrationalism', trans. Mary Tiles, *Radical Philosophy* 173 (May 2012).

39   Dominique Lecourt summarizes 'the philosophical thesis that underpins all of Bachelard's epistemological work: the truth of a scientific truth "*imposes itself*" by itself. In Spinozist terms: *veritas norma sui* (the truth is its own measure). In Leninist terminology: Bachelard is posing the thesis of the objectivity of scientific knowledges. He is posing it, not discussing it. He does not seek to found, to *guarantee* this objectivity. He is not concerned to pose to scientific knowledge the traditional question of its claims to validity' (Lecourt, *Marxism and Epistemology: Bachelard, Canguilhem, and Foucault*, trans. Ben Brewster [London: NLB, 1975], 12).

40   Bachelard, *The New Scientific Spirit* [1934], trans. Arthur Goldhammer (Boston: Beacon Press, 1984), 43, 54; *The Philosophy of No*, 52. Cf. Balibar, 'From Bachelard to Althusser: The Concept of "Epistemological Break"', 208.

must first destroy to clear a space for its constructions.'[41] Again, the criteria that validate a new break or rectification are determined not through approximation with lived experience but through relative adequation to previously undetected structures and complexity, and are thus 'guided by a kind of autonomous necessity.'[42] The *Cahiers pour l'Analyse*, like Althusser before them and Badiou after them, are an emphatic affirmation of the new theoretical horizons that may open up on the basis of an epistemological break in this sense.

Following Bachelard, Georges Canguilhem insists that 'science explains experience'[43] and that this explanation advances across discontinuous leaps and breaks, rather than as a gradual and progressive 'recapitulation' of accumulated certainties. Again, the objects of science are not given in nature or experience but are expressly constituted by scientific practices themselves,[44] through purification, manipulation, experimentation and so on, such that only science can provide the criterion for any genuine knowledge. 'Knowledge which is not scientific is no knowledge at all.'[45] One of the main things that Canguilhem adds to this Bachelardian valorization of science is a sharper distinction between *concepts* on the one hand and explanatory frameworks or *theories* on the other. Concepts – for instance the concept of motion in classical physics, or the concept of a reflex action in early modern physiology, or the biological concept of a cell – have a history of their own, one that is deeper than and relatively independent of the various theories subsequently devised to account for them. (Contrary to retrospective assumptions, for instance, the concept of reflex was not the product of mechanistic theories of natural causality widely accepted in the seventeenth century, but actually arose, with Thomas Willis, in a vitalist context[46]). A concept emerges as a problem that invites competing theoretical solutions, and from one

---

41   Bachelard, *Le Matérialisme r   nnel*, 207; Bachelard, *La Dialectique de la durée* (Paris: Boivin, 1936), 14.

42   Bachelard, 'Epistemology and ⁀he History of the Sciences' [1951], *Phenomenology and the Natural Sciences*, ed. Joseph Kockelmans and Theodore Kisiel (Evanston,: Northwestern University Press, 1970), 345. For Bachelard, 'every particular science produces at each moment of its history its own norms of truth' (Lecourt, *Marxism and Epistemology*, 164). Or as Althusser will argue: science per se is not part of the 'superstructural' components of a society (and thus not subject to the 'common fate' of historico-economic change that transforms both structure and superstructure) but rather, on account of the epistemological break that inaugurates it, a self-validating discourse that prescribes for itself a 'new form of historical existence and temporality' (RC, 133).

43   Georges Canguilhem, *The Normal and the Pathological*, trans. Carolyn R. Fawcett (New York: Zone Books, 1989), 198.

44   'Every science more or less gives itself its given' (Canguilhem, 'What is Psychology', CpA 2.1:78).

45   Canguilhem, interview with Alain Badiou, 1965, cited in Balibar, 'Science et vérité dans la philosophie de Georges Canguilhem', in *Georges Canguilhem, Philosophe, historien des sciences* (Paris: Albin Michel, 1993), 58–59.

46   Canguilhem, *La Formation du concept de réflexe aux XVIIe et XVIIIe siècles* (Paris: PUF, 1955), 66.

explanation to another 'the problem itself persists.'[47] As Althusser's student Pierre Macherey puts it, in one of the first studies of Canguilhem's work, 'the birth of a concept is thus an absolute commencement: the theories which are its "consciousness" only come after.' A philosophy of the concept would in this sense be 'the science of problems independent of their solution.'[48] A science thus proceeds – always at the risk of slipping into 'ideological' generalizations beyond its legitimate domain – on the basis of an ongoing and relatively autonomous pursuit of the problem as such, or as the 'critical rectification' of the explanations it proposes for the concepts it works or works on.[49] 'To work a concept [*travailler un concept*]', as Canguilhem put it in a text that would be reprinted at the front of every volume of the *Cahiers*, 'is to vary its extension and comprehension, to generalise it through the incorporation of exceptional traits, to export it beyond its region of origin, to take it as a model or on the contrary to seek a model for it – to work a concept, in short, is progressively to confer upon it, through regulated transformations, the function of a form.'[50]

II ALTHUSSER

What students at the ENS in the early 1960s found in Louis Althusser, first and foremost, was a comparable but more extreme, more uncompromising (and by all accounts more exhilarating) affirmation of science. Althusser assumes that whereas a 'reactionary bourgeois' establishment 'prefers half-knowledge in all things, the *revolutionary* cause, on the contrary, is always indissolubly linked with knowledge, in other words *science*.'[51] Given the importance of these political stakes, what is at issue is a yet more abrupt and intransigent 'passage from ignorance to knowledge.'[52] Building on Marx's

---

47   Canguilhem, *The Normal and the Pathological*, 76.

48   'Passing behind the accumulation of theories and responses, history is really *in search of forgotten problems, up to their solutions*' (Macherey, 'Georges Canguilhem's Philosophy of Science: Epistemology and History of Science', in Macherey, *In a Materialist Way*, 177). Or in Althusser's terms: 'the theory of a science at a given moment in its history is no more than the *theoretical matrix of the type of questions* the science poses its object' (RC, 155); cf. Patrice Maniglier, 'What is a Problematic?', *Radical Philosophy* 173 (May 2012).

49   Canguilhem, *Idéologie et rationalité dans l'histoire des sciences de la vie* (Paris: Vrin, 1981), 21. On Althusser's 'incalculable debt' to Canguilhem see his 'Letter to the Translator', FM, 257.

50   Georges Canguilhem, 'Dialectique et philosophie du non chez Gaston Bachelard', *Revue Internationale de Philosophie* 66 (1963), 452; cf. Jacques-Alain Miller, 'Action de la structure', CpA 9.6:94.

51   Althusser, 'Problèmes étudiants', *La Nouvelle Critique* 152 (January 1964), 94.

52   HC, 265. The further and peculiar privilege of Marx's discovery of a 'new scientific continent' (through historical materialism), is that it also includes an account of the history of knowledge itself, i.e. (through dialectical materialism) a theory of 'the *process of production of knowledge*' in general (PSPS, 8; cf. Althusser, 'Matérialisme historique et matérialisme dialectique', *Cahiers Marxistes-Léninistes* 11 [1966], 97).

assertion that 'it is not the consciousness of men that determines their being but on the contrary it is their social being that determines their consciousness', Althusser presumes that the structuring principles that shape a complex social configuration are not directly accessible from within the experience of those living in that society.[53] The experience of time endured by workers under capitalism, for instance, does not overlap with 'the time of social labour' through which hidden surplus value is produced any more than it coincides with 'the cyclical time of the turnover of capital', and therefore the objective 'time of the capitalist economic production [. . .] must be *constructed* in its concept' rather than recognized in its experience.[54] What is *lived* is merely the ideological mis-representation of these structuring principles, arranged in ways that serve to protect or 'cement' the social order they structure. Ideology circumscribes the sphere of experience in which objects can be re-cognized (and thus accepted) rather than truly cognized (and thus transformed).[55] In fact, as Althusser understands it ideology is nothing other than the imaginary and '"lived" relation between people and the world' as such, and is thus an irreducible, '*organic part of every social totality.*' All societies 'secrete ideology as the very element and atmosphere indispensable to their historical respiration and life' (FM, 232). They secrete, more precisely, all the deluded, mystifying forms of lived experience that lead people to endure and accept the 'roles and functions' to which they are condemned by that society.[56]

By the same token, since 'there are no subjects except for and by their subjection' (LP, 169), any adequately scientific or non-ideological account of a historical process must grasp it as a 'process without a subject'[57] and as irreducible to relations between subjects.

The structure of the relations of production determines the *places* and *functions* occupied and adopted by the agents of production, who are never anything more than the occupants of these places, insofar as they are the

---

53   Karl Marx, 'Preface', in *A Contribution to the Critique of Political Economy* [1859] (Beijing: Foreign Languages Press, 1976), 3.

54   RC, 299, 101. 'In no sense is it a time that can be *read immediately* in the flow of any given process. It is an invisible time, essentially illegible, as invisible and as opaque as the reality of the total capitalist production process itself. This time, as a complex "intersection" of the different times, rhythms, turnovers, etc., is only accessible in *its concept*, which, like every concept is never immediately "given", never *legible* in visible reality: like every concept this concept must be *produced, constructed*' (RC, 101).

55   See in particular Badiou, 'Le (Re)commencement du matérialisme dialectique', *Critique* 240 (May 1967), 449.

56   Althusser, PSPS, 24-25, 28; LP, 168-70; cf. Rancière, 'Le Concept de critique et la critique de l'économie politique des *Manuscrits* de 1844 au *Capital*', in Althusser et al., *Lire le Capital* (Paris: Maspero, 1965), 168-169.

57   Balibar, RC, 271; cf. FM, 121; LP, 121-124; ESC, 51, 94ff.

'supports' (*Träger*) of these functions. The true 'subjects' (in the sense of constitutive subjects of the process) are therefore not these occupants or functionaries, are not, despite all appearances, the 'obviousnesses' of the 'given' of naïve anthropology, 'concrete individuals', 'real men' – but *the definition and distribution of these places and functions. The true 'subjects ' are these definers and distributors: the relations of production* (and political and ideological social relations).[58]

The subject in the usual sense of the term is merely a derivative effect of structuring forces operating on a level beyond its grasp, i.e. a level that cannot be understood in any sense as 'inter-subjective' (RC, 140, 180, 220). Comparably extra-subjective forces also shape the domain of comprehension or knowledge itself. In any 'process of real transformation of the means of production of knowledge, the claims of a constitutive subject are as vain as are the claims of the subject of vision in the production of the visible', and in the 'mutation of a theoretical structure [. . .] the subject plays, not the part it believes it is playing, but the part which is assigned to it by the mechanism of the process.'[59]

As long as it remains sufficiently distant from such subjective delusions, scientific analysis can penetrate the veil of ideological or imaginary mystification and grasp the objective order of things. This antithesis of science and

---

58   RC, 180. Balibar generalizes the point, arguing that each of the elements (labour, means of production, raw materials, etc.) that combine to determine a given mode of production 'undoubtedly has a kind of "history", but it is *a history without any locatable subject*: the real subject of each component history is the *combination* on which depend the elements and their relations, i.e., it is *something which is not a subject* [. . .]. There is no reason why the elements, which are thus determined in different ways, should *coincide* in the unity of concrete individuals, who would then appear as the local, miniature reproduction of the whole social articulation. The supposition of such a common support is, on the contrary, the product of a psychological ideology, in exactly the same way as linear time is the product of a historical ideology' (Balibar, RC, 252–253). In 1970 Althusser would make the point still more emphatically: 'the category of the subject is only constitutive of ideology insofar as all ideology has the function (which defines it) of "constituting" concrete individuals as subjects' (Althusser, 'Ideology and Ideological State Apparatuses', LP, 171).

59   RC, 27. Althusser's own relation to structuralism in general and to Lévi-Strauss in particular is complicated. On the one hand, as G.M. Goshgarian notes, Althusser 'had been decrying structuralism, "idealism's last hope"', as a philosophical fraud since his 1962–63 seminar [at the ENS] on the subject' (Althusser, *The Humanist Controversy and Other Writings*, trans. G.M. Goshgarian [London: Verso, 2003], xii; cf. xli); in a text he circulated in the summer of 1966 Althusser condemned Lévi-Strauss, lacking any concept of a mode of production, as trapped within ideology 'without knowing it' (Althusser, 'On Lévi-Strauss' [20 August 1966], HC, 24–25). On the other hand, like Lévi-Strauss, Althusser also embraced a scientific anti-humanism based on the systematic analysis of the elements of a purely synchronic system, to the exclusion of any genetic or historicizing explanation (RC, 65; cf. 234, 298), and as Gregory Elliott demonstrates, Althusser's actual proximity to structuralist methods in his writings of 1964–65 far exceeds the 'mere "flirt" with structuralist terminology' to which he reduced this episode in his later auto-critique' (Elliott, *Althusser: The Detour of Theory* [1987] [Leiden: Brill, 2006], 47).

ideology provides the 'cardinal principle' of Althusserian theory,[60] one that would be developed with dizzying virtuosity by several key contributions to the *Cahiers* (perhaps most notably in François Regnault's 'Dialectic of Epistemologies', CpA 9.4). An ideological representation of reality 'is necessarily distorted, because it is not an objective but a *subjective* representation of reality [...]. Science, in contrast, exists only on condition that it struggles against all forms of subjectivity, class subjectivity included [...]; science is objective. Science provides knowledge of reality independent of "subjective" class interests.'[61] Against the legacy of Zhdanov and Lysenko, scientific knowledge is neither 'bourgeois' or 'proletarian' but simply knowledge as such. What science most definitely cannot be, however, is pseudo-knowledge of an object as it is given or lived, e.g. an object as it is spontaneously 'seen' by a subject.[62] A science comes into existence when it is capable of constituting its own strictly theoretical or intelligible object, on the now-familiar model of non-intuitable mathematical objects – for instance the unconscious as theorized by Freud and Lacan (at a maximum distance from the 'concrete' psychology of a Sartre or Politzer), or the capitalist mode of production as theorized by Marx (organized around the 'imperceptible' accumulation of surplus value). 'What makes any theory a theory', as Althusser will explain in the autumn of 1966 (in terms directly influenced by his students' work in the *Cahiers*), is that

> it takes as its object not this or that real object, but an object of knowledge (and thus a theoretical object); it produces the knowledge of the (determinate) *possibility* of the *effects*, and thus of the *possible effects* of this object in its *real* forms of existence. Every theory, then, goes beyond the *real* object that constitutes the empirical 'point of departure' for the historical constitution of the theory (in Freud, this point of departure is the 'talking cure') and produces its own theoretical object as well as knowledge of it, which is knowledge of the *possibilities* of this object, and the forms of existence in which these determinate possibilities are realized, that is, exist as *real* objects.[63]

So strict a scientism has far-reaching political and epistemological implications. The political implication, of course, is a radicalization of Lenin's assumption that, prior to its illumination by Marxist science, working class experience

---

60   Althusser, PSPS, 42; cf. FM, 167–168.

61   Althusser, 'The Historical Task of Marxist Philosophy', HC, 191 note h.

62   Liberated from any phenomenological relation to a given object, the theoretical insight that structures a scientific field is 'no longer the act of an individual subject, endowed with the faculty of vision' but rather the 'act of its structural conditions', a matter of strictly 'immanent reflection', such that it's not 'the eye of a subject which *sees* what exists in the field [...], it is this field itself which *sees itself* in the objects or problems it defines' (RC, 25).

63   Althusser, 'Three Notes on the Theory of Discourses' [October 1966], HC, 39. In this sense, 'the theory of the unconscious is, in principle, the *theory of all the possible effects* of the unconscious – in the cure, outside the cure, in "pathological" as well as "normal" cases' (39).

can only generate the sorts of 'utopian or reformist' consciousness that reinforce rather than overthrow the structures of oppression in which they are forced to live (PSPS, 16; cf. 30–33). The epistemological implication is the apparent irrelevance of any merely 'empirical' verification of Marxist theory, i.e. the foreclosure of any risk of extra-theoretical falsification.[64] As we shall see, this theoretical configuration will receive a kind of 'practical' confirmation in due course, precisely when it is interrupted in May 68.

A science of history is concerned, more specifically, with the structuring principles that *cause* a society to take on its particular shape. For Althusser and his students (Miller, Rancière, Balibar, Duroux . . .) this defines the central problem that social science must address. Determined in the last instance by economic factors, a 'structural causality' is one that produces the various dimensions, instances and subjects of a society as its effects. Contra Lévi-Strauss and his 'vulgarized structuralism', history itself can therefore be grasped as an intelligible domain amenable to scientific analysis, but (contra Hegel and *gauchiste* neo-Hegelians like Lukács, Gramsci, or Sartre) the secret of this intelligibility will not normally be accessible to the subjects whose roles it determines. For the same reason, the sort of causality that works through the relatively autonomous instances and practices which combine in a social form can be neither merely 'transitive' or mechanical on the one hand (the linear determination of an effect by a cause that remains external to it) nor 'expressive' on the other (the self-actualization of a unified i.e. 'non-structured' spirit or whole). A scientific conception of historical causality must be adequate to *complex* or structured totalities, as distinct both from integrated wholes or mere aggregations of elements (RC, 186). 'In structural causality', Althusser explains, 'we find something that resembles the problem (often invoked by biologists) of the causality of the "whole upon its parts", with the difference that the "Marxist" whole is not a biological, organic whole, but a complex structure that itself contains structured levels (the infrastructure, the superstructure). Structural causality designates the very particular causality of a structure upon its elements.'[65] Modelled on the relation Spinoza posits between God or substance and its various modal modifications, a properly 'structural causality' is thus both 'absent' from its effects (since the economic 'last instance' never asserts itself directly) and yet fully 'immanent' to them:

---

64   'Marx's method', Balibar argues after Althusser, 'completely *abolishes* the problem of "reference", of the empirical designation of the object of a theoretical knowledge' (RC, 249; cf. 59–60). 'In Althusser's work, the possibility of a "feedback" from experience to theory is entirely excluded' (Peter Dews, 'Althusser, Structuralism, and the French Epistemological Tradition', in *Althusser: A Critical Reader*, ed. Gregory Elliott [Oxford: Blackwell, 1994], 124; cf. Elliott, *Althusser: The Detour of Theory*, 88ff, 146, 187; Lewis, *Althusser*, 170.

65   Althusser, 'The Historical Task of Marxist Philosophy', HC, 200.

The absence of the cause in the structure's 'metonymic causality' on its effects is not
the fault of the exteriority of the structure with respect to the economic phenomena;
on the contrary, it is the very form of the interiority of the structure, as a structure,
in its effects. This implies therefore that the effects are not outside the structure, are
not a pre-existing object, element or space in which the structure arrives to *imprint
its mark*; on the contrary, it implies that the structure is immanent in its effects, a
cause immanent in its effects in the Spinozist sense of the term, that *the whole existence of the structure consists of its effects*, in short that the structure, which is merely
a specific combination of its peculiar elements, is nothing outside its effects.[66]

What structures the capitalist mode of production, for instance, are the
coercive relations of exploitation that generate a complex set of mechanisms for
resolving the various forms of class conflict they provoke. The forced extraction
of surplus value figures as 'the very structure that dominates the process in the
totality of its development and of its existence': whereas mere 'instruments of
production' (tools, raw materials, etc.) are visible 'things' and wages or prices
are measurable 'facts', the economists who measure them can no more 'see' the
relations of production that structure them 'than the pre-Newtonian "physicist"
could "see" the law of attraction in falling bodies or the pre-Lavoisierian chem-
ist could "see" oxygen in "dephlogisticated" air.'[67]

The field illuminated by analysis of structural causality is thus a field
purged of those deluded subjects who assume that 'the "actors" of history are

---

66   RC, 188–189; cf. ESC, 126–127; Lewis, *Althusser*, 174–177. As Badiou was quick to
recognize, 'the further progress of dialectical materialism depends on the solving or at least on the
positing of the problem of structural causality' (Badiou, 'Le (Re)commencement du matérialisme
dialectique', 458). Pushed to its limit, Rancière will later suggest, the Althusserian conception of
structure 'confronts us with a truism: the structure is defined by nothing more than the opacity
manifested in its effects. In other words, the structure's opacity is what renders it opaque' (Rancière,
Althusser's Lesson [1974], trans. Emiliano Battista [London: Continuum, 2011], 133). That the
'hopeless' circularity of this apparent equation of cause and effect was 'not more frequently appreciated at the time', Peter Dews argues, 'may be attributed to the fact that Althusser tacitly adopts the
Spinozist assumption of the metaphysical identity of logical and causal relations. He can therefore
speak indifferently either of the deterministic mechanism of the social formation itself, or of the
logical implications of the "theoretical object" which corresponds to it [. . .]. It is for the same
reason that Althusser never appears unduly concerned about the relation, which many commentators have found highly problematic, between the "real object", which remains in its self-identity
outside thought, and the theoretical object of Marxist science' (Dews, 'Althusser, Structuralism,
and the French Epistemological Tradition', 116).

67   RC, 181; cf. 222. 'The fact that surplus-value is not a measurable reality arises from the
fact that it is not a thing, but the concept of a relationship, the concept of an existing social
structure of production, of an existence visible and measurable *only in its* "*effects*", in the sense
we shall soon define. The fact that it only exists in its effects does not mean that it can be grasped
completely in any one of its determinate effects: for that it would have to be *completely present* in
that effect, whereas it is only present there, as a structure, in its *determinate* absence. It is only
present in the totality, in the total movement of its effects, in what Marx calls the "developed
totality of its form of existence", for reasons bound up with its very nature' (RC, 180).

the authors of its text, the subjects of its production', subjects who, ignorant of the structuring work of history's invisible 'stage director', believe themselves capable of undertaking the work of their own self-emancipation.[68] Althusserian analysis applies instead to the direction or '*mise en scène* of a theatre which is simultaneously its own stage, its own script, its own actors', i.e. to what is 'in essence an *authorless theatre*' (RC, 193). Such elimination of the author, however, need not imply passivity in the face of historical destiny. On the contrary, the whole purpose of Althusser's intervention was to renew the openly revolutionary dimension of Marxist politics, at a time when both the Soviet and the French communist parties had come to embrace reformist positions. To some extent, at least, Althusser can afford to discount the subject in theory insofar as he remains in practice a *party* theorist. The strategic corollary of structural analysis was practical intervention, along Leninist lines, at the 'weakest link' in the chains of domination.[69] Whereas ideology preserves the status quo in its repetitive inertia, science allows us to understand and thus change the world, the world in its full complex reality, in which class antagonisms don't often take a merely confrontational form. Science enables us not only 'to anticipate the future [. . .] but also and above all the roads and means that will secure us its reality'.[70] Marxist knowledge, in short, should allow us to 'define the appropriate *means of action* for "making the revolution."'[71]

---

68   RC, 139; *pace* Althusser, Marx himself was one such deluded subject (see for instance Marx, *The Poverty of Philosophy* [1847] [Beijing: Foreign Languages Press, 1966], 109).

69   FM, 95–99, 104; cf. Bruno Bosteels, 'Alain Badiou's Theory of the Subject, Part I: The Recommencement of Dialectical Materialism?', *Pli* 12 (2001), 210–212; Duroux, 'Strong Structuralism, Weak Subject', CF2, 193. And Badiou: 'I think that Althusser found the Maoist theory of contradiction at the exact moment when he was trying, with considerable difficulties I should add, to determine the point where the structure is in excess over itself, the point which he sought for in the Leninist theory of the weakest link, in the question of overdetermination, and, finally, in the theory of the principal aspect of the contradiction according to Mao. All this means pinning down the structural point which is also at the same time the point of breakdown of the structure' (interview with Bosteels, 'Can Change be Thought?', in *Alain Badiou: Philosophy and its Conditions*, ed. Gabriel Riera [New York: SUNY, 2005], 244).

70   RC, 198. 'The number one strategic task for Marxist philosophy is to become a true theory, in the strong sense, so that it can struggle and prevail against bourgeois ideology and its influence on the revolutionary workers' movement' (HC, 194).

71   PSPS, 3–4. As Rancière would later acknowledge, 'it is *precisely* the "theoreticist" discourse of *For Marx* and of *Reading Capital* that produced political effects, both on the practices of communist organizations and on the student uprisings' (Rancière, *Althusser's Lesson*, 23). 'One has to understand', he reminds us, that 'to choose the camp of theory and of science was *also* to choose the camp of rupture, of revolution, the camp of Marxism's autonomy, of its exteriority to the Communist Party's political apparatus [. . .]. Don't forget that what is at stake at the heart of Althusserianism [. . .] is still a refutation of evolutionist theories [. . .]. Theory says that the revolution can only proceed in the form of rupture, and not in the form of a peaceful evolution' (Rancière, 'Only in the Form of Rupture', CF2, 264). Cf. Guy Lardreau, *Le Singe d'or: Essai sur le concept d'étape du marxisme* (Paris: Mercure de France, 1973), 22–23.

III THE *CAHIERS MARXISTES-LÉNINISTES*

The 'rigour' of Althusser's version of revolutionary theory was all the more appealing to the students who entered the École Normale in the early and mid 1960s, as an alternative to the general sense of political torpor and complacency characteristic of the years that followed the end of the Algerian War. In order to make sense of first the theoretical appeal of Althusser and then the practical appeal of Maoism, Badiou points out, 'you have to remember just what the established Gaullist regime was like, in the early 1960s. You need to remember its oppressiveness, and the extraordinarily marginal or minoritarian character – in a way we can scarcely imagine today – of the protest movements, of radical or critical currents, confronted with the triumphalism of Pompidolian propertied capitalism. And you need to have lived through that society, a society which saw itself as having no more problems . . .'[72] A sign of the times was the dissolution in 1965 of the journal *Socialisme ou barbarie* and the withdrawal of its editors Claude Lefort and Cornelius Castoriadis from revolutionary politics: as Castoriadis explained in 1967, the review had become redundant because 'in modern capitalist societies political activity properly speaking tends to disappear.'[73] In its congresses of 1956 and 1961, the once-revolutionary PCF had committed itself to 'peaceful coexistence' between East and West, and opted to follow a 'peaceful transition to socialism'. The 'new social movements' that would emerge after 1968, meanwhile, had hardly begun to exist. Given the range of concrete alternatives available to them, perhaps it's not surprising that Althusser's students developed a highly abstract conception of politics.

Two political developments in the pivotal years of 1964–66 took some of the edge off this abstraction, one of parochial and the other of global significance: the takeover of the École Normale's branch (the 'Cercle d'Ulm') of the Union des Étudiants Communistes (UEC) by Althusserians, and the explosion of cultural revolution in China.

In the spring of 1965, Althusser concluded one of the sections of *Reading Capital* with a word of sympathy for his predecessor: forced to work 'alone, Marx looked around him for allies and supporters', and in his isolation was obliged to look for theoretical support wherever he could find it (RC, 193). In the years before he made this acknowledgement, Althusser himself (though certainly no stranger to isolation and discouragement) enjoyed a very different situation. From the late 1950s, there gathered round him one of the most

---

72   Badiou, 'Politics and Philosophy', in *Ethics*, trans. Peter Hallward (London: Verso, 2001), 124tm.

73   Cornelius Castoriadis, 'The Suspension of Publication of *Socialisme ou barbarie*', in *Political and Social Writings vol. 3, 1961–1979* (Minneapolis: Minnesota University Press, 1992), 119–120.

remarkable groups of students of philosophy ever to assemble at the École Normale or indeed anywhere else. Alain Badiou and Emmanuel Terray left the ENS in 1961, followed by François Regnault in 1962 and Pierre Macherey in 1963; Etienne Balibar, Yves Duroux and Jacques Rancière arrived in 1960, Jean-Claude Milner in 1961, Jacques-Alain Miller and Alain Grosrichard in 1962 and Robert Linhart in 1963. Benny Lévy and Dominique Lecourt arrived in October 1965.[74] In the autumn of 1961, Althusser began organizing with his students a series of open seminars over several years, on the young Marx (in 1961–62), on the origins of structuralism (1962–63, with sessions on Foucault, Descartes, Montesquieu, Dumézil, Lévi-Strauss, and Barthes, among others), on Lacan and psychoanalysis (1963–64), and then the seminar published as *Reading Capital* (1964–65).[75] As everyone involved confirms, these years were marked by a sense of collective enthusiasm occasionally bordering on exaltation – Linhart, for instance, remembers his time at the ENS (1963–68) as 'years of mad elation, of delirium, of an unimaginable freedom.'[76] Althusser himself was delighted (if not intimidated) by his precocious young collaborators,[77] whose new sense of mission and *esprit de corps*, reinforced by their institutional credentials, soon gave them considerable influence in the Union of Communist Students (UEC). At the time, the UEC enjoyed a significant amount of autonomy in relation to the PCF itself, and it remained 'a place of great freedom which the party considered with a great deal of mistrust.'[78] At the UEC's eighth congress, in March 1965, the reformist ('pro-Italian', pro-Khrushchev) leadership was pushed out and the Cercle d'Ulm found itself drawn into an increasingly complex war of manoeuvre between the various factions fighting

---

74   Cf. Duroux, 'Élèves d'Althusser', *Magazine littéraire* 304 (November 1992), 48.

75   Balibar, 'A Philosophical Conjuncture', CF2; cf. Edward Baring, *The Young Derrida and French Philosophy, 1945–1968* (Cambridge: Cambridge University Press, 2011), 277–278.

76   Robert Linhart, cited in Edouard Launet, 'Rétabli: Portrait de Robert Linhart', *Libération* 17 May 2010.

77   'These kids are incredible', Althusser wrote to his lover Franca Madonia. 'I need to get my ass in gear [*il faut que je cravache*] if I don't want to be left behind' (Letter to Franca, 21 January 1964, *Lettres à Franca*, 505). An anecdote gives a good sense of the prevailing mindset: on the eve of Lacan's first lecture at the ENS, Althusser's students told him what they were planning to do. 'Tomorrow, they will intervene when Lacan, having finished his lecture, asks: "Are there any questions?" [. . .] One of them will stand up and say: "We have no questions to ask you. What we want is to answer the questions you ask without knowing it, the questions you ask yourself, unbeknownst to you, that is to say, the questions you don't ask, because you haven't asked them yet. We'll ask these questions, ask them of ourselves, because we have the answers, and what we are about to say will give both the questions and the answers. So listen, and if afterwards you have questions to ask of us, we'll listen to you . . ." Funny, don't you think? They're amazing' (Althusser, letter to Franca Madonia, 21 January 1964, *Lettres à Franca*, 506). According to André Green's recollection, in 1962 Miller and Milner had made a less favourable impression on Roland Barthes: 'they come to all my seminars, they torture me, they argue with me in a completely unpleasant way, they want to rip me apart' (Green, interview with Dosse, in Dosse, *History of Structuralism* vol. 1, 76).

78   Duroux, 'Strong Structuralism, Weak Subject', CF2, 198.

to determine the future orientation of the PCF.[79] Althusser celebrated their success: 'my young dogs, who are also young lions' (he wrote to Franca Madonia), strengthened by their 'correct conception of things', appear set to make a 'direct transition from theory to politics'.[80]

Led by Miller, Linhart and Rancière, in late 1964 the Cercle d'Ulm decided to reinforce its growing political influence with the establishment of a new student-run journal, the *Cahiers Marxistes-Léninistes*.[81] Conceived along rigorously Althusserian lines, the journal was designed to complement the creation of well-attended 'theoretical schools' for the transmission of Marxist science. The most urgent priority, as Althusser had repeatedly insisted, was the 'theoretical training [*formation*]' of a new revolutionary generation, one whose grasp of Marxist science would reverse the disastrous revisionist steps taken by the older generation and return the party to its proper course. The goal should be to 'extend the broadest possible *theoretical training* to the greatest possible number of militants', 'to educate them constantly in theory, to make them militants in the full sense of the term', in other words 'militants capable of one day becoming men and women of science. To attain this goal one cannot aim too high.'[82] Only appropriate theoretical training and the 'importation' of Marxist science can guard against the expression of ideological or spontaneous i.e. untrained reflexes (veering from utopian-anarchist to chastened-reformist) among students and workers alike. Given the shadow it

---

79   Elliott summarizes the sequence: 'At the Eighth Congress of the UEC in March 1965, the right-wing leadership was unseated and a new *bureau national* loyal to the PCF installed. Accounts were now settled with the "Trotskyist" Left; open opposition to Communist support for Mitterrand's Atlanticist presidential candidacy led to the disciplining of the *Lettres* section. The Althusserians, preoccupied with the seminar that produced *Reading Capital*, declined to adopt a public position on the Mitterrand issue. The diverse pro-Chinese currents in the PCF were divided between those who believed the eventual foundation of a new "Marxist-Leninist" party openly affiliated to Peking to be necessary, and those who deemed *lutte interne* (internal struggle) for the reformation of the Party the most appropriate course of action. Among the latter were Althusser's students and disciples, who proposed to combat the PCF's current orientation by defending and disseminating Marxist theory' (Elliott, *Althusser*, 171).

80   Althusser, letter to Franca Madonia, 18 March 1965, *Lettres à Franca*, 608.

81   Other influential members of the editorial team were Roger Establet, Dominique Lecourt, Georges Rougemont, and Christian Riss. The most detailed study is Frédéric Chateigner's unpublished DEA dissertation, 'D'Althusser à Mao: Les *Cahiers Marxistes-Léninistes* (1964–1968)' (École Normale Supérieure – École des Hautes Études en Sciences Sociales, October 2004), 72 pages; an abbreviated version was published as 'D'Althusser à Mao', in *Dissidences* 8 (2010), 66–80. Cf. Virginie Linhart, *Volontaires pour l'usine: Vies d'établis 1967–1977* (Paris: Seuil, 1994), 24–25; Jean-Pierre Le Dantec, *Les Dangers du soleil* (Paris: Presses d'aujourd'hui, 1978), 61–65; Daniel Bensaïd and Henri Weber, *Mai 68: Une Répétition générale* (Paris: Maspero, 1968), 43–45.

82   Althusser, 'Theory, Theoretical Practice and Theoretical Formation', PSPS, 40; cf. Althusser, letter to Lacan, 4 December 1963, *Writings on Psychoanalysis*, trans. Jeffrey Mehlman (New York: Columbia University Press, 1996), 154. The only redeeming feature of Marx's own philosophical background in Hegel and Feuerbach, according to Althusser, was the way it had at least given him a *formation à la théorie*, a training or 'formation for theory' (FM, 85).

casts over his students' work, Althusser's definition of such training is worth citing at length:

> By *theoretical training*, we understand the process of education, study and work by which a militant is put in possession – *not only of the conclusions* of the two sciences of Marxist theory (historical materialism and dialectical materialism), *not only of their theoretical principles*, not only of some detailed analyses and demonstrations – but of *the totality* of the theory, of all its content, all its analyses and demonstrations, all its principles and all its conclusions, in their indissoluble scientific bond. We literally understand, then, a *thorough study and assimilation* of all the scientific works of primary importance on which the knowledge of Marxist theory rests. [. . .] Theoretical training is thus something entirely different from simple economic, political or ideological training. These must be preliminary stages of theoretical training; they must be clarified by theoretical training and founded upon it, but cannot be confused with it, because they are only *partial* stages of it. [. . .] Why attach such importance to theoretical training? Because it represents the *decisive intermediary link* by which it is possible both to develop Marxist theory itself, and to develop the influence of Marxist theory on the entire practice of the Communist Party and thus on the profound transformation of the ideology of the working class.[83]

The first issue of the *Cahiers Marxistes-Léninistes* came out in December 1964, with contributions by Miller, Milner, Rancière, and Linhart, dedicated to the Althusserian problematic par excellence: 'science and ideologies'. A first edition of 1000 copies sold out in a matter of days. A total of 17 issues of the *Cahiers Marxistes-Léninistes* subsequently appeared over the next three and a half years, through to May 1968, on topics including Algeria and India (issue 2), agriculture (issue 3), revolutionary perspectives in Latin America (4), Leninism (9–10), and art and language (12–13). Along with Miller and Milner, Duroux and Regnault also worked on these first *Cahiers*. Althusser himself contributed two articles, including the substantial 'Historical Materialism and Dialectical Materialism' in issue 11 (April 1966).[84]

Robert Linhart, soon to be joined by Jacques Broyelle and Benny Lévy, quickly became the animating spirit of the *Cahiers Marxistes-Léninistes*. Linhart was committed body and soul to Althusser's reformulation of Lenin's

---

83   PSPS, 39–41; cf. the Cercle d'Ulm, 'Faut-il réviser la théorie Marxiste-léniniste?' [April 1966], *Que faire?* 1 (April 1966), in *Le Mouvement maoïste en France, textes et documents*, vol 1, ed. Patrick Kessel (Paris: Union Générale d'Éditions, 1972) 155, 160.

84   Most new articles in the *Cahiers Marxistes-Léninistes* were unsigned, and presented as contributions to a collective scientific endeavour, partly sanctioned by reference to the authority of the ENS itself (cf. Chateigner, 'D'Althusser à Mao', 17–18).

dictum: 'without revolutionary theory there can be no revolutionary movement.'[85] As Rancière remembers, 'Linhart's big project in the UEC circle was this: first we need to take care of theoretical training' and to 'teach Marxism, considered as an existing science, to militants', so as to intensify a commitment to revolutionary practice.[86] Linhart's close friend Jacques-Alain Miller, meanwhile, was perhaps the most precocious and ambitious of all Althusser's students during these years, and the most committed to the primacy of theory per se. Miller's initial contribution to this first set of Cahiers at the ENS was substantial. Among other things, he proposed the quotation from Lenin which appears on the cover of each issue of the journal ('Marx's theory is omnipotent because it is true'[87]), and he drafted the agenda-setting introduction to its inaugural volume, fittingly entitled 'The Function of Theoretical Training'.

Like Miller's other texts of this period, his introduction to the Cahiers Marxistes-Léninistes asserts principles and priorities that, a year later, in yet more purely 'theoretical' form, would apply again to the establishment of the Cahiers pour l'Analyse. 'Marxist-Leninist theory', he begins,

> requires a form of teaching that is not reducible to the communication of a set of statements and bits of information constituted as knowledge [savoir]. This is because Marxist-Leninism provides the principle of a new organization of the conceptual field, which breaks with the most constant but less obvious references of our intellectual moment – to teach it is to engage in the enterprise of changing those who receive it. We propose to call the process of this transformation: theoretical training.[88]

What most members of the UEC need today, Miller argues, is not simply to learn about Marxism but actually to become Marxists, i.e. to be trained and prepared [formés] as Marxists, somewhat in the way that one might train a missionary or evangelist.

---

85   Lenin, What is to be Done? [1902], in Collected Works, vol. 5, 369; cf. Althusser, PSPS, 5; Althusser, 'Matérialisme historique et matérialisme dialectique', Cahiers Marxistes-Léninistes 11 (April 1966), 105.

86   Rancière, 'Only in the Form of Rupture', CF2, 261; Rancière, Althusser's Lesson, 44. Jean-Pierre Le Dantec remembers that when Linhart spoke at the UEC's eighth congress, in early March 1965, he urged the congress to abstain from petty party politics and to concentrate exclusively on theory, so as to 'transform the UEC into a vast school of communism' (Le Dantec, Les Dangers du soleil, 61).

87   Lenin, 'The Three Sources and Three Component Parts of Marxism' [1913], in Collected Works vol. 19 (Moscow: Progress Publishers, 1968), 23; cf. Althusser, HC, 218; Lacan, 'La Science et la vérité', CpA 1.1:20; E, 869/738.

88   Jacques-Alain Miller, 'Fonction de la formation théorique' (présentation des Cahiers Marxistes-Léninistes, vol. 1 (December 1964), reprinted in Miller, Un Début dans la vie (Paris: Gallimard, 2002), 86.

The first and most important step in this 'combative' training or formation, of course, is to break with ideology. Ideology is the 'primary' concern, because 'in the structural system through which a specific mode of production is articulated, the sphere in which the subject moves – insofar as it draws on the level of the present or actual [*l'actuel*], i.e. insofar as the structure concedes to the subject perception of his state (of his apparent movement) while concealing its system – is defined as illusion.' The more powerful the system of ideological illusion, the more profoundly 'the subject reflects it, signifies it, in brief redoubles it.' The structuring level of the economy, by contrast, since it is determinant in the last instance and thus serves as the 'reference of all the manifestations of social practice', is 'radically foreign to the dimension of the actual, and is only accessible through its effects.' This 'absence of cause' ensures that what is experienced at the level of individual consciousness is the 'inversion of structural determinations. Inversion as perception is illusion. As discourse, inversion is ideology.' Thus the primary 'task of theoretical training is to *convert* perception and *reform* discourse.' This task, Miller continues, should be carried out by a 'particular commission', in close and unceasing connection with communist militants – non-communists are condemned to remain 'on the threshold of science'. By the same token, although Marxist theory has political economy as its primary field, it exceeds it insofar as it also presumes and 'involves a general theory of science', i.e. the theoretical elements required for 'the analysis of the constitutive process of science as such, and thus for an understanding of the difference between science and ideology'.[89]

For the best part of 1965, the agenda set by such 'theoretical training' served as a common programme that united both the most committed political activists and the most 'abstract' theorists at the ENS. Theoretical training allowed a neo-Bachelardian emphasis on Marxist science to be read alongside the anti-humanist works of Foucault, Lacan, Barthes and Derrida as contributions to a shared anti-ideological project; Miller and Linhart, Rancière and Balibar – in the spring of 1965, it seems they were all on the same page. It was also an agenda that rapidly gained some traction in the wider Paris student movement. As Julian Bourg observes, in the mid 1960s the assault on reformist humanism and the critique of a conservative university establishment were intimately connected, and the affirmation of a 'theoretical practice' uncoupled from the stifling authority of tradition was as much a matter of pedagogical as of political liberation.[90]

89   Miller, 'Fonction de la formation théorique', 87–89.

90   Julian Bourg, 'The Red Guards of Paris: French Student Maoism of the 1960s', *History of European Ideas* 31:4 (2005), 483. In this context, Bourg continues, 'the project of "theoretical education" caught on, the ideas of Althusser and his students showing up in the schools of theory [that] were set up in almost all the universities of Paris. Althusserianism became a veritable phenomenon among left-leaning students who [. . .] were stuck with a [French Communist] Party

It wasn't long, however, before Althusser's students paid him the proverbial 'highest compliment', and began to outflank him in both practice and theory.

In the domain of practice, the pace of events was determined by the intensification of the Sino-Soviet split over the course of 1965, and the explosion of cultural revolution in China the following year. The Chinese party had called the question, obliging communists to make a decision 'whether or not to accept the universal truth of Marxism-Leninism' and to pursue its revolutionary mission 'to the end'.[91] In keeping with their mentor's example, the Cercle d'Ulm and their *Cahiers Marxistes-Léninistes* initially hoped to answer this question by gaining influence on the PCF from the inside, via the UEC. Over the course of 1966, however, it became clear that this road would lead nowhere. In January, Roger Garaudy and his allies condemned Althusserian anti-humanism and 'theoreticism' at a gathering of party intellectuals at Choisy-le-Roi. In March, a decisive meeting of the PCF's Central Committee at Argenteuil reaffirmed its commitment to 'the humanism of our time' and condemned the anti-humanism championed by both Althusser and the Chinese party in unequivocal terms.[92] After Argenteuil, most partisans of *la théorie* concluded they would have to complete their training outside the PCF. Although Althusser appeared to accept the censure in silence, his students reacted more quickly and more forcefully. Three days after Argenteuil, Althusser's students in the UEC adopted an effectively mutinous text entitled 'Marxism is not a Humanism', which accused the party's Central Committee of 'exercising a right that it does not have: that of liquidating Marxist-Leninist theory'.[93] A few months later the PCF moved to dissolve the Cercle d'Ulm.

After a good deal of debate Althusser and Balibar eventually decided to submit to party discipline and remain in the PCF, but in the last months of 1966 many of the more militant members of the group (including Robert Linhart, Benny Lévy, Jacques Broyelle, Dominique Lecourt, Guy Lardreau and Christian Jambet) left the party to create the first openly Maoist student organization in France, the Union des Jeunesses Communistes – marxistes-léninistes

---

whose mythical role in the Resistance paled before its pitiful response to the Algerian War and its seeming abandonment of the world revolutionary cause' (482). On the complex political (and pedagogical) relation between Althusserianism and broader student political demands in 1964–65 see Elliott, *Althusser*, 169–70; Rancière, *Althusser's Lesson*, 136–137; Warren Montag, 'Introduction to Althusser's "Student Problems"', *Radical Philosophy* 170 (November 2011), 8–10.

91   Communist Party of China, *The Polemic on the General Line of the International Communist Movement* (Beijing: Foreign Languages Press, 1965), 4–5, cited in Elliott, *Althusser*, 6.

92   Elliott, *Althusser*, 172; Goshgarian, 'Introduction', in Althusser, HC, xxx–xxxi, xxxv–xxxvi.

93   Quoted in Kessel, *Le Mouvement maoïste en France* vol. 1, 148; see also the Cercle d'Ulm's subsequent tirade against Garaudiste humanism, 'Faut-il réviser la théorie Marxiste-léniniste?' (April 1966), in Kessel, Le Mouvement maoïste en France, 149–161.

(UJC[ml]).[94] The UJC took the *Cahiers Marxistes-Léninistes* with them, and dedicated its next several issues to the revolution under way in China; issue 14 (November 1966) included an unsigned article by Althusser himself 'On the Cultural Revolution', celebrating it as an *'unprecedented* fact' of 'intense *theoretical* interest.'[95] During this same period, growing numbers of Mao's young admirers in France set themselves further apart from the PCF by campaigning not just for peace but for communist victory in Vietnam. More important than the policy, as Kristin Ross notes, was the change in tactics it instigated. Inspired by

---

94   The first congress of the UJC(ml) was held on 10–11 December 1966, and the organization soon included several hundred militants in the Paris region. As Bourg notes, 'the founding text of the UJC(ml) stressed the immediate theoretical struggle against revisionist "theoretical fools"; the need for a Leninist form of organization stressing "unity of thought and action"; and the link between Chinese and French Marxist–Leninists: "For the world Proletarian revolution, the red base of the People's Republic of China is the fulcrum. The advanced front of the Proletarian Revolution in France are the Marxist-Leninists who struggle and organize themselves everywhere. [. . . A] revolutionary force, lead justly and solidly founded, is invincible"' (Bourg, 'The Red Guards of Paris', 485–486). The first resolutions of the UJC, taken in December 1966, commit it to 'leading the class struggle in the university and among young people' by opposing 'revisionist bourgeois ideology' and by 'developing the ideas of scientific communism', by 'continuing with the theoretical and political training of its militants' ('Résolution politique de la première session du premier congrès de l'UJC(ml)', in Kessel, *Le Mouvement maoïste en France* vol. 1, 205). Although not a member himself, Badiou remembers the UJC as 'a thoroughly unique phenomenon, one that brought together all that was most "modernist", so to speak, most concentrated, in the French intelligentsia' (Badiou, 'Theory from Structure to Subject', 276).
     For more details see UJC documents posted at archivescommunistes.chez-alice.fr/ujcml/ujcml.html; 'Une Catastrophe pour le révisionisme français; une grande victoire du marxisme-léninisme!', in Kessel, *Le Mouvement maoïste en France* vol. 1, 199–203; 'Résolution politique de la première session du premier congrès de l'UJC(ml)', *Cahiers Marxistes-Léninistes* 15 (January 1967); Bensaïd and Weber, *Une Répétition générale*, 50, 63–74; Virginie Linhart, *Volontaires pour l'usine*, 25–27; Hervé Hamon and Patrick Rotman, *Génération* vol. 1, *Les Années de rêve* (Paris: Seuil, 1987), 328ff; Le Dantec, *Les Dangers du soleil*, 86–98.
     95   See Althusser, 'On the Cultural Revolution' [*Cahiers Marxistes-Léninistes* 14 (1966)], trans. Jason E. Smith, *Décalages* 1:1 (February 2010), 1–2. Althusser concludes 'that every great revolution can only be the work of the masses, and that the role of revolutionary leaders, while giving the masses the means to orient and organize themselves, while giving them Marxism-Leninism as compass and law, is to attend the school of the masses, in order to help them express their will and solve their problems' (18).
     Although never prepared to make an open break with the PCF, in 1966–68 Althusser's own theoretical position evolved more or less in line with that of the UJC, and by 1967 he had moved away from his 1965 definition of philosophy as pure 'theoretical practice' to take up an emphatically 'partisan' position whereby 'philosophy represents the class struggle in theory' (LP, 18). He now recognizes as the 'two great principles of Marxism': (i) 'it is the masses that make history'; and (ii) 'it is the class struggle that is the motor of history' (PSPS, 163; cf. LP, 20–21). Philosophy is thus the 'continuation of politics' in theory, 'philosophy represents politics in the domain of theory or to be more precise: *with the sciences* – and, *vice versa,* philosophy represents scientificity in politics, with the classes engaged in class struggle' (LP, 65).
     Linhart, Rancière, and Badiou would soon attack Althusser for not going far enough down the Maoist path; Balibar and then Elliott, among others, would fault him for going too far down it, for conceding too much to his post-68 critics and thereby swapping his earlier theoreticism for a new politicism – at risk of returning to the Zhdanovist heresy he had originally condemned (Balibar and Macherey, 'Interview', *Diacritics* 12 [1982], 48; Elliott, *Althusser*, 179, 188).

Chinese example the new Comités de Vietnam de Base 'began to conduct a different kind of political organizing: direct contact, leaving the territory of the university, organizing regularly in workers' housing, outside the gates of factories, in cafes in immigrant suburbs – outside of the Latin Quarter and outside, that is, of the PCF's definition of the way politics was to be conducted.'[96]

In the domain of theory, likewise, even before the founders of the UJC broke away to form their own organization, tensions developed within the *Cahiers Marxistes-Léninistes* group between those who (like Linhart, and Benny Lévy) prioritized political practice and those who (like Miller, Milner and Regnault) sought to privilege a broader theoretical-epistemological agenda. In the summer of 1965 Miller, disappointed by Althusser's decision to make the *Reading Capital* seminars open to the public (which he then refused to attend), launched a furious attack on Rancière and Althusser for apparently drawing, without acknowledgement, on the concept of metonymic or structural causality he had helped to formulate in the still-unpublished text that would soon serve as the unofficial manifesto of the *Cahiers pour l'Analyse* ('The Action of the Structure', CpA 9.6, drafted in September 1964).[97] Things came to a head in the last months of 1965, and crystalized in a row over the eighth issue of the *Cahiers Marxistes-Léninistes*. The issue was prepared by Miller, Milner and Macherey on the 'Powers of Literature', with articles on experimental works by Borges, Gombrowicz and Aragon. Miller's introduction to the issue announced its concern with what 'literature can do on its own and upon itself,' at the level of pure 'signification' or of 'the treatment of language by its structure', without appeal to Marx or any 'outside' reference.[98] Dominique Lecourt found their approach 'totally esoteric', and Linhart was appalled by such apolitical and scholastic use of the *Cahiers*; after accusing Miller of seeking only to secure a 'bourgeois position of authority' he blocked its distribution.[99] Miller, Milner and Grosrichard immediately resigned from the journal, and in January 1966 launched a new set of *Cahiers*, the *Cahiers pour l'Analyse*, as a less 'doctrinal' forum in which to consolidate the primacy of science. (As for the *Cahiers Marxistes-Léninistes*, they countered their new rivals, the following month, with a double issue entitled 'Vive le léninisme!')

---

96   Kristin Ross, *May '68 and its Afterlives* (Chicago: University of Chicago Press, 2002), 90; cf. Kessel, *Le Mouvement maoïste en France* vol. 1, 209–212.

97   Duroux, 'Strong Structuralism, Weak Subject', CF2; Rancière, 'Only in the Form of Rupture', CF2; Althusser, *The Future Lasts Forever*, 209, 353. Perhaps it's no accident that this most anti-subjective concept, one conceived to help bury the old notion of authorial 'paternity' once and for all, should so quickly have become the object of such a quarrel.

98   Miller, 'Les Pouvoirs de la littérature', *Cahiers Marxistes-Léninistes* 8 (December 1965, suppressed), reprinted in *Un Début dans la vie*, 90–94.

99   Dominique Lecourt, interview with Dosse, in Dosse, *History of Structuralism* vol. 1, 282; Linhart, cited by Hamon and Rotman, *Génération* vol. 1, 313.

IV   FOUCAULT AND LACAN

Both the *Cahiers Marxistes-Léninistes* and the *Cahiers pour l'Analyse* should be understood as pursuing the general Althusserian project of a *formation théorique*, i.e. as trying to provide that theoretical supplement required to develop the more general 'philosophy', left undeveloped both by Marx and his followers, that would secure the science of historical materialism. But whereas the first *Cahiers* inherited the problem in terms defined by that science in particular, the new *Cahiers* begin with 'theory' in a much wider epistemological sense.[100] As even a superficial review of the contents of the *Cahiers pour l'Analyse* will show, what is immediately striking about them, in relation to the more directly political concerns of the predecessor, is that their range of theoretical reference is much broader and that, alongside articles on logic and the history of the sciences, the privileged point of theoretical reference is less historical materialism than psychoanalysis. Over the course of the trajectory that leads from Cavaillès and Bachelard through Canguilhem and Althusser to Lacan and these new *Cahiers*, the scope of scientific analysis – always in its implacable distinction from lived experience or ideology – shifts from its foundations in pure mathematics, to mathematized physics, to biology and the life sciences, to historical materialism, before culminating at the edge of what for so long had marked an apparent limit for scientific investigation – the domain of the psyche, of the imaginary, the fantasmatic, and so on. As we'll soon see in more detail, the *Cahiers*' ambition is to develop a general 'theory of discourse' that might be adequate both to the most abstract operations of logic, the most fundamental configurations of speech, and the most elusive operations of the unconscious.

The broader epistemological agenda is suggested by the *Cahiers* editors' enthusiasm for Foucault; the more specific theoretical inflection, especially in the first few issues, is signalled by their fascination with Lacan.

Like Canguilhem and Althusser, Foucault insists on the qualitative gap between the 'self-evident' clarity of what appears as 'given' and the actual epistemological process that produces this evidence. Since there is no 'heaven that glitters through the grid of all astronomies', so then 'it is not enough for us to open our eyes, to pay attention, or to be aware, for new objects suddenly to light up and emerge.'[101] Before we can open our eyes we must first reconstruct the historical processes that, one way or another, have effectively closed our minds – for instance the processes that have led to a certain way of distinguishing between reason and madness (such that madness comes to figure, after

---

100   See Althusser, FM, 30–31; RC, 121, 143.
101   Foucault, *The Archaeology of Knowledge* [1969], trans. Alan Sheridan Smith (New York: Pantheon, 1972), 191, 44–45; cf. RC, 45.

Descartes, as mere absence of reason, and thus as a mere defect to be corrected)[102], or a certain way of thinking the relation between general scientific categories and individual 'cases' (as when, in the early nineteenth century, clinical medicine devises new ways of looking at an individual patient 'in his irreducible quality', and thereby demonstrates that 'one could at last hold a scientifically structured discourse about an individual'[103]). For Althusser and his students, Foucault's work offers a privileged demonstration of the complex historicity at work in the 'production of knowledge' in general: puncturing any ideological pretension that knowledges accumulate gradually and continuously, Foucault exposes the discontinuous and 'absolutely unexpected temporality' of actual processes of cultural development (RC, 103). More importantly, this 'archaeological' Foucault uncovers, in the most radically anti-humanist terms, the fundamental gap that separates the domain of conscious motivation and speech from the anonymous system of rules that configure a particular discursive formation. 'Discourse is not life: its time is not your time.'[104] Rather than reconstruct the 'signified' or intended meanings of a speaker, rigorous 'structural analysis of discourses' should approach their elements

> not as autonomous nuclei of multiple significations, but as events and functional segments gradually coming together to form a system. The meaning of a statement would be defined not by the treasure of intentions that it might contain, revealing and concealing it at the same time, but by the difference that articulates it upon the other real or possible statements, which are contemporary to it or to which it is opposed in the linear series of time.

On this basis, 'a systematic history of discourses would then become possible', and with it a renewal of 'the task of transforming them.'[105] The 'subjects' of speech themselves, however, can no more serve as the agent of such transformation than can, in Althusser's conception of things, the 'supports' or effects of a given mode of production direct the action that will overthrow it. A subject here is not the author, cause or origin of a statement, understood as something he or she 'meant' to say; rather, a legitimate statement, for a specific discourse, is a proposition to which, by the rules that define this discourse, 'the position of

---

102   With Descartes and the establishment of modern scientific reason, 'madness has been banished. While *man* can still go mad, *thought*, as the sovereign exercise carried out by a subject seeking the truth, can no longer be devoid of reason. A new dividing line has appeared, rendering that experience so familiar to the Renaissance – unreasonable Reason, or reasoned Unreason – impossible' (Foucault, *History of Madness* [1961], trans. Jonathan Murphy and Jean Khalfa [London: Routledge, 2006], 44–47; cf. 157).

103   Foucault, *The Birth of the Clinic* [1963], trans. Alan Sheridan (London: Taylor & Francis, 2003), xix.

104   Foucault, *The Archaeology of Knowledge*, 275/211.

105   Foucault, *The Birth of the Clinic*, xvii, xix.

the subject can be assigned. To describe a formulation qua statement does not consist in analyzing the relations between the author and what he says (or wanted to say, or said without wanting to), but in determining what position can and must be occupied by any individual if he is to be the subject of it.'[106]

Although perhaps not as profound as the first issues of the journal might suggest (given the constraints on what even the most precocious non-analysts can make of a discourse based on clinical practice[107]), Lacan's influence on the *Cahiers* demands detailed study on its own right,[108] and there is only space here to consider a couple of the most essential points.

In one sense, Lacan's conception of discourse and of science is broadly consistent with the anti-humanism championed by Foucault and Althusser. After Freud, conscious agents no longer figure as the centre of their world or the author of their words, and what Lacan offered Althusser's students in the mid 1960s, first and foremost, was a suitably i.e. remorselessly 'rigorous' way of coming to terms with this displacement.[109] The point of departure for an analysis of the 'truth' of speech is that the signifying or 'symbolic order is absolutely irreducible to what is commonly called human experience' (S2, 320). Both of Lacan's two contributions to the *Cahiers* insist on the exclusion of 'man' and 'humanist references' from science (CpA 1.1:9, 11; CpA 3.1:12), and in keeping with neo-Bachelardian epistemology Lacan rejects any conception of the unconscious that considers it as some sort of 'given' reality, something like an underlying or 'inner' bundle of instinctual impulses, more or less adapted to a

---

106   Foucault, *The Archaeology of Knowledge*, 95–96; cf. Emile Benveniste, 'De la subjectivité dans le language,' in *Problèmes de linguistique générale* (Paris: Gallimard, 1966), 259–260). Hence the importance, in Foucault's *The Order of Things* (1966), of those transitional moments (the moments he associates with Sade, with Cervantes, and then with himself and his contemporaries) in which the structured field starts to break up, in which discourse is liberated from the established rules.

107   Miller often told Badiou that '"we tried to declare that we were stronger than Lacan, for being able to create a Lacanianism without having to pass through all the trouble of psychoanalysis [. . .]. Miller told me several times that Lacan was a bit vexed by the *Cahiers pour l'Analyse*. He saw them as a presumptuous attempt to escape from the rigours of psychoanalytic training' (Badiou, 'Theory from Structure to Subject', CF2, 285; cf. Duroux, 'A Philosophical Conjuncture', CF2; Milner, *L'Oeuvre claire* [Paris: Seuil, 1995], 111–112).

108   See Adrian Johnston, 'Affects Are Signifiers', and Tracy McNulty, 'Desuturing Desire', in CF2; Tom Eyers, 'Psychoanalytic Structuralism', *Angelaki* 18:1 (2013).

109   As Peter Starr notes, Lacan's 'privileged instrument' for grasping the tragic fate of human desire was 'logic' as such, i.e. logic conceived as '"science of the real because it places access to the Real in the mode of the impossible." From the logic of specular doubling in Lacan's work of the 1940s and 1950s to the mathemes of the 1970s, there is a consistent linkage between the "logical" and the specific aims of Lacan's tragic ethic. No single word better captures the intimacy of this linkage than one whose centrality to the work of both Lacan and Althusser would have a decisive impact on Marxist (and specifically Maoist) theory in the post-May '68 period – that is, the word "rigour" [*la rigueur*]' (Starr, *Logics of Failed Revolt : French Theory after May '68* [Stanford: Stanford University Press, 1995], 48).

world in which they gradually evolved or 'developed'.[110] No less than Bachelard, Lacan insists that 'all scientific progress consists in making the object as such fade away' and in replacing it with formal symbolic or signifying constructions (S2, 104; cf. 136). 'Recourse to the signifier [provides] the sole foundation of all conceivable scientific structuration' (S3, 191). More precisely, 'what is distinctive about positive science, modern science, isn't quantification, but mathematization and specifically combinatory that is to say linguistic mathematization' (S3, 238). Only in mathematics can science realise its goal of an 'integral transmission' of knowledge (S20, 100), and thus 'mathematical formalization is our goal, our ideal'.[111] The matheme is language literalized, language purged of image and intuition.

By the same token, what is at stake in speech is less the communication of deliberate meanings or intentions than participation in a discursive logic inaccessible to conscious reflection. 'Language exists completely independently of us. Numbers have properties which are absolute. They are, whether we're here or not' (S2, 284). It is this 'world of words that creates the world of things', so if 'man speaks' it is because the signifying 'symbol has made him man'.[112] Again, 'the signifier doesn't just provide an envelope, a receptacle for meaning. It polarizes it, structures it, and brings it into existence'.[113] The unconscious is thus 'structured like a language', in Lacan's famous formulation, for the same reason that the subject's desire is 'the desire of the Other'

---

110   'It is not the instinctual effects in their primary force that Freud tries to treat. That which is analyzable is so, because it is already articulated in what determines the singularity of the subject's history. If the subject can recognize himself in it, this is insofar as psychoanalysis allows the 'transference' of this articulation. In other words, when the subject "represses" something, this does not mean that the subject refuses to become conscious of something that might be like an instinct – say, for example, a sexual instinct that might manifest itself in a homosexual form – no, the subject does not repress his homosexuality, he represses the speech where this homosexuality has the role of a signifier. You see, it is not something vague or confused which is repressed; it's not a sort of need, or tendency, that would have to be articulated (but that can't then be articulated since it is repressed); it is a discourse that is already articulated, already formulated in a way of speaking [dans un language]. Everything is there' (Lacan, 'Les clefs de la psychanalyse: Entretien avec Madeleine Chapsal', L'Express 310 [31 May 1957], reprinted in Chapsal, Envoyez la petite musique [Paris: Grasset, 1984], 229–230).

111   Lacan, S20, 108; cf. S3, 227, S7, 236. 'There is no such thing as a truth which is not "mathematized", that is [. . .], which is not based, qua Truth, solely upon axioms. Which is to say that there is truth but of that which has no meaning' (S21, 11 December 1973, cited in Bruce Fink, The Lacanian Subject [Princeton: Princeton University Press, 1995], 121). As Badiou observes, 'Lacan holds mathematization to be the key to any thinkable relation to the real; he never changed his mind on this point' (Badiou, 'Lacan et les présocratiques' [1990 ms.], 3–4).

112   Lacan, 'The Function and Field of Speech and Language in Psychoanalysis', E, 276/229. 'Language is not to be confused with the various psychical and somatic functions that serve it in the speaking subject [. . .;] language, with its structure, exists prior to each subject's entry into it' (Lacan, 'The Instance of the Letter in the Unconscious', E, 495/413).

113   Lacan, S3, 260. 'The signifier doesn't depend on meaning but is the source of meaning' (S3, 248; cf. 292).

– existing before and independently of any self, 'language is constituted in such a way as to found us in the Other, while radically preventing us from understanding him' (S2, 286). As Lacan will insist in ever more strident terms over the course of the 1950s and early 1960s, the signifier and its symbolic order 'cannot be conceived of as constituted by man but must rather be conceived of as constituting him.'[114] In rather the same way that for Althusser the subject is a category of ideology, for Lacan the conscious 'self' or 'ego' is an imaginary projection, a merely 'structured' rather than structuring configuration, in short a 'sum of prejudices' (S2, 41), fundamentally distinct from the true i.e. unconscious or repressed subject of discourse. 'The unconscious is the unknown subject of the ego.'[115]

What then speaks through discourse is not the self but this repressed subject that cannot by definition articulate itself directly. What speaks are the words or 'signifiers' that, precisely because they pre-exist the self and shape its world, always say more than what the speaker consciously means. If following Freud we should 'grant priority to the signifier over the subject' this is because, as illustrated in dreams, slips of the tongue and 'unintended' puns, 'the signifier plays and wins [. . .] before the subject is aware of it.'[116] What speaks, in other words, is the subject of the signifier, the subject subjected by the signifier – or more precisely, what speaks is 'the signifier that represents a subject to another signifier.'[117] Like a social formation as analyzed by Althusser and Balibar (RC, 249), Lacan's subject is not directly determined by some underlying instinct or impulse, but by a complex combination of objects, drives, resistances, etc., whose 'immanent causal' configuration in the 'chain of signifiers' that constitutes speech can only be properly understood by those who know how to analyze its effects, by those who resist the temptation to refer speech back to some external i.e. linear or transitive causal power. Rather like Foucault, therefore, Lacan says that in analysis 'I don't ask myself "who speaks?" [. . . but] "from where does it [ça] speak?"'. The goal is to locate the repressed truth of desire, so as to help an analysand 'to settle in this place, this place where he was no longer, replaced by this anonymous word that we call the "it".'[118] It's perhaps not surprising that Foucault recognized himself in this apparent mirror, suggesting in 1966 that 'Lacan is important because he has shown how [. . .] structures, the very system of language itself – and not the subject – are what

---

114   Lacan, 'Seminar on "The Purloined Letter"', E, 46/34.

115   Lacan, S2, 43. And thus 'one trains analysts so that there are subjects in whom the ego is absent. That is the ideal of analysis, which, of course, remains virtual. There is never a subject without an ego, [i.e.,] a fully realized subject, but that in fact is what one must aim to obtain from the subject in analysis' (S2, 246).

116   Lacan, 'Position of the Unconscious', E, 840/712; cf. Bertrand Ogilvie, Lacan: le sujet (Paris: PUF, 1987), 91–92.

117   Lacan, E, 818/694; cf. E, 840/713; S11, 207; S20, 49.

118   Lacan, 'Interview with Chapsal', L'Express (1957).

speak through the discourse of the patient and the symptoms of his neurosis', such that what thinks is 'anonymous thought' and 'knowledge without subject'.[119]

Unlike both Foucault and Althusser, however, Lacan's primary clinical concern still remains this decentred *subject* per se, the subject trying to come to terms with the unconscious 'truth' revealed by the signifiers representing it. From start to finish, Lacan recognizes that 'the quest for truth is not entirely reducible to the objective, and objectifying, quest of ordinary scientific method. What is at stake is the realization of the truth of the subject, as a dimension peculiar to it' (S1, 21). Lacan acknowledges, in an important passage, that philosophers had certainly made 'important corrections' to a naïve Cartesian version of the cogito, recognizing that 'in that which is thinking [*cogitans*], I am never doing anything but constituting myself as an object [*cogitatum*].' Nevertheless, he continues,

> the fact remains that through this extreme purification of the transcendental subject, my existential link to its project seems irrefutable, at least in the form of its actuality, and that '*cogito ergo sum*' *ubi cogito, ibi sum*, overcomes this objection.
>
> Of course, this limits me to being there in my being only insofar as I think that I am in my thought; to what extent I really think this concerns me alone and, if I say it, interests no one.
>
> Yet to avoid it on the pretext of its philosophical semblances is simply to demonstrate one's inhibition. *For the notion of the subject is indispensable* even to the workings of a science such as strategy in the modern sense, whose calculations exclude all subjectivism.
>
> It is also to deny oneself access to what might be called the Freudian universe – in the sense in which we speak of the Copernican universe. Indeed, Freud himself compared his discovery to the so-called Copernican revolution, emphasizing that what was at stake was once again the place man assigns himself at the centre of a universe.[120]

As understood through analysis, the speech or movement of the signifier that assigns a subject's place 'is not a play of signs, it is to be located, not on the level of information, but on that of truth' (S1, 251). Elusive 'effect of the signifier', the 'subject is this emergence which, just before, as subject, was nothing, but which, having scarcely appeared, solidifies into a signifier,'[121] such that psychoanalysis

119   Foucault, 'Entretien avec Madeleine Chapsal' (1966), *Dits et écrits* vol. 1, 515.

120   Lacan, 'The Instance of the Letter in the Unconscious' [1957], E, 516/429, my emphasis; cf. Regnault, 'The Thought of the Prince', CpA 6.2:39.

121   Lacan, S11, 199. As Bertrand Ogilvie notes, up to a point Foucault here attributes to Lacan 'the opposite of what he says' (Ogilvie, *Lacan*, 42; cf. 118).

is the practice that exposes how '*I* can come to be by disappearing from what I said.'[122]

By the same token, however, this unconscious subject of the signifier enjoys only a 'fading', flickering existence, an existence 'barred' from conscious articulation. Representing a subject for another signifier, 'the signifier, producing itself in the field of the Other, makes manifest the subject of its signification. But it functions as a signifier only to reduce the subject in question to being no more than a signifier, to petrify the subject in the same movement in which it calls the subject to function, to speak, as subject' (S11, 207). An individual becomes a subject through subjection to speech and the signifier, i.e. in the gap between 'itself' and the structuring action of the signifier that represents it. And since signifiers only represent a subject in the differential movement that skips from one signifier to another, so then the place of the subject is properly the gap that separates 'its' signifiers from others. If then for Lacan a version of Descartes' cogito offers a way of evoking the scientific 'truth' of this elusive, vanishing subject (CpA 1.1:8), it is only insofar as the 'I' that doubts and thinks is distinguished from any sort of thinking 'substance', consciousness or freedom.[123]

The great effort of the *Cahiers pour l'Analyse* was to develop, on the basis of an Althusserian conception of structure and a Lacanian 'logic of the signifier', a general theory of discourse that includes a place for the subject in this implacably evanescent and in-substantial sense. The *Cahiers* writers, as Badiou remembers, 'sought to find in scientism itself, in the extreme forms of formal thought, something to support the Lacanian theory of the subject', on the assumption that 'it's not because one engages in the most extreme formal rigour and takes up the intellectual power of mathematics, of logic, etc., that one must necessarily erase or abolish the category of the subject. I think that was Lacan's major philosophical influence.' (For much the same reason, Badiou goes on to

---

122   Lacan, 'Subversion of the Subject', E, 801/678. 'The subject is subject only from being subjected to the field of the Other' (S11, 188), but 'the relation of the subject to the Other is entirely produced in a process of gap' (S11, 206).

123   S11, 126; cf. 140–141; E, 831/705. As Mladen Dolar puts it, 'in the place of the supposed certainty of the subject's being, there is just a void. It is not the same subject that thinks and that is; the one that is is not the one that thinks, even more, the one that is is ultimately not a subject at all' (Dolar, "Cogito as the Subject of the Unconscious" in *Cogito and the Unconscious*, ed. Slavoj Žižek [Durham: Duke University Press, 1998], 19). Since speech can never present the 'substantial' truth of its subject, truth cannot be a matter of full presentation or speech; as a matter of course, 'words fail' (Lacan, *Television*, ed. Joan Copjec, trans. Denis Hollier et al., [New York: Norton, 1990], 9). But as Peter Starr notes, in terms that apply equally well to the *Cahiers*, in the later Lacan 'it is precisely through this material failure, this lack of material, that the truth participates in the "real". The great originality of Lacan's project lay in the lengths to which he would go to mimic this lack, reproducing the equivocation and indirection of unconscious discourse in a style, both analytic and pedagogical, that he called "mid-speak" [*le mi-dire*]' (Starr, *Logics of Failed Revolt*, 37–38).

argue, in May 68 it would be the *Cahiers* Lacanians, more than either the Sartreans or the orthodox Althusserians, who embraced Maoism with the greatest enthusiasm).[124]

V THE *CAHIERS POUR L'ANALYSE*

The specific sequence that led to the creation of the *Cahiers pour l'Analyse* by Miller and his associates overlaps to a large extent with the conjunctural sequence, at the ENS, that led them from Althusser to Lacan. Miller enrolled at the ENS in the autumn of 1962, a year after his friend Milner. At the time, Lacan's teaching was still mainly confined to a clinical audience, and his work remained almost unknown in philosophical circles – no doubt its daunting reputation and semi-clandestine status helps account for some of the fascination it soon exerted among the trail-blazing *normaliens*, the first non-analysts to engage with it in any depth. In his final year at the ENS (1960–61) Badiou gave his first presentation on Lacan's work, and Althusser subsequently introduced his students to Lacan with a seminar on psychoanalysis in 1963–64. As Balibar and Regnault remember, it was Althusser himself who pushed them to study Lacan's work in detail, and who in 1963 arranged for a couple of closed seminars with Lacan and a small hand-picked group (Miller, Milner, Duroux, Rancière, Balibar).[125] Althusser's own personal investment in and experience of psychoanalysis was already profound, and his article on 'Freud and Lacan', written in January 1964, applauds psychoanalysis as a genuine science, i.e. as a discourse capable of producing its own object of knowledge (the unconscious), distinct from any merely 'given' object and from any merely 'ideological' conception of the subject.[126] More precisely, Althusser found in Lacan's approach a convincing response to a standard Marxist objection to psychoanalysis (one made most forcefully by Georges Politzer in his influential *Critique of the Foundations of Psychology* [1928]), an objection that served to valorize the 'concrete' or 'lived' dimension of the unconscious: as Duroux recalls, it was the 1961 critique of Politzer made by Lacan's students Jean Laplanche and Serge Leclaire that 'turned his ideas about psychoanalysis (and thus also about Lacan) upside down.'[127]

---

124   Badiou, 'Theory from Structure to Subject', CF2; cf. Badiou and Bosteels, 'Can Politics be Thought?', 243.

125   Balibar, 'A Philosophical Conjuncture', CF2.

126   Althusser, 'Freud and Lacan', LP, 200–201.

127   Duroux, 'Strong Structuralism, Weak Subject', 197; cf. RC, 39n.18; Jean Laplanche and Serge Leclaire, 'L'Inconscient: Une étude psychanalytique', *Les Temps Modernes* 183 (1961); 'The Unconscious: A Psychoanalytic Study', trans. Patrick Coleman, *Yale French Studies* 48 (1972), 118–175. Laplanche and Leclaire emphasize 'how far the contribution of psychoanalysis is from descriptions given in the realm of phenomenology' (129); as conceived by Freud, the unconscious 'is radically and scandalously intolerant of any attempt at interpretation by the conceptual tools of

Meanwhile by 1963 Lacan himself had reached a critical juncture. After losing patience with some of the apparent liberties he took with his patients, in October the International Psychoanalytic Association struck him off its list of training analysts. In protest, Lacan resigned his post at the Sainte-Anne hospital, the venue that had hosted his weekly seminar since it began in 1953. Many veterans in the French branch of the IPA had turned against him, and by the end of the year, his biographer notes, he was in a 'state of dreadful agitation', threatening suicide and 'fulminating against his banishment' from the psychoanalytic establishment.[128] When Althusser met with him in December, Lacan quickly accepted an invitation to relaunch his seminar at the ENS, and to present his ideas to a much wider audience. The first session of Lacan's new seminar took place at the ENS on 15 January 1964, and for Jacques-Alain Miller in particular it cemented a conversion that affected every dimension of his life.[129] As Elizabeth Roudinesco observes, Lacan himself 'wasn't at all interested in Althusser's philosophy' but he was certainly interested in the influential 'student body at the ENS. He knew they'd been awakened to his ideas by Althusser and hoped they might prove to be potential disciples, familiar enough with philosophy to be able not only to understand his work but also to give a new impetus to his thought and his movement.'[130] Sure enough, in Miller Lacan found more than he could ever have bargained for: the most enthusiastic, most brilliant and most forceful of his disciples, soon to become the editor of his words, husband of his daughter, and custodian of his legacy. For the next ten years this young

---

a psychology of consciousness' (128). Laplanche and Leclaire formulate their Freud-Politzer distinction in terms that anticipate the 'theory of discourse' proposed in the *Cahiers pour l'Analyse*. For Freud, against Politzer, 'the unconscious is rigorously distinguished from the manifest text, and it is precisely for that reason that it can enter into relation with it: (a) The unconscious is not coextensive to the manifest as its meaning: it must be interpolated in the lacunae of the manifest text. (b) What is unconscious is in relation to the manifest not as a meaning to a letter, but on the same level of reality. It is what allows us to conceive of a dynamic relationship between the manifest text and what is absent from and must be interpolated in it: it is a fragment of discourse that must find its place in the discourse as a whole' (126).

128   Roudinesco, *Jacques Lacan*, trans. Barbara Bray (Cambridge: Polity, 1997), 301; cf. Althusser, 'Correspondence with Jacques Lacan' [1963–1969], in *Writings on Psychoanalysis*, ed. Olivier Corpet and François Matheron, trans. Jeffrey Mehlman (New York: Columbia University Press, 1996), 145–174.

129   According to Roudinesco, when Althusser suggested to Miller that he begin reading Lacan, in late 1963, 'he went at once to the PUF bookshop, bought every issue they had of *La Psychanalyse*, and then shut himself up in his room to puzzle them out. He emerged dazzled: "I had just come upon something extraordinary". An immediate convert, the nineteen-year-old [Miller] was further impressed by Lacan's seminar [at the ENS] on "Excommunication". On 21 January 1964, at the ENS, Miller presented his first paper on the master's work', followed by two further presentations in successive weeks (Roudinesco, *Lacan*, 305).

130   Roudinesco, *Lacan*, 300. In a terse note to Althusser, Lacan himself wasted few words on Miller ('Rather good, your guy. Thanks'), but when Althusser showed it to him it was enough for Miller: 'Here, a spark fixated something for me' (Lacan, letter to Althusser, 22 January 1964, in Althusser, *Writings on Psychoanalysis*, 169, 184n.18tm).

philosopher who had never undergone analysis would act, Roudinesco notes, 'against the practitioners of the unconscious, as an "extra-therapeutic" subject, that is, as chief spokesman for Lacanianism's "scientific" truth.'[131]

A few months after his move to the ENS, Lacan established his own new school, the École Freudienne de Paris, and opened its membership to non-analysts. Combining his most faithful adherents from Sainte-Anne with an eclectic mix of philosophers, mathematicians, literary critics and linguists, with its shift to the ENS 'the Freudian cause ceased to be exclusively in the hands of specialists.'[132] In order to apply to the new school, would-be members had to form a distinctive 'cartel', and over the summer of 1964 Miller, Milner, and Duroux formed a group dedicated to 'the theory of discourse', drafting a short article entitled 'Action of the Structure' (CpA 9.6) to serve as its programme.[133] In the first months of 1965 (i.e. overlapping with sessions of the *Reading Capital* seminar), in order to consolidate the institutional standing of his new school and to strengthen his teaching against the neo-Freudian alternative promoted by his rival Daniel Lagache, Lacan began to rework his doctrine in terms that drew directly on the sort 'formalization' or 'scientifization' now dominant at the ENS. In February he invited Duroux and Miller to make presentations on Frege's logic (subsequently published as CpA 1.2 and 1.3), and in turn they invited Lacan's disciple Serge Leclaire to give a series of lectures on the relation between the theory and practice of analysis (subsequently published as CpA 1.5, 3.6, 8.6). Over the course of 1965, as Miller and his friends threw themselves into Lacan's seminar, their theoretical priorities began to move

---

131   Roudinesco, *Jacques Lacan & Co.: A History of Psychoanalysis in France, 1925–1985*, trans. Jeffrey Mehlman (London: Free Association, 1990), 404.

132   Jacques-Alain Miller, 'The Non-Existent Seminar' [1992], *The Symptom* 11 (2010), www.lacan.com/symptom11/?p=26, accessed 3 October 2011; cf. Roudinesco, *Jacques Lacan & Co.*, 399ff. Miller's move from Althusser to Lacan also involved moving Althusser into Lacan, so to speak, a neo-Althusserian injection of science and 'rigour' into Lacanian doctrine, such that, for the first time, Lacan's critics 'could be identified and labelled "deviationist" in relation to a pure and absolute doctrinal norm. While Lacan produced concepts that were deliberately ambiguous and open to multiple interpretation, Miller sought to rationalise them. This "corrected", more "coherent" version of Lacan facilitated attacks on now more easily identifiable theoretical enemies. Before this period Lacan had not used the term "deviation" to describe wayward disciples. In his very first presentation at Lacan's seminar, however, Miller applied this politicized language to attack theoretical impurities in the work of Lacan's followers, and specifically that of the analyst Piera Aulagnier. Aulagnier had refused Lacan's invitation to respond, claiming that the charge of deviationism had no meaning in a clinical context. From this first interchange, Miller established a pattern that was to be fateful for the history of the Freudian School: a "scientific" philosophical language was pitted against "impure" clinical discourse' (Sherry Turkle, 'Dynasty: Review of Roudinesco, *Jacques Lacan & Co*', London Review of Books, 6 December 1990; cf. Sherry Turkle, *Psychoanalytic Politics: Jacques Lacan and Freud's French Revolution* [1978] (New York: Guilford Press, 1992).

133   Roudinesco lists, as ancillary members of this cartel, Balibar, Grosrichard, Macherey, Jean Mathiot, Jean Mosconi, Rancière, Regnault, and Jean-Marie Villégier (Roudinesco, *Jacques Lacan & Co.*, 383).

further and further away from the 'narrow' concerns of the *Cahiers Marxistes-Léninistes* and by the end of the year they were ready to expand their group to form a 'Cercle d'Épistémologie' and to launch their own journal.[134]

All the pieces were now in place: with Bachelard-Canguilhem on scientific methodology, Althusser on the theoretical training of political militants, Foucault on the archaeology of discourse and Lacan on the signifier and its subject, by the end of 1965 Miller's group had everything they needed to undertake the analysis of discourse in the most anti-humanist or 'structuralist' sense of the term. It was now possible to consider, from several distinct perspectives and on the broadest (or most abstract) epistemological basis, how best to think together the theoretical projects of historical materialism and psychoanalysis, with the former serving to elucidate 'particular signifying orders (ideologies), and the latter producing the structures of their efficacy, the laws of entry and connection through which the places allocated by ideology are eventually occupied.'[135] As Miller puts it, in the *Cahiers'* founding document, if 'Marxist discourse has today been liberated by Louis Althusser of the obstacle that burdened it with a conception of society as historical subject, just as [Freudian discourse] has been liberated by Jacques Lacan from the interpretation of the individual as psychological subject, – we think that it is now possible to join these two discourses. We maintain that the discourses of Marx and Freud might communicate with each other via regulated transformations, and might reflect one another in a unitary theoretical discourse.'[136]

Looking at the ten issues of the *Cahiers pour l'Analyse* as a whole, we might roughly distinguish between three sorts of article published by the journal. There are, first of all, some programmatic pieces, dealing with the general theory of discourse or science, with fundamental issues like logic, the subject, the signifier, representation, and so on; in the final issues of the journal, this category bleeds into still broader reflections on the status and history of science, and recent developments in formal logic. Then there are articles dealing with psychoanalysis more specifically, as a privileged sphere for the application of discourse theory. Finally there's a more open-ended series of somewhat eclectic investigations, determined by intersection of the journal's theoretical agenda together with contingent editorial requirements (the need to find suitable copy, issue by issue) – here we find articles on various aspects of the history of philosophy, political or deconstructive readings of philosophers like Hume, Rousseau or Fichte, appreciative readings of recent experimental fiction, and so on. These three categories overlap, of course, but the assumption behind the selection translated in the present volume (together with what remains of this

---

134   Cf. Roudinesco, *Jacques Lacan & Co.*, 398–406.
135   Badiou, 'Mark and Lack', CpA 10.8:162.
136   Miller, 'Action of the Structure', CpA 9.6:103.

introduction) is that it's the first sort of article that's likely to remain of most general interest today.

Miller's brief introductory text to the first volume of the *Cahiers* (January 1966) explains that the journal will publish (and in some cases republish) a wide range of texts 'relating to logic, to linguistics, to psychoanalysis, to all sciences of analysis – in view of contributing to the constitution of a theory of discourse.' Miller then defines some key terms in the sort of clipped, neo-Lacanian style that will characterize much of the work that will appear in the *Cahiers* over the next three years. 'By discourse, we mean a process of language [*langage*] that truth constrains'; a subsequent *avertissement* will define 'a discourse [as] a sequence, discrete in essence, incommensurable with the continuum of consciousness' (CpA 8.Intro). By epistemology, Miller means 'the history and theory of the d ourse of science', in the singular [*la science*] (CpA 1.Intro). By analysis, Mi r means 'all discourse insofar as it can be reduced to putting unities in place that produce themselves and repeat themselves, whatever the principle may be that it assigns to the transformations at play in its system'; analysis is 'the theory that deals with concepts of element and their combinations.' More precisely, the analysis at issue here 'chiefly concerns dialectical materialism' as conceived by Althusser, and though 'nothing in our project holds to the particularity of a doctrine', the priority remains a matter of *la formation théorique*. 'What is at stake for us is simply a matter of training ourselves, following our teachers, in line with the rigour of the concept' (CpA 1.Intro).

In one sense, the programme for the new *Cahiers* remains perfectly consistent with Althusser's long-standing priorities. If 'theoretical research begins only in the zone that separates those knowledges already acquired and deeply assimilated from knowledges not yet acquired', Althusser had argued, such 'research demands a very strong theoretical formation simply to be possible', i.e. 'possession of a high degree not only of Marxist culture (which is absolutely indispensable) but also of scientific and philosophical culture in general.'[137] The new *Cahiers* would provide a forum for such 'general education' and would frame it, against the 'closure' of humanism and ideology, in terms of that '*openness* typical of a scientific field' (RC, 308). It makes sense to read the *Cahiers*, accordingly, alongside the semi-clandestine effort of Althusser and a small

---

137   Althusser, 'Theory, Theoretical Practice and Theoretical Formation', PSPS, 20. The *Cahiers* project is also consistent with Althusser's conception of theory more generally, as sketched in his presentation of the *Théorie* book series at Maspéro. As Elliott summarizes it, Marxist philosophy should comprise: '(i) a theory of scientific and ideological discourse: theoretical practice – and what distinguished this practice from other practices; (ii) a theory of the history of the sciences – as distinct from other forms of history; and (iii) a theory of the structure and history of the other – non-theoretical – social practices with which theoretical practice is "articulated"' (Elliott, *Althusser*, 75).

group of his students, including *Cahiers* collaborators Duroux, Badiou and Tort, to work out for both historical materialism and psychoanalysis the relation between their 'general theory' and the various 'regional theories' (e.g. of capitalism, ideology, the unconscious, etc.) they include, and thereby – as Althusser told Franca Madonia in September 1966 – distinguish psychoanalysis per se from 'the general theory of the signifier, which studies the mechanisms and possible effects of every discourse.'[138] An 'epistemological' or analytical approach to discourse, moreover, for Althusser as much as for Lacan, is an approach attuned to the gaps and silences that expose the structuring forces at work in it, repressed forces inaccessible to the experience they structure. 'In an epistemological and critical reading we cannot but hear behind the proffered word the silence it conceals, see the blank of suspended rigour, scarcely the time of a lightning-flash in the darkness of the text: correlatively, we cannot but hear behind this discourse which seems continuous but is really interrupted and governed by the threatened irruption of a repressive discourse, the silent voice of the real discourse' underlying it (RC, 143).

In another sense, however, Miller and his main collaborators take their distance from Althusser via Lacan and the subject. 'There is no such thing as a science of man', Lacan argues, 'because science's man does not exist, only its subject does' (CpA 1.1:11/730) – Althusser and an Althusserian like Badiou could agree with the first part of the proposition but not the second. From a rigorously Althusserian position, the subject can *only* perform an ideological function.[139] As Regnault remembers, 'the greatest différend between us and "the others" concerned the subject. It served as a shibboleth between psychoanalysis and materialist philosophy, between Lacanians and Althusserians, between

---

138   'If all this is true', Althusser continues in a style that gives some indication of the atmosphere in which these questions were pursued, 'it should, despite its aridity, have the effect of a bomb. I'm going to get as many guarantees as I can by consulting a few, but only a very few, knowledgeable young lads before publishing it, in a form I've yet to decide on. For I'm advancing here in a field bristling with people packing pistols of every imaginable calibre; they fire without warning and without mercy, and, if I don't watch out, I risk being shot down in cold blood' (Althusser, letter to Franca Madonia, 13 September 1966, *Lettres à Franca*, 711–712, cited in HC, 35–36).

139   Althusser himself toyed for a brief moment in 1966, in response to the challenge posed by psychoanalysis, with acknowledging a place for the subject in terms that appear similar to those defended by Miller and his associates, but soon changed his mind. In a draft text he discussed that autumn with a small group of confidants including Badiou and Duroux, entitled 'Three Notes on the Theory of Discourses', Althusser recognized a need to account for 'subjectivity-effects' not only in the domain of ideology but also in scientific, artistic and psychoanalytic discourses (Althusser, 'Three Notes on the Theory of Discourses', HC, 48). By the time he wrote a cover letter for his essay (dated 28 October 1966), however, he admits that 'everything I have said about the place of the "subject" in every one of the discourses must be revised. The more I work on it, the more I think that the category of the subject is absolutely fundamental to ideological discourse' in particular, such that it is not legitimate to speak (as Lacan does) of a subject of science, or of the unconscious (HC, 37–38).

Althusser's process without subject and the procedures of the barred subject, between the logic of the signifier and a certain scientific positivism.'[140]

More than anything else, it's this general question – how best to think the relation between science and subject – that figures as the guiding concern of the *Cahiers* as a whole. If we formulate the general issue in terms wide enough to embrace Hegel and Kierkegaard on the one hand and Sartre or Lacan on the other, we can still say that, at a minimum, unlike an object, a subject is something that doesn't simply coincide with itself, and thus has no stable relation with itself (whether this non-self-coincidence is then thought in terms of freedom or existence or alterity or drive, etc., is at this level a secondary issue).[141] But if this 'negative' dimension of the subject can't be thought from within science, science won't then be able to explain the movement from structure (e.g. linguistic or kinship or class structures) to actual spoken discourse or social practice. What's required, therefore, is a theory of the subject that acknowledges the primacy of science while enabling the inclusion, within science, of that subjective dimension it appears to exclude. In brief, and to put it in canonical structuralist terms: if every element of a signifying system is defined solely by the relations that distinguish it from other elements, the 'subject' will be that element that is both included in the system yet defined by a 'vanishing' or 'impossible' relation to itself.

The general stakes of the question are especially clear in the confrontation that pits the science of psychoanalysis against mere psychology, in Milner's introduction to the second issue of the journal. The general thrust of the *Cahiers'* approach to psychology, and in particular of 'experimental psychology', is consistent with Canguilhem's critique of behaviourism and instrumentalism (as contributing to 'barbarism'[142]) and Lacan's critique of 'ego-psychology' (the version of psychoanalysis, dominant in the contemporary United States, concerned with strengthening the 'autonomous' ego and its conscious defences, with enhancing its capacity to adapt to its circumstances, and so on[143]). Psychology is an ideological rather than scientific discipline. Since 'consciousness constitutes itself in excluding desire from its field', experimental study of consciousness can never access the real object of analysis. Psychology effectively reduces the subject to the status of thing or 'tool', in order to put the speaking

---

140   Regnault, essay, CF2; cf. Wahl, *Qu'est-ce que le structuralisme?*, 342n.2.

141   I draw here on discussions with Patrice Maniglier, and on his article 'The Structuralist Legacy', in *The History of Continental Philosophy* vol. 7, ed. Alan Schrift (London: Acumen, 2010), 55–82.

142   Canguilhem, 'Qu'est-ce que la psychologie?' [1956], CpA 2.1; Canguilhem, 'Brain and Thought' [1980], trans. Steven Corcoran and Peter Hallward, *Radical Philosophy* 148 (March 2008), 17–18.

143   See for instance Lacan, E, 87/70, 116/94–95, 178/146. 'The dimension discovered by analysis is the opposite of anything which progresses through adaptation' (S2, 86; cf. S2, 11), and as far as psychoanalysis is concerned 'it is not a question of adapting to [reality], but of showing [the ego] that it is only too well adapted, since it assists in the fabrication of that very reality' (E, 596/498tm; cf. Philippe van Haute, *Against Adaptation: Lacan's 'Subversion of the Subject'* (New York: Other Press, 2002).

subject in the position of 'a thing that responds' to questions, rather than a person who raises them. What is at stake, Milner suggests, anticipating Grosrichard's contribution to this issue, is the reduction of the subject to the manipulation of a 'rationalized political system, one regulated according to a grid of needs and capacities'. In order that people be reduced to the status of things or tools who 'freely' sell their labour-power, Marx showed, they must first be made 'master of themselves.'[144] In this way 'the subject of science' itself becomes merely the object of a science which believes that it can know everything about the subject, and thus condemns itself to ignorance of the real subject at issue here, the unconscious subject of desire.

By contrast, genuine i.e. Lacanian psychoanalysis strips the conscious ego of its apparent mastery and awareness, and reconceives it as a 'function of misunderstanding and mirage, ransom of the imaginary that science, returning to its own *subjectum*, must pay as the price of the exclusion with which it encircles it [the subject].' Psychoanalysis will thus dedicate itself to an analysis of those drives that the subject can only access via the bar of repression. To analyze psychology as a *discourse* in Miller's sense of the term, then, is to 'delimitate in it the element that induces silence' and misunderstanding, and 'to specify this element as the self or ego [*moi*] of synthesis and mastery.'[145] By the same token, Regnault explains, the unconscious subject accessed through psychoanalysis, 'far from being a unity, a centre, a power of synthesis, is divided, split [*refendu*]. It is the effect of the signifier', i.e. an effect of the process whereby it is represented by one signifier to another and thereby 'sends a message' that calls for analysis. 'All you need are two signifiers side by side in order to produce the effect of the subject: it is in the interstice of the two, but also disappears there, such that they miss or lack it.'[146]

---

144 Milner, 'Avertissement', CpA 2.Intro:74; cf. Grosrichard, 'An Eighteenth-Century Psychological Experiment', CpA 2.3:110.

145 CpA 2.Intro:74. This basic alternative between psychology (i.e. ideology) and psychoanalysis (i.e. science) reappears, in issue seven, in the alternative between the novel and myth. If myth is distinguished by its evocation of a depersonalizing 'cause without reason' or 'irrational determinism', what the novel does is 'rationalize' such a cause by lending it 'motivation' (at the level of both narrative and characterization). It thereby introduces into the scenario of myth a 'psychological and juridical calculus of interest, i.e. motivation and judgment'; it introduces enough 'sufficient reason' to enable 'interpretation' of a character's behaviour (as more or less adapted to the situation). But as the trajectory that runs from myth to novel reaches its extreme limit, it begins to double back on itself. In the experimental novels by Aragon and Gombrowicz considered in this issue, characters begin to lose their apparent unity, and their actions lose some of their superficial intelligibility. They resist the sort of interpretation at issue in that 'experimental psychology' so firmly condemned throughout the *Cahiers*. As Regnault and Miller conclude, 'to put psychology and its sufficient reasons at such distance, this is surely a return to myth' (CpA 7.Intro).

146 'I will remind you', Regnault continues, 'of the simplest example: you go to see someone, a friend, and you are surprised to find yourself at their door with your own key in hand, ready to enter their house. "How silly I am!", you say to yourself. Well! The subject of the unconscious is this subject, unknown by you, immediately effaced, which, for an instant, allowed you to glimpse ... And it is up to you to interpret it: "I am breaking into the other's home, I am at home with the other, etc." The first signifier: my key; the second: his or her lock!' (Regnault, 'Structure and Subject', CF2, 21).

VI SCIENCE, STRUCTURE, SUBJECT

The problematic relation between science and subject not only informs many of the articles and debates in the *Cahiers*, it also underlies the journal's inception, as anticipated in what retrospectively came to be recognized as its inaugural document – the text 'Action of the Structure' (CpA 9.6) written by Miller with Duroux and Milner in September 1964, pondered in detail by the participants of Althusser's *Reading Capital* seminar in the spring of 1965, and eventually published, on the eve of 1968, in its penultimate issue. This is the text that frames the broader *Cahiers* effort to incorporate a subjective dimension within the structuralist project, and there is only space in what remains of this introduction to consider this article and some of its implications.

'Action of the Structure' sets out to build on the achievements of Lacan and Althusser, and to combine the insights of structuralist Marxism and Freudianism in a new 'unitary theoretical discourse' (CpA 9.6:103). The unity of this discourse will result from the way it accommodates a place for the subject in a suitably scientific analysis of 'structuring structure' (95). In keeping with the anti-humanism now dominant at the ENS, the point of departure is not what is 'given' or 'lived' in experience (97) but the effort to grasp what structures such experience, with the proviso that 'structure here will not reserve a place for anything that might be above and beyond scientific discourse' (94). It isn't enough, though, simply to exclude the lived or to replace it with an abstract model: 'an exact integration of the lived into the structural must now be made to operate.' Psychoanalysis, Miller argues, is especially suited to perform this integration, in the spirit of Freud's famous formula *Wo es war, soll ich werden* – where it (i.e. an unconscious drive) was, there I (i.e. the subject) should come to be.[147] Unlike forms of structuralism modelled on Saussurean linguistics, which emphasize formal rules and ordering principles without reference to a speaker or subject, a Lacanian psychoanalytic structuralism recognizes subjectivity as 'ineliminable': although subjective 'experience itself will appear in it only through its concept', psychoanalysis allows for a definition of structure as 'that which puts in place an experience for the subject that it includes' (95).

As with any conception of structure, this definition allows for a distinction between 'structuring' and 'structured' dimensions. The distinction only becomes significant, however, to the degree that the structure includes something that interrupts its action, i.e. insofar as the structure includes a reflexive element, 'an element that turns back on reality and perceives it, reflects it and signifies it, an

---

147   CpA 9.6:103; cf. Lacan, E, 416/347ff, 801/678.

element capable of redoubling itself on its own account.'[148] (As Duroux will subsequently explain, what distinguishes the 'strong structuralism' embraced by Lacan and the *Cahiers* from the 'weak' structuralism of Lévi-Strauss, Barthes or generalized semiotics is its insistence on including such an element[149]). This element introduces a gap or absence into the structuring process, something that structure 'misses'. On the level of what is structured or lived, this absence is generally covered over by imaginary or ideological representations of fullness and coherence. Such 'representations are put into play by what they conceal' (i.e. 'their own structuring structure'), such that *they exist only in order to hide the reason for their existence*' (CpA 9.6:96). They accomplish this by including, in the continuum of representations, not a representation of the lack itself (which is unrepresentable by definition) but of an element which 'takes the place of the lack', a sort of 'decoy' [*leurre*]. Every structure must incorporate some such placeholder for the lack it includes, which serves to 'sew up' or 'suture' the lack, and by thus assigning it a place, absorbs it into an imaginary continuum.[150]

Considered on the level of the structuring process itself, the gap or lack appears as its 'utopic' point, a point that 'should not be there' and that is 'impossible to occupy', in other words a point that defies any sort of recognition or representation (CpA 9.6:97). It is here, at this point, that 'the spread-out space of structure and the "transcendental" space of the structuring interconnect and are articulated.' Inaccessible to structured perception by definition, this utopic point can only be perceived through a 'conversion of perspective', one organized by the logic of that placeholder which appears on the level of structured representation. Such conversion allows us to see how the utopic point identifies the

148   CpA 9.6:95. Jean-Toussaint Desanti later made a similar point: 'The necessity of having to link instances of conduct to the determination of an underlying structure once again poses the question of the subject. The subject is not abolished, since if the structure signifies nothing there is no structure. Where experience is missing, there is no structure' (Jean-Toussaint Desanti, interview with Dosse, in Dosse, *History of Structuralism* vol. 1, 286tm).

149   Duroux, 'Strong Structuralism, Weak Subject', CF2. It's a measure of how influential this 'strong' version subsequently became that when Étienne Balibar came to reconsider the relation between subject and structure, in 2003, he characterized the 'typical movement of structuralism' not as a mere 'destitution of the subject' but as a 'simultaneous operation of *deconstruction* and *reconstruction of the subject*, or deconstruction of the subject as *arche* (cause, principle, origin) and reconstruction of subjectivity as an *effect*, or in yet another formulation, a passage from constitutive to constituted subjectivity. But this first, decisive, and spectacular movement is only meaningful to the extent that it is overdetermined and rectified by a second one, which seems to me to correspond to the *alteration of subjectivity* in the various modalities of a denaturation, an excess, or a supplement' (Balibar, 'Structuralism: A Destitution of the Subject? *differences* 14:1 (2003), 10–11).

150   CpA 9.6:96; cf. Milner, 'The Point of the Signifier', CpA 3.5:78–80. And Badiou: 'The fundamental problem of *every* structuralism is that of a dual-function term that determines the belonging of the other terms to the structure insofar as it is itself excluded from it by the specific operation that makes it figure in the structure only under the guise of its *representative* or *placeholder* (its *lieu-tenant*, adopt a concept from Lacan)' (Badiou, 'Le (Re)commencement', 457n.23).

'weakest link' in the causal chain that defines a structure, and opens the door to an analysis that might grasp and transform it:

> We will then immediately see space [*l'espace*] pivot around on itself, and through a complete rotation that accomplishes its division, expose the internal rule of its law, and the order that secretly adjusts what is offered to the gaze. [. . .] Every activity that does not play out solely in the imaginary, but which instead transforms a state of the structure, sets out from the utopic point, a strategic post, specific to each of the levels in which the structuring lacks (97).

At each level, what structure misses or lacks is concealed by ideology but can be exposed through science. Concealed by imaginary representations, the lack can be grasped through analysis, Duroux explains, as 'the pivoting point of the structure', e.g. the point indicated through psychoanalytic identification of primary signifiers, or 'the point touched by the analysis of the extortion of surplus labour in Marx' (an extortion that is not itself accessible to normal experience or perception). In either case, 'analysis means: to seek out the point by which the imaginary element of the structure is made to topple over'.[151]

By 'starting from structure' in this sense, Miller continues, we can theorize the 'insertion' of the subject in structure. Since 'structure alone is originary' there can be no question of referring back to a causal, constituent, phenomenological or 'immediate' subject. Subjectivity figures here not as 'regent' or as 'stage director', but only as *subjected* [*sujette*]. The subject's 'conscious being is distributed across each of the levels induced by the imaginary in structured reality; as for its unity, it depends on its localization, its localization in the structuring structure. The subject in the structure thus retains none of the attributes of the psychological subject' (98). In that sense, most of the work of this 'theory of the subject' is negative – it should 'refute' phenomenology, reject psychological attempts to 'adapt' an 'adjusted' or 'happy' subject to its position, resist a merely 'reciprocal' account of intersubjectivity, and contest 'all liberal or humanist politics' along with any neo-Hegelian notion of alienation and its overcoming. Illuminated by science, the subject must come to terms with its structured i.e. derivative status, and accept restoration of its activities 'to their radical dependence with regard to the action of the structuring process'.[152] Or as

---

151   Duroux, 'Strong Structuralism, Weak Subject', CF2, 187. 'For Althusser, the word was theory, for us it was analysis, but it was the same thing, the same thing that we sought to make more operational. Analysis was the grasping of this utopian point, the deployment of the structure, in order, let's say, to open a place for action *on* the structure' (191).

152   CpA 9.6:100; hence, as Miller later puts it, 'the equivalency of the subject and object *a*', since 'it is object *a*'s subtraction from reality that frames it. The subject, as barred subject – as want-of-being – is this hole. As being, it is nothing but the subtracted bit' (Jacques-Alain Miller, 'Montré à prémontré', *Analytica* 37 [1984], 29). 'We search in vain for [object *a*] in positive reality', Žižek adds, 'because it has no positive consistency – because it is just an objectification of a void, of a

Althusser will say, following here in Miller's footsteps, ideological subjects may appear 'present in person' in (illusory) ideological discourse, but 'the subject of scientific discourse, in contrast, is *absent in person*, for there is no signifier designating it (it is an evanescent subject which is inscribed in a signifier only on condition that it disappear from the signifying chain the moment it appears there – otherwise science slides into ideology).'[153]

On this basis, a 'science' or 'analysis' of discourse should provide an interpretation of discourse that 'searches throughout its placeholding [*tenant-lieu*] for the specific lack that supports the structuring function.' The goal is not to make audible a repressed or silent speech, but rather to pinpoint that lack or 'hidden place that cannot be illuminated because it is on the basis of its absence that the text was possible, and that discourses were uttered: an Other scene or stage where the eclipsed subject situates itself, from where it speaks, for which it speaks' (for instance the scene that stages class antagonism, or the lack of relation between the sexes). The goal is not only to analyze what a discourse

> means to say but above all what it does not say, to the degree that it *means* not to say it. We will therefore consider the whole of a text as the circling [*l'entour*] of a lack, principle of the action of the structure, which thus bears the marks of the action that it accomplishes: *the suture*. Starting from the placeholder towards which the disorders of the statement of its contradictions converge, tilting the plane of the statement must reveal the discourse of the subject as the discourse of the miscognition pertaining to the place where, as an element, or support, it is situated in the structuring structure (102).

In terms that would soon be taken up by Althusser and Rancière (and subsequently reworked by Žižek and Badiou), Miller goes on to characterize the sort of causality responsible for such 'displacement of determination'. 'At once univocal, repressed and interior, withdrawn and declared, only *metonymic* causality might qualify it. The cause is metaphorized in a discourse, and in general in any structure for the necessary condition of the functioning of structural causality

---

discontinuity opened in reality by the emergence of the signifier' (Žižek, *The Sublime Object of Ideology* [London: Verso, 1989], 95). Once the subject is understood first and foremost as the gap that 'emerges as a result of the failure of [social] substance in the process of its self-constitution', Ernesto Laclau argues (after Žižek), once '"subject" is nothing but the name for this inner distance of the "substance" towards itself', so then the 'traditional debate as to the relationship between agent and structure thus appears fundamentally displaced: the issue is no longer a problem of *autonomy*, of determinism versus free will', but rather how best (drawing on 'the theory of deconstruction') to acknowledge the primordial indeterminacy of the subject as such (Laclau, 'Preface', in Žižek, ibid., xiv–xv; cf. Laclau and Chantal Mouffe, *Hegemony and Socialist Strategy* [London: Verso, 1985], 2, 152ff; Bosteels, 'Badiou's Theory of the Subject, Part I', 223).

153 Althusser, 'Three Notes on the Theory of Discourses' [October 1966], HC, 49.

is that the subject takes the effect *for the cause*. Fundamental law of the action of the structure.'[154]

The further question that arises concerns the sort of discourse that might articulate such action and thus qualify as science. Since science (for familiar Bachelardian-Althusserian reasons) cannot involve any mere 'return to a reality beyond discourse', what distinguishes science and establishes its adequacy is instead its capacity, on the basis of the 'epistemological break' that establishes it, to 'expel lack' and close itself in such a way as to eliminate the gap that characterizes non-scientific discourse. Unlike an ideological discourse, a scientific discourse 'includes no utopic element' (102). Science, in short, lacks any lack. But since '*the lack of a lack is also a lack*', science can then only relate to what it excludes – i.e. the domain of imaginary/ideological experience structured around lack – in terms of 'foreclosure' or exclusion as such. Insofar as a science 'forecloses' such experience, Miller concludes, 'every science is structured like a psychosis: the foreclosed returns under the form of the impossible.'[155]

When Duroux and Miller return a few months later (in a session of Lacan's seminar in late February 1965) to the 'suture' that links the subject to the lack in a structure, they draw on Frege's theory of numbers in order to formalize the 'logic of the signifier' that determines the relationship.[156] The basic configuration, Miller argues, can be expressed in terms of the elementary difference between the numbers zero and one. For Frege, following Leibniz, any concept can only subsume an object insofar as that object can indeed be treated as *an*

---

154   CpA 9.6:102; cf. RC, 188n45; Badiou, 'Le (Re)commencement', 457–458. Deleuze offers a helpful gloss: 'Structures are unconscious, necessarily overlaid by their products or effects. An economic structure never exists in a pure form, but is covered over by the juridical, political and ideological relations in which it is incarnated. One can only *read,* find, retrieve the structures through these effects. The terms and relations which actualize them, the species and parts that realize them, are as much forms of interference *[brouillage]* as forms of expression. This is why one of Lacan's disciples, J.-A. Miller, develops the concept of a "metonymic causality," or Althusser, the concept of a properly structural causality, in order to account for the very particular presence of a structure in its effects, and for the way in which it differenciates these effects, at the same time as these latter assimilate and integrate it. The unconscious of the structure is a differential unconscious' (Deleuze, 'How Do We Recognize Structuralism?', 181; cf. Milner, *Le Périple structural*, 160).

155   CpA 9.6:103. As Bosteels summarizes this approach, 'to become consistent, not just a psychotic but any symbolic order needs to foreclose a key element which paradoxically "incompletes" the structure by being "included out". The structure is not all: there is always a gap, a leftover, a remainder or, if we slightly change the perspective, an excess, a surplus, something that sticks out' (Bosteels, 'Badiou's Theory of the Subject', 221).

156   CpA 1.2, CpA 1.3. In his 'Mark and Lack' (CpA 10.8), Badiou reads Miller's 'Suture' as an essentially extra-scientific or 'intra-ideological' exercise (CpA 10.8:151; cf. Badiou, 'Le (Re) commencement', 457n.23; Hallward, 'Badiou and the Logic of Interruption', CF2. In 1990 Badiou returns to Miller's article ('the first great Lacanian text not to be written by Lacan himself') in order to criticize its essentially 'constructivist' logic as a misreading of Frege, as a misunderstanding of the ontological status of zero, and as inimical to the possibility of a transformative event (Badiou, 'Additional Note on a Contemporary Usage of Frege', *Number and Numbers* [1990], trans. Robin Mackay [Cambridge: Polity, 2008], 24–30).

object, i.e. as *a* self-identical unit or 'one'. Anything that counts as a thing counts insofar as it can be counted as one thing, and science (or true discourse) excludes anything that does not count in this way. The number zero, then, can be assigned to the number of things that do not thus count, i.e. that are not self-identical: there are *none* such things.[157] But there is also only *one* number that quantifies this absence, i.e. there is only one zero. We can thus derive the number one as the 'proper name' of the number zero,[158] and by repeating this derivation (i.e. by repeating the exclusion of the non-identical) we can generate the unending numerical succession of 1+1+1 . . .

Moving from Frege to Lacan, Miller proceeds to identify this 'impossible object', which the discourse of logic summons as the not-identical-to-itself and then rejects', precisely as the *subject*. We can then 'recognize in the zero number the suturing stand-in for the lack' (CpA 1.3:46), i.e. that 'placeholder' evoked in 'Action of the Structure'. Zero is all that be represented of the subject as such, i.e. of the gap in the structure, but, given this gap, a signifier can represent it as *a* (or one) gap for another signifier, and can do so indefinitely. If we conceive the relation of 0 to 1 and 1+1+1 . . . in terms of this Lacanian logic of the signifier, i.e. in terms structured by processes of metaphor and metonymy respectively, Miller suggests, we might sketch the general relation between subject and signifier as follows:

> If the series of numbers, metonymy of the zero, begins with its metaphor, if the 0 member of the series as number is only the standing-in-place suturing the absence (of the absolute zero) which moves beneath the chain according to the alternation of a representation and an exclusion – then what is there to stop us from seeing in the restored relation of the zero to the series of numbers the most elementary artic-ulation of the subject's relation to the signifying chain?[159]

---

157   CpA 1.3:44. '0 is the number that belongs to the concept "not identical with itself"' (Frege, *The Foundations of Arithmetic* [1884], trans. J.L. Austin [New York: Harper, 1960], §74).

158   CpA 1.3:46. '1 is the number which belongs to the concept "identical with 0"' (Frege, *The Foundations of Arithmetic* §77). Deleuze reads Miller's 'zero position, defined as lacking its own identity', as exemplary of that 'object = x' which, for any structured domain, 'constitutes the differenciating element of difference itself [. . .]. The object = *x* is not distinguishable from its place, but it is characteristic of this place that it constantly displaces itself' (Deleuze, 'How Do We Recognize Structuralism?', 186).

159   CpA 1.3:47. Lacan's version of this argument, in 1960, ran as follows: 'The effect of language is to introduce the cause into the subject. Through this effect, he is not the cause of himself; he bears within himself the worm of the cause that splits him. For his cause is the signifier, without which there would be no subject in the real. [. . . The subject per se does not speak, and] one does not therefore speak to the subject. *It* speaks of him, and this is how he apprehends himself; he does all the more necessarily in that, before he disappears as a subject beneath the signifier he becomes, due to the simple fact that it addresses him, he is absolutely nothing. But this nothing is sustained by his advent, now produced by the appeal made in the Other to the second signifier.

As an effect of language, in that he is born of this early split, the subject translates a signifying synchrony into the primordial temporal pulsation that is the constitutive fading of his identifica-tion. This is the first movement.

In other words, from one link to another of a signifying chain, a signifier represents, places or 'sutures' (i.e. treats-as-identical or counts-as-one), for another signifier, that essential lack of self-identity or place which is all that can be represented of the subject qua subject. 'Suture names the relation of the subject to the chain of its discourse', by treating its absence or lack of place as *a* lack of place, i.e. by subsuming it 'in the form of a placeholder [*tenant-lieu*]' (39). And by thus 'crossing logical discourse at its point of least resistance, that of its suture, you can see articulated the structure of the subject: as a "flickering in eclipses", like the movement which opens and closes the number, and delivers up the lack in the form of the 1 in order to abolish it in the successor' (49).

Once again, analysis of this sutured place, this point of least resistance or this weakest link in the chain, is meant to yield an understanding of 'structural causality (causality in the structure insofar as the subject is implicated in it)' (49) and thereby open the way to its transformation. Writing under the pseudonym of Thomas Herbert, Michel Pêcheux's contributions to the *Cahiers* will likewise seek to develop an account of ideological discourse, informed by the emerging sciences of linguistics, psychoanalysis and historical materialism, in terms that would allow 'political practice' to understand and transform it, in somewhat the same way that analysis allows for the understanding and transformation of a neurosis.[160]

VII FROM THEORY TO PRACTICE (MAY 68)

What these founding texts of the *Cahiers* did *not* include was any detailed account of the political practice that might actually take the work of such transformation in hand.[161] As we have seen, the same omission characterizes Althusser's texts during these same years, although in 1965 Althusser could at least fall back on the implication that his theory, as a contribution to the strategic re-orientation of a revolutionary political party, confirmed this party in its practical role as vanguard and leader, as the head of a chain 'without weak links' (cf. FM, 97–98). As Althusser's students moved away from the PCF over the

---

But in the second, desire – bedding down in the signifying cut in which metonymy occurs, the diachrony (called "history") that was inscribed in fading – returns to the kind of fixity Freud grants unconscious wishes (see the last sentence of the *Traumdeutung* [*The Interpretation of Dreams*]).

This secondary subornation not only closes the effect of the first by projecting the topology of the subject into the instant of fantasy; it seals it, refusing to allow the subject of desire to realize that he is an effect of speech, to realize, in other words, what he is in being but the Other's desire ('The Position of the Unconscious', E, 835/708–709).

160   Thomas Herbert, 'Réflexions sur la situation théorique des sciences sociales', CpA 2.6:160, 164.

161   Duroux: 'The idea is ultimately that the rigorous traversal of the imaginary was what authorized all practice. We said nothing about practice as such. [. . .] We said that we would authorize practice, but what, which practice?' (Duroux, 'Strong Structuralism, Weak Subject', 192).

course of 1966 they moved away from this 'classical Leninist' solution to the old theory-practice question as well. And it is this question, returning now to conclude our micro-history of the ENS in the run-up to May 68, that first divided and then reunited the two Althusserian groups with their parallel sets of *Cahiers*.

Once the editors of the *Cahiers Marxistes-Léninistes* broke openly with the PCF and established their own Maoist organization (the UJC[ml]), in late 1966, they began to embrace a logic that, in keeping with the slogans of China's Cultural Revolution, effectively inverted their earlier understanding of theory and practice. Three of the last four issues of the *Cahiers Marxistes-Léninistes* (issues 14, 15 and 17) are dedicated to the *Grande Révolution Culturelle Prolétarienne*, and downplay talk of 'theoretical training' in favour of Mao's call for concrete and detailed 'investigations' [*enquêtes*] of the socio-political terrain. By February 1967, struggling with one of his periodic bouts of depression, Althusser regretted that his young 'whelps' were now 'completely out of his control', and criticized their renunciation of the PCF as a form of 'infantile leftism'.[162] Under the pressure of criticism from people like Linhart and Debray, however, Althusser himself had already begun to discount the privilege of science in favour of the practical imperatives of class struggle.[163] That summer, Linhart and Broyelle visited China as guests of the Chinese Communist Party and returned as ardent advocates for the political priority of the masses over the intellectuals, and the need for the latter to re-educate themselves through alignment with popular instincts, via direct '*établissement*' in factories or farms. Although such rigid workerism discouraged the UJC from initially embracing the student mobilization when it began in May 68 (provoking arguments and self-criticisms that soon dissolved the organization), most of its members soon rallied in unconditional support of *les événements* and many then played leading roles in several new Maoist groups that emerged later that year, including Gauche Prolétarienne (GP).[164]

The *Cahiers pour l'Analyse*, meanwhile, pursued more or less the opposite trajectory. Already well known as an avant-garde novelist (a 'celebrity', as Althusser put it in late 1964[165]), Badiou joined the editorial team in 1967, at a time when Miller's own theoretical priorities were also becoming increasingly 'pure' or abstract; the last two issues of the *Cahiers* consist of rigorous if not forbidding discussions of the status and history of science, and of pivotal

---

162   Althusser, letter to Michel Verret, 25 February 1967, cited in Goshgarian, 'Introduction', in Althusser, HC, xxxvii; cf. Althusser, *The Future Lasts Forever*, 353–354.

163   Cf. Althusser, 'Philosophy as a Revolutionary Weapon' [February 1968], LP, 21.

164   Cf. Hamon and Rotman, *Génération* vol. 1, 468–470, 579ff; Kessel, *Le Mouvement maoïste en France* vol. 1, 422–437; vol. 2, 96–107; 235–252; Virginie Linhart, *Volontaires pour l'usine*, 38–45.

165   Althusser, letter to Franca Medonia, 7 November 1964, *Lettres à Franca*, 576.

moments in the development of modern mathematical logic. The penultimate article to appear in the journal, Badiou's 'Mark and Lack', offered the most forceful version of a conclusion implied in other late contributions, confirming once again an absolute break between ideology and science, and with it the foreclosing or 'psychotic' quality of the latter (CpA 10.8: 162). The only place such a science might acknowledge for popular political practice seemed to be the place offered by exclusion pure and simple, the position of an absolute outside.

As far as Badiou and his colleagues were concerned, then, when an explosion of such practice duly erupted in May 68 it could only be interpreted as a sort of invasion of the outside as such. That which the theory of discourse had excluded from consideration arose from this position of exclusion, 'from nowhere', to interrupt the discourse of theory. In one sense, what happened thereby confirmed a principle of the theory itself, insofar as what happened was indeed 'impossible': a practice banished to the outside of theory, precisely qua outside, had abruptly forced its way inside the discourse that excluded it. As Regnault had already observed, in his article on politics and philosophy (which concludes the present volume), any 'materialism *of* history' recognizes it as 'something *encountered, given*, instead of being an object to be constructed', and theoretical questions of political power are indeed resolved, in practice, in the more or less brutal terms of power and its appropriation.[166] No doubt Badiou is right to suggest that this logic of radical interruption remains to this day a guiding motif for him and for several of his contemporaries.[167] In another sense, however, May's interruption of theory was also simply that, an interruption: faced with this dramatic indication of its apparent redundancy, the programme of theoretical training came to an abrupt halt and at a combative editorial meeting held in the autumn of 1968 it was decided to terminate publication of the *Cahiers pour l'Analyse* without further explanation or ado.[168] As Regnault remembers, 'the *Cahiers* thus died of an external cause, which is a perfectly Spinozist outcome, and should have pleased us well.'[169]

Interrupted from without, the theoretical project expired – to be resurrected no less abruptly in practice. By the middle of 1968 many of the *Cahiers* Lacanians (including Miller, Milner, Grosrichard, Regnault and Badiou himself) had already thrown themselves unreservedly into the Maoist camp, and by joining Gauche Prolétarienne, Miller and Milner found themselves once again members of the same organization as Linhart, Rancière and Benny Lévy. In its newly inverted form, for a few years after 1968 Lacano-Althusserian structuralism came to exercise something close to hegemonic influence in the French

---

166   Cf. Regnault, 'The Politics of the Prince', CpA 6.2:41, 44–47.
167   Badiou, 'Theory from Subject to Science', CF2.
168   Ibid.
169   Regnault, 'Structure and Subject', CF2, 24.

academy, as its leading figures gained control of institutions ranging from the Collège de France to the universities at Nanterre and Vincennes.[170]

The sense of shared revolutionary purpose that had crystallized around theoretical training in 1963–66 thus returned temporarily after 1968 in the form of a political practice that now staked everything on the *untrained* reflexes of the masses. Where before it was theory that guided the party which in turn guided the people, now it is the people who know best and who dispense with any need for theory. Where before only complex analysis of a structural cause offered any political grip on a situation, now practice could rely on the entrenched wisdom of workers and farmers, trusting that (as Mao liked to say) *l'oeil du paysan voit juste* [the peasant sees things clearly]. Where before only scientific reason could guide any attempt to challenge the status quo, now reason itself – extrapolating from Mao's dictum that '*on a raison de se révolter* [it is right to rebel]' – figures as derivative of popular revolt.[171] In his 1973 book *Le Singe d'or* Guy Lardreau distilled the general outlook of Gauche Prolétarienne, at the moment of its dissolution, when he combined a sharp critique of Althusser's reduction of Marxism to a science ('all science is science against the people') with an affirmation of revolution as a 'work of faith', an unconditional wager on the rectitude of the masses and the 'necessary justice' of their desire and will; when it comes to fighting oppression 'the masses never make mistakes.'[172] The following year, Rancière pushed a similar though less exalted version of the argument to its conclusion when, condemning Althusserianism as a 'philosophy of order' and a pedagogy of oppression, he affirmed instead the untutored 'discourse of revolt' put forward by workers and students in the terms and places of their own making, in keeping with Mao's insistence that 'the

---

170   As Dosse notes, May 68 was followed by 'a "wave of rationalism that drove masses of students into courses on logic." Epistemology and the theory of science were the only subjects that attracted students' (Dosse, *History of Structuralism* vol. 2, 128, citing Hervé Le Bras). In 1969, remembers Roger Pol-Droit, 'not to be an Althussero-Lacanian was to be an *Untermensch*, less than a man' (Pol-Droit, 'Curriculum vitae et cogitatorum', *La Liberté de l'esprit* 17 [winter 1988], 18, cited in Dosse, *History* vol. 2, 124).

171   See for instance, Lardreau, *Le Singe d'or*, 24; Badiou, *Théorie de la contradiction* (Paris: Maspéro, 1975), 21, 58 – its first chapter is translated by Alberto Toscano as 'An Essential Philosophical Thesis: "It Is Right to Rebel against the Reactionaries"', *Positions* 13:3 [2005], 669–677). As Benny Lévy put it, the 'philosophical foundation' of Gauche Prolétarienne is built on the assumption that 'the principal current of the mass movement is always reasonable' (Pierre Victor [Benny Lévy], 'Etre prets pour une crise sociale ouverte', in *Les Maos en France*, ed. Michele Manceaux [Paris: Gallimard, 1972], 232; Lévy, 'Investigation into the Maoists in France' [1971], trans. Mitchell Abidor, 2007, online at marxists.org, accessed 3 October 2011).

172   Lardreau, *Le Singe d'or*, 89, 124. By 1975–76, Lardreau and Jambet had reached a point where they could only affirm this wager by pushing its spiritual orientation to the limit, recasting the revolutionary masses in a literally angelic role: 'once again we will make the senseless wager: the Angel has always been defeated – but he will triumph, in the end, in an unprecedented revolution' (Lardreau and Christian Jambet, *L'Ange: Ontologie de la révolution tome 1* [Paris: Grasset, 1976], 152; cf. 36–37, 79; Hallward, introduction to Lardreau, 'The Problem of Great Politics', *Angelaki* 8:2 [2003], 85–89).

people, and the people alone, are the motive force of world history.'[173] Foucault summarised the growing objection many of his contemporaries addressed to Marxism by 1976 when he denounced its pretension to be a 'science' and debunked its claims to the hierarchical, centralizing, 'vanguard' authority associated with science.[174] Mandarin 'heory had replaced popular practice in the old position of exclusion and redui ncy. In the Maoist engagement that continued for a few years after 1968, we might say, the Althusserian project continued by turning itself inside out.

Then it splintered. Gauche Prolétarienne dissolved in 1973, and after leaving the GP Miller devoted much of his energy to consolidating his institutional position at the new University of Paris VIII and in Lacan's school (before its own dissolution in 1979), leaving it to his student and analysand Slavoj Žižek to pursue some of the political implications of the account of structure and subject he had sketched in the pages of the *Cahiers*. His nerves shattered by the re-education imposed on him after May 68, Linhart never recovered the revolutionary *élan* he enjoyed as leader of the UJC,[175] and many of his former GP comrades soon joined in the hysterical chorus of self-incriminating voices that began to denounce, in 1975, both the theory and the practice of Marxism as a criminal violation of the rights of man.[176] Less frenzied attacks on 1960s antihumanism followed in due course, and in some ways continue unabated to this day.[177] Benny Lévy and then Jean-Claude Milner moved on to embrace forms of Zionism. Regnault moved away from philosophy and politics in favour of psychoanalysis and theatre, while Duroux has rarely broken the self-imposed

---

173   Rancière, *Althusser's Lesson*, 119, 14. After the self-emancipatory mobilization in 1973 of workers at the Lip watch factory in Besançon, in particular, 'it seemed quite clear that the ability to systematize class struggles was held by those who actually fought them', rather than by the theoreticians who tried to make sense of them from a distance (119). Althusser himself, long after he had missed his own opportunity to affirm May 68 and its consequences, eventually admitted what his *gauchiste* critics had been saying for years: thanks to its 'leadership's deep-rooted, tenacious and inveterate distrust of the masses', in and after 1968, 'the party deliberately cut itself off from the student and petty-bourgeois masses, *because it did not have control over them*, and pressurized the working class to restrict its activity to material demands' (Althusser, 'What Must Change in the Party', trans. Patrick Camiller, *New Left Review* I/109 [May 1978], 43, 41).

174   Foucault, *Power/Knowledge – Selected Interviews and Other Writings 1972–1977*, ed. Colin Gordon (Brighton: Harvester Press, 1980), 84–85.

175   Cf. Virginie Linhart, *Le Jour où mon père s'est tu* (Paris: Seuil, 2008), 31–32.

176   See in particular André Glucksmann, *La Cuisinière et le mangeur d'hommes* (Paris: Seuil, 1975); Glucksmann, *Les Maîtres penseurs* (Paris: Grasset, 1977); Claudie and Jacques Broyelle, *Deuxième retour de Chine* (Paris: Seuil, 1977); Claudie et Jacques Broyelle, *Apocalypse Mao* (Paris: Grasset, 1980).

177   Luc Ferry and Alain Renaut, *La Pensée 68: essai sur l'anti-humanisme contemporain* (Paris: Gallimard, 1985); Jürgen Habermas, *The Philosophical Discourse of Modernity* [1985], trans. Frederick Lawrence (Cambridge, Mass.: MIT Press, 1987); Peter Dews, *Logics of Disintegration: Post-Structuralist Thought and the Claims of Critical Theory* (London: Verso, 1987). The current state of the debate is suggested by the reactionary inflection of recent attacks on Badiou's philosophy, for instance by Eric Marty, Mehdi Belhaj Kacem, and François Laruelle.

silence that has characterized his whole post-Althusserian career. Rancière has persevered in his anti-theoreticist appreciation of popular political discourse but in order to find people better suited to play the subversive role thus assigned to them he began to look for them more in the historical past than in the political present. More orthodox Althusserians like Balibar and Macherey have to a certain extent continued to follow in their teacher's footsteps, while taking their distance from his revolutionary priorities. Arguably, only Badiou has remained faithful to the original Althusserian-Lacanian project, precisely by embracing the logic of interruption that ended it.[178]

As for what remains significant about this revolutionary project today, the least that can be said is that the verdict no longer appears as clear-cut as it did to the jaded proponents of *la nouvelle philosophie* in the late 1970s and the liberals who followed them in the 1980s and 90s. No doubt it is too early to say, towards the end of a tumultuous 2011, that the question of revolutionary change has returned to a prominent place in the philosophical agenda. But after decades dominated by the myriad forms of a backlash against radical politics (liberalism, deconstruction, 'ethics', historicism, cynicism . . .), many younger thinkers and activists are at least more receptive now to the basic problem that 'theoretical training' was meant to solve in the 1960s: how might we think and work towards radical change in conditions of economic inertia, political complacency and popular disempowerment, compounded by the absence of an appropriately oriented political organization? Today's answer to this old question may depend on a different account of the relation between structure and subject, drawing on a more dialectical conception of the former and a more assertive (if not 'voluntarist') conception of the latter. We have much to gain, however, by paying more careful attention to the way this question was formulated, in the mid 1960s, in the run-up to Europe's last great revolutionary sequence.

---

178   Cf. Hallward, 'Badiou and the Interruptions of Science', CF2.

CHAPTER ONE

Forewords to the *Cahiers* volumes 1–9

FOREWORD, VOLUME 1: TRUTH

[2] The *Cahiers pour l'Analyse*, published by the École Normale Supérieure's Cercle d'Épistémologie, aim to present new and previously published texts dealing with logic, linguistics, psychoanalysis, and all the sciences of analysis, in order to help constitute a theory of discourse.

Without wanting to sacrifice any of the generality of such a project, here is how we understand some of the terms we will use.

We define epistemology as the history and theory of the discourse of science [la *science*] (its birth justifies this use of the singular).

By discourse, we mean a process of language that truth constrains. That what this design implies is in our view a suture will be clear from the texts that comprise this first issue.

We dub analytical, finally, any discourse whose function can be reduced to that of putting into place units that produce themselves and repeat themselves, whatever the principle may be that it assigns to the transformations at play in its system. What is at issue is analysis properly speaking, i.e. the theory that deals with concepts of element and combination [*combinatoire*] as such.

Who could doubt that this research chiefly concerns dialectical materialism, given the scope of its significance today, and Louis Althusser's recognition of its import?

The reader will find a justification of these proposals in the present volume. The subsequent issues will follow their own distinctive paths: there is nothing about our project that clings to the particularity of a doctrine. For us it is only a matter of training ourselves [*de nous former*], following our teachers, in line with the rigour of the concept.

For the editorial board: Jacques-Alain Miller, 1 January 1966

FOREWORD, VOLUME 2: WHAT IS PSYCHOLOGY?

[73] If consciousness constitutes itself by excluding desire from its field, and by reducing its subjective correlate to something with the impact of a punctuality, then experimental psychology is a paradoxical enterprise, insofar as it seeks to return to what it grasps as the site of the excluded, so as thereby to submit it to the very laws that cut it away – that is, the person and its equation, source of error and of passion.

If we are right to recognize that the scientific knowledge claimed by experimental psychology applies to a world in which truth can only be said of things, is it surprising that, on the terms of such knowledge, in order to obtain the truth of he who questions things, one must first make of him a thing that answers questions?

Georges Canguilhem guides us here, by showing what psychology intends: to lend to the object of things – man is a tool – function and permanence: man is a fixed place in the network of exchanges.

These include exchanges with the biological environment, but also exchanges with his social partners: this nucleus that is gripped ever more tightly by the interlocking tests, must we not recognize in it the deductible element [*l'élément décomptable*] of a rationalized politics, regulated in line with the grid of needs and capacities? We are then better placed to understand that, from the beginning, experimentation is indissolubly tied in a double rapport, whereby, as psychology provides a subject to a rational politics, politics will prove itself rational by securing for psychology its means to progress (Alain Grosrichard).

To this conjunction, psychology cannot help but lend its support, confirming the efficacy of its practices through the self-evidence of an apparatus that guarantees the permanence and usability of its object: what is at stake [74] here is the position of an ego [*un moi*] of mastery and synthesis, the basis of all instrumental servitudes (since as Marx demonstrated, in order for man to become a tool he must become master of himself): the subject of science, condensed, is rendered fit to be handled by science itself, science that is henceforth assured that there is nothing it cannot know about what it excludes.

There is no better way for psychoanalysis to mark its position here than by situating this ego as a function of misunderstanding and mirage, as the ransom that science, returning to its own *subjectum*, must pay to the imaginary as the price of the exclusion through which it circumscribes it [this ego].

It is hard to see how one might demonstrate the point more clearly than at the level of the drive, introduced by Freud precisely in terms of stimulus and response, so as to understand all the better that there are stimuli in relation to which the subject, far from experiencing itself as a synthetic nucleus, or as possessing an organism with denumerable faculties, instead can only respond – as Dr. Serge Leclaire shows us – by barring itself from the lack of a difference [*se barrer du manque d'une différence*].

It is hard to see how one might better demonstrate the point than at this level where all those deviations that re-centre the subject on a nuclear ego appear. This, then, is where the singular relation that psychoanalysis maintains with psychology is formed: if in fact the latter is indeed this strange return of science to what it excludes, then for psychoanalysis it must trace the geometric place of its wanderings or aberrations [*égarements*], a place that receives its unity by roaming the borders of that hole of exclusion into which psychoanalysis must insert its relation with science – a relation on which Freud, thanks to his 'scientism', never ceases to insist, albeit only in order that we might discover its eccentricity.

Perhaps in this way we can better understand the necessity with which anyone who tries to speak rigorously of psychology must locate in it the dimension of a silence: the silence that experimental psychology must keep with respect to the statement that founds it, the silence of a social psychology that, while stating clearly what is hidden from a philosophy that rejects it, thereby says nothing about the link that unites them insolubly (Thomas Herbert).

In this silence, unknown or disregarded as such, we are summoned to recognize psychology as a discourse. To analyze this discourse would be to delimit in it the element that induces silence, and that disguises it; to specify this element as the ego of synthesis and mastery has now become a necessary task, and the reader will find here the means to accomplish it.

For the editorial board: Jean-Claude Milner, 1 March 1966

FOREWORD, VOLUME 3: ON THE OBJECT OF PSYCHOANALYSIS

[iii] If it is to question the point at which it aims, in other words its object, a discourse is obliged to recognize a space whose depth is regulated by this point, a space that is its domain, its extension and its laws.

We will help establish the laws of the domain of psychoanalysis by stating more clearly the signifying structuration of the subject, either by constituting the latter in its singular relation to the object, or, without recourse to any form of geneticism, by articulating the succession of states through which it passes in the instauration of the forms of communication that locate and mark it [*qui le repèrent*].

We will test the boundaries of this domain by pushing its concepts to the point of analyzing, without recourse to any form of positivism, the chain of a theoretical discourse, so as to perceive in it, through reversal, the very lineaments of their logic.

Whether this double movement amounts only to one, whether we recognize the authority or agency [*instance*] of the signifier everywhere its effects can be discerned, it still belongs to analysis both to measure and construct the domain, to distinguish and elucidate the object – since these [operations] only ever call for, and are only founded by, enunciation of the fissured structuration of the subject; this unity can only be read from one point: it was up to Jacques Lacan to place it.[1]

For the editorial board: Jean-Claude Milner

---

1   TN: The full French passage reads: 'Que ce double mouvement n'en soit qu'un, que reconnaître l'instance du signifiant partout où les effets s'en peuvent déceler, est toujours de l'analyse, à la fois, mensurer et construire le domaine, distinguer et élucider l'objet – puisque ce n'est jamais qu'énoncer la structuration fissurée du sujet qu'ils appellent et qui les fonde – cette unité ne peut se lire que d'un point seulement: il appartenait à Jacques Lacan de le placer.'

FOREWORD, VOLUME 4: LÉVI-STRAUSS IN
THE EIGHTEENTH CENTURY

[3] The metaphor that might describe without fault or mistake the genealogy of a text still cannot be formulated. In its syntax and in its vocabulary, in its spacing, through its punctuation, its gaps, its margins, the historical belonging of a text is never a matter of direct descendance. Nor a simple accumulation of layers. Nor pure juxtaposition of borrowed pieces. And if a text always gives itself a certain representation of its own roots, these only live off this representation, which is to say on condition that they never touch the ground. This no doubt destroys their *radical essence*, but not the necessity of their *rooting function*. To say that we only ever intertwine roots ad infinitum, bending them to take root in roots, to pass through the same points, to redouble ancient adhesions, to circulate between their differences, to coil up in themselves or to envelop each other reciprocally, to say that a text is only ever a *system of roots*, is no doubt to contradict both the concept of system and the schema of a root. But for it not to be merely apparent, this contradiction only acquires the sense of a contradiction, and receives its 'illogicism', as a result of being thought in a finite configuration – the history of metaphysics – taken from inside a system of roots that never ends and that still has no name.

The text's consciousness of itself, however, i.e. the circumscribed discourse in which is articulated its genealogical representation (for example a certain conception of the 'eighteenth century' that Lévi-Strauss constitutes and lays claim to), without collapsing into this genealogy per se, plays an organizing role, precisely through this gap, in the structure of the text. Even if we had the right to speak of retrospective illusion, such illusion would not be an accident or a theoretical waste [*déchet*]; we would have to account for its necessity and for its positive effects. And this genealogical representation of itself is itself already a representation [4] of a representation of self: that which the 'French eighteenth century', for example, if such a thing exists, already constructed as its own provenance and its own presence.

The play of these belongings, so manifest in the texts of anthropology and of the 'human sciences', is it produced entirely within a 'history of metaphysics'? Does it somewhere enforce its closure? Such is perhaps the larger horizon of the questions that will be considered here on the basis of some examples. To which we can give proper names: the holders of discourse, Condillac, Rousseau, Lévi-Strauss; or common names: the concepts of analysis, of genesis, of origin, of nature, of culture, of sign, of speech, of writing, etc . . . – in the end the common name of proper name [*le nom commun de nom propre*].

Jacques Derrida

FOREWORD, VOLUME 5: THE CONCEPT OF PUNCTUATION

[3] We consider the concept of punctuation to be central to the theory of reading, if this theory is to be con-scious or con-scientious with the science [*consciente avec la science*] of structure that progresses here, on the basis of the signifying chain.

To state that the structure is to be grasped within the time of its action obliges us to follow that which *perpetuates* itself of the structuring operation in that which *results* from it.

The difference between these two terms comes down to nothing in classical physics, which takes the exhaustion of a cause in its effect to be the necessary condition of the rationality of the real. To a full cause corresponds a total effect, says Leibniz, refuting Descartes in principle.

Yet, when we acknowledge a surplus of force in the cause, by which it signs its product, splitting it through its mark, what happens to the rational real? It must reconcile itself to an effect that is, if you like, irrational.

If we then misjudge or miscognize [*méconnaître*] the disparity that results, this is because it falls in the zero of the chain, which identifies it with insignificance as far as signification is concerned.

To point to this place in a text is not to deny the rigour of explicit deductions. But, by returning to the dead letter the accent that eludes it, the new punctuation sometimes discovers the principles [that are] the effects of their consequences. Michel Foucault's work on [Descartes'] *First Meditation* is exemplary in this respect (*History of Madness* [1961], pp. 54–57). No doubt he calls Descartes' rigour *into question*, but certainly not in the way that metaphysicians might want.

– We invite [our readers] here to read what Freud read, and to read Freud, as Freud would read [*lisait*]: by transferring the accent to the annulled excess.

Jacques-Alain Miller

FOREWORD, VOLUME 6: THE POLITICS OF READING

[iii] 1. A philosopher poses his problems. To silence the fact that at the same time he inscribes them on the text of another philosopher, however, would be to tolerate the arbitrariness of a reading without recall or memory. The earlier philosopher is enriched by his epigone, and by the credit he gives him for having found more knots than he himself severed.

Between two philosophies the rapport is thus not one of *reference* (whereby one would be the thing of which the other would say the word; to the same question, one would say yes the other no), but of *difference* (between a concept and its absence from the other; between a word, and the same in the other [*entre un mot, et le même chez l'autre*]). Since Saussure, we have indeed been missing a difference among signifiers[2]; yet another difference may also be lacking from between the problems in the history of philosophy: the aporiae would then be resolved, from the feigned literalities of erudition (considered as a means of measuring doctrines and their intervals) to the diversions and overtakings the mind thinks it takes (considered as psychology, and thus as the psychologization of theories).

2. In the simpler case where the one philosopher reads the other, the difference passes between them, although lightly; the difference presses more strongly when it passes over wholly from the former, or wholly from the latter's reading of the former. It is up to the one who reads this reading to detect the difference in its greatest effects, and to make between the two the most effective distribution of shares.

Martial Gueroult here teases apart the strings of the tangle, strings knotted around Rousseau's concept of the state of nature: how the Fichte of before 1794 reads the later Rousseau, then the later Fichte, and the equivocation of the two Rousseaus; that Fichte saw Rousseau as double leads us to see Fichte as similarly double.

Having come to the end of these reduplications, it turns out that, as in Plato, the deployment of exhaustive, disjunctive dichotomies chase difference to its thinnest edge – to the point of a concept, if not a word – and that punctuation (a concept introduced elsewhere[3]) admits the *recurrence* of its [iv] transfer right up until the final excess or surplus. Halfway down the path of the tortoise, we can still take a shortcut [*coupe encore par le plus court*].

This calculation of what the area [*l'aire*] of a system or of an argument suffers or sustains is the concern of the other readings presented here: sometimes readings of readings, of Rousseau by Fichte, of Machiavelli by Descartes, differential readings of Fichte opposed to himself; of Hume, opposed to Locke and to Hobbes, in spite of the phrase 'social contract'.

3. In the particular case where *politics* is the field of answers, if not the field of questions, difference again excludes reference and referendum. If we maintain that the philosophers under consideration here wrote under a sovereign, we merely recognize that they share this point in common before settling for an assessment of their opinions as *partes extra partes*, i.e. a distribution of political theses without intersections or gaps [*vides*]. But the city did not obey the rules of a Euclidian space: writing under their sovereign, philosophers were therefore

---

2   TN: The French reads: '*Il s'en faut en effet d'une différence, depuis Saussure, entre les signifiants*'.

3   Jacques-Alain Miller, 'Foreword, volume 5: The Concept of Punctuation', see above, 61.

also obliged to subsume their problematics, with these subsumptions taking the form of a theory of divine right, or a theory of origins, or of obedience, or of the taking of power – whereby we can reveal who does theology, who does philosophy, who psychology and who science.

Moreover, that the centre should always be occupied implied in turn a hierarchy of places around it, and that the space should be closed implied a lack of place: whence displacements (promotion, demotion) and 'condensations' (contraction, enlargement).

4. Politics and reading can then be shown to obey analogous laws: the politics of a philosopher is his reading of another philosopher. To claim that, under these laws, at least the objects differ, would be to take for granted production of the object of a politics as science: but this is precisely what is in question here, to know whether there ever was a Copernican revolution in politics, or merely a succession of recuperations by the *subject* (of the sovereign or of ideology) of the place it loses again and again. Politics would then only ever have been the metaphor of the subject, *that* which accompanies it in its displacements.

5. But in return, if a politics as science has been or was invented, far from rendering the old problems obsolete it would *re*read them better: it is precisely of politics (in the singular) that the philosophers will have spoken, and the difference of a reading between two philosophers will have been a matter of difference in politics itself.

François Regnault

FOREWORD, VOLUME 7: THE ORIENTATION OF THE NOVEL

[3] The novel is not interminable.

A literary genre, it began one day. Having been born condemned it to die, and all along the path of its development it confronts the law that commands its extinction: after having passed through a finite number of states, it finds its position of rest. This arrest [*arrêt*⁴] gives it a destiny. By destiny one must understand a system – though not one so perfect that it does not also admit that residual contingency⁵ from which the manifest imbroglio of literary history results.

We would like here to exemplify the novel's initial investigation

---

4   TN: The French term *arrêt* means both a stop or arrest of movement, but also a decree or a ruling, and an arrest in the police sense of the word.

5   'Die in jenen Systemen zurückbleibende Zufälligkeit' (Hegel, *Elements of the Philosophy of Right*, §188).

[*information*], namely what it transforms in order to begin its process: myth – and its conclusive investigation – when, having run its course, it treats its own law, which the process it commands then comes to transform.

The self-application of the novel henceforth forbids it to stop. Terminated, but indefinite, it enters the interminable.

That the novel transforms myth is something we can see in the substitutions of *tukhè* for *anankè*, of freely taken heroic chances for the injunctive word of the oracles, of intimate and demonic certainties for the constraints of theogonic knowledge[6] – so many mutations in the driving force [*ressort*] that leave the scenario unchanged. What distinguishes [4] a mythical narrative, therefore, is the fact that in it there functions a cause without reason (something Georges Dumézil indicates in *furor*, the principle of an 'irrational determinism'). The novel defines itself then by motivating this cause so as to rationalize it: consecution (the sequence of episodes) tolerates, undisturbed, the displacement of the consequence,[7] while the inherited figuration finds a way to deploy itself in the new genre. Thus the figure of the wanton woman – here an Irish queen who shocks the hero and blunts his desires, there a most Roman lover [*amante plus que romaine*] who excites him.

The novel's rationalization is thus the introduction, into the scenario of myth, of psychological and juridical calculations of interest, thus of motivation and judgment, a double discrimination that consecrates Horatius as responsible and that makes of him a person properly speaking. And on the contrary, what *furor* shows is the depersonalization of the hero.[8]

Motivation implies interpretation, which justifies Livy in always accommodating by a *sive . . . sive . . .* [whether . . . or . . .] both the mythical version and a prosaic solution that is itself often plural. Interpretation implies equivocity: it implies, in a character, the tension of different possibilities and a convergence of opposed traits that the person renders compatible. Myth separates this mixture: we will see examples of this in India (Indra delegates to Trita the guilt of his participation in a necessary crime) and in Persia (double heroes, double exploits, double story). Myth lacks the sleight of hand of Roman law, which drives a guilty Horatius to his death – in order to save in extremis a glorious Horatius.

At the other end of this trajectory, Aragon and Gombrowicz will be appreciated for having begun to reintroduce similar scissions in some of their heroes, whereby the novel captures its double. Aragon will make Ant(h)oine lose his

---

6   Cf. Pierre Grimal, Introduction to *Romans grecs et latins*, éd. de la Pléiade (Paris: Gallimard, 1958).

7   On consecution and consequence see Roland Barthes, *Communications No. 8. Introduction à l'analyse structurale des récits* (1966), 10, 12.

8   TN: See Georges Dumézil, 'Horace et le furor', in his 'Lecture de Tite-Live' §3, CpA 7.1.

reflection in the mirror, along with the insignia of his unity. Gombrowicz will render Skuziak's participation in the plot superfluous, and his act gratuitous.

To put psychology and its sufficient reasons at such a distance is surely to revert to myth.

Jacques-Alain Miller and François Regnault

FOREWORD, VOLUME 8: THE NATURE OF THE UNTHOUGHT

[3] How to transform an objectively given collection of statements into a homogenous and complete body, if not by recomposing the set of rules that produce them, in such a way as to verify their compatibility, establish their order, and effectuate their power, that is to say: to extend, through the exercise of syntax, the actuality of their sequence [*suite*], in view of increasing their quantity to the point where the virtual dissipates?

Once it has been followed through to the end, this operation of *maximum effectuation* is the absolute determination of the field. To call it positive is to deny that the inactual reforms itself as one draws on it [*l'épuise*], and to deny that new statements are forever yet to come from an unthought forever to be reached, like the self-renewing half [*la moitié renaissante*] of the Eleatic paradoxes[9] – because a discourse is a sequence, one that is essentially discrete and incommensurable with the continuum of consciousness.

If there is thus no unthought to be thought, [a discourse] is now an integral chain that sets itself apart from its environment so as to subsist as a body of arguments arranged in a *process of validation*.[10] Each argument implies the preceding one that governs it, except the one that, as principle of the validation, governs itself. In this respect, the latter is [4] *the autonomous statement*, the one that asserts its own position, implied by all the others, validated by itself alone, that is to say *the self-evident*, the unperceived point of the decision.

Since its deduction is missing from every discourse, it is destined to be *the un-thought of that which goes without saying*. This is not to deny that it may be said – on the contrary: whether occasional or repeated, making it explicit has no consequences [*son explicite ne tire pas à conséquence*]. But this is to maintain that, present in each thought, it cannot itself be thought, and that it opens, outside of possible consciousness, onto that which determines the thesis of the discourse.

Unthought determination – whose quasi-transparency authorizes the

---

9   The undetermined environment stretches out, moreover, to infinity. This vague horizon, forever incapable of a total determination, is necessarily there (Husserl, *Idées directrices pour une phénoménologie*, trad. Paul Ricoeur [Paris: Gallimard, 1950], §27, p. 89).

10   Martial Gueroult, *Descartes selon l'ordre des raisons*, vol. 1, (Paris: Aubier-Montaigne, 1953), 11.

illusion of the autonomy of the process – is here *unthought,* since incompatible with actual statements, such that its validation would immediately invalidate them. As we know, the cause (practical conjuncture, or epoch of the concept) only takes effect by lending itself to misunderstanding.

What I think is only the effect of what I un-think [*im-pense*].

Jacques-Alain Miller and Jean-Claude Milner

FOREWORD, VOLUME 9: POSITION OF
THE GENEALOGY OF SCIENCES

[3] Nothing can be said that goes to the essence of the sciences if it is not based in a science of sciences [*s'il n'est pas de science des sciences*]. Their syntax is such that one can only treat them as the object of a way of speaking [*un langage*] either by approaching them from the perspective whereby they are still to come (this is the discipline known as the history of the sciences, which deals only with their prehistory or progression), or by effacing what distinguishes them in the universe of discourse (by recourse to archaeology, the opposite of the sciences[11]).

For one should see the sciences from the perspective whereby, lacking memory, they have no history, and live an eternal Present. This is an effect of the eternal Return of their birth, an infinitesimal time in which they incessantly render themselves independent of that which determines them to be [*ce qui les détermine à être*], and renounce their lineage.

Genealogy here serves as a reminder of this forgotten lineage, in keeping with an inscription that is sufficiently neutral so as to annul the difference between the archaeologist and the historian.

We say: genealogy of the sciences, but science can also figure in the singular, so long as we take care to remember that this singular is plural. 'All science, as research, is founded on the project of [clarifying] a delimited sector of objectivity; it is thus necessarily a particular science' (Heidegger).

If the specialization (the pluralization) of science is thus implied in its concept a function is correlative to it, one that can be distinguished as its *Ideal,* which is to say that impossible point from which it sees, as if it were complete and entire, its divided body. Hence the mirage of an *ideal science,* a mirage that one can recognize at every theoretical conjuncture by the fact that a science reigns there, astronomy, physics or biology: by giving its partners the universal idiom in which they are translatable, this ideal science represents for them the fact that they are unities and in themselves whole [*leur représente qu'elles sont*

---

11   TN: The reference is to 'archaeology' in Michel Foucault's sense of the term: cf. Foucault, 'Sur l'archéologie des sciences', CpA 9.1.

unes et en elles entières].

In the play of mirrors that links the point of the Ideal to its imaged effect as ideal science, the names have varied: in classical times, the first was called God and the second geometry: but it fell to modern scientism to have closed this space and to have given the impossible point the traits of its imaginary correlate, by understanding it as *Science*. [4]

Confronted by so strong a knot of misunderstanding and of knowledge, genealogy must turn itself into forcing [*se faire forçage*]; faced with the beautiful continuity and mastery characteristic of Science, it may instead, at this price, emphasize the rupture and dependence it implies. It will hold the scientist himself accountable – the virtuous scientist (since he is upright, objective and liberal), and the egalitarian scientist (since in his eyes all have an equal right to truth). It will ask him about the fate of his desire, ransom of his virtues, and it will ask about the conditions under which he can maintain that all are equal before the truth.

At this point, genealogy must turn itself into the doctrine of foreclosure, even if this requires pursuing it not only in the subjective position it establishes, but also in the politics that insinuates itself there.

CHAPTER TWO

Jacques-Alain Miller
Action of the Structure[1]

[93] FOREWORD

This text needs to be introduced with reference to its circumstances. On 27 June 1964, Jacques Lacan founded the École Freudienne de Paris, opening it up to non-analysts. A few students of the École Normale, supporting the new school, grouped themselves, in keeping with its statutes, into a 'cartel' identified by the object of its interest: Theory of Discourse. The pages that you are about to read were initially written in order to justify the name the members of this group took on in order to inscribe their work, and to mark it as a tributary that originates in that same conceptual field. The initial plan was to publish them in the *Annuaire de l'École Freudienne*, but this turned out to be no more than a list of names, and so they were left stranded.

If I am publishing these pages now, it is because it seems to me that despite the time that has passed, despite the seminars of all kinds recently devoted to deciphering Freud, Marx and Lacan, in which hitherto difficult truths [*des vérités difficiles il y a peu*] have been made accessible for all and sundry, and despite all that the *Cahiers pour l'Analyse* have already made known – what was articulated in this text concerning the relations between the structure of the subject and the structure of science has not yet been made generally available.

PREAMBLE

Psychoanalysis, like Marxism, provides the principle for a new organization of the conceptual field. This is why it still is not understood, and is reduced to silence, or else, through an interior repression, welcomed while being conjured away, narrated in theoretical terms that predate it, or that it opposes – the terms of psychology, biology, and the philosophy of mind. Its name is thus usurped, and its truth forced into exile.

To recall this today is a task that is as untimely as it has ever been.

For our part, we subscribe to this reorganization and aim to assess its implications. You might think that we have been blind to the limits that our ignorance of psychoanalytic practice necessarily sets on our discourse. But no: it

---

1 TN: First published as: Jacques-Alain Miller, 'Action de la structure', CpA 9.6 (summer 1968): 93–105. Translated by Christian Kerslake, revised by Peter Hallward.

seems to us that by recognizing our limits we do not abolish the legitimacy we attribute to psychoanalysis but on the contrary found it, and protect it from any possible intemperance in our presumptions. [94] The only vocation that the discourse whose project we are conceiving here can assume in the Freudian field will be a critical one, and experience itself will appear in it only through its concept. Our intervention thus hangs on the mediation of a discourse that precedes it, and which we have identified right from the beginning, since it is the only one to set out from an idea of the specificity of Freudian theory via the work of Jacques Lacan. Our first undertaking – and it is not the least ambitious of our undertakings – was to arrive at an understanding of this discourse, and to put it to the test by providing a systematic exposition of it. What we are trying to think through here is an extension of the consequences of this discourse, we are trying to join it up with other discourses that intersect with it and to elaborate their unitary theory, so as then to distribute the power of such a theory in various spaces, some of which will already be circumscribed in what follows. The whole of this conceptual labour will adopt as its slogan Georges Canguilhem's definition: 'To work a concept [*travailler un concept*] is to vary its extension and comprehension, to generalize it through the incorporation of exceptional traits, to export it beyond its region of origin, to take it as a model or on the contrary to seek a model for it – to work a concept, in short, is progressively to confer upon it, through regulated transformations, the function of a form.'[2]

Critique can no doubt lay claim to the freedom with which it establishes itself; the only tribunal to which it is summoned is that of its own rigour. When this happens, however, it receives the confession [*aveu*] and sanction of its discourse-object, and is quickly led to borrow from it the means of its progress, including the very concept of its exercise; critique soon realizes that it is not only authorized by but is already thought by what it thinks, that it is already called up and indeed already broached [*entamée*], that it is not adventitious in relation to its discourse-object: that it doubles it without exceeding it. Little by little, this discovery becomes its theme. What is proper to Jacques Lacan's discourse, for having been tutor to its critique, stems first and foremost from the concept he has created and put to work, the concept of structure.

STRUCTURE

As understood here, structure will not reserve a place for anything that might be above and beyond scientific discourse.

The distance from experience over which models prevail, while at the same time acting as its rigorous guardian (by including what is irreducible about it in

---

2   Georges Canguilhem, 'Dialectique et philosophie du non chez Gaston Bachelard', *Revue Internationale de Philosophie* 66 (1963), 452.

their definition) – this distance must now disappear, and an exact integration of the lived into the structural must now be made to operate.

Structure no more subtracts an 'empirical' content from a 'natural' object than it adds 'the intelligible' to it. If we remain content with articulating objects within the dimension of a network in order to describe how its elements are combined, then we isolate the product from its production, we establish between them a relation of exteriority, and in order to pay no attention to the cause we end up understanding [95] it merely as the expedient guardian of its effects: only mechanistic thought authorizes such an approach.

When structuralist activity rejects temporality and subjectivity from the neutralized space of the cause, it obliges itself to guarantee its already-constituted objects by referring them back to the categories of 'social life', 'culture', 'anthropology', if not to biology, or to mind [l'esprit]. It makes an illegitimate appeal to linguistic structuralism: the latter, by opening its field of analysis through the preliminary exclusion of any relation that the subject entertains with its speech, prohibits itself from saying anything about it. As long as the *alteration* brought about by this exclusion of the speaking subject is not annulled, linguistic structures do not apply beyond their region of origin. Psychoanalytic structuralism legitimately exports them, in our opinion, because its objects are experiences – or because an ineliminable subjectivity is situated in these experiences, and they unfold according to their own interior time, *indiscernible from the progress of their constitution*. The topology of the structure no longer contradicts its dynamic, which the displacement of its elements articulates [*scande*].

Structure, then: that which puts in place an experience for the subject that it includes.

Two functions qualify our concept of structure: structuration, or the *action* of the structure, and subjectivity, *subjected* [*assujettie*].

Drawing the consequences of such a hypothesis generates [*engendre*] the structure.

It is clear, to begin with, that the first function requires that it be divided between, on the one hand, an actual plane, in which it is given to the observer, and which constitutes its state, and on the other hand, a virtual dimension, through which all its states are capable of being deduced. We must therefore distinguish between a *structuring* structure and a *structured* structure.

Up to this point, the first is related to the second as its immanent condition or clause [*clause*], which is to say: the point of view taken in an investigation which explicates itself [*se désimpliquant*] so as to pass from a description to a knowledge [*connaissance*]. The two orders are continuous with each other, their relation is simple, their division is merely relative to a method, there is no delay, and so no structural time, and a movement established in the structure will be only apparent.

But if we now assume the presence of an element that turns back on reality and perceives it, reflects it and signifies it, an element capable of redoubling itself on its own account, then a general distortion ensues, one which affects the whole structural economy and recomposes it according to new laws. From the moment that the structure involves the element we have mentioned,

- its actuality becomes an experience or experiment,
- the virtuality of the structuring [*le structurant*] is converted into an absence,
- this absence is produced in the real order of the structure: the action of the structure comes to be supported by a lack.

The structuring [*le structurant*], *by not being there*, governs the real. It is here that we find the driving discordance: for the introduction of this reflexive element, which suffices to institute the dimension of the structured-insofar-as-it-lives-it, as taking its effects only from itself, arranges an *imaginary* organization, contemporaneous with [96] and distinct from the real order yet nevertheless coordinated with it, and henceforth an intrinsic part of reality. A tertiary, imaginary structure constitutes itself in the real. As a result the reduplication of the structural system, which was merely ideal at the outset, is accomplished. This duplicity in turn afflicts the reflexive element which provokes it – insofar as at the structuring level there is no reflexivity –, which then defines it as a subject, reflexive in the imaginary, non-reflexive in the structuring.

In this second status [*statut*], its subjection reduces it to being nothing more than a support. The relation of the subject to the structure, a relation that is circular insofar as each of its terms owes its definition to the others, but that is dissymmetrical since it is an insertion, proves to be inconceivable without the mediation of an imaginary function of *miscognition* [*méconnaissance*], re-establishing reality in its continuity by means of the production of representations that respond to the absence in the structuring, and compensate for the production of lack. Structuration functions covertly, and in this sense the imaginary is its means. But it is at the same time its effect: the representations are put into play by what they conceal – by what they have the function of concealing, so that *they exist only in order to hide the reason for their existence*. It is their own structuring structure that they conceal, for what structures reality structures them. That their reflection in subjectivity grants them a coherence (another name for their inertia), constitutes them in systems, and incessantly works to make them independent of the action of the structuring, implies that the lack that they ward off summons them inwardly.[3]

---

3   TN: the French reads: 'Que leur réflexion dans la subjectivité leur assure une cohérence, autre nom de leur inertie, les constitue en systèmes, et s'emploie incessamment à les rendre indépendants de l'action du structurant, implique que c'est intérieurement que le manque auquel elles parent, les intime.'

The cause is reflected among the effects that it determines and which are not understood as such [*qui s'ignorent comme tels*]. It follows that their subordination to the structuring transformations is necessarily indirect. The action of the structuring, depending on the resistance of representations or of systems of representations, is exercised unequally upon the imaginary, and thus upon the real, and differentiates and multiplies the levels of the structured in its totality. We call *overdetermination* the structuring determination which, by being exercised through the biases of the imaginary, becomes indirect, unequal and eccentric in relation to its effects.

In order to reconstitute the totality of the structure, we must make these effects correspond with their lateral cause in this permanent space of distortions and general discrepancies [*décalages*], measure its incidence, and relate it back to lack [*manque*] as to its principle.

And yet lack is never apparent, since what is structured [*le structuré*] miscognizes the action which forms it, presenting instead what appears at first glance to be a form of coherence or homogeneity. We must deduce from this that, in this place where the lack of the cause is produced in the space of its effects, an element interposes itself that accomplishes its suturation.

Every structure, in our sense of the term, thus includes a lure or decoy [*leurre*] which takes the place of the lack, which is linked to what is perceived, but which is the weakest link of the given sequence, a vacillating point which belongs only in appearance to the plane of actuality: the whole virtual plane (the plane of the structuring space) *crushes* down at that point [*s'y écrase*]. This element [**97**], which is precisely *irrational* in [the domain of] reality, exposes, by inserting itself into it, the place of the lack.

We can further distinguish the function of this element that never tallies and that always misleads the eye, and by virtue of which all perception becomes miscognition, by naming as its place *the utopic point* [*le point utopique*] of the structure, its improper point, or its point *at infinity*.

A positivist investigation would no doubt be deluded and eluded by this point, since nothing can fall into the net of such an investigation that exceeds the flat surface over which its gaze roams. A conversion of perspective is necessary in order to perceive the utopic point. This place that is impossible to occupy then indicates itself by its singular and contradictory allure, unequal to the plane on which it appears; the element that masks it now indicates, by a certain bending of its configuration, that its presence is unjustified, and that it should not be there. But it is at this point, precisely there where the spread-out space of structure and the 'transcendental' space of the structuring interconnect and are articulated, that we must regulate our gaze, and adopt as our principle of organization the placeholder itself. We will then immediately see the space [*l'espace*] pivot around on itself, and through a complete rotation that accomplishes its division, expose the internal rule of its law, and the order that secretly adjusts what is offered to the gaze. The translation of the structure opens it up to a diagonal reading. The topology that might possibly figure it would have to be constructed in a space whose centre is united, in a punctual convergence, to the exteriority of its circumscription: its peripheral exterior is its central exterior. The outside passes into the inside.

Every activity that does not play out solely in the imaginary but which instead transforms a state of the structure, sets out from the utopic point, a strategic post, specific to each of the levels in which the structuring lacks. It goes without saying that the subject which devises this efficacious practice is not thereby exempt from the miscognition pertaining to its place.

SUBJECT

It is by starting from structure that we must enter into the theory of the subject, which takes its insertion for granted. It is essential to preserve the order here, which goes from structure to subject. This is enough to ruin the possibility of any discourse that seeks its foundation in the sphere of the immediately given, at the end – at the origin – of the historical or methodological journey of consciousness, its detour that is both preambular and essential. If on the contrary structure alone is originary, if no return of consciousness to itself allows it to discover its organization, then the immediate is no more ultimate than it is initial; it is not then a matter of rediscovering or of waiting for the immediate, and reality is not something to be 'disinterred' or overcome, it is something we must traverse, and force into its retreat that which puts it in place. If therefore, against the philosophy [98] of structuralism, we require a notion of subjectivity, this subjectivity will figure not as regent but as subjected [*sujette*]. Although it is required by representation, this subjectivity is not required to occupy the position of a foundation, with the function of a cause. Its gap or deficiency distributes its conscious being at each of the levels induced by the imaginary in structured reality; as for its unity, it depends on its localization, its localization in the structuring structure. The subject in the structure thus retains none of the attributes of the psychological subject, it escapes from the latter's definition, and is never stabilized between the theory of knowledge, morality, politics and law.

The tasks of the theory of the subject are as follows. It must first of all refute the phenomenological attempt to rediscover the naïve or primitive state of the world by means of an archaeological investigation of perception. Phenomenology hopes that by reducing the visible to the visible it can secure the donation of a secret unchanging and ahistorical foundation for knowledge and history; anything invisible that it would encounter would only be the underside of an ultimately miraculous visibility. But if, on the contrary, the invisible accommodates a structure that systematizes the visible that hides it, if it is the invisible that varies and transforms the visible, then this is the basis for a truly radical archaeology of perceptions that are historical through and through, that are absolutely specified, that are structured like a discourse, an archaeology that returns seeing and saying to their essential identity. The work of Michel Foucault today gives us the first example of such an archaeology.[4]

We must also treat in detail the psychological analyses of the subject. What is common to such analyses is that they assign it, in the end, a statutorily identical position before the objects of the world, and they reduce its function to that of collecting these objects within a parenthesis in order to constitute their consistent unity under the name of reality – this latter serving, in turn, as the corrective measure of subjective functioning. The discourse of overdetermination, on the contrary, leads us to the point where we can recognize as spontaneous the subject's orientation towards the decoy [leurre]. Fundamentally, the subject is deceived: *its misunderstanding or mistake is constitutive*. This does not prevent it from registering and capitalizing its experiences, and of having at its disposal, in reality, a system of reference [repérage] by means of which its existence adapts and perseveres. But nothing can render this adaptation to the real natural or innate. It cannot be thought according to models which hold good for the animal world, it proceeds through the secondary intervention of a corrective system. We must then distinguish between an adequate miscognition, necessary to the action of the structure, and an inadequate miscognition, which damages the subject's subsistence; from the standpoint of our current perspective, all perception and ideology, as well as everything we might call sensibility, are gathered together in the sole concept of miscognition.

Miscognition [méconnaissance] is not the exact opposite of cognition or knowledge [connaissance], and 'coming [99] to consciousness' – i.e. the operation through which what is lived is made explicit – does not end miscognition. On the contrary: miscognition is a part of knowledge, and the formation of any conceptual system, closed or as good as closed, continues the dimension of the imaginary. The psychological sphere, that of volitions and appetites, in other words of motivations, is derived from the functional miscognition of the structuring, with the result that people always act in light of an end, i.e. in light of what they perceive as useful. Since the adequate systems that elaborate this miscognition of the cause form, for Claude Lévi-Strauss, the object of ethnology, this latter remains a psychology, and we must rely on psychoanalysis to delimit the field of psychology.

---

4   This is the explicit theme of *The Birth of the Clinic*. Our aim is less to discredit phenomenological discourse (that of Maurice Merleau-Ponty in particular), which remains positivistic insofar as it blinds itself to all mutation of invisible structures, than to take it up again so as to give it a new foundation: as rigorous discourse, in the imaginary, of the imaginary.

The theory of the subject prepares the way for a doctrine of intersubjectivity, which we already know cannot be articulated in simply reciprocal terms. The relation established between one subject and another is no more reversible than it is exclusively dependent on either one of them: this simple alterity, twin-like or fissiparous [*scissipare*], inhabits the imaginary, and the hopeless impossibility of deducing its configuration from one of the terms leads to its description as miraculous. That which unites them, and arranges their relations, of which we only perceive the effects, is tied up and decided on an Other Scene, and refers them to an absolute alterity in absence that is, so to speak, exponentialized.[5] This alterity is never given in the present, and yet there is no presence which does not pass through it, or that is not constituted in it.

No relationship between a subject and another subject, or between a subject and an object, fills the lack, except by an imaginary formation that sutures it; the lack persists inside the subject [*il se retrouve en son intérieur*]. Contestation of the moment of reciprocity affirmed in the psychologies of intersubjectivity should be correlative to a refutation of all liberal or humanist politics; we are entitled to say that such politics are derived from reciprocity, and they search indefinitely for that object that might come to fill in what they conceive as human 'dissatisfaction' (such is Lockean *uneasiness*), and guarantee the transparency of interhuman relations. Once we know that it is no longer in accordance with a 'having' [*avoir*] that man has anything, but according to his 'being' [*être*], or, without recourse to metaphor, once we know that the imaginary is the means of determining a structure that includes a subject, then we must consider any notion of a politics of happiness, i.e. of adjustment, as the surest way of reinforcing the inadequation of the subject to the structure.

The final task is to unite all these analyses in a doctrine of alienation, in open conflict with Hegel and neo-Hegelianism. For a subjectivity that cannot be defined in terms of reflexivity, alienation cannot be treated as that hell from which it should liberate itself so as to possess itself and enjoy its own activity – this is something that could only be conceived for an autonomous sphere of self-consciousness, and not for a reduplicated and therefore lacunary subject, the imaginary subject-agent of the structured, the subject-support, element, of the structuring, which only appears as a subject in the real by miscognizing itself in the imaginary as element in the structuring. But an alienation is essential to the subject since it can only be effectuated as an agent in the imaginary [100], by taking account of the effects of the structuring, in which he or she is

---

5   TN: the French reads: 'Ce qui les unit et arrange leurs liens, et dont nous voyons uniquement les effets, se noue et se décide sur une Autre Scène, et les réfère à une altérité absolue en absence, pour ainsi dire exponentiée.'

already accounted for [*compté*]. An actor, the subject is a director in his fantasy.[6]

SCIENCE

Now, once the undertakings of the subject are restored to their radical dependence with regard to the action of the structuring, and once alienation is defined as constitutive of the subjected subject, how are we to understand the possibility of a discourse that gives itself an adequate object, and that develops its own norms? And first: how is a discourse of overdetermination itself even possible? The sole fact that it is exposed to encountering (or rather necessarily invokes in its advance), beyond the problem of scientificity in general, the problem of its own possibility, makes manifest the singular circuit of a reflected implication: the status of this discourse is the concern of a doctrine of science through which its reason is grounded, but in which the discourse alone is entitled to assign its own place, to constrain the concept, and to dictate the categorical terms. It is from this problem that is precisely ultimate and primary, that we intend to make the thematic departure on the basis of which we will order our procedure.

If we might agree to call the field of the statement [*énoncé*] the field where logic establishes itself, and the field of speech [*parole*] that of psychoanalysis – then, anticipating our future knowledge, we will declare the need for a new position in the space of language, and will produce this proposition: that any field in which the question 'is it scientific or not?' has cardinal importance is to be constituted as a field of discourse.

When logic constructs a formalized system, it expresses the alphabet of its symbols, an initial set of formulas and rules for their formation and their deduction, such that the statements it produces do not double themselves with any virtual dimension; when a logical activity is attached to systems that it has not itself engendered, this dimension remains always reducible in principle. By contrast, statements isolated in the linguistic field are referred back to a code whose virtuality is essential, and which defines them as messages. But communication itself is not taken into account, and both the emission as well as the reception [of messages] serve more to fix the limits of the field, rather than form a part of it.

If now we try to derive from the linguistic relation a subject that would be capable of sustaining it, it cannot be the indivisible medium or support [*support*] of the message and of the code, it will not entertain the same relation with one and the other: the code, necessary to the production of speech but absent from the speech enunciated by the subject, does not belong to the emitting subject, and cannot be situated in his place; reception requires it as well, and it is

---

6   TN: 'Acteur, il est metteur en scène dans son fantasme.'

necessary to situate it in the exponentialized dimension of alterity that we evoked above. The topological distribution that is thus sketched disconnects the plane on which the subject is effectuated in the first [101] person, and the place of that code to which he is rendered [*rendu*], but where as subject-agent, precisely, he is elided, and from where his speech originates, only to be inverted as soon as it is uttered, and to where it ultimately returns, since it is the place which guarantees its intellection and its truth. The lack of the code at the level of speech, and the lack of the subject-agent in the place of the code, which are correlative to each other, open up the splitting [*refente*] of the unconscious within the interior of language. We can now say: *the subject is capable of an unconscious.*

In this splitting, psychoanalysis articulates this Other scene in which the speech of the subject is decided and structured, where this latter figures in a passive function, like an element whose transitivity is ruled by a quaternary combination – another Scene that draws the human animal into language, and towards which its speech (left to its own devices) returns, as if towards its most primordial and generative dependency.

But other circuits branch out of this splitting. As for us, we attend to this speech constrained by the conscious aim of its goal as veracity [*véridicité*], which we name discourse. The topology remains, but the connection is only established here through a secondary selection from the primordial Other scene, or in other words: depending on the mode of language, the connection can be made with *other Other scenes*, grafted upon the place of the code. For example: the Other scene of the class struggle, whose combinatory deals with 'class-interests'. A specification of lacks [*manques*] gets under way.

The fundamental articulation that structures discourses as instances of constrained speech prescribes a reading of them which is neither a commentary nor an interpretation. It is not a commentary because it is not in search of a meaning that might abstain from the text by virtue of a misfortune inseparable from the word, but which the text nevertheless invokes and necessarily implies, and which we might restore and multiply indefinitely through recourse to the tacit ground of speech, which no amount of exploitation can exhaust. Nor is it a question of making a meaning pass from one text to another, and, for example, of translating it into the vocabulary of an already constituted philosophy, without excluding possibilities for other interpretations; such a discourse would be like a neutral element in relation to the first discourse, established upon it like a parasite. To take up a statement by referring it to other statements closer to the mystery of its meaning presupposes the kind of relation to the letter that Spinoza criticized in biblical exegesis. Lastly, it is not enough to restore to a text its continuity, its logical simultaneity, spelling out its surface. 'Structuralism' at the level of the statement should only be a moment for a reading which searches throughout its placeholding [*tenant-lieu*] for the specific lack that supports the structuring function. For this transgressive reading that traverses the statement towards the enunciation, the name of *analysis* strikes us as appropriate.

The lack at issue here is not a silent speech that it might suffice to bring to light, it is not some impotence of the word or a ruse of the author; it is silence, the defect [*défaut*] that organizes enunciated speech, it is the hidden place that [102] cannot be illuminated because it is on the basis of its absence that the text was possible, and that discourses were uttered: that Other scene where the eclipsed subject situates himself, from where he speaks, for which he speaks. The exteriority of discourse is central, this distance is interior. We must break the reciprocal determination whereby the elements of an object are orchestrated into a structured network: we seek a univocal determination – we seek not only what it [*ça*] means to say, but above all what it does not say, to the degree that it *means* not to say it.[7] We will therefore consider the whole of a text as the circling of a lack, principle of the action of the structure, which thus bears the marks of the action that it accomplishes: *the suture*. Starting from the place-holder towards which the disorders of the statement of its contradictions converge, pivoting [*faire pivoter*] the plane of the statement must reveal the discourse of the subject as the discourse of the miscognition pertaining to the place where, as an element, or support, he [*il*] is situated in the structuring structure. The discourse that the subject emits, he also receives, and the determination inverts itself through being made in the first person [*la détermination s'inverse de se faire en première personne*]. We will thus explore the space of the determination's displacement. At once univocal, repressed and interior, withdrawn and declared, only *metonymic* causality might qualify it. The cause is metaphorized in a discourse, and in general in any structure – for the necessary condition of the functioning of structural causality is that the subject takes the effect *for the cause*. Fundamental law of the action of the structure.

So how, then, is such a discourse possible, a discourse which only takes orders from itself, a flat discourse, without unconscious, adequate to its object? It is clear that it is not the return to a reality beyond discourse, an explicit [*désimpliquée*] and simply positive attention, that opens up its field; rather, it is again a singular state of the structuring, a particular position of the subject in relation to the place of truth, that closes speech upon itself. This closing of scientific discourse should not be confused with the suture of non-scientific discourse, because it actually expels lack, reduces its central exteriority, disconnects it from every other Scene. Thought from within the field it circumscribes, this closing [*fermeture*] will be given the name: *closure* [*clôture*]. But the limit of this circumscription has a density, it has an exterior; in other words, scientific

---

7   TN: '. . . nous cherchons une détermination univoque, – non seulement ce que ça veut dire, mais surtout ce que ça ne dit pas, dans la mesure où ça veut ne pas le dire.' 'Ça', French for Freud's *Id* [*das Es*], may also denote the unconscious.

discourse is not stricken with a simple lack – *rather the lack of a lack is also a lack.*

Double negation confers a positivity to its field, but at the periphery of this field one must acknowledge the structure that makes it possible, and from which its development is nevertheless not independent. The lack of the lack leaves open in every scientific discourse the place of the miscognition, and of the ideology that accompanies it, without being intrinsic to it: a scientific discourse as such includes no utopic element. We would need to envisage two superposed spaces, without quilting point [*point de capiton*], without slippage (lapsus) from the one to the other. The closure proper to science therefore operates a redistribution between a closed field, on the one hand, of which one perceives no limit if one considers it from the inside, and a foreclosed space on the other. *Foreclosure* is the other side of closure. [103] This term will suffice to indicate that every science is structured like a psychosis: the foreclosed returns under the form of the impossible.

It is in fact the epistemological break that we rediscover here, but by approaching it from its exterior side we should recognize the privilege and novel scientific status of a discourse of overdetermination which constitutes its field at the exterior limit of all science in general, whose theoretical as well as practical (therapeutic or political) injunction is given by the Freudian '*Wo es war, soll ich werden*', which for us summons the scientific subject to pull himself together.

We know of two discourses of overdetermination: the Marxist discourse and the Freudian discourse. Since the first has today been liberated by Louis Althusser of the obstacle that burdened it with a conception of society as historical subject, just as the second has been liberated by Jacques Lacan from the interpretation of the individual as psychological subject – we think that it is now possible to join these two discourses. We maintain that the discourses of Marx and Freud might communicate with each other via regulated transformations, and might reflect one another in a unitary theoretical discourse.

September 1964

NOTE ON THE CAUSES OF SCIENCE

The crucial problem for the Doctrine of science, the very problem that defines it, concerns its own status.

It is indeed alone in its ability to provide this status, since unlike any particular science it has no exterior: the principles that govern it fall under their own jurisdiction. The Doctrine cannot then posit that it should not be counted among the number of its objects; if it has no outside it is internal to itself. The introjection that it suffers as soon as it establishes itself condemns it to all the phenomena of self-reflexivity.

The consequences of this property are as follows: the Doctrine has no meaning [*sens*], or at least it does not have any that can be stated. As such, it cannot be said, because it cannot be constructed. From the outset, to expound it, that is to say, to explicate it, unfold it, spread it out, is, by right, impossible. And if nothing can be that cannot be said, that is because if *nothing is without a name* (this is our version of the principle of reason, and there are two ways of understanding it according to its punctuation – Heidegger demonstrates it in the case of Leibniz), [then] the project of a Doctrine of science is impossible, it has the name of the unnameable: the *Anonymous Doctrine*.[8]

Consequently, every statement which aims at it will be preambular and peripheral, and [104] at the same time, this Doctrine is itself nothing but preambular and peripheral: it is sucked [*aspirée*] into its surroundings. The discourse adequate to it is always to one side of it, because it is nowhere, and thus everywhere.

These marvellous properties ensue from one alone: its self-reflexivity, which, by forbidding the division of its enunciation, renders meta-language indiscernible from the language-object in its field.[9] It would therefore contradict the concept of the Anonymous Doctrine if one could isolate it in any given place of the Universe of discourse. To expound it, in other words to miss it [*la manquer*], so as to produce its absence in language by providing it with surroundings, is an infinite enterprise.

This is no doubt why Fichte, who wanted what I have just described, is first of all a philosopher who speaks, and for whom books constitute nothing more than the residue of speech. In a certain sense, his discourse should not be conserved, it is proffered with a view to its own disappearance, and always bears the clause of annulment laid down by Wittgenstein in 6.54 of the *Tractatus*:[10] Fichte's *Principles of the Doctrine of Science* of 1794[11] is a 'manual for auditors', and the various expositions of the Doctrine rework his lectures. We should not doubt that the internal failure of the Doctrine is not accidental: dispersion is its sole possible form. There is no meta-language of the Doctrine, and so what is

---

8   TN: 'Et si rien n'est qui ne peut être dit, c'est si *rien n'est sans nom* (c'est là notre version du principe de raison, et il y a deux façons de l'entendre selon la ponctuation – Heidegger le démontre pour Leibniz), le projet d'une Doctrine de la science est impossible, elle a le nom de l'innommable: la *Doctrine Anonyme*.'

9   TN: 'son auto-réflexivité qui, d'interdire à son énonciation de se diviser, fait en son champ le méta-langage indiscernable du langage-objet.'

10   TN: 'My propositions serve as elucidations in the following way: anyone who understands me eventually recognizes them as nonsensical, when he has used them – as steps – to climb up beyond them. (He must, so to speak, throw away the ladder after he has climbed up it.) He must transcend these propositions, and then he will see the world aright' (Ludwig Wittgenstein, *Tractatus Logico-Philosophicus* [1921], trans. D. F. Pears and B. F. McGuinness [London: Routledge Classics, 2001], 6.54).

11   TN: Johann Gottlieb Fichte, *The Science of Knowledge* [*Wissenschaftslehre*, 1794], trans. Peter Heath and John Lachs (Cambridge: Cambridge University Press, 1982).

essential is never said, or it is said at each moment, always present, but never there. And those who listen to it do not amount to an audience [*un public*], rather each, confronted with it, is self-confiding and solitary. Discourse does not do the thinking for those who listen to it, in their place, from outside of them; but each listener must, on his own account and each time as if for the first time, bring about the annulment of the process of enunciation, for the process only terminates at the moment it is found to be interminable, when the operator sees that he did not construct the Doctrine in himself, but rather that it was constructing itself in him. So it is the same thing to say that the Doctrine is impossible, or that its exposition is infinite, or that it precedes everything that bears on it, or that it envelops everything that wants to envelop it. And we can see that, to whoever lives and moves in it, and who wants to speak or write it, the Discourse will present itself as an effort, 'not a reality that *is*, but something that we ought to, and yet cannot, produce.'[12]

What is being stated here depends on a *law*, a law of reason *a priori*, or a law *a posteriori* of the sign: a self-reflexive and thus self-reproducing object has for its correlate an impossible construction, or an infinite activity. *This is why we can just as well say that it does not exist, or that it is indestructible.*

Freud must have had some knowledge of this object, whose self-reproduction is not a division but rather a repetition, since it is indivisible, in order to have been able to have recognized desire[13] as indestructible, and to have withdrawn the unconscious from the principle of contradiction. As for analysis, its termination has nothing in common with the end of any physical process, for its movement is perpetual. [105]

I add, in order to mark the place where other developments might be inserted, that the proposition of Fichte which I cite above situates the point where his discourse joins that of Spinoza.

'We necessarily arrive at Spinozism, if we exceed the *I am*'[14], and to hold oneself to the *I am* as if it were an Unconditioned amounts to giving the absolute I the properties of substance, as Schelling's first text (*On the I as the Principle of Philosophy*) indicates: 'Spinoza has characterized the unconditioned in a perfect manner, for everything that he says of substance can apply word for word to the absolute I.' We should nevertheless draw attention to the fact that, since God is not self-conscious, Spinoza expounds his theory in a definitive text.

Perhaps the coordinates that I give here, in passing, to Fichte – i.e. Spinoza and Freud – will forestall laughter from those who think they have recognized, in the aporia of the Doctrine, something like, what exactly? An ideology!

---

12   TN: Fichte, *The Science of Knowledge* I, 101/102tm.
13   *Perseveration* in Spinoza's sense is an identical effect.
14   TN: Fichte, *The Science of Knowledge* I, 101/102tm.

To make it clear that in my view what is at stake here is not this, I will say that we must take up the four problems identified by Fichte in his opuscule of 1794, 'Concerning the Concept of the *Doctrine of Science* or, of So-Called "Philosophy"'[15], and I take them up again, turning them to my own ends.

How is the Doctrine sure that it exhausts science, including the science to come? It is because it must discover its causes. How is it distinguished from particular sciences? By the way it thinks what they cannot integrate into their field – the decisions that institute their principles. How is it distinguished from logic? As logic of the signifier. How does it conduct itself in relation to its object? The Doctrine is antinomical to the object, i.e. they are mutually incompatible, whether the former absorbs the latter, or the latter vanishes in the former: they only exist in the non-relation, as incommensurable.

These responses should not be taken for the Doctrine itself: I am only declaring what this Doctrine must be. But if it is already clear that we must not understand by science the indistinct totality of all human knowledge (i.e. that which for Kant begins with but does not derive from experience[16]), but rather the thought that calculates, verifies and experiments, to the exclusion of perception, of consciousness, and of all the modes of feeling [*sentiment*], then space is made in the Doctrine for the history of the sciences insofar as it teaches which *position* of the subject makes science possible.

What must be known in order to situate the position of a subject in any conjuncture are the relations it entertains with the authority of the guarantee [*instance de la garantie*], with its statements, with their object. If we can clarify the modes whereby the subject correlative to science relates to these three determinations, we will be able to know the causes of science.

---

15   TN: Fichte, 'Concerning the Concept of the *Wissenschaftslehre*', in *Early Philosophical Writings*, trans. & ed. Daniel Breazeale (Ithaca: Cornell University Press, 1988), 94–135.

16   TN: Immanuel Kant, *Critique of Pure Reason*, A1/B1.

CHAPTER THREE

Yves Duroux
Psychology and Logic[1]

[31] My presentation is based on a reading of Frege's *Grundlagen der Arithmetik* (Breslau, 1884).[2]

The object of this investigation is what we might call the natural progression of whole numbers. We can study the properties or the nature of number. But the properties of number conceal its nature.

By a property of number I mean what mathematicians do in a domain delimited by Peano's axioms.[3] The properties of whole numbers are drawn from these axioms. But in order for these axioms to function and to produce these properties, it is necessary that a certain number of questions are excluded from the field, questions whose terms, given as self-evident, concern the nature of the number. There are three such questions:

1. What is a number? (Peano's axiom takes it for granted that one knows what a number is).
2. What is zero?
3. What is the successor?

It is on the basis of these three questions that responses regarding the nature of whole numbers can vary.

For my part, I will look at the way Frege, criticizing a tradition, articulates his response. The whole of this critique [32] and of this response, as I will present them here, will constitute the foundation [*butée*] on the basis of which Jacques-Alain Miller will develop his presentation.[4]

---

1 This is the account of a presentation given on 27 January 1965 at the seminar of Dr. Jacques Lacan [at the École Normale Supérieure]; it has not been subsequently revised by the author. TN: First published as Yves Duroux, 'Psychologie et logique', CpA 1.2 (January 1966): 31–36. Translated by Cécile Malaspina, revised by Peter Hallward.

2 TN: Gottlob Frege, *The Foundations of Arithmetic* [1884], trans. J.L. Austin (New York: Harper, 1960). In the fourth chapter of this book (sections 72–80), Frege presents a logical construction of the series of whole or 'counting' numbers, derived from the definition of zero, the number one, and the 'successor function' (denoted by the + sign).

3 TN: In his *Principles of Arithmetic Presented by a New method* (1889) Giuseppe Peano lists the axioms that determine the sequence of whole numbers. Among other things, these axioms characterize the relation of equality (as reflexive, symmetric and transitive), and they assert that every number has just one successor, that no two numbers share the same successor, and that 0 is a number that is not the successor of any other number.

4 TN: This presentation was subsequently published as 'Suture' (CpA 1.3).

If zero is not reflected in a function that is different from the other numbers (if it is not taken as a point from which a succession is possible), if zero is not given a prevailing function – then the two other questions may be stated as follows:

1. How do we pass from a collection of things to a number that is the number of these things?
2. How do we pass from one number to another?

These two operations, one of collection [*rassemblement*], the other of addition, are treated by a long empiricist tradition as operations that can be referred back to the activity of a psychological subject. This whole translation plays on the word *Einheit*, which in German means 'unit [*unité*]', such that it is from a *play on words* on this word that a series of ambiguities regarding the functions of successors and of number becomes possible.

An *Einheit* is first of all an undifferentiated and undetermined element of any given set [*ensemble*]. But an *Einheit* can also be the name *One* [*Un*], name of the number 1.[5]

When we say one/a [*un*] horse and one horse and one horse, the *one* can indicate a unit, that is to say one element in a set where '3' horses are posited, one beside the other. But as long as these units are taken as elements and gathered together in the collection, we absolutely cannot infer that there is thus a result to which the number 3 can be attributed – unless we impose by force this designation on the collection.

In order to be able to say one horse and one horse and one horse = three horses, we must proceed on the basis of two modifications. It must be the case:

1. that the *one* [*un*] is conceived as a number.
2. that the *and* is transformed into the sign +.

But of course, once we have carried out this second operation, we still will not have explained anything: we will [only] have posed the real problem, which is to know how 1 plus 1 plus 1 make 3, once we no longer confuse the number 3 with the collecting of three units.

The source of the problem is that the recurrence [*retour*] of number brings with it a radically new signification, which is not the simple repetition of a unit. How can this return of the number understood as the sudden emergence of a new signification be thought, so long as we have not resolved the problem of the difference between equal elements [33], posited one beside the other, and their number?

5   TN: The French indefinite article 'un/une' can be translated either as 'a' or as 'one'.

A whole empiricist tradition contents itself by relating the emergence of a new signification to a specific activity (a function of inertia) of the psychological subject, which would consist in adding (along a temporal line of succession) and naming.

Frege cites a number of important texts that all come down to promoting imaginary operations: collecting, adding, naming. To support these functions, which mask the real problem, one must *suppose* a psychological subject that operates and states them. If the real problem is to discover what is specific to the sign + and to the *successor* operation, we must tear the concept of number away from psychological determination.

Here is where Frege's original enterprise begins in its own right. This reduction of the psychological proceeds in two stages:

1. Frege enacts a separation in the domain of what he calls the domain of *Vorstellungen* [representations]: on one side he puts what he calls psychological, subjective *Vorstellungen,* and on the other side what he calls objective *Vorstellungen.* This separation aims to *efface* all reference to a subject and to treat these objective representations according to laws that deserve to be called logical.

In these objective representations the *concept* and the *object* must be distinguished. Close attention must be paid to the fact that concept and object cannot be separated; the function that Frege assigns them is no different from the function of the predicate with respect to a subject, it is nothing other than a monadic relation (Russell), or a relation of function to argument.

2. Building on this first distinction, Frege effects a second one that allows him to relate a number, no longer to a subjective representation as the empiricist tradition tried to do, but to an objective representation, which is the concept. The diversity of possible numerations cannot be founded on a diversity of objects. It is simply the indication of a substitution of the concepts to which number applies.

Frege gives a rather paradoxical example. He takes the sentence: 'Venus has no moon [*aucune lune*].' To what should we attribute the determination 'no'? Frege says that we do not attribute 'no' to the object 'moon' – and with good reason, since there is none. Nevertheless *zero* is a numeration; we thus attribute it to the *concept* 'moon of Venus'. The concept 'moon of Venus' is related to an object which is the object 'moon', and this relation is such that there is no moon. [34]

It is on the basis of this double reduction that Frege obtains his first definition of number (the various different definitions of number only serve to ground the successor operation). First definition of number [*le nombre*]: number belongs to a concept.

But this definition is still incapable of giving us what Frege calls an individual number, that is to say a number that possesses a definite article: *the one, the two, the three,* which are unique as individual numbers (there are not several *ones,* there is only *one one, one two*).

We still have nothing that would allow us to determine whether that which is attributed to a concept is this number which is the unique number preceded by the definite article.

To help us understand the need for another way of reaching this individual number, Frege takes another example of planets and their moons, and this time it is: 'Jupiter has four moons.'

'Jupiter has four moons' can be converted into this other sentence: 'the number of Jupiter's moons is four.' The *is* that links the number of Jupiter's moons to four is absolutely not analogous to the *is* of the sentence 'the sky is blue': it is not a copula, it is a function of equality. The number *four* is the number one must posit as equal (identical) to the number of Jupiter's moons; to the concept 'Jupiter's moons' is attributed the number *four.*

This detour obliges Frege to posit a primordial operation that allows him to link numbers to a purely logical relation. This operation – I will not describe it in detail here – is an operation of 'equivalence'[6], a logical relation that enables one to order objects or concepts in a one-to-one correspondence (this 'or concepts' need not worry us insofar as, for Frege – at least at this stage of his thought – each relation of equality between concepts equally orders the objects falling under these concepts according to the same relation of equality).

Once this relation of 'equivalence' has been posited one can arrive at a second, the genuine definition of the number: 'the number that belongs to the concept f is the extension of the concept equivalent to the concept F.' [35]

This means: we have posited a determined concept F; we have determined, through the relation of equivalence, all the equivalences of this concept F; we then define the number as the extension of this concept equivalent to the concept F (all the equivalences of the concept F).

Frege's thinking will then proceed on the basis of a machine that we might arrange along two axes: a horizontal axis upon which the relation of equivalence comes into play, and a vertical axis which is the specific axis of the relation between concept and object (we can always, from the moment we have a concept, transform it into the object of a new concept, since the rapport between the concept and the object is a purely logical rapport of relation). It is on the basis of his relational machine that Frege now claims to demarcate [*cerner*] the various numbers, the individual numbers, which in a certain way he places at the end of his investigation, as the crowning of his system of equivalence. To demarcate the various numbers comes down to defining zero and the successor.

---

6   Or again of 'identity'.

In order to obtain the number zero, Frege forges the concept of 'not-identical to itself', which is defined by him as a contradictory concept, and he declares that, to whichever contradictory concept (and he evokes the commonplace contradictory concepts of traditional logic, the square circle or the wooden metal), to whichever concept under which no object falls, is attributed the name: 'zero'.[7] Zero is defined by logical contradiction, which guarantees non-existence of the object. There is a referral from the non-existence of the object, which is certified, decreed (since one says that there is no centaur or unicorn), to the logical contradiction of centaur or unicorn.

The second operation, which allows us to generate the entire series of numbers, is the successor operation. Frege defines at one and the same time the *one* and the successor operation.

For the successor operation I will give only Frege's definition, which he posits before the one; then I will show how he can only avail himself of this successor operation because he provides himself with this relation of one to zero.

The successor operation is defined simply as follows:

We say that a number immediately follows another number in a series if this number is attributed to a concept under which falls an object (x), and that there is another number (this is the number which the first number follows such that it is attributed to the concept 'falling under the preceding concept, but not identical to (x)').

This definition is purely formal. Frege grounds it, immediately afterwards, by defining the one. The one is defined on the basis [36] of the concept 'equal to zero'. What object falls under this concept? The object zero. Frege then says: '1 follows 0 insofar as 1 is attributed to the concept "equal to 0"'.[8]

So: the successor operation is generated by a double play of contradiction in the passage from zero to one. We might say, without going far beyond Frege's own field, that the reduction of the successor operation is accomplished by the operation of a double contradiction. Zero is given as contradictory; the passage from zero to one is given as a contradictory contradiction. The motor that animates succession in Frege is purely a negation of the negation. The apparatus that enables the definition of number functions very well. But is it capable of answering the following question: 'how, after 0, is there 1?' I will not question the legitimacy of the operation here. I will leave Jacques-Alain Miller to attend to this.

I would just like to make two remarks:

---

7   TN: '0 is the number that belongs to the concept "not identical with itself"' (Frege, *The Foundations of Arithmetic* §74).

8   TN: '1 is the number that belongs to the concept "identical with 0"' (Frege, *The Foundations of Arithmetic* §77).

1. For the empiricists, as for Frege, the name of [a] number (which Frege calls an individual name) is only obtained, in the end, by a *coup de force*, like a seal that the sealed might apply to itself.

2. For Frege, as for the empiricists, number is always captured by an operation whose *function is to fill up* [*de faire le plein*]⁹, through a collecting, or by this operation that Frege calls one-to-one correspondence and which has precisely the function of exhaustively collecting a whole field of objects. The activity of a subject on the one hand, and the logical operation of equivalence on the other, have the same function. We will have to draw the consequences of this.

---

9   TN: The phrase '*faire le plein*' means to fill up a car at a petrol station.

CHAPTER FOUR

Jacques-Alain Miller
Suture (Elements of the Logic of the Signifier)[1]

[37] No one without those precise conceptions of analysis which only a personal analysis can provide has any right to concern himself (or herself) with it. Ladies and Gentlemen, doubtless you fully conform to the strength of that ruling by Freud in the *New Introductory Lectures*.

Thus, articulated as a dilemma, a question raises itself for me in your regard.

If, contravening this injunction, it is of psychoanalysis that I am going to speak, – then, by listening to someone whom you know to be incapable of producing the credentials which alone would authorize your assent, *what are you doing here*?

Or, if my subject is not psychoanalysis, – then you who so faithfully attend here in order to become conversant with the problems which relate to the Freudian field, *what are you doing here*?

And you above all, Ladies and Gentlemen the analysts, what are *you* doing here, you to whom Freud specifically addressed the warning not to rely on those who are not confirmed in the practice of your science, on those so-called authorities, those literary intellectuals, who bring their soup to warm at your fire, without so much as recognizing your hospitality? Even if he who reigns in your kitchens [38] as head chef could amuse himself by letting someone lower than the lowest kitchen boy get hold of the pot with which you are so naturally concerned since it is from it that you draw your sustenance, it would still be uncertain – and I confess that I myself doubted – that you would be ready to drink in a soup merely cooked up in that way. And yet you are here. Permit me to marvel a moment at your presence, and at the privilege of your having lent me for a while that most precious of the organs at your disposal, your ear.

Which I must now attempt to justify to it, and with reasons which are at least admissible [*avouables*].

I will not keep you waiting. The justification lies in this, which will come as no surprise after the developments which have so enchanted your hearing at this seminar since the start of the academic year, that *the Freudian field is not representable as*

---

1   TN: This article was first presented in Lacan's Seminar XII, in the session of 24 February 1965, and was first published as Jacques-Alain Miller, 'La Suture (Éléments de la logique du signifiant)', CpA 1.3 (January 1966), 37–49. This translation by Jacqueline Rose first appeared in *Screen* 18:4 (Winter 1977–78), 24–34, and is reproduced here with permission. The translation appears unaltered but we have added a few fragments of the original French, in parentheses or footnotes.

a closed surface. The opening up of psychoanalysis is not the effect of the liberalism, the whim, the blindness even of he who has set himself as its guardian. For, if not being situated on the inside does not relegate you to the outside, it is because at a certain point, excluded from a two-dimensional topology, the two surfaces join up and the periphery or outer edge crosses over the circumscription.

That I can recognize and occupy that point is what releases you from the dilemma I presented to you, and entitles you to be listening to me today. Which will enable you to grasp, Ladies and Gentlemen, to what extent you are implicated in my undertaking and how far its successful outcome concerns you.

CONCEPT OF THE LOGIC OF THE SIGNIFIER

What I am aiming to restore, piecing together indications dispersed through the work of Jacques Lacan, is to be designated the logic of the signifier – it is a general logic in that its functioning is formal in relation to all fields of knowledge including that of psychoanalysis which, in acquiring a specificity there, it governs; it is a minimal logic in that within it are given those pieces only which are necessary to assure it a progression reduced to a linear movement, uniformally generated at each point of its necessary sequence. That this logic should be called the logic of the signifier avoids the partiality of the conception which [39] would limit its validity to the field in which it was first produced as a category; to correct its linguistic declension is to prepare the way for its importation into other discourses, an importation which we will not fail to carry out once we have grasped its essentials here.

The chief advantage to be gained from this process of minimization is the greatest economy of conceptual expenditure, which is then in danger of obscuring to you that the conjunctions which it effects between certain functions are so essential that to neglect them is to compromise analytic reasoning proper.

By considering the relationship between this logic and that which I will call logician's logic, we see that its particularity lies in the fact that the first treats of the emergence of the second, and should be conceived of as the logic of the origin of logic – which is to say, that it does not follow its laws, but that, prescribing their jurisdiction, itself falls outside that jurisdiction.

This dimension of the archaeological can be grasped most succinctly through a movement back from the field of logic itself, where its miscognition [*méconnaissance*], at its most radical because it is closest to its recognition, is effected.

That this step repeats something of that which Derrida has shown to be exemplary to phenomenology[2] will conceal to none but the most hasty this

---

2   Edmund Husserl, *L'Origine de la géométrie*, translation and introduction by Jacques Derrida (Paris: PUF, 1962); Jacques Derrida, *Edmund Husserl's Origin of Geometry: An Introduction*, trans. John P. Leavey, Jr. (Lincoln: University of Nebraska Press, 1989).

crucial difference, that here miscognition finds its point of departure in the production of meaning. We can say that it is constituted not as a forgetting, but as a repression [*refoulement*].

To designate it I choose the name of *suture*. Suture names the relation of the subject to the chain of its discourse; we shall see that it figures there as the element which is lacking, in the form of a stand-in [*tenant-lieu*].[3] For, while there lacking, it is not purely and simply absent. Suture, by extension – the general relation of lack to the structure – of which it is an element, inasmuch as it implies the position of a taking-the-place-of [*tenant-lieu*].

It is the objective of this paper to articulate the concept of suture which, if it is not named explicitly as such by Jacques Lacan, is constantly present in his system.

Let it be absolutely clear that it is not as philosopher or philosopher's apprentice that I am speaking here – if the philosopher is as characterized by Heinrich Heine in a sentence quoted by Freud, 'with his [40] nightcaps and the tatters of his dressing-gown, patching up the gaps in the structure of the universe.' But take care not to think that the function of suturation is peculiar to the philosopher: what is specific to the philosopher is the determination of the field in which he operates as a 'universal structure'. It is important that you realize that the logician, like the linguist, also sutures at his particular level. And, quite as much, anyone who says 'I'.

In order to grasp suture we must cut across what a discourse makes explicit of itself, and distinguish from its meaning, its letter. This paper is concerned with a letter – a dead letter. It should come as no surprise if the meaning then dies.

The main thread of this analysis will be Gottlob Frege's argument in *Grundlagen der Arithmetik*,[4] crucial here because it puts into question those terms which in Peano's axiomatic, adequate for a construction of a theory of natural numbers, are taken as primary – that is, the zero, the number, the successor.[5] This calling into question of the theory, by disintricating, from the axiomatic where the theory is consolidated, the suturing, delivers up this last.[6]

---

3   TN: The French gives '*tenant-lieu*', literally a 'holding-the-place-of', in the sense of substitute; it has been variously translated as 'stand-in', 'taking-the-place-of', etc.

4   German text with English translation published under the title *The Foundations of Arithmetic* (Oxford: Basil Blackwell, 1953).

5   Our reading will not concern itself with any of Frege's various inflections of his basic purpose, and will therefore keep outside the thematization of the difference of meaning and reference, as well as of the later definition of the concept in terms of predication, from which is deduced its non-saturation [*non-saturation*]. TN: The English has 'following in a series' as substantive ('*der Folgen in einer Reihe*'), cf. Frege, *Foundations* §79, 'Definition of following in a series'.

6   TN: the French reads: 'Cette mise en cause de la théorie, à déboîter, de l'axiomatique où elle se consolide, son suturant, le livre.'

THE ZERO AND THE ONE

Here then is the question posed in its most general form:

> *what is it* that functions in the series of whole natural numbers to which we can assign their progression?

And the answer, which I shall give at once before establishing it:

> in the process of the constitution of the series, in the genesis of progression, *the function of the subject*, miscognized, is operative. [41]

This proposition will certainly appear as a paradox to anyone who knows that the logical discourse of Frege opens with the exclusion of that which is held by empiricist theory to be essential for the passage of the thing to the unit [*unité*], and of the set [*collection*] of units to the unit of number: that is, the function of the subject, as support of the operations of abstraction and unification.

For the unity which is thus assured both for the individual and the set, it only holds insofar as the number functions as its *name*. Whence originates the ideology which makes of the subject the producer of fictions, short of recognizing it as the product of its product – an ideology in which logical and psychological discourse are wedded, with political discourse occupying the key position, which can be seen admitted in Ockham, concealed in Locke, and miscognized thereafter.

A subject therefore, defined by attributes whose other side is political, disposing as of powers,[7] of a faculty of memory necessary to close the set without the loss of any of the interchangeable elements, and a faculty of repetition which operates inductively. There is no doubt that it is this subject which Frege, setting himself from the start against the empiricist foundation of arithmetic, excludes from the field in which the concept of the number is to appear.

But if it is held that the subject is not reducible, in its most essential function, to the psychological, then its *exclusion* from the field of number is assimilable to *repetition* [*s'identifie à la répétition*]. Which is what I have to demonstrate.

You will be aware that Frege's discourse starts from the fundamental system comprising the three concepts of the concept, the object and the number, and two relations, that of the concept to the object, which is called subsumption and that of the concept to the number which I will call assignation. A number is assigned to a concept which subsumes objects.

---

7   TN: '. . . disposant comme de pouvoirs d'une faculté de mémoire . . .'.

What is specifically logical about this system is that each concept is only defined and exists solely through the relation which it maintains as subsumer with that which it subsumes. Similarly, an object only has existence insofar as it falls under a concept, there being no other determination involved in its logical existence, so that the object takes its meaning from its difference to the thing integrated, by its spatio-temporal localization, to the real.[8]

Whence you can see the disappearance of the thing which must be effected in order for it to appear as object – which is *the thing insofar as it is one.* [42]

It is clear that the concept which operates in the system, formed solely through the determination of subsumption, is a redoubled concept: *the concept of identity to a concept.*

This redoubling, induced in the concept by identity, engenders the logical dimension, because in effecting the disappearance of the thing it gives rise to the emergence of the numerable.

For example, if I group what falls under the concept 'child of Agamemnon and Cassandra', I summon in order to subsume them Pelops and Teledamus. To this set I can only assign a number if I put into play the concept 'identical to the concept: child of Agamemnon and Cassandra'. Through the effect of the fiction of this concept, the children now intervene insofar as each one is, so to speak, applied to itself – which transforms it into a unit, and gives to it the status of an object which is numerable as such. It is this one of the singular unit, this one of identity of the subsumed, which is common to all numbers insofar as they are first constituted as units.

From this can be deduced the definition of the assignation of number: according to Frege 'the number assigned to the concept F is the extension of the concept "identical to the concept F"'. Frege's ternary system has as its effect that all that is left to the thing is the support of its identity with itself, by which it is the object of the operative concept, and hence numerable.

The process that I have just set out authorizes me to conclude the following proposition, whose relevance will emerge later – the unit which could be called *unifying* of the concept insofar as it is assigned by the number is subordinate to the unit as *distinctive* insofar as it supports the number.

As for the position of the distinctive unit, its foundation is to be situated in the function of identity which, conferring on each thing of the world the property of being one, effects its transformation into an object of the (logical) concept.

At this point in the construction, you will sense all the importance of the definition of identity which I am going to present.

---

8   TN: '. . . l'objet prend son sens de sa différence d'avec la chose intégrée, par sa localisation spatio-temporelle, au réel.'

This definition which must give its true meaning to the concept of number, must borrow nothing from it[9] – precisely in order to engender numeration. [43]

This definition, which is pivotal to his system, Frege takes from Leibniz. It is contained in this statement: *eadem sunt quorum unum potest substitui alteri salva veritate*. Those things are identical of which one can be substituted for the other *salva veritate*, without loss of truth. Doubtless you can estimate the crucial importance of what is effected by this statement: the emergence of the function of truth. Yet what it assumes is more important than what it expresses. That is, identity-with-itself. That a thing cannot be substituted for itself, then where does this leave truth? Absolute is its subversion.[10]

If we follow Leibniz's argument, the failing of truth whose possibility is opened up for an instant, its loss through the substitution for one thing of another, would be followed by its immediate reconstitution in a new relation: truth is recovered because the substituted thing, in that it is identical with itself, can be the object of a judgement and enter into the order of discourse: identical with itself, it can be articulated.

But that a thing should not be identical with itself subverts the field of truth, ruins it and abolishes it.

You will grasp to what extent the preservation of truth is implicated in this identity with itself which connotes the passage from the thing to the object. Identity-with-itself is essential if truth is to be saved.

Truth is. Each thing is identical with itself.

Let us now put into operation Frege's schema, that is, go through the three-stage itinerary which he prescribes to us. Let there be a thing X of the world. Let there be the empirical concept of this X. The concept which finds a place in the schema is not this empirical concept but that which redoubles it, being 'identical with the concept of X'. The object which falls under this concept is X itself, as a unit. In this the number, which is the third term of the sequence, to be assigned to the concept of X will be the number 1. Which means that this function of the number 1 is repetitive for all things of the world. It is in this sense that this 1 is only the unit which constitutes [the] number [*le nombre*] as such, and not the 1 in its personal identity as a number with its own particular place and a proper name in the series of numbers. Furthermore, its construction demands that, in order to transform it, we call upon a thing of the world – which, according to Frege, cannot be [done]: the logic must be sustained through nothing but itself.

In order for the number to pass from the repetition of the 1 of the identical to that of its ordered succession, in order for the logical dimension to gain

---

9   Which is why we must say identity and not equality.

10   TN: 'Qu'une chose ne puisse être substituée à elle-même, et qu'en est-il de la vérité? Absolue est sa subversion.'

its autonomy definitively, without any reference to the real the zero has to appear. [44]

Which appearance is obtained because truth is. Zero is the number assigned to the concept 'not identical with itself'. In effect, let there be the concept 'not identical with itself'. This concept, by virtue of being a concept, has an extension, subsumes an object. *Which object? None.* Since truth is, no object falls into the place of the subsumed of this concept, and the number which qualifies its extension is zero.

In this engendering of the zero, I have stressed that it is supported by the proposition that truth is. If no object falls under the concept of non-identical-with-itself, it is because truth must be saved. If there are no things which are not identical with themselves, it is because non-identity with itself is contradictory to the very dimension of truth. To its concept, we assign the zero.

It is this decisive proposition that *the concept of not-identical-with-itself is assigned by the number zero* which sutures logical discourse.

For, and here I am working across Frege's text, in the autonomous construction of the logical through itself, it has been necessary, in order to exclude any reference to the real, to evoke on the level of the concept an object *not-identical-with-itself*, to be subsequently rejected from the dimension of truth.

The zero which is inscribed in the place of the number consummates the exclusion of this object. As for this place, marked out by subsumption, in which the object is lacking, there nothing can be *written*, and if a 0 must be traced, it is merely in order to figure a *blank*, to render visible the lack.

From the zero lack [*zéro manque*] to the zero number, the non-conceptualizable is conceptualised.

Let us now set aside the zero lack in order to consider only that which is produced by the alternation of its evocation and its revocation, the zero number.

The zero understood as a number, which assigns to the subsuming concept the lack of an object, is as such a thing – *the first non-real thing in thought.*

If of the number zero we construct the concept, it subsumes as its sole object the number zero. The number which assigns it is therefore 1.

Frege's system works by the circulation of an element, at each of the places it fixes: from the number zero to its concept, from this concept to its object and to its number – a circulation which produces the 1.[11] [45]

This system is thus so constituted *with the 0 counting as 1.* The counting of the 0 as 1 (whereas the concept of the zero subsumes nothing in the real but a blank) is the general support of the series of numbers.

It is this which is demonstrated by Frege's analysis of the operation of the successor, which consists of obtaining the number which follows *n* by adding to

---

11   I leave aside the commentary of paragraph 76 [of Frege's *Foundations*] which gives the abstract definition of contiguity.

it a unit: n' the successor of n, is equal to $n + 1$, that is, $\ldots n \ldots (n + 1) = n' \ldots$ Frege opens out the $n + 1$ in order to discover what is involved in the passage from n to its successor.

You will grasp the paradox of this engendering as soon as I produce the most general formula for the successor which Frege arrives at: 'the Number assigned to the concept "member of the series of natural numbers ending with n" follows in the series of natural numbers directly after n.'

Let us take a number. The number three. It will serve to constitute the concept 'member of the series of natural numbers ending with three'. We find that the number assigned to this concept is four. Here then is the 1 of $n + 1$. Where does it come from? Assigned to its redoubled concept, the number 3 functions as the unifying name of a set: as reserve.[12] In the concept of 'member of the series of natural numbers ending with 3', it is the term [*il est terme*] (in the sense both of element and of final element).

In the order of the real, the 3 subsumes 3 objects. In the order of number, which is that of discourse bound by truth, it is numbers which are counted: before the 3 , there are 3 numbers – it is therefore the fourth.

In the order of number, *there is in addition the 0* and the 0 counts for 1. The displacement of a number, from the function of reserve to that of term, implies the summation of the 0. Whence the successor. That which in the real is pure and simple absence finds itself through the fact of number (through the instance [*instance*][13] of truth) noted 0 and counted for 1.

Which is why we say the object not-identical with itself invoked-rejected by truth, instituted-annulled by discourse (subsumption as such) – in a word, sutured.

The emergence of the lack as 0, and of 0 as 1 determines the appearance of the successor. Let there be n; the lack is fixed as 0 which is fixed as 1: $n + 1$; which is added in order to give n' – which absorbs the 1. [**46**]

Certainly, if the 1 of $n + 1$ is nothing other than the counting of the zero, the function of addition of the sign + is superfatory [*superfétatoire*], and we must restore to the horizontal representation of the engendering its verticality: the 1 is to be taken as the primary symbol of the emergence of lack in the field of truth, and the sign + indicates the crossing, the transgression through which the 0 lack comes to be represented as 1, producing, through this difference of n to n' which you have seen to be an effect of meaning, the name of a number.

Logical representation collapses this three-level construction. The operation I have effected opens it out. If you consider the opposition of these two

---

12   TN: '. . . le nombre 3 fonctionne comme le nom unifiant d'une collection: réserve.'

13   TN: The French word *instance* can be translated as 'authority', in the sense of legal authority, or as 'agency'.

axes, you will understand what is at stake in logical suturing, and the difference of the logic which I am putting forward to logician's logic.

That zero is a number: such is the proposition which assures the logical dimension of its closure.

Our purpose has been to recognize in the zero number the suturing stand-in for the lack.

Remember here the hesitation perpetuated in the work of Bertrand Russell concerning its localization (interior? or exterior to the series of numbers?).

The generating repetition of the series of numbers is sustained by this, that the zero lack passes, first along a vertical axis, across the bar which limits the field of truth in order to be represented there as one, subsequently cancelling out as meaning in each of the names of the numbers which are caught up in the metonymic chain of successional progression.

Just as the zero as lack *of* the contradictory object must be distinguished from that which sutures this absence in the series of numbers, so the 1, as the proper name of a number, is to be distinguished from that which comes to fix in a trait the zero of the not-identical with itself sutured by the identity with itself, which is the law of discourse in the field of truth. The central paradox to be grasped (which as you will see in a moment is the paradox of the signifier in the sense of Lacan) is that the trait of the identical represents the non-identical, whence is deduced the impossibility of its redoubling,[14] and from that impossibility the structure of *repetition*, as the process of differentiation of the identical. [47]

Now, if the series of numbers, metonymy of the zero, begins with its metaphor, if the 0 member of the series as number is only the standing-in-place suturing the absence (of the absolute zero) which moves beneath the chain according to the alternation of a representation and an exclusion – then what is there to stop us from seeing in the restored relation of the zero to the series of numbers the most elementary articulation of the subject's relation to the signifying chain?

The impossible object, which the discourse of logic summons as the not-identical with itself and then rejects as the pure negative, which it summons and rejects in order to constitute itself as that which it is, which it summons and rejects *wanting to know nothing of it*, we name this object, insofar as it functions as the excess which operates in the series of numbers, the subject.

Its exclusion from the discourse which internally it intimates is suture.[15]

If we now determine the trait as the signifier, and ascribe to the number the position of signified, the relation of lack to the trait should be considered as the logic of the signifier.

---

14   And, at another level, the impossibility of meta-language (cf. Jacques Lacan, 'La Science et la vérité', CpA 1.1 [1966]: 7–28).

15   TN: 'Son exclusion hors du discours qu'intérieurement il intime est: suture.'

RELATION OF SUBJECT AND SIGNIFIER

In effect, what in Lacanian algebra is called the relation of the subject to the field of the Other (as the locus of truth) can be identified with the relation which the zero entertains with the identity of the unique as the support of truth. This relation, insofar as it is matrical [*matriciel*], cannot be integrated into any definition of objectivity – this being the doctrine of Dr. Lacan. The engendering of the zero, from this not-identical with itself under which no thing of the world falls, illustrates this to you.

What constitutes this relation as the matrix of the chain must be isolated in the implication which makes the determinant of the exclusion of the subject outside the field of the Other its representation in that field in the form of the one of the unique, the one of distinctive unity, which is called 'unary' by Lacan. In his algebra, this exclusion is marked by the bar which strikes the S of the subject in front of the capital A,[16] and which is displaced by the identity of the subject onto the A, according to the fundamental exchange of the logic of the signifier, a displacement whose effect is the emergence of signification signified to the subject.

Untouched by the exchange of the bar, this exteriority of the subject to the Other is maintained, which institutes the unconscious. [48]

For: – if it is clear that the tripartition which divides (1) the signified-to-the-subject, (2) the signifying chain whose radical alterity in relation to the subject cuts off the subject from its field, and finally (3) the external field of this reject [*rejet*], cannot be covered by the linguistic dichotomy of signified and signifier; – if the consciousness of the subject is to be situated on the level of the effects of signification, governed, so much so that they could even be called its reflections, by the repetition of the signifier: – if repetition itself is produced by the vanishing of the subject and its passage as lack – then only the unconscious can name the progression which constitutes the chain in the order of thought.

On the level of this constitution, the definition of the subject comes down to *the possibility of one signifier more*.

Is it not ultimately to this function of excess that can be referred the power of thematization, which Dedekind assigns to the subject in order to give to set theory its theorem of existence? The possibility of existence of an enumerable infinity can be explained by this, that 'from the moment that one proposition is true, I can always produce a second, that is, that the first is true and so on to infinity.'[17]

In order to ensure that this recourse to the subject as the founder of iteration is not a recourse to psychology, we simply substitute for thematization the

---

16   TN: 'A' stands for *Autre*; in English it would be capital 'O', for the big Other.
17   Richard Dedekind, quoted by Jean Cavaillès, *Philosophie mathémathique* (Paris: Hermann, 1962), 124.

representation of the subject (as signifier) which excludes consciousness because it is not effected for someone, but, in the chain, in the field of truth, *for* the signifier which precedes it. When Lacan faces the definition of the sign as that which represents something for someone, with that of the signifier as that which represents the subject for another signifier, he is stressing that insofar as the signifying chain is concerned, it is on the level of its effects and not of its cause that consciousness is to be situated. The insertion of the subject into the chain is representation, necessarily correlative to an exclusion which is a vanishing [*évanouissement*].

If now we were to try and develop in time the relation which engenders and supports the signifying chain, we would have to take into account the fact that temporal succession is under the dependency of the linearity of the chain. The time of engendering can only be [49] circular – which is why both these propositions are true at one and the same time, that subject is anterior to signifier and that signifier is anterior to subject – but only appears as such after the introduction of the signifier. The retroaction consists essentially of this: the birth of linear time. We must hold together the definitions which make the subject *the effect of the signifier* and the signifier *the representative of the subject*: it is a circular, though non-reciprocal, relation.

By crossing logical discourse at its point of least resistance, that of its suture, you can see articulated the structure of the subject as a 'flickering in eclipses', like the movement which opens and closes [the] number, and delivers up the lack in the form of the 1 in order to abolish it in the successor.

As for the + you have understood the unprecedented function which it takes on in the logic of the signifier (a sign, no longer of addition, but of that summation of the subject in the field of the Other, which calls for its *annulment*). It remains to disarticulate it in order to separate the unary trait of emergence, and the bar of the reject: thereby making manifest the *division* of the subject which is the other name for its *alienation*.

It will be deduced from this that the signifying chain is *structure of the structure*.

If structural causality (causality in the structure insofar as the subject is implicated in it) is not an empty expression, it is from the minimal logic which I have developed here that it will find its status.

We leave for another time the construction of its concept.

CHAPTER FIVE

Serge Leclaire
The Analyst in His Place?[1]

[50] I am going to try to say in what sense the position of the psychoanalyst is irreducible to all others, and is perhaps, strictly speaking, inconceivable, taking as my point of departure Jacques-Alain Miller's exposition of 24 February [1965].[2]

In his enterprise of interrogating the foundations of logic, of what he calls the logic of logicians, and in gathering together from the work of Lacan the elements of a logic of the signifier, Miller himself comes to present us with a logical discourse, or even an archaeological discourse, as he puts it, one capable of comprehending the discourse that issues from the analytic experience.

Now to arrive at such a discourse it is necessary, if I may say so, to hold firmly to the point that makes the articulation of a logical discourse possible, that is, the point that Miller presents to us both as the weak point and as the crucial point of every discourse, namely the point of suture [le point de suture].

We need to understand, Miller reminds us, that 'the function of suturation is not peculiar to the philosopher'. 'It is important that you are persuaded', he insists, 'that the logician, like the linguist, also sutures at his own particular level' [CpA 1.3:40].

I am quite persuaded of it. *It is clear that Miller, as a logician, or archaeologist, himself also sutures.* But here is the difference: the analyst, whether he likes it or not and even when he attempts to [51] discourse upon psychoanalysis, *the analyst does not suture*, or at least he ought to strive to be wary of this passion [passion].

I could stop there. This would obviously be the most concise form. Nevertheless, I would like to try to take my argument a bit further. Of what does the point of suture evoked here consist?

One of the pivotal propositions of Miller's exposition is as follows: 'It is this decisive proposition that *the concept of not-identical-with-itself is assigned by the number zero* which sutures logical discourse' [CpA 1.3:44].

Far be it from me to contest the importance of this remark. But I would like to go further.[3] The introduction of this concept of non-identity to itself follows

---

1   TN: A version of this article was first presented in Lacan's Seminar XII, *Crucial Problems For Psychoanalysis* (1964–65), in the session of 24 March 1965, and it was first published as Serge Leclaire, 'L'Analyste à sa place?', CpA 1.4 (January 1966): 50–52. Translated by Christian Kerslake, revised by Peter Hallward.

2   TN: The reference is to Jacques-Alain Miller, 'Suture', CpA 1.3.

3   TN: the text here omits a phrase included in the version transcribed in Cormac Gallagher's unofficial translation of Lacan, S12 (online at lacaninireland.com), 301: 'and to question Miller's interest in the concept of non-identity to itself'.

on from the Leibnizian concept of identity-to-self advanced by Frege, namely: 'those things are identical of which one can be substituted for the other without the truth being lost.' It is starting from there that one arrives at this other proposition: 'The truth is: each thing is identical to itself.' What is this thing that is identical to itself? It is the thing insofar as it is one [*une*], namely, the object. That everything is identical to itself is what permits the object (the thing insofar as it is one) to fall under a concept. *It must be* that the thing is identical to itself so that truth can be saved: here, we might discover the major accent not only of Frege's book, but also of Miller's exposition, namely, the saving of the truth. However, the analyst, *for his part*, is not necessarily concerned with saving the truth.

The analyst will happily admit, or at least I would, that 'truth *also* is [*la vérité est* aussi].' But reality *is* also. And reality, for the analyst, forces him to envisage the thing insofar as it is not one, to envisage the possibility of the non-identical to itself.

Frege certainly does this, but by blocking immediately, as Miller shows, the non-identical to itself with the number zero.

If we renounce, for a moment, the saving of the Truth, then what appears? I would say that for me it is radical difference, otherwise known as sexual difference.

We can find an extremely precise reference to this in the work of Freud. At the moment in the 'Observation' in the *Wolf Man* when he discusses the reality of the primal scene, he focuses on the problematic of castration in its relations with anal eroticism, and comes up with the curious expression of an '*unconscious concept*'. [52]

This concept certainly involves a unity, but one that covers things that are non-identical to themselves: his examples include the faeces, the child, or the penis, or why not, the finger, the cut finger, the little spot on the nose, or indeed the nose itself. The notion of an unconscious concept emerges from Freud's pen to connote the unity of things that are small or indifferent, but which can be separated from the body. Perhaps we have here the concept, the reality of a thing that is non-identical to itself.[4]

---

4   Doctor Leclaire here gives another example that we do not reproduce here: it will be the theme of a session of his seminar at the ENS.

TN: The example, Freud's analysis of the Wolfman, is taken up in Leclaire's essay 'The Elements at Play in a Psychoanalysis' (CpA 5.1), but the transcription of Leclaire's presentation of the example in the version of this paper given at Lacan's Seminar XII is already illuminating. Cormac Gallagher's rough translation of this passage runs as follows:

'[. . . I]n the experience of the Wolfman, there are many moments where his experience pivots, turns upside down, where something changes radically.

In the supplement to the history of an infantile neurosis, that Ruth Mack Brunswick has given us, she signals textually one of these moments where the world pivots on its axis, where the structure of the world, the order of the world seems to vanish. It is the moment when, uneasy about the

When I say that the analyst does not suture, it is because for him, in his experience, it is necessary that not even the zero serve to hide the truth of a radical difference, of a difference to self [*une différence à soi*] that asserts itself in the last analysis in the face of the irreducibility of sexual reality.

Whoever does not suture is able to see the reality of sex sus-tained [*sous-tendue*] by fundamental castration. He can envisage the enigma of generation. Not only that of the engendering of the sequence of numbers, but also of the generation of people.

The domain of the analyst is a domain that is necessarily a-veridical [*a-véridique*], at least in its exercise. The analyst refuses to suture, I have told you. In fact, he does not construct a discourse, even when he speaks. Fundamentally, and it is in this sense that the question of the analyst is irreducible, the analyst listens [*est à l'écoute*]. Listens to what? To the discourse of his patient, and what interests him in the discourse of his patient is precisely to know what is fixed for him at the point of suture. That for his part Miller situates himself, in order to speak to us, at a topological point that is neither open nor closed, we grant him that – but the analyst, on the other hand, is more like the subject of the unconscious, which is to say that he has no place and cannot have one.

I imagine that this position or this non-position of the analyst might give vertigo to the logician, the one whose passion is for the truth. For it is indeed what testifies in his action to this radical difference between a sutured desiring [*un désirant suturé*] and one that refuses to suture, a non-suturing, a desiring-not-to-suture. I know very well that in a certain sense this position is intolerable. But I believe that, whatever we make of it, we are not done with it, and nor are you Miller, you are not yet done with trying to put the analyst in his place,

---

presence of this pimple on his nose, the Wolfman having questioned the dermatologist, hears it being said that nothing can be done, the pimple will remain the same, it will not change, there is nothing to do, there is no need to treat it or to take it off.

You will tell me, this pimple is therefore precisely one of these things, like that, which is found to coincide with itself. Does that mean that it is identical, that it can be located as identical? I do not think so at all. The proof is that he goes to see another dermatologist, has the pimple removed, experiences moreover an acute ecstasy at the moment that this pimple is removed. He is relieved about it for a while. The veil which separates him from the world is once again torn, and he is once again present to the world.

But, of course, this does not last. And what replaces the pimple is a hole. And of course his delusional preoccupation – in fact the delusion is not one that would frighten us – is going to be what is going to happen to this hole, this little scar, this little scratch, which cannot be seen, but he, at his mirror where he constantly looks at his nose sees this hole.

The decisive moment, another decisive moment, which this time decides him to begin a new slice of analysis, is when he is told that the scars will never disappear.

There again it is the same thing: whether what is involved is the pimple or the scar of the pimple; different things, they are nevertheless the same things. For him also, here the world pivots on its axis, he can no longer live like that, it is completely intolerable' (S12, session 20, 302–303).

or as is said, to return [*remettre*] the analyst to his place.[5] Fortunately, as it happens. If he puts himself there all by himself, then this results from lassitude, or because he is compelled to do so. Only one thing is sure: the day the analyst is in his place, there will no longer be any analysis.

5   TN: '. . . de mettre, ou comme on dit, remettre l'analyste à sa place.'

CHAPTER SIX

Jean-Claude Milner
The Point of the Signifier[1]

[73] We have inherited a relation between being and computation – this point is sufficiently demonstrated by ancient doxography, which, relaying opinions on being, can only state them as enumerations, and in order to list them, can only follow the sequence of numbers. Isocrates relates, for example, that 'for one group, the ancient sophists, there are an infinity of beings; for Empedocles, there are four; for Ion, only three, for Alcmaeon, just two; for Parmenides, one; and for Gorgias, absolutely none' (Isocrates, Or. XV, 268; cited p. 345 of the Diès edition).[2]

This relation, which the anecdote describes, also delimits [cerne] the hypothesis supporting Plato's movement in the *Sophist*, where he desires to establish the status of non-being. Placing himself in the succession of opinions, since he aims to conclude it – between Parmenides' 'one', which summarizes all the positive countings [les comptes positifs], and Gorgias' 'absolutely none', which erases them all – all he can do is enumerate non-being, provoking its emergence with a calculation.[3]

Consider the *genera* [or general 'kinds' of things] then, as the elements of the collection to be deduced or deducted [à décompter], out of which non-being should arise through e-numeration: 'Among the genera, [. . .] some may participate in a mutual community, and others not; certain of them will accept it with

---

1   This is a revised version of a text delivered on 2 June 1965 at the Seminar of Doctor Lacan. We must thank Dr. Audouard, who, speaking before us, presented us with more than a point of departure: while taking a different approach, we have done nothing more than recognize, following him, the foundational points he had already marked with the doctrine of the signifier.

TN: First published as Jean-Claude Milner, 'Le Point du signifiant', CpA 3.5 (May–June 1966): 73–82. Translated by Christian Kerslake, revised by Knox Peden. In Cormac Gallagher's rough translation of Lacan's *Seminar XII: Crucial Problems for Psychoanalysis* (1964–65), Milner's presentation runs from pages 334 to 339, online at lacaninireland.com.

2   TN: The reference is to Isocrates' *Antidosis*, cited in Auguste Diès' edition of Plato, *Oeuvres complètes*, tome VIII, part 3 [1925]: *Le Sophiste*, 4th edition (Paris: Les Belles Lettres, 1963), 341. The full passage from Isocrates reads, in the most recent English translation: 'I would advise the young to spend some time in these subjects but not to allow their natures to become withered up by them or stranded in the discourses of the old sophists, of whom one said the number of elements is infinite; Empedocles, that it is four, among which are strife and love; Ion, that it is not more than three; Alcmaeon, that it is only two; Parmenides and Melissus, that it is one; and Gorgias, [that it is] none at all' (Isocrates, *Antidosis*, 268; in Yun Lee Too, *A Commentary on Isocrates'* [Oxford: Oxford University Press, 2008], 75).

3   TN: We have translated quotations from Plato directly from Milner's French, but have included some passages from the English translation by Nicholas White (in Plato, *Complete Works*, ed. John M. Cooper [Indianapolis: Hackett, 1997]) in the notes.

some, while still others, penetrating everywhere, find nothing to prevent them from entering into community [74] with everything' (254b).[4] Through this opposition between mixture [*le mélange*] and non-mixture, between what lends itself to community and what does not, a distinctive trait is defined, which allows for the introduction among the genera of an order and classes: a hierarchy.

Since the procedure of enumerating a collection – by assigning a given genus to a class and situating it in the order – is now known, Plato is able to delimit arbitrarily a series by selecting from among the genera a certain number of them: the three largest, i.e. *being, rest, movement*. It is as if, instead of searching for non-being in some given collection (no doubt confident that he would not find it there), Plato meant to take the opposite course, and to produce non-being in the succession of states of a constructed collection.

Apparently arbitrary, the selected collection is in fact sustained by formal properties: if, among the three selected genera, rest and movement cannot mix or blend with one another, whereas being mixes with both, then Plato has in effect constituted the minimal series needed to support the binary opposition between mixture and non-mixture, which is the very law of the entire collection.

---

4   TN: Nicholas White's translation of this passage, in the Cooper edition of Plato's *Complete Works*, reads as follows:

'VISITOR: We've agreed on this: some kinds will associate with each other and some won't, some will to a small extent and others will associate a great deal, nothing prevents still others from being all-pervading – from being associated with everyone of them. So next let's pursue our account together this way. Let's not talk about every form. That way we won't be thrown off by dealing with too many of them. Instead let's choose some of the most important ones. First we'll ask what they're like, and next we'll ask about their ability to associate with each other. Even if our grasp of *that which is* and *that which is not* isn't completely clear, our aim will be to avoid being totally without an account of them – so far as that's allowed by our present line of inquiry – and see whether we can get away with saying that *that which is not* really is that which is not.
THEAETETUS: That's what we have to do.
VISITOR: The most important kinds we've just been discussing are *that which is, rest,* and *change.*
THEAETETUS: Yes, by far.
VISITOR: And we say that two of them don't blend with each other.
THEAETETUS: Definitely not.
VISITOR: But *that which is* blends with both of them, since presumably both of them are.
THEAETETUS: Of course.
VISITOR: We do have three of them.
THEAETETUS: Yes.
VISITOR: So each of them is different from two of them, but is the same as itself.
THEAETETUS: Yes.
VISITOR: But what in the world are *the same* and *the different* that we've been speaking of? Are they two kinds other than those three but necessarily always blending with them? And do we have to think of them all as being five and not three? Or have what we've been calling *the same* and *the different* turned out, without our realizing it, to be among those three?' (Plato, *Sophist*, 254b-255a).

In actual fact, the initial distinction is between two [terms], mixture and non-mixture, but whereas one term suffices to represent mixture, two are required to support non-mixture. Suppose that movement and being are the only genera given. In this case being, which by definition involves everything, would mix with movement and movement's distinctive trait of evading any kind of mixing within its own order would be abolished: all that would appear in the series is mixture. In order to make non-mixture manifest, then, two mutually exclusive terms in addition to being are necessary: rest and movement. This gives us a minimal series of three terms (254d).

But scarcely are three terms posited before their trinity calls upon two supplementary terms to maintain itself as a series in which 'each is other than two of them, but the same as itself' (254d): these terms are the *same* and the *other*. In order to articulate the binary positions of mixture and non-mixture, a minimal series of five terms must be constituted: 'it is indeed impossible for us to consent to reducing this number' (256d).

But this minimal series cannot be closed off in a saturated cycle since, by the very play of the binary law of mixture that governs it, it allows for the appearance of an internal dissymmetry: all the terms fall under the law of mixture and that of non-mixture at the same time, except for one. To each term another is opposed which enters into a specific relation of non-mixture with it: rest against movement, the other against the same. It is only being that mixes with everything, finding no point of resistance, escaping a pairing with a term that would limit it. [75] It is in this dissymmetry that the place of non-being must be found.

Alone among the terms, being must support the founding opposition's binarity through an alternating duality of functions: mixing with everything, it effectuates [*effectue*] the trait that defines it as a term assignable to the class of mixture; yet in the very same movement it ceases to subsist as the delimited term [*terme cerné*] this effectuated trait sought to define.

Being spreads throughout the whole series. It is the very element of its own development since all the terms, as terms, have being. But through this expansion it cannot but make manifest the distinctive trait that situates it in a binary opposition between what blends or mixes and what does not blend: in short, through the modality of its expansion being becomes a term that can be delimited in its singular concentration.

Spreading itself, being presents or posits itself [*se pose*] as being. Now, if being posits itself, then by this fact alone it falls within the register of the other: becoming, through its self-positing, a term within the series, it posits, as its others, all the terms that it is not. 'So we see that to the extent that these others are, being is then not to the same extent; for it is not them, but its own

unique self, and in their infinite number, for their part, the others are not'
(257a).[5]

It is no doubt true that every term of the series participates in the same and
the other: in the same, such that it gathers itself; in the other, such that, through
the very act of gathering itself, it posits itself as an other (256b). But only being,
which as a result of its limitless expansion sees its function split into two [*se
dédoubler*], can, in its double participation, invoke a new term, as an other it is
powerless to deny or refuse: *non-being*.

Through the vacillation of being as expansion and being as term, through
the play of being and the other, non-being is henceforth generated. 'Having
shown [. . .] that there is a nature of the other, and that it is distributed among
all beings in their mutual relations, from each part of the other that opposes
itself to being, we have the audacity to say – this here is what non-being really
is' (258e).[6]

And yet, having accorded non-being the status of this new unity, Plato does
not add it to the sum of genera, and in no way suggests that the minimal number
needed to support the original binary opposition must be raised from five to six.
This is because he needs to maintain simultaneously both that the genera are the
points where being is bound [*se noue*], through which the articulation of the
discourse on being is compelled to pass, and that they are also equally points
wherein being disappears. Emerging through this operation of passage via the
other, and of binding [*nouage*] via the same, non-being arises in the series of
genera under a singular mode. In the series that must be unfolded to support
the opposition of mixture and non-mixture, non-being has no assigned place,
other than those points of inflection [*fléchissement*] where the limiting shape
[*cerne*] shows itself to be passage.[7] [**76**]

Unable to continue without vacillation, the series is now confirmed as a
chain whose elements entertain relations that are irreducible to a simple succession. Some relations of dependence are revealed, which, on the basis of the
sequential linearity of the series, outline a space deep enough for the play of

---

5   TN: White's version reads: 'So we have to say that *that which is* itself is different from the
others. [. . .] So even *that which is* is not, in as many applications as there are of the others, since,
not being them, it is one thing, namely itself, and on the other hand it is not those others, which
are an indefinite number' (Plato, *Sophist*, 257a).

6   TN: White's version reads: 'Since we showed that the nature of *the different* is, chopped
up among all beings in relation to each other, we dared to say that *that which is not* really is just
this, namely, each part of the nature of the different that's set over against *that which is*' (Plato,
Sophist, 258e).

7   TN: The French reads: '*il n'a pas de place assignée, sinon les points de fléchissement, où le
cerne se révèle passage.*' Use of the term *le cerne* (a ring or circle that encloses or demarcates something) here echoes Milner's use of the verb *cerner* elsewhere in this text, which we have translated
as 'to delimit'; for consistency we have translated *le cerne* as 'delimitation' or 'limit'. The term
fléchissement also recurs; it evokes 'bending' or 'flexing' as well as 'yielding' or 'weakening'. We have
translated it as 'inflection' throughout, but the connotation of 'yielding' should be retained as well.

cycles that, in regulated alternations, posit and suppress the same, the other, being and non-being.

Each time that being, passing from one term to another ('others have just as much'), confirms its function of expansion, it denies itself as a delimitable term: at each passage, it makes non-being emerge in the form of repetition ('as many times that being is not'). On the other hand, when being, defined through this very capacity of expansion, gathers in on itself as a term, as a countable unity ('it is its unique self'), it denies its expansion, refuses itself to other terms, and rejects them into non-being as if into an abyss in which every chain and every deduction [décompte] vanishes ('the others are not').

Through a correlative movement veiled by the smooth statement that posits it as an 'integrating unity among the number [. . .] of forms' (258c), non-being is split;[8] it is the abyss which erases all terms ('the others are not'), but it is also the term repeated, each time the genera are deduced, as the delimitation [cerne] isolating the deducted term ('as many times, being is not'). Insofar as it is a term in the chain, it is a delimitation repeated without a fixed place, the displacement of a scrap of being; on the other hand, to fix it to a place is to renounce it as a delimitable term, since it cannot be fixed without becoming the abyss in which every series of terms is abolished. To count [compter] non-being as a unity 'among the number of forms' can only mean counting it in the chain as that which obliterates any account or deduction [décompte].

It is now possible to scan through the cycle in which non-being is enumerated:

- Being as a term is defined by its ability to mix through expansion with any term whatsoever.
- Being, functioning as expansion, is attributable to all the terms, which thereby come to be.
- The terms, coming to be, deny being as a term (this is the moment of the other); non-being appears under all the terms as a term without fixed place, as a repeated limit or delimitation [cerne].
- Being as a term refuses or withholds itself from [se refuse à] all terms (this is the moment of the same); non-being fixes itself as the abyss absorbing all terms.

(At this point, the cycle can resume, since being is only a distinct term via its property of expansion).

---

8   TN: White's version of the discussion of the being of non-being, or 'that which is not', reads: 'Then does it have just as much being as any of the others, as you said it did? Should we work up the courage now to say that *that which is not* definitely is something that has its own nature? Should we say that just as *the large* was large, *the beautiful* was beautiful, *the not large* was not large, and *the not beautiful* was not beautiful, in the same way that *'which is not* also was and is not being, and is one form among the many *that are?'* (*Sophist*, 258b–c).

Non-being is thus developed through a play of vacillations between expansion and term, between place and repetition, between the function of abyss and the function of limit [*cerne*]: [77]

- As term, it is repetition, without assigned place, since it is determined by the spreading out of being.
- As place, it becomes absorption, effacement, since it is determined by being presenting or positing itself as term and refusing itself.

In this way, non-being is each time the inverted reprise of a property of being: the double use that must be granted it – at once a term of the chain, and, as term, the collapse of any chain – is none other than the reverse side of being's violent division [*écartèlement*] as at once term and expansion, and which, as a term of the chain, designates in the chain the possibility of any chain.

Perhaps here it is necessary, following Jacques-Alain Miller, to recognize the powers of the chain, the only space that can support the play of vacillation, and that also can induce such play. Indeed, any movement that replaces an element in the linearity of a sequence that, as element, transgresses it – either because it must situate its foundational authority or agency [*instance*], or because it indicates the place of its erasure – induces there this double formal dependence that we name vacillation, retroactively defining this sequence as a chain.

But to what does this movement of linearization refer, if not to the resonance [*prégnance*] of the unknown or disregarded order of the signifier from which being and non-being would regain their traits, those traits whose very coupling guarantees truth and authorizes discourse?

The signifying order develops as a chain, and every chain bears the specific marks of its formality:

- vacillation of the element, an effect of a singular property of the signifier, which, as element and order all at once, cannot be the one except through the other, and demands for its development a space – supported by the chain – whose laws are production and repetition; being and non-being recover this relation through their inverse symmetry, dividing themselves between term and expansion, between delimitation and abyss.
- vacillation of the cause, in which being and non-being never stop overflowing into one another, each one only able to posit itself as cause by revealing itself to be the effect of the other.
- vacillation of the transgression, finally, which recapitulates them all, in which the term that situates as a term (thereby transgressing the sequence) the authority [*instance*] that founds all the terms, summons [*appelle*] the term that might take up or recover transgression itself as a term, an authority that annuls every chain.

A formal system is [thereby] constituted, and the ways it might be inter-preted can now be specified. How can we not read, in their double dependence, being as the order of the signifier, the radical register of all computations, the set of all chains, and also [as] 'one' of the signifier, unity of computation, element of the chain? And non-being [78] as the signifier of the subject, reappearing each time that discourse, continuing on, overcomes an inflection that confirms its discrete character – and [also as] reprise of the specific power of the subject to annul every signifying chain?

But might we not also be permitted to formalize along these lines the object (a), which can be described as being, in the form of stasis, the cyclical repetition of a fall?[9] It is as if we are in possession of a logic capable of situating the formal properties of any term submitted to an operation of fission [*fission*],[10] but not one capable of marking out specificities.

Unlike Frege's articulation, which reduces the chain to its minimal couple,[11] the interpretation of a less summary formalism is perhaps not univocal. What we might touch upon here, in the form of a system of fission, without being able to specify them further, are the lineaments of a logic of the signifier, and the source of all the mirage-effects that its miscognition [*méconnaissance*] induces.

It is even possible to perceive the necessity whereby this miscognition must summon the symmetry of the mirage to produce its effects, and to see that this necessity authorizes the conferral, upon any balancing [*balancement*], of the significance of an indication or sign:[12] the relation of being to non-being already bore all its traits, and it was by right the critical point in which the signifier could be localized.

We need not be reluctant to recognize the deduction of non-being as a formal system, if we observe that Plato himself appears to rely on a formal system in order to lead the dialogue to its end or term. Superimposed on the chains of the genera, other chains unfold wherein he is able to articulate the status of the sophist, who must be delimited [*cerné*] by discourse at the precise point where he denies discourse the power of delimiting anything; and there is the status of discourse itself, which Plato must open to the statement of non-being, to the lies of the sophist, in order to delimit the sophist and his power for truth.

---

9   TN: The French reads: '*l'objet (a), qui se décrit d'être comme stase la répétition cyclique d'une chute*'.

10   I hope we might be allowed to collect under this unitary term, chosen to suggest their formal homology, the splitting of the subject, the evacuation [*déjection*] of the (a), and the distri-butions [*partages*] of being and non-being.

11   Jacques-Alain Miller, 'Suture', CpA 1.3:57.

12   TN: '*Il est possible même d'apercevoir la nécessité que cette méconnaissance appelle pour ses effets la symétrie du mirage, et que cette nécessité autorise à conférer à tout balancement la portée d'un indice*'.

A double connection is instituted in this way: a thematic relation by which Plato reconnects the theme of non-being to that of the sophist through the mediations of lie and error; and a homological relation where, in its register, each theme requires a vacillation to be posited, with the sophist and his lying, counterparts of non-being, unable to place themselves except by effacing all place. But in order to draw up this homology, it is necessary to constitute the chains in which it will act. [79]

The object of the dialogue is the *onoma* [name or character] of the sophist, and the infallible sign that the latter will have been discovered will be that the sophist will have to cease being the sophist, that in escaping the circle traced by his definition, he will cease to be at the moment the *onoma* seizes him.

In the course of the dialogue, the sophist consequently appears at the points where he is pursued, pushed from definition to definition, surviving its inflections [*fléchissements*]. If he is spoken of, by the very rules of dialogical exchange, his presence must be that of a *he*, as opposed to an *I* and a *you*, pronouns specifically designating the partners of speech. But this is still not enough to situate his place in the dialogue.

We have to emphasize, in fact, the need to analyse closely a language with regard to this point, which, in contrast to the *I* and *you*, represents the one spoken of with a unique sign, whether or not it can enter into the dialogue as a partner through some sort of arrangement [*montage*]. Although devoid of pertinence at the linguistic level, his potential insertion in these partners' game is essential in order to be able to detach from the *he* of a partner another *he* with different properties.

Now, Plato provides an indication that he is operating with such a distinction when in 246e, arriving at the refutation of two philosophically opposed schools, he charges Theaetetus with the task of rendering them present: 'Demand that they answer you [. . .] and then interpret what they say' (τὸ λεχθὲν παρ' αὐτῶν ἀφερμήνευε).[13]

The ἑρμηνεύειν [*hermeneuein*], this position of Hermes, the herald, the medium that lends his mouth to another voice, this is what clearly signals that this *he*, this absent one who is spoken of, belongs to those who can on occasion insert themselves into dialogue and take up their place therein.

But the sophist is excluded from this ἑρμηνεύειν. No one lends him their mouth, he is excluded from replying, and yet he is present at every articulation, since at each level the Stranger appoints him judge of the definition: the sophist

---

13   TN: White's version: 'VISITOR: [. . .] Something that better people agree to is worth more than what worse ones agree to. Anyway we're not concerned with the people; we're looking for what's true.

THEAETETUS: That's absolutely right.

VISITOR: Then tell the better people to answer you and interpret what they say' (*Sophist*, 246d-e).

is in fact this other *he*, the one who is both pretext for the discourse as well as its measure [*pesée*]. In the dialogue, his place is in the horizontality of a chain at its points of passage, and his function is purely one of form, such that this place and function need not rest on any turn of speech.

But if the sophist is the formal figure of the dialogue, it is because he has made his *techne* [craft] from a property of the discourse that must define him. As a result, every definition of the sophist opens on to a definition of the discourse, which will situate in it a potential community between being and non-being.

The thematic relation, however, can only be maintained by a homology. As with non-being among the genera, and as with the sophist in the dialogue, the statement of non-being can only enter discourse through the possibility created by an inflection. [80]

The itinerary here is the inverse of the first one, and can serve as its confirmation. From the other, we were led to non-being; from non-being, now given, we are led to install alterity at the heart of discourse by defining it as an assemblage (σύνθεσις, 263d) of classes of incommensurable words.

No doubt the sequence established toward this end will be indifferent to developments in the sequence of genera. This is because here again Plato is concerned with the minimal: since by definition discourse must be the intertwining of elements to be distinguished within it, the alterity that emerges will be subjected to mixture, but two terms now suffice to maintain it: the name or noun [*le nom*] and the verb (262a)[14] – with no need for three, as before, and above all without having to give an exhaustive analysis of discourse.

We see then that it would be absurd to search for Plato's teaching on the parts of discourse here, and to imagine that, at the level of the *sophist*, he would posit two of them. All he is telling us with this number is that discourse is divisible, but he stops well short of actually making the deduction himself.

For if the theory of the parts of discourse is exemplary for linguistics, this is precisely insofar as it has become a calculation forgetful of its point of departure, such that in this closed and declinable list a deduction of the elements of discourse is possible wherein the subject, misrecognized, becomes a term (namely, in particular, a pronoun).

With Plato, we find ourselves at the origin of this deduction, and its point of departure is still palpable: we know non-being is not yet an element like the others, but rather an element that, if made to appear or arise [*surgir*], makes discourse disappear. If discourse is made to appear, then non-being subsists only as an inflection, at once limit [*cerne*] and passage from one term to the

---

14   TN: White's version: 'There are two ways to use your voice to indicate something about being [. . .]. One kind is called names, and the other is called verbs' (*Sophist*, 262a).

other, i.e. the dimension of alterity through which discourse defines itself as assemblage.

It is perhaps insofar as a miscognition is not fully achieved or completed that there can be no representing the subject here by an enumerable term in a list: the non-being in which we have read its appearance cannot take its place in this sequence, henceforth impossible to conclude – it must be made to fall into what lies beneath [*dans les dessous*].

But then a new operation develops, where the sequence of the dialogue seems to encounter a point of regression.

If what is at stake is indeed the ability to utter a false discourse, of being able to say what is not, this is in any case only possible through statements about what is, since discourse always bears upon a being. 'If it discourses about no-one, [. . .] discourse will not be discourse at all. We have indeed showed that it is impossible for there to be discourse that is not discourse on some subject' (the Stranger at 263c).[15] [**81**]

And it is perhaps here that the true implication of Plato's apparently arbitrary choice is revealed. Is it by chance that the example used to show the possibility of a false discourse is a statement bearing on a proper name, 'Theaetetus flies' (263a)? It seems that, tied here to the verb designating an action which is not, arriving at this place where being must give non-being a support of predication, the name must be set as a proper name.

For, after all, it was possible for the Stranger to speak in the first person: πέτομαι, 'I fly', an inverted version of the Cogito. We must acknowledge in this avoidance of the grammatical person the resonance [*prégnance*] of the proper name as such. If it can mark the place where non-being disappears, it is because, designating the subject as irreplaceable, as now able – in Jacques Lacan's terms – to come to lack [*venir à manquer*], it also locates it precisely as not lacking. In the sequence of words, non-being, revolving around the proper name, seems to flow back upon itself and to condense: the subject, fixed, takes on the characteristics of plenitude; the sequence of words, as soon as it is posited as a chain, becomes again a series without vacillation, with the name, as a part of discourse, being absorbed into the proper name.

In this avoidance of the grammatical person (no doubt prior to any historical process), through which the category was defined as such, coming to fix the subject in a misrecognition, we nonetheless witness the recovery and the covering-up [*recouvrement*] of the vacillation: with the statement 'Theaetetus flies',

---

15   TN: White's version: 'And if it were not of anything it would not be speech at all [. . .]. But if someone says things about you, but says different things as the same or not beings as beings, then it definitely seems that false speech really and truly arises from that kind of putting together of verbs and names' (Plato, *Sophist*, 263c–d).

thanks to the plenitude of the proper name, non-being of non-being, discourse establishes itself as a reign of unshakeable knowledge.

Everything proceeds as if, at the end of the *Sophist*, it was necessary to turn around and go back and erase non-being itself in discourse, even though it had been necessary to make it present there to ground the properties of truth. The cycles of being and non-being now acquire the status of 'hypotheses' condemned to the silence of the statements they support.

For the superimposition of interpretations within the same formal system, we must substitute the image of an itinerary of recovery and covering-up [*une itinéraire de recouvrement*], where the homologies were only able to develop so as to be broken: the chain has become a series again; hardly opened, the register of the signifier slams shut, and the term that carries the cause of all the effects of fault and lack [*défaut*] itself comes to lack.[16]

Whereas being, restored, reveals its relation to discourse, insofar as it concentrates its properties in a truth that is henceforth assured, non-being, considered as a species of the false, fixes around the proper name those vacillations through which it had received its definition. It becomes at once the point where the register we should recognize as anchoring a logic of the signifier can be situated, and by this very fact, the point where its misrecognition must be marked. [82]

But the actual [*effectif*] movement is the inverse: the signifier and its logic may have provided a key, but this was at the cost of accepting that our commentary plays out in a circle, and that in order to support its claims, discerns in a smoothly polished text [*un texte lisse*] signs of closure that we have emphasized as misrecognitions and suturations. Here we did not have to read a suture but rather to invent one in order to render a statement legible: we have had recourse to the figure of the chain.

Chain of genera, chain of dialogue, vanishing chain of classes of words: each time, it has been possible to target a point where we can read the logic of the signifier – going so far as to recognize the limit where, we must realize, the introduction of this logic requires us to leave it behind – going so far as to establish anew in the wake of *The Sophist* the hidden and unpredictable adventure [*péripétie*] of an eclipse of the signifier.

From the point of departure, no doubt, everything was already given in the anecdote about the calculation of being, where the arithmetic of the ancient sophists offered an immediate support for the model of the chain. This was to invent everything, with regard to Plato above all, who did not miscognize the structure of the zero but simply knew nothing of it. But this does nothing but remind us that when Plato speaks of being, he seeks his own discourse in its very possibility, insofar as truth can constrain its discrete articulation.

---

16   TN: '*le terme porteur de la cause de tous les effets de défaut, vient lui-même à faire défaut*.'

If in its deduction from being, the latter connects, via the mediation of truth, the fate of the assertion and that of the thing which is its object, then what is at stake in being is also immediately at stake in discourse:[17] Plato, speaking about being in a discourse that reclaims truth, examines in detail the laws of a site where discourse as the assertion of truth may be possible.

To make this appear as the diffracted reflection of the signifier requires that we imagine Plato turning a blind eye toward a point whose unicity, position, and validity can only subsist as foreign to the gaze itself, just shy of a miscognition.

'To locate the point that makes the object come alive', Breton tells us, 'the candle must be well placed.'[18]

---

17   TN: *'l'enjeu de l'être est immédiatement aussi celui du discours'*.

18   TN: The citation is from André Breton's 'Ideas of a Painter', on the work of André Derain: 'The object whose being I paint only lives insofar as I can make a "white or blank point [*point blanc*]" appear. Everything depends on placing the candle well' (Breton, *Oeuvres complètes*, vol. 1 [Paris: Gallimard, Pléiade, 1988], 248).

CHAPTER SEVEN

François Regnault
Dialectic of Epistemologies[1]

[45] *We offer here an exercise of pure dialectics*: to enumerate all the possible relations between science and epistemology. How do we find the law of this enumeration? If we vary our two selected terms according to whether or not they exist and according to their number, we clearly obtain several possible cases: if science exists or does not exist, we have what results from this for epistemology, and vice versa; if we take science in the singular or the plural, we have what results from this for epistemology, and vice versa. We can of course also anticipate the aberrant or unproductive cases that may present themselves: What is the epistemology of a non-science? What are the epistemologies of science [in the singular]? Which science corresponds to a non-epistemology? etc. However we want to posit the following restrictive hypothesis: we define epistemology as *relative* to science or to the sciences. In other words, we impose a univocal trajectory from 'science' to 'epistemology', with the latter receiving the minimal definition of 'discourse on science (or the sciences)'. We can concretely imagine this orientation of the vector in the sense [*sens*] that one might say that there is a delay of consciousness or awareness about science [*conscience sur la science*], that epistemology comes too late. The question to be asked is thus: in restricting the number of possible relations in this way (since the choice of one direction [*sens*] for the trajectory excludes all the possible relations based on the opposite direction) do we not limit the interest of the exercise? Do we not contaminate the sense of the chosen terms? Can the law still be applied, or does the number of exclusions paralyze its effects? To begin with, we

---

1   TN: First published as François Regnault, 'Dialectique d'épistémologies', CpA 9.4 (summer 1968): 45–73. Translated by Knox Peden and Peter Hallward.

We should draw attention to some of our translation choices here. Although 'meaning' would often be the more natural translation for *sens*, we generally translate it as 'sense', in order to serve as a reminder of the double meaning (frequently evoked here) of the French term, as both meaning or signification and as direction or orientation. For the sake of consistency, we have translated all instances of *Un* or *un* as 'one' (or occasionally 'oneness'), and all instances of *être* as 'being'. French allows for the distinction between the infinitive *être* and the participle *étant*: the first normally translates as 'being as such' (or as to be), the second as being in the sense of 'a being', or as existing; where necessary we will include *étant* in brackets.

We have translated most of Regnault's references to Plato's *Parmenides* from the French version he usually refers to (Auguste Diès' edition of Plato, *Parménide* [Paris: Les Belles Lettres], 1923), but where he refers directly to F.M. Cornford's translation we have followed suit (Francis MacDonald Cornford, *Plato and Parmenides* [London: Routledge & Kegan Paul, 1939]). We have also drawn on Mary Louise Gill and Paul Ryan's translation of *Plato: Parmenides* (Indianapolis: Hackett, 1996). Wherever one or both of these translations is used it will be signalled in the notes.

respond as follows:

- If we examine all the possible cases of relations resulting from the position according to the existence and number of the two terms, we will leave no remainder as regards the nature of the relation; in the preceding hypothesis, we have prejudged only its direction. It is clear that even if one of the two terms disappears, or even both of them, the relation itself remains formally oriented, even if it is from one nothingness to another nothingness. The direction [*sens*] of the vector does not prejudge its value or intensity. Why choose this direction then? This is the second response:

- For reasons primarily of linguistic facility, because epistemology is defined via [*par*] science and not the inverse. We will shortly provide [46] confirmation of this facility in the matrix we have chosen for the law of enumeration.

Where do we find this matrix? We borrow it, rigorously and textually, from the second part of Plato's *Parmenides*, the part that includes the celebrated eight (or nine) Hypotheses. Such a choice for the present project cannot be justified without, at some point, forcing the argument [*un coup de force*]. It is not a question of denying it, but of assigning it its exact place, and consequently its exact remit, which we do not intend to be any weightier than when one chooses, in the application of some equation, a certain value (say 3) for an unknown *x*. On either side of the point where we have forced the argument, we should list each of the justifications we can give. Here they are,[2] in order of increasing importance.

a) We draw first on the authority of Jean Cavaillès, who, in his *On Logic and the Theory of Science*,[3] cites a passage from the second Hypothesis of the *Parmenides* (142d-143a) in order to illustrate the workings of a theory that he describes as paradigmatic of science. It is true that what is at issue is the specific object of a science more than its relations with its theory. However, in the case under consideration, the science guides and envelops the theory.

b) The authority of Parmenides in Plato's writings; and here Parmenides presents the dialectical exercise as necessary from the point of view of philosophical pedagogy, as formal from the point of method, and as safe from the point of view of its results (135c to 137e): 'If you want to be thoroughly exercised, you must not merely make the supposition that such and such a thing *is* and then consider the consequences; you must also take the supposition that that same thing is *not*. [. . .] In a word, whenever you suppose that anything whatsoever exists or does not exist or has any other character, you ought to consider the consequences with reference to itself and to any one of the other

---

2   The reader can easily skip over the preliminaries that follow and pass directly to the application of the Hypotheses.

3   Jean Cavaillès, *Sur la logique et la théorie de la science* (Paris: PUF, 1946), 27–28.

things that you may select, or several of them, or all of them together; and again you must study these others with reference both to one another and to any one thing you may select, whether you have assumed the thing to exist or not to exist, if you are really going to make out the truth after a complete course of discipline' (135e; 136b-c).[4]

These passages designate an empty operation, a matrix of matrices, so to speak. In order for an effective exercise to take place, Parmenides himself needs to posit a hypothesis, or more precisely one or several terms that might enter into one or several axiomatics. 'Would you like me, since we are committed to playing out this laborious game, to begin with myself and my own original supposition? Shall I take the One itself and consider the consequences of assuming that there is, or is not, a One?' (137b).[5] What results from this choice are the (eight or) nine final Hypotheses, which vary according to their nature and number. We may be reproached then for producing an indefensible allegory by requiring the position of [47] science and of epistemology to entail as many hypotheses as the One (and moreover the same hypotheses). To be more precise:

1. Let there be an object. What are the results for it and for some other object according to whether this first one exists or not? The minimal matrix contains two values (0 and 1 for example).

2. The posited object can be taken in several senses; this is what leads to a much greater number of hypotheses than two, in principle a multiple of two, $2n$ if n is the number of different senses of the object.

3. Let us posit the One (Parmenides' choice). If we consider it broadly, in four different senses, we will obtain eight different axiomatics along with their consequences (plus one more, which can be considered as the variant of another, and thus nine in total). In fact, since the being and the non-being that we attribute to the One can themselves be taken in different senses, there is no need to go as far as the four senses of the One to obtain the eight hypotheses. A combination of different senses of the two terms suffices (i.e., an *a priori* deduction).

4. Take the objects 'science' and 'epistemology'. By what right will the matrix of the One function for these new objects?

Several arrangements are conceivable, but not all are legitimate:

First arrangement: For semantic reasons we can make the One correspond to science and being to epistemology. A weak pretext for this would be that the One tends to be the object of science, and that being tends to be rather the

---

4   TN: Cornford, *Plato and Parmenides*, 104–105.
5   TN: Ibid., 108.

object of metaphysics, which would at least have the epistemological status of being a discourse on science (in Aristotle, for example). We cannot stop here because the semantic convergence is subordinated to the syntactical or rather axiomatic functioning of each term in each hypothesis. Even if the proximity of place between science and the One were to be conserved, it is the sense or direction [*sens*] of the One that would be lost from one hypothesis to another. The proportion alone would remain constant.

So a much stronger pretext would be that, in the Hypotheses of the *Parmenides*, being is defined as a function of the One, the vector goes from the One to being: the One commands being. In this case, nothing of the sense of the terms is retained, science and epistemology safely translate One and being, the allegory is legitimate though weak. We indeed obtain eight or nine relations between science and epistemology (i.e., perhaps nine possible epistemologies), but we must provide everything ourselves. In order for it to be genuinely a question of *science* and *epistemology* (and not of a spoon and fork), their properties must be introduced from elsewhere, i.e. from a place where they are already defined or presupposed. But then the matrix is not only weak, but also useless; whatever one would hope to gain in its formalism is lost elsewhere in the imported properties. Moreover (and in fact), in the *Parmenides* the One and being do not really operate in a purely formal way, as each Hypothesis introduces a certain number of predicates ('finite, contiguous, temporal . . .') or relations ('identical, similar . . .') authorized by the senses given to each of the two terms in the [48] axioms in which they figure together. And these properties and these relations may prove awkward for those properties and relations of science and epistemology that are otherwise widely accepted. For example, if we say of the One that it is 'without figure', or 'contiguous with itself', and if we make the One equivalent to science, we will either be obliged to leave these properties aside and to replace them with the properties of science, put forward for the occasion and drawn from elsewhere, or instead to attribute these same properties of the One to science itself, which would lead to countless difficulties, plays on words, blind windows and absurdities.

The allegory might yet be successful however: we will see how, for instance, the first Hypothesis, which posits the One absolutely and totally refuses the multiple, comes down to positing the One as a pure signifier for which any other can be substituted, as far as their sense is concerned. Nothing can be said about the One thus posited, and in this case, we are certainly entitled to substitute, for the One, 'science' or indeed any other signifier. But in this way we obtain nothing but a purely negative confirmation of our allegory. Reference to this allegory serves only to generalize it along these lines: even if, pragmatically, the results of all these hypotheses might for whatever reason confirm the allegory as in this example, nevertheless this could only be the result of chance, and the principles stated above would render the allegorical operation illegitimate. So we must renounce it.

* * *

Second arrangement: We might take into account the nature of the One and that of being and consider these terms as so general that they can work with any possible subject. To be sure, it would not then matter very much that science and epistemology were the terms substituted for them, since here any object that could be said to be or to be one would do the trick. There is nothing to gain, then, from a semantic convergence. We might stand to gain, instead, from the logical privilege of seeing the One and being attributed to all things, up to and including the multiple itself for the One, and up to and including non-being itself for being – inasmuch as, like Aristotle says, 'it is impossible to think anything [or to think nothing], if one thinks nothing of one'[6] (thus not even the multiple), and inasmuch as, like one sees in *The Sophist*, we must attribute some sort of status to non-being if only to be able to speak of it. In this sense, we only ever *think* something as one, and we only *name* something as a being [*en tant qu'étant*]. In other words, 'Being and the One are what are most universal and, if there is no One in itself nor Being in itself, we do not see how there could be some other being outside of individual things.'[7] As a result, if we were to apply this universality to science and epistemology, it would in no sense be a matter of allegory. In this second arrangement, there would clearly be nothing in principle to justify science's playing the role of the One and epistemology that of being, since the One and being apply equally to both terms. We would only need [49] to take account of the fact that, in the *Parmenides*, since it is the One that has been chosen for the dialectical exercise, being finds itself in the position of receiving its status from the sense given to the One. The relation is thus well and truly oriented; being depends on the One. This would be a convenient reason for choosing the One for science and being for epistemology, thereby conserving the unequal relation evoked at the outset. But can we be content with this formal analogy between two inequalities, and, giving a general sense to the One and to being, can we conserve the respective correspondences? The question should be examined as follows.

Whereas in the first arrangement the semantic correspondence at issue was presented from the point of view of science (the One is its object) and from the point of view of epistemology (being is its horizon), a different correspondence is given here, with more justification, from the point of view of the One and

---

6   TN: The French reads '*il est impossible de rien penser, si l'on ne pense rien d'un.*'

7   Aristotle, *Metaphysics*, book IV, 1001a (citing Jules Tricot's translation of Aristotle, *La Métaphysique* [Paris: Vrin, 1933/1962], II, 156). TN: W.D. Ross' English translation of this passage (in *The Complete Works Of Aristotle: The Revised Oxford Translation*, vol. 2, ed. Jonathan Barnes [Princeton: Princeton University Press, 1984]) reads: 'If we do not suppose unity and being to be substances, it follows that none of the other universals is a substance; for these are most universal of all. If there is no unity-itself or being-itself, there will scarcely be in any other case anything apart from what are called the individuals.'

being, and rightly so: it's a matter of interrogating science (or epistemology) as one [*une*] (or as multiple), and as existing [*étant*] (or not existing). We momentarily rid the One and being of their properties as objects of two disciplines when we evoked their apparent functioning in the axiomatic of the Hypotheses; this was done in order to find in this very functioning predicates that did not fit with this proposal. It is not the same in this second arrangement. To be sure, to begin with, the One and being have no sense other than what they receive in each hypothesis taken separately;[8] but, taken as terms of general logic, they are also found to retain a general sense that at the very least prevents them from being interchangeable:

1. If sometimes they were to receive their sense only as a function of one another, as signs receive their values in Saussure, they would not, for all that, change places: one is a father only of a son, and a son only of a father, but not as one is a brother of a brother.

2. Were the One to lose all sense, as in the first Hypothesis, and become a pure signifier, the signifier of being would not for all that be substitutable for it. For in its materiality, the signifier of the one cannot see itself substituted for another and thus any term other than the 'One' retains a value in that its signifier differs from that of the One.

3. Finally, if it is the case that the One is not, it should be added that it is only as a function of being that is not, and that *being* can be defined as not being [*étant*] the One in the first place, even *before* being [*être*] eminently (Hypothesis VI, 162*a*), of not participating in the One (VII, 163*c*), of being wholly to the Others (VIII, 165*c*), or even of not being, just like the One (IX, 166*c*).

In short, the One and being retain a dissymmetry sufficient to distinguish and place them. But since they also retain, if not in all the Hypotheses, at least in several among them – and that is enough – more sense than their opposition, dissymmetry, and placements alone would let them produce, and since it is precisely [50] on this surfeit of sense that the possibility relies of conferring properties (size, place, movement) and relations (dissimilarity, equality, contiguity) upon them, not always but often – and that is enough –, the result is that these properties and relations will once more repel those that are peculiar to science and epistemology, should we invoke them again. Of course, this invocation does not resemble the preceding one. In the first arrangement, the poverty of the matrix *compelled* us to borrow the properties of science and epistemology from another theoretical field. So these properties were positive, already formed elsewhere. Everything was said, and the matrix came too late. In the second arrangement, in which the matrix (of the One and of being) is richer, we only invoke the potential properties of science and epistemology so as to enrich them in the

---

8   On this formalism, see Cornford, *Plato and Parmenides*, 111ff.

mould of this matrix. So these properties are no longer real, but only possible; they leave the matter of constituting their positivity to the jurisdiction of the matrix. But the difficulty relative to this second arrangement subsists: there is no reason for science and epistemology to receive any positive properties from properties that would be the exclusive privilege of the One and being; just as it would be normal for the One and being to pass on to the science and epistemology that hold their place only the properties that they receive from their opposition (with the added benefit, moreover, of an identity of asymmetry between the two orders of oriented trajectories), so it is illegitimate for the One and being to impose on our two terms properties that they owe to their concepts alone. And so, as may sometimes happen, if the One has some dalliances [*aventures*] that it owes not to its encounter with being, but for example with place, time, etc., then its universality, its applicability to every term, would be compromised.

We will lessen the difficulty of this second arrangement if we make an effort to distinguish the One taken as substantive from the one taken as attribute. For all our difficulties have sprung not from the fact that the term 'one' can be applied to any subject [*tout sujet*], for we cannot then be reproached for applying it to science for example, but from the fact that we have identified science with the One itself and epistemology with being. The key thing is that the One is the subject on which bears the theory of *that which* is one, of a predicated one. The adventures of the trait of unity are lent by the dialectic of Hypotheses to a unity chosen for this end, the One. It is from the *excess* of the One, taken as subject, over the simple predicate of unity, attributable to any object, that the surfeit of properties comes which renders troublesome the substitution of science's *salva veritate* for Plato's chosen term. This is why we must slightly correct Cornford's formalism that declares: 'In a modern book it would be natural, in certain contexts, to substitute letters, e.g., "*A*" for "the One" and "not-*A*", or "*B*", or some such symbol for "the Others".'[9]

A remark concerning Plato's dichotomies is necessary here. We [51] know that they are binary (every ternary can be divided into two binaries, one of which commands the other; ternarity is permitted, if need be: cf. Plato's *Statesman*, 287c[10]) and disjunctive, but an equality of the two distinguished essences is also required (this is what is shown by the counter-example of the crane who wrongly classes animals as either animals or cranes, *ibid.* 263c). Now, this equality can in fact be calculated in the case of numerable examples (the animals), but it cannot be done for qualitative essences; we must then vouch for the equality in *importance* or in *value* between two essences, which is

---

9   Ibid., 112.
10   TN: 'VISITOR: Then let's divide them limb by limb, like a sacrificial animal, since we can't do it into two. For we must always cut into the nearest number so far as we can' (Plato, *Statesman*, 287c, trans. C.J. Rowe, in Plato, *Complete Works*).

something that can only be intuited. The same applies here insofar as we are not so much making a theory of what is one [*ce qui est un*] (a predicate defined by a dichotomous opposition) as of the One [*l'Un*] (substance defined by itself). 'We must not,' Plato says with regard to two opposed terms, 'suppose them to exist only in relation to each other, but rather as we have now said, that we should speak of their existing in one way in relation to each other, and in another in relation to what is in due measure' (*Statesman*, 283*e*, trans. Rowe).

Third arrangement: The third arrangement follows from the critique of the preceding two. They have allowed us to see the conditions required in order to apply the Platonic model to the question of science and epistemology.

1. The correspondence of these two terms to the One and being respectively must be abandoned.

2. The functions of the One and being must no longer be delegated to science and epistemology, but to the unity and to the being of science *or* of epistemology. Which of the two?

3. If we retain our initial postulate according to which there is an ordered trajectory that runs from science toward epistemology, and our definition of epistemology as the discourse on science, then it follows that the functions of the One and being must henceforth be delegated to science alone. Two consequences result from this:

a) The Platonist model, if it is complete, is going to allow us to establish the enumeration of all the possible theories of the unity (or non-unity) of the concept of science. If Plato provides a theory of the One, he provides in the same stroke the theory of the one of science insofar as it is one [*en tant qu'une*]. The same applies, albeit less directly, in the case of being. Thus the surfeit of properties of the One, (of being), its semantic contaminations, and the formalism of its oppositional functioning are no longer a problem for science, since the theory only concerns science in the form of its unity, (of its being), and so these features of the One can be fully preserved. We will need only to concern ourselves with their consequences.

b) The status of epistemology follows from this: if it is the discourse on science (or on the sciences), it will be *explicitly sustained*, we will see it at work, according to whether science is said to be one or not, whether it is or is not. The chances are that the existence or inexistence, the unity or multiplicity of science govern in a radical way all epistemological discourse. Broadly speaking, there will then be as many epistemologies [52] as there are different conceptions of this existence and this unity. We will therefore retain the relation postulated at the outset, without making it correspond to that of the One and of being.

Were it to be objected that we have already prejudged the nature of epistemology by defining its discourse only as explicitly involved in the hypotheses of the unity and existence of science, we will respond that, if the model is well made and considers *all the possible cases*, we will have traversed, with the aid of

the combinatory alone, the whole possible space of the problem, and that consequently there is no epistemology outside of these considered cases, since they
are all radically pertinent to it.

Were one to object, as at the outset, that we prejudge the nature of epistemology by defining it as the discourse on science, we would say again that, if the model
is well made and considers the cases of science's *existence* as well as its *non-
existence*, of its *unity* as well as its *multiplicity*, we will have effectively neutralized
the danger of presupposition. If science disappears, as being and as one, there
admittedly remains this subordination to that *Unding* [absurdity] of the discourse
that says it, but at the same time the relation is reduced to the minimum, perhaps
even to a state of indetermination. Furthermore, inverting the sense or direction of
the relation and reversing the whole operation, we could also apply the One and
being to the unity and the existence of epistemology alone, but in that case all that
is said of the One or being would concern epistemology, and we would find
ourselves maintaining a discourse *on* epistemology, an epistemology of epistemology if you like. We would then wholly miss or lose its relation to science; inversely,
in the choice made here, we no doubt miss the relation of science to its object or
objects, but we do not miss the science/epistemology relation that we have decided
to focus on. So we in no way limit our presuppositions, other than to the relation
of a metalanguage to a language, when we propose the following single postulate:
any statement on science (or the sciences) belongs to what we will call epistemology, which is thereby defined as the domain of these statements.

There are thus as many epistemologies as there are discourses sustained in
this way; we indeed have a dialectic of epistemologies.

Incidentally, we need not fear making unwarranted [*intempestives*] presuppositions since the combinatory treatment, even if it were to retain the positivity
of the relation in each case, would not fail to displace its sense from case to case.
The result of this would be that a problematic implicit in the question would
become clear through its explicit treatment: we might discover between the lines
other true relations among the chosen terms; we could in any event handle the
potential equivocities wrapped up in the concepts. Such is in fact the law of the
Platonist dialectic, which several authors have drawn attention to, and which
Cornford has illustrated with regard to the *Parmenides*. We can describe it thus:
an aporetic dialogue is not aporetic for everyone; one must know how to draw the
implicit solution out from under the explicit confusion of difficulties. And so with
the *Parmenides*, and even more so since it culminates in a complete aporia (166c),
the attentive reader will have [53] had to locate throughout the work the different
possible senses of the One and being, senses whose attribution is only justified by
the various axioms that inaugurate each hypothesis (Example: Hypothesis I: if the
One is one, εἰ ἓν ἔστιν – Hypothesis II: if the One is: ἓν εἰ ἔστιν), and which are
then developed in the properties, and then in the relations that are attributed to
the terms. We will briefly specify the correlative principles of this reading, i.e. of

this specific interpretation of Plato, chosen among several others in order to the respond to the requirements of this dialectic of epistemologies.

1) Whether or not the dialogue succeeds is a function of the method employed by the interlocutors and not a lack of the true [un défaut du vrai].[11] Through the aporia, we perceive the solution. As it happens, this might be, setting aside the contemplation of essence, a recapitulation of the different meanings [sens] of the words. Cornford provides an example with regard to being and the One,[12] and shows that Aristotle's Metaphysics is situated in this line of thinking and that it completes the project of the separation or defusion [désintrication][13] of meanings.

2) The hypotheses of the Parmenides are thus not a 'parody'[14] of logic, destined to become muddled in the ironies of Zenonian arguments, nor are they a series of sophisms, nor an esoteric or mystical text, as certain neo-Platonists have supposed.[15] This means that the ludic or esoteric interpretations must be subordinated to a logical or dialectical interpretation. To accuse the series of Hypotheses of being a game is to overlook the laws of this game; the argument that eliminates the sophisms in principle is one Plato suggests himself: 'If One is, we are saying, aren't we, that we must agree on the consequences for it, whatever they happen to be [ποῖά ποτε τυγχάνει ὄντα]?' (142b).[16] This law of writing separates the thinkable or the non-contradictory from what can solely be inscribed or said; we must work through [prononcer] the hypothesis to the end, even if we can no longer totally think it. Sophisms could only be attributed to the thinkable per se. Secondly, these are just the kind of laws that a theologizing interpretation will tend to misunderstand, unless it preserves the logical core: and so, to assimilate, as Plotinus does, the One of the first Hypothesis to the Good, that of the second to the Noῦς, and that of the third to the Soul of the world, is formally permitted if nothing in the allegory goes against the laws of the axiomatic core.[17]

---

11   This point has been established by Victor Goldschmidt, Les Dialogues de Platon (Paris: PUF, 1947); see in particular sections 1, 6, and 13–16. See also, for Plato's Meno, Alexandre Koyré, Introduction à la lecture de Platon [1945] (Paris: Gallimard, 1962).

12   Cornford, Plato and Parmenides, 111.

13   TN: Laplanche and Pontalis present the Freudian concept of Triebentmischung in French as désintrication or désunion and in English as 'defusion'. They write: 'defusion signifies a process tending to produce a situation in which the two sorts of instincts [i.e. the life instinct and the death instinct] would operate separately, each pursuing its own aim independent of the other' (Jean-Laplanche and Jean-Bertrand Pontalis, The Language of Psychoanalysis [1967], trans. Donald Nicholson-Smith [London: Hogarth Press, 1973], 180).

14   Alfred Edward Taylor, ed. and trans., The Parmenides of Plato (Oxford: Oxford University Press, 1934), 10.

15   Cornford, Plato and Parmenides, vi, 113.

16   TN: Based on Gill and Ryan's translation (147), rather than Cornford (136) who omits 'whatever they happen to be.'

17   '[Our] teachings are, therefore, no novelties, no inventions of today, but long since stated, if not stressed; our doctrine here is the explanation of an earlier and can show the antiquity of these opinions on the testimony of Plato himself' (Plotinus, Enneads V, 1, §8, trans. Stephen Mackenna and B. S. Page [London: Faber, 1969]).

3) Whence the result that, if the method is the cause of aporiae (though these are pregnant with truth [*grosses de la vérité*]), and if the dialectical exercise is not a parodic addition, the [54] section that discusses the Hypotheses (135c to the end) yields a solution that was implicit in the difficulties discovered by Zeno and Socrates at the outset; in other words, this is one single dialogue, such that the arguments of the Hypotheses are directed against those of Parmenides and Zeno no less than against the theory Socrates expounds at its beginning. But we will leave this point aside in what follows.[18]

These principles authorize our return to Cornford's book for the detail on the Hypotheses. How should we generate this detail?

A. If we consider the One, one can conceive it as being [*étant*] or as not being, which makes for two hypotheses.

B. If we consider the One as either absolutely one, or as relative to being or as accepting participation in it [*participable*], this gives us two more hypotheses, which yields four when combined with the preceding two.

C. If we no longer consider this minimal dialectic of the One in itself, but in relation to the Others, this makes four new hypotheses (the One being absolute, or being relative; the absolute One not being, or the relative One not being; and at each point seen from the point of view of the Others), which, when added to the previous results, gives us eight.

Finally, between the second hypothesis and the one that would be the third, there is, according to Cornford, another that sneaks in as a corollary to the second[19] for semantic reasons, and which always lags behind. We will in fact find a more formal status for it. In sum, nine Hypotheses, according to the following schema:

$$(2 \times 2) + (2 \times 2) + 1 = 9$$

Now, this third series of hypotheses (part C) is presented as that of the Others considered with respect to their positive properties on the one hand, and their negative properties on the other.[20] And this is how we would obtain Hypotheses IV and V in the rubric of the One being [*étant*], and VIII and IX in that of the One not being. In fact, the Others are defined each time only as a function of the nature of the One:

a) In the rubric of the One as being [*l'Un étant*] (part A), the position of the absolute One and that of the relative One form the first two Hypotheses; once the non-participable absolute One is posited again, we can then only think the

---

18   See Cornford, *Plato and Parmenides*, 106, 134, etc.

19   This is why Cornford counts eight hypotheses in total, and numbers them accordingly. We will preserve this numbering, to run now from 1 to 9.

20   Cf. the subtitles of Léon Robin's translation (Paris: Gallimard, La Pléiade, 1950). Auguste Diès gives a convincing explanation ('Notice' in his edition of Plato's *Parménide* [Paris: Les Belles Lettres, 1923], 35). What leads Plato to consider the Others in relation to themselves, in Hypotheses V and IX, is precisely the fact that the One, whether it is or is not, is non-participable [*non-participable*]. Cf. Diès, *Parménide*, 36, and Cornford's analysis of each Hypothesis.

negative properties of the Others: 'The One is *apart* from the Others, and the Others are *apart* from the One' (159c, Hyp. V). When the relative One is reintroduced, we can think the Others in relation to it. So they acquire positive properties: 'they partake of it in a way' (157c, Hyp. IV). **[55]**

b) In the rubric of the One as not being (part B), the position of the absolute One and that of the relative One form the Hypotheses VI and VII. When we again posit the non-participable absolute One, we obtain the Others without relation: 'there is no one among the Others' (165e, Hyp. IX). In fact, when we reintroduce the relative One, the Others retain some of their positive properties, albeit fleetingly (since the One is not). This is why Plato does not mark their participation in the One, even when the One is understood as participable. However, the Others, instead of being considered as not being (Hyp. IX), are considered as *being* [*étant*] in opposition to the One – 'it is necessary *first of all* [μέν] to assume that there are others' (164b, Hyp. VIII) – even if subsequently we insist more on the One as not being than as having at first conferred upon them their precarious though preliminary existence.

But we can, more simply,[21] present the set of Hypotheses under a dichotomous form,[22] i.e. according to the schema:

$$2^3 = 8 \text{ or } 2^3(+1) = 9$$

We then have:

	the One/the Others	absolute	Hyp.	I
The One is		relative		II
	the Others/the One	absolute		V
		relative		IV
	the One/ the Others	absolute		VII
		relative		VI
The One is not	the Others/the One	absolute		IX
		relative		VIII

(+ III) appears beside the "the Others/the One" group in the upper ("The One is") section.

---

21   Whatever the law is, it surely rests on the (axiomatic) equivocity of the concepts of the one and of being [*d'être*], as was seen by Proclus, who said that there are nine hypotheses because 'One' and 'being' have more than one meaning (see the beginning of book VI of his *Commentary*). A translator and commentator on the *Parmenides* who was a contemporary of Victor Cousin, J.A. Schwalbé, suggests that we might conceive of the One in three ways (absolute, relative to being, relative to the other), and non-being in two ways (partial, total). 'From there,' he adds, 'nine hypotheses result', and he enumerates them – though we do not perceive a law, but solely the aggregate: $(3 + 2) + (2 + 2) = 9$.

22   A dichotomy that is combinatory and not classificatory like Plato's, since it can be grasped in arbitrarily choosing the order of the three criteria.

[56] Or better yet the following schema, which more clearly shows the relations between the Hypotheses:

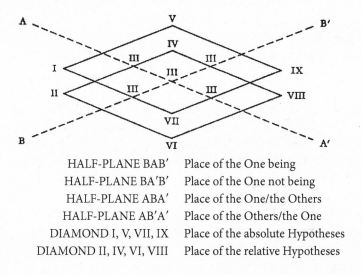

HALF-PLANE BAB′	Place of the One being
HALF-PLANE BA′B′	Place of the One not being
HALF-PLANE ABA′	Place of the One/the Others
HALF-PLANE AB′A′	Place of the Others/the One
DIAMOND I, V, VII, IX	Place of the absolute Hypotheses
DIAMOND II, IV, VI, VIII	Place of the relative Hypotheses

HYPOTHESIS III (The One is 'is not' [*L'Un est n'est pas*]), 'corollary' of the second, would be situated at the juncture of the One as being and the One as not being, but just as well at that of the One and the Others, since this is the Hypothesis of becoming. The combination of the two gives it four possible positions on the schema, which could come together in the centre, etc. Plato would only have placed it at the spot where he would have encountered it for the first time. In any event, for structural reasons and in order to *pass* from any given half of one of the three dichotomies to the other half, it is necessary to posit this multi-functional Hypothesis. There are thus indeed nine of them.

We could group the Hypotheses together in many different ways. We would prefer to retain roughly the Platonist order. However, for reasons that will become clear in what follows, we have decided to have each Hypothesis bearing on the One taken in itself and with regard to the Others follow from the Hypothesis *corresponding* to the Others, taken in themselves and with regard to it. The study of Hyp. I will thus be followed by that of Hyp. V; II will be followed by IV; then III alone, then VI will be followed by VIII; finally VII by IX.

We now have at our disposal a matrix for enumerating the possible relations between epistemology and science, the latter being considered from the points of view of its unity and its existence. This is the only way we have forced the argument.[23]

---

23   TN: '*En cela réside le seul coup de force.*'

HYPOTHESIS I (THE ONE. IS THE ONE/
THE OTHERS. THE ABSOLUTE ONE)

Axioms:[24] *The One is one and is in no way multiple. It has no parts and is not a whole* [tout].

Properties: *It has neither beginning, nor end. It is unlimited, without figure, neither in anything other than itself nor in itself,*[25] *neither motionless nor in motion.* [57]

Relations: *It is neither identical to something other than itself, nor to itself, neither different from itself nor from something other than itself, neither dissimilar nor similar to itself, nor to something other than itself; it is neither equal to itself nor something other than itself, neither older nor younger than itself, nor than something other than itself. It has neither been, nor become, nor is. 'Thus it does not even have enough being to be one.' Concerning it, there is neither 'science, nor sensation, nor opinion.'*

Science is absolutely one; its unity is [*son unité est*]. No multiplicity of sciences makes sense, so there are not sciences in the plural. Science has no parts: scientificity cannot be divided; it is whole in itself. If only mathematics or mathematical logic can satisfy such a requisite, then these are identical to scientificity itself. So it is not only the case that 'in any special doctrine of nature there can be only as much *proper* science as there is *mathematics* therein,'[26] but we should even say here that everything that is not included in this scientificity is nothing, is a nothingness from the perspective of the absolute.

No beginning can be attributed to this mathematics (neither from Egyptian practices of measurement, nor from any ideology, nor from any psychological or transcendental deduction). It entertains no relation (resemblance, difference) with anything that is external to it: no experimentation, no application. We cannot even say of this essence that it is perfectly identical to itself, but the introduction of its non-identity to itself withdraws it (or excludes it) from the real and leaves it to thought alone: it is a 'non-real thing in thought.'[27] We can take Plato's formula in this sense: 'the object under consideration does not even have enough being to be

---

24   To make things easier, we will summarize the theses of each Hypothesis each time. The translation used is that of Auguste Diès (Platon, *La Parménide* [Paris: Les Belles Lettres], 1923).

25   Concerning space and time, we can just as easily consider 'being in', 'aging', etc. as properties or as relations. The distinctions are not very rigorous here.

26   Immanuel Kant, *Metaphysical Foundations of Natural Science*, trans. Michael Friedman (Cambridge: Cambridge University Press, 2004), AK 4:470.

27   See Jacques-Alain Miller, 'Suture,' CpA 1.3:46. In principle, the whole of his analysis should be applicable here.

one'[28] (οὐδ' ἄρα οὕτως ἔστιν ὥστε ἓν εἶναι, 141e).[29] In this way the plane of language[30] is deduced or designated, in which what remains is the signifier science, which refuses all predicates. It counts then solely as a signifier, and any other signifier would do the trick just as well. This signifier has no proper signifier of its own, then. It is the signifier of a non-signifier.

We understand – and Cornford underscores the point[31] – that this 'one' of the first Hypothesis cannot be assimilated to Parmenidean being, closed, homogeneous, absolutely one and absolutely being [étant], which 'is without lack', since 'not being, it would lack everything' ['n'étant pas, il manquerait de tout'].[32] Parmenidean being lacks nothing, whereas the Platonic One here lacks even this lacking nothing – it lacks being, precisely. The unity of science thus cannot be assimilated to a Parmenidean sphere. It would have instead the status Cavaillès assigned it with respect to Bernard Bolzano's project:

> Science is perhaps for the first time [58] no longer considered as a simple intermediary between the human mind [esprit] and being in itself, equally dependent on both and lacking its own reality, but rather as an object sui generis, original in its essence, autonomous in its movement. [. . .] A theory of science can only be a theory of the unity of science. [. . .] As a uniquely autonomous progress, a dynamism closed in on itself with neither absolute beginning nor term, science moves outside of time [. . .]. If total knowledge [savoir] has no sense – with an absolute consciousness there exists a hiatus or in-between as real as with opinion, in such a way that there can be no question of either preparing for it or starting from it – neither does a radical extra-scientific knowledge. [. . .] Science is a Riemannian volume that can be at once closed and exterior to itself.[33]

The question arises of the possibility of a discourse on this absolute unity of science. 'The difficulty', Cavaillès writes, 'of situating the discipline that posits [these characteristics]' – of science according to Bolzano – 'appears straight

---

28   TN: This translates Regnault's French text. Cornford has: 'It cannot, then, "be" even to the extent of "being" one' (129). Gill and Ryan have: 'Therefore the one in no way partakes of being' (146).

29   On the issue of introducing such a function of the zero in a Greek text that was unaware of it, see Jean-Claude Milner, 'The Point of the Signifier', CpA 3.5:82, and the whole analysis that leads up to it.

30   'The mode of reality belonging to language differs from that belonging to other substances, and visible objects differ absolutely from words' (Sextus Empiricus, Contre les logiciens, I, 80).

31   Cornford, Plato and Parmenides, 134.

32   Parmenides, On Nature, fragment 8, line 33. (Regnault cites the French edition of the Poème de la Nature, trans. Jean Beaufret and Jean-Jacques Riniéri [Paris: PUF, 1955]).

33   Cavaillès, Sur la logique, 21–24; we follow several of his analyses here.

away.'[34] As it is a matter then of considering what is at least named as the other of the one, the fifth Hypothesis, correlative to the first, must be introduced.

HYPOTHESIS V (THE ONE IS. THE OTHERS/ THE ONE. THE ABSOLUTE ONE.)

Axioms: *The one is apart from the Others. Exclusion of any middle or third solution (there is only the One or the Others).*

Properties: *They have no common link. The One is not in the Others. The Others are neither one nor a plurality, neither immobile nor in motion.*

Relations: *They are neither similar nor dissimilar to the One, neither identical, nor different, neither becoming in it, nor smaller, nor larger.*

If unity is posited in its absoluteness, and without exterior, the only place for the epistemological discourse that is correlative to it is within it and identified with it, or else it is 'external' to this unity but without any relation being assigned to it, and with no status other than that of language being assigned, in its turn, to epistemology. The first case is the limit of Bolzanoan epistemology, the second that of logical neo-positivism.[35]

In the first case, epistemology is the science of science, since it is identical to science; if we raise it to the level of a metalanguage of science, it is the signifier of the signifier that has no signifier. Inversely, science is wholly its epistemology, or 'if there is science, it is in its entirety demonstration, which is to say logical.'[36] But then epistemology [59] must account for its pretension to identify itself with scientificity; precisely, the necessity of assigning it the status of a metalanguage renders it *relative* to that for which its exact function is to demonstrate that it is deprived of relations. It becomes the name for that to which 'no name belongs' (142*a*). It becomes secondary: 'Without having resolved these problems, scientific epistemology is unable to constitute itself directly as primary, as was its ambition. Rather it is posterior to the analytic which provides the content of its object, as well as to the ontology which completes its being.'[37]

The 'exterior' is thus reintroduced in the unity of science as the impossible, i.e. as the unnamed naming the name of science; it only indicates it, but having no other property than the deictic, it loses everything, even its signifier. Hence the absence of properties that Plato assigns it in this new hypothesis. We obtain

---

34 Cavaillès, *Sur la logique*, 24.

35 Let it be made clear at once that the minimal character of the hypotheses considered here ensures that our references to actual epistemological discourses cannot be anything other than formal. We proceed as with regulative ideas. Any real epistemology is a mixture [*un mixte*]. What is more, not all mixtures can figure here – hence the absence of certain names of the first importance.

36 Cavaillès, *Sur la logique*, 25.

37 Ibid., 26.

the 'discourse' without properties on science that closes Wittgenstein's *Tractatus Logico-Philosophicus*: 'The right method of philosophy would be this. To say nothing except what can be said, i.e. the propositions of natural science [. . .] and then always, when someone wished to say something metaphysical, to demonstrate to him that he had given no meaning to certain signs in his propositions.'

'My propositions serve as elucidations in the following way: anyone who understands me eventually recognizes them as nonsensical, when he has used them – as steps – to climb up beyond them. (He must, so to speak, throw away the ladder after he has climbed up it).'[38]

- In Bachelardian terms, it will be said that science is *cut off* from everything, that there is thus no error that is not a nothingness; or in other terms, there is no ideology that is external to science, nor one that must be referred back to it as the retroactive proof of its falsity.

- In Lacanian terms,[39] it will be said that scientificity can be defined on the basis of the foreclosure from its field of a lack (it constitutes itself in this way); science in this sense lacks a lack.[40] And yet, this is what is excluded here in its turn; the One of scientificity is thus here the lack of this lack of a lack, since outside of science taken in the sense of this first Hypothesis there is nothing. Instead of excluding *to* the exterior, science excludes the exterior itself. This foreclosure of foreclosure, according to operations we can define, comes down to a suture, which consists in the reintroduction into science of an exteriority whereby it annuls itself as the subject of its discourse.[41] But this suture within a science (in the Lacanian sense at present, and no longer that of the Hypothesis) of what is excluded from it; its reintroduced exterior, although it is the suture of a foreclosure, is [60] not the suture of a subject: here it is precisely foreclosure that plays the role of the subject. In order to understand such an 'anomaly' (the foreclosure is a suture), we must distinguish between the structure of this One of the first Hypothesis, which is a structure *of subject*, and that which we making it bear here, the name of a supposed foreclosure.

Here science excludes itself from the discourse about it as the subject of its own discourse, but if we want to persist in giving it the name science, and the name of epistemology to this discourse, then it is this discourse that plays the role of science; it is, like science, desutured, but desutured here precisely from

---

38   TN: Ludwig Wittgenstein, *Tractatus Logico-Philosophicus* [1921/1961], trans. D. F. Pears and B. F. McGuinness (London: Routledge Classics, 2001), 6.53–6.54.

39   What follows involves transformations of Lacanian operations. They only function in their pure state in Hyp. II (with the One operating a foreclosure, and the Others being sutured).

40   For an explanation of these concepts, see Jacques Lacan's *Ecrits* (Paris: Seuil, 1966), and Jacques-Alain Miller's 'Action of the Structure' (CpA 9.6) in the present volume of the *Cahiers*.

41   This is what justifies, though in terms of lack, the reintroduction of an 'exterior' to the One, developed above in terms of language.

science. It is at once science, the supreme truth (Bolzano), and it is also, since we do not allow it to retain either the name or the properties of science, wholly destitute, like the Others of the One (neither one, nor multiple, nor similar, nor dissimilar, neither in motion, nor at rest, having with the One no common link). Such is the discourse of the *Tractatus*, which absolutely guarantees the truth of which it speaks – 'the *truth* of the thoughts communicated here seems to me unassailable and definitive'[42] – but at the same time this discourse is totally deprived of sense, it is *'nonsensical'*.

If, structurally, the One and the Others do not have the same function, they have the same properties, and their difference is absolute and non-attributable [*inassignable*].

We should add that these Hypotheses I and V, in which the absolute idealism of science is confined to an ineffable negative theology of science,[43] will serve as a limit to the correlative Hypotheses IX and VII.

The passage to a second hypothesis is justified by the necessity of conferring properties on the One, but we must not claim to deduce it from the first.[44] All the hypotheses are thinkable, or if they are not, they can be stated (as well-formed expressions): the contradictions they entail, should they arise, are irrelevant. We can only say that some of them are aporetic, and this is what renders the transition from one to another impossible. It is thus by consideration of the matrix alone that we now attribute being to the One in a positive way.

HYPOTHESIS II (THE ONE IS. THE ONE/ THE OTHERS. THE RELATIVE ONE.)

Axioms: *It is, but does not merge with being, nor does being with it: 'their subject alone is identical, namely "the One that is"'* (142d). *Each part possesses at once being and oneness, and so on to infinity. There will be an infinite multiplicity of beings* [êtres].

Properties: *Infinite multiplicity of the One in itself. It is limited, has beginning and end, and shape; it is in itself and in something other than itself, immobile and in motion.*

Relations: *It is identical to itself and different from itself, identical to the Others and different from the Others, similar and dissimilar to itself and the Others, contiguous* [61] *and non-contiguous to itself and the Others, equal and unequal to itself and the Others (smaller and larger too). It participates in Time (is older and younger, etc.).*

---

42   Wittgenstein, *Tractatus*, preface.

43   Many commentators, both neo-Platonist and not, have rightly traced the origins of negative theology to this first hypothesis.

44   Plato, *Parmenides*, trans. Diès, 32; trans. Schwalbé, 339; Cornford, *Plato and Parmenides*, 134–135.

It becomes, it has been and it is. There can thus be 'science, and opinion, and sensation' of it.

The unity of science is, but not in the sense that it is one. It is 'the One that is', nevertheless, that is the sole subject both of the One and of being; it is the unity of science – let us call it scientificity here – that is sometimes one and sometimes something other. We could call it existent, but it would be better not to restrain the meaning of the word being to existence alone.[45] This is why we will say: science is science and much more, which means that one can attribute limits to it, a beginning, an end, a configuration, a space and a history. For example, we can say, referring to time: Greek science, classic science, but this multiplicity will not be a discontinuous dispersal. The category of science will be rightfully preserved in all cases.

We might also refer to space: mathematics, physics, etc. But here too we are not condemned to a pure multiplicity, otherwise there would not only be no reason to call these particular beings science, but equally, we would be authorized to call anything science. This Hypothesis leads then to a regionalizing epistemology, like Bachelard's, but it does not authorize dispersion. It guarantees the properties common to each particular science, and precisely those properties we were entitled to confer right away upon scientificity in general. All sciences have in common their scientificity, and this cannot amount to nothing: 'the one that is, must it not itself, since it is one being, be a whole, and the parts of this whole be oneness and being?' (142d).[46] Consequently, if it is said that the One has a beginning and a history, the same will have to be said of all the ones that follow from it. It is a question here of a conceptual deduction rather than a historical development. As such, it will not be said that mathematics has *given rise to* physics, and then to chemistry, etc. It will be said rather, for example, to use Bachelard's concepts, that scientificity (what he calls the *esprit scientifique*) institutes itself via an epistemological rupture with the 'web of errors' that precedes it, and that one must mark this rupture in each particular science, and each particular science will possess scientificity for itself (it is indeed *ones* that the One engenders). This is how it works in Auguste Comte's classification of the sciences, which *are* sciences (they all have criteria of positivity), yet which have a well-ordered filiation among them. [62]

If we add to this engendering of the one part of the One the parallel engendering of its other part, then a field of science opens that does not coincide with

---

45   Cornford prefers to avoid the meaning of existence in this hypothesis, and rightly insists: '"Being" is to be taken in the widest sense [. . .] as belonging to anything about which any true statement can be made' (*Plato and Parmenides*, 136).

46   TN: Plato, *Parmenides*, trans. Gill and Ryan, 148.

scientificity itself, and which renders possible the movement of this scientificity.

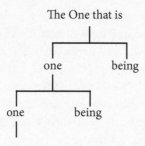

We still have to distinguish the One with respect to being from the One with respect to the Others: 'Supp e we take a selection of terms, say, being and the different, or being and the One, or the One and the different' (143*b–c*). This leads us to three different dialectics:

(a) that of the One and being: the unity of science or of each science can encroach upon being and produce a rejection of being [*un rejeté d'être*], 'being' being the name of the formally rejected term. Along these lines, Bachelard says: 'science creates philosophy';[47] we could call this rejection the *spontaneous philosophy of the scientists* [*savants*] to use Louis Althusser's expression.[48] For example, Newton gives space and time the purely mathematical character of independent variables of movement of the body of reference (in scientificity), but he adds to them the metaphysical character of absoluteness (in being).[49]

Inversely, it will be said that there is no being or metaphysical statement that does not owe something to a potential scientificity, 'for the One is always pregnant with being [*gros de l'être*], and being pregnant with the One' (142*e*).[50] This is what is expressed for example in the claim that metaphysics only begins with Greek science.

Cavaillès describes this process in a more pertinent and intrinsic way when he uses this Hypothesis of the *Parmenides* to think what he calls a paradigmatic conception of thought. 'Synthesis is coextensive to the engendering [*l'engendrement*] of the synthesized [. . .]. There is no sense without an act, and

---

47   Gaston Bachelard, *Le nouvel esprit scientifique* (Paris: PUF, 1934), 3; *The New Scientific Spirit*, trans. Arthur Goldhammer (Boston: Beacon Press, 1984), 3tm.

48   TN: Cf. Louis Althusser, *Philosophy and the Spontaneous Philosophy of the Scientists & Other Essays*, ed. Gregory Elliott (London: Verso, 1990).

49   Isaac Newton, in *Philosophiæ Naturalis Principia Mathematica*, 'Definitions, Scholium', trans. Andrew Motte, revised and ed. Florian Cajori (Berkeley: University of California Press, 1962), I, 6.

50   TN: Cornford has: 'for a "one" always has being, and a "being" always has unity' (138). Gill and Ryan have: 'since oneness always possesses being and being always possesses oneness' (148).

no new act without the sense that engenders it.'[51] But the Bachelardian relation between a science and the quantity of metaphysics it contains (and jettisons) is at bottom the same referred back to its core[52]; for if pure scientificity defines itself solely by the foreclosure of being, as scientificity in its becoming, by contrast, it unceasingly rejects being. The history of the sciences [63] is the sequence of these rejections. There is only the first or primary One [*l'Un premier*] that functions as the ideal of science; all the rest is weighed down with being.

(b) *that of the One and the Others*: this necessitates, as with the first hypothesis, that we add to this second one its correlative (The Others/the One), Hypothesis IV.

HYPOTHESIS IV (THE ONE IS. THE OTHERS/
THE ONE. THE RELATIVE ONE.)

Axioms: *The One is. The others are part of it; they have community with it and with themselves.*
Properties: *They are a whole, and are multiple, limited and unlimited.*
Relations: *They are similar and dissimilar to themselves and to each other.*

(b) (*continued*): Because it does not coincide with being, the One engenders an alterity. Being is the name of this alterity as it is referred back to this One (it is pregnant with the One). But we can also consider this alterity as *alterity* (of the One) rather than as alterity *of* the One. So the other of scientificity taken as a whole is the prescientific domain, which receives its status and its space from the cut that the One carries out with it; this is how Galilean science reveals the medieval physics of the *impetus* to be prescientific. Hence, it is the whole oneness of the One that determines and circumscribes its specific alterity: to each science there corresponds the ideology with which it has ruptured. The Others, or the ideologies (here *deduced*) thus do indeed have 'community with the One' (158d) (alchemy is the other of chemistry, not physics) 'and with themselves', and the ones with the others (all ideologies have common characteristics, if only as a result of their retrospective re-absorptions in configurations that are always larger: alchemy rejoins the pseudo-physics of the *impetus*). We are thus entitled to speak of a science that is contiguous and non-contiguous (148d-149d) to its other to describe the relation of cut [*rapport de coupure*] that it maintains with its ideology.

If then we take all the relations that Plato, in either Hypothesis II or IV, posits between the One and its others, we can, by adding dialectic *(a)* and

---

51   Cavaillès, *Sur la logique*, 26–30.
52   TN: '*Mais le rapport bachelardien d'une science à la quantité de métaphysique qu'elle contient (et dont elle se déleste) est au fond le même rapporté à son noyau.*'

dialectic *(b)*, apply them just as well to a science in becoming and to its ideal scientificity as to this same science and its ideology of rupture:

- The One is self-identical = all science is its scientificity;
- The One is different from itself = the state of knowledge [*savoir*] does not coincide with the ideal of science;
- The One is identical to the Others = there is only ideology if there is science. They are identical insofar as we name them together and separate them from the rest;
- The One is different from the Others = a science is not its ideology, etc.

Moreover, the multiplication of dialectic *(a)* by dialectic *(b)* induces a third dialectic: [**64**]

(c) that of being and of the Others; being, or here, the rejected, the foreclosed of science,[53] is not identical to what is cut from science. This can account for the fact that Galileo for example was able to proffer a metaphysics (the Universe is written in a mathematical Language) that was not incompatible with his physics,[54] whereas he could not endorse the pseudo-physics of his predecessors – which does not prevent the metaphysics compatible with the state of a science from becoming incompatible with a subsequent state of this same science, as when Bachelard explains that Cartesian epistemology does not work with modern physics. In that case, metaphysics falls back into the field of ideologies, it becomes a movement of being toward the others of the One, of the foreclosed toward the simply renounced. A science simultaneously breaks with its prehistory and excludes itself from the metaphysics that accompanies it.

– In Comtean terms, the positive state breaks with the theological state and distinguishes itself from the metaphysical state. This latter vacillates between the other two. It can only be the effect of the positive on the theological.

– In Lacanian terms, the foreclosure of foreclosed being determines the latter to relate incessantly to the space that excludes it; it is by this impossible suture to a foreclosure that it manages to exclude its real suture to another space, that of the Others of Science, which is sutured by nature, the space of the subject. Being is still pregnant with the One, and claims like the One to lack lack, but it is also itself thrown back as if its oneness is annulled,[55] it comes to lack *tout court*, which no longer serves then to distinguish it from the subject.

---

53   We will see in Judith Miller's article [in this same issue of the *Cahiers*] how, in Galilean physics, relation precisely excludes being (CpA 9.9). In our second Hypothesis, the One signifies science and being thus signifies being, but the coincidence is fortuitous in principle, and we cannot be accused of allegory: we arrive at this coincidence, we do not posit it.

54   On this subject, see the analyses of Alexandre Koyré in his *Études Galiléenes* (1939), *Études d'histoire de la pensée scientifique* (1966), etc.

55   TN: '*il est aussi renvoyé lui-même comme annulé de son un*'.

Thus Newton's absolute space, however far from any subject, and referred to the big Other of the *sensorium Dei* alone, has, since relativity, fallen into the space of the small others, of *impetus*, of nature's abhorrence of a vacuum, and of phlogiston theory. It will be said that this space, foreclosed from science ('*écarté par le bras du secret qu'il détient*') and at the same time emerging from the depths of an otherwise suturing space ('*naufrage cela direct de l'homme*'),[56] is that of overdetermination.[57]

That there is a tenable discourse on these three dialectics and that it has its place here is further attested to by Plato: 'So there can be science, opinion, and sensation of it [of the One]; since we in fact are now exercising all these activities with respect to it' (155*d*).[58] Epistemology is its name, but this discourse comes to be held under the authority of different proper names assigned to this Hypothesis. [65]

HYPOTHESIS III (THE ONE IS AND IS NOT, ABSOLUTE AND RELATIVE, ETC.).

Axioms: *The One is one and multiple. It is and is not.*

Properties: *cannot be assigned.*

Relations: *It becomes similar and dissimilar, larger and smaller; in motion, it immobilizes itself, immobilized, it moves, etc.*

In the preceding Hypothesis, there was knowledge of the One because at each step of its multiplication [*démultiplication*] to infinity, we could actually distinguish its part of oneness [*d'un*] and its part of being, the stable part of its scientificity and the vacillating part of what it was excluding from itself. In introducing several other determinations than those that the sole category of unity allows, we could describe the actual or effective configurations of science, or of each science, and find for them stable states. But if we reduce each configuration to the formal punctuality of the One alone, the division between the oneness of the One and its being will multiply to infinity in an instant, and we are no longer able to assign any possible proposition to the One nor to being. In that case the One is one and multiple, it is and is not, the state of science and the sciences becomes liquid. Science is reduced to its denomination alone; without properties, it can be attributed to any object whatsoever. This comes to pass when one proclaims to be science all that emerges at the vanishing limit between the space of scientificity and the space of ideology. In the space – this means that we will

---

56   TN: These references are to Stéphane Mallarmé's poem *Un coup de dès*.

57   Cf. Jacques-Alain Miller, 'Action of the Structure' (CpA 9.6), in which epistemology is defined as a discourse of overdetermination.

58   TN: Cornford, *Plato and Parmenides*, 193tm.

call science any branch of a science, and any branch of a branch, to infinity. In the terms of temporal development, a science will be born each day.[59] Or again, and without going to this extreme, we can detect in what could be called a minimal positivism (and echoes of which we find in Claude Bernard) the idea that science is the vanishing present instant that renders null all that preceded it and ratifies all that follows: science is the future of science. Its development is reduced to the pure development of a cursor on the line of time: 'Medicine is directed toward its *definitive* scientific path. By the *natural* march of its evolution alone, it thus abandons *little by little* the region of systems to assume *more and more* the analytic form, and return *gradually* to the method of investigation common to the experimental sciences.'[60]

This third Hypothesis can be applied in turn to the fourth, already envisaged. We consider then the Others than the One, but these have no more stability than it. Ideologies no longer have any properties in this case, and they cannot be distinguished from sciences; henceforth their characteristics can be attributed to the sciences themselves in the indistinction of properties. Scepticism arises here; this is the moment of the evil genius, when [66] Descartes accuses all the sciences themselves of nullity, including mathematical certainty itself, in the name of a more powerful hypothesis.

It has been noted that this is the same third Hypothesis that, when applied to the second, established the reign of the 'everything is science' or 'everything can pass for science', and when applied to the fourth, the reduction of even the best sciences to nothing, by a decision of the subject. An absolute suture excludes all foreclosures, but all sutures as well.

We will not add very much to the almost empty content of this Hypothesis, except to say that it is that of *all transition* from one Hypothesis to another, since it consists in making the status of the One vanish: 'it cannot even change without making a change' (156c).[61] The result is that one can in principle find this same Hypothesis III between Hypotheses II and IV, IV and VIII, VI and VIII, II and VI, between Hypotheses I and V, V and IX, IX and VII, VII and III.

Reduced to pure vacillation, it serves as a common place for all the Hypotheses (the One at once is and is not, is one [*un*] and multiple, etc.); it is the multiple root of all the equations, or the mediation of all proceedings [*instances*]. Their dialectic is thus of a Hegelian order.[62]

---

59   This is encountered in numerous cases of the human sciences. All epistemological interrogation is thereby reduced to a pure question of designation.

60   Claude Bernard, *Introduction à l'étude de la medicine expérimentale* [1865], introduction; emphasis added.

61   TN: Cornford has: 'On the other hand it does not change without making a transition' (200).

62   We can thus confer upon the third the status of a real Hypothesis (the traditional solution), or that of a corollary to the second. This is Cornford's solution, which however restrains its function, since in our view it can circulate. Furthermore, he refuses to accord to it the role of

From here we are going to enter into the field of the One as not being [*l'Un n'étant pas*]. If we translate this as meaning that the unity of science is not, we can understand this as implying either that science as such is in its essence multiple, that there are only sciences, or that there is no science at all. The first case corresponds in general with Hypotheses VI and VIII, of relative negation, and the second to Hypotheses VII and IX, of absolute negation. With the former, it is the unity that is lost, and scientificity fractures into particular objects. With the latter, it is scientificity itself that comes to be lacking, which implies, at the limit, a radically pluralist epistemology in the former case, and a thoroughly sceptical one in the latter.

HYPOTHESIS VI (THE ONE IS NOT. THE ONE/
THE OTHERS. THE RELATIVE ONE.)

Axioms: *It is the One that is not. It is knowable, different from the Others (it's to the extent that it is* [en tant qu'il est] *that non-being is attributed to it: it participates in being 'in some way'* ('Πη', 161e)).

Properties: *It has a large number of them, for it participates in all kinds of things, it is in motion and at rest.*

Relations: *It is different from the Others, dissimilar from the Others, resembles itself, unequal to the Others, but equal to itself (large and small). It is an object of science.* [67]

This Hypothesis, which allows the One to participate in certain properties even while refusing it being, is symmetrical with Hypothesis II. The One is evoked only to be dismissed as an existent [*existant*] straight away. There is not really a unity of science, so we must now only speak of sciences. By what right? At least their signifier gathers their plurality. The unity of sciences is not, but it has a being of language or of illusion. The non-being of unity resembles that of the *Sophist*, introduced precisely in order to define the status of the image.

Unity is thus only posited as a name. This name can serve as a commonplace for many objects deprived of properties, but it is only a name indefinitely repeated with regard to each among them. We can thus speak of it, 'there is science of it' (160d), but this is not to say anything else about it, except that it circulates from object to object, assuring only their liaison without predicates, and in consequence their pure difference: 'so, in addition to science, difference

---

synthesis in the Hegelian sense. But then he refuses *a priori* any proximity to Hegel. It is true that he grants Plato everything he denies Hegel (195, 202): he is opposed on this point by the authority of Hegel himself, who often specified what he owed (or didn't) to the *Parmenides*. For example: Hegel, *Science of Logic*, trans. George di Giovanni (Cambridge: Cambridge University Press, 2010; the pagination here refers to the German *Gesammelte Werke*), introduction, 21:40; chapter 1, 21:70, 76, etc.

also applies to it' (160*d*). Equal to itself alone, it is the difference of the Others. It plays exactly the same role as Mind [*Esprit*] in epistemologies such as those proposed by Brunschvicg, Lalande, etc. For it is not the unity of science that is one, it is the unity of a something about which one can say nothing, but of which the sciences give a different version at every moment. The unity of science is outside of science, if we understand by science the rigid configurations wherein the perpetual spontaneity of reason is paralyzed from moment to moment. 'Reacting against the logicism coming from Frege and Russell, which it regarded as a renewal of the Aristotelian tradition, [Brunschvicg's epistemology] sets thought as a creation escaping all norms against its linguistic expression, which, as a social phenomenon, immediately falls prey to both the illusions of the city and the laws of nature.'[63] Similarly, Lalande distinguishes reasoning reason [*la raison raisonnante*], a pure spontaneity always at work in science yet deprived of all properties (the One not being [*étant*], but being in a certain way) from reasoned reason [*la raison raisonnée*], the system of visible consequences of the invisible activity of Mind.

This epistemology is in one sense the culmination of Kantianism: the understanding, or the capacity for rules, does indeed have formal though positive properties in Kant, and scie   is subordinated to this capacity, even if the question of its actual regularity o everity [*sévérité*] is not in doubt.[64] However: 'There is no science *qua* autonomous reality, and describable as such, but rather a rational unification of diversity that is already organized by the understanding according to a set pattern, or gleaned from a body of evidence with neither plan nor discovery.'[65] This position straddling the second Hypothesis (the unity is [68] real) and the sixth (there is no unity) thus accentuates unity, even though this unity is not precisely that of science. But if we withdraw unity's properties from it – and this is the whole meaning of Brunschvicg's critique of Kantian categories – then we open the sciences up to an actual history, but we have not for all that abandoned their subordination to the unity of a fixed term, at once being and not being, even if we should be unable to say anything about it.

Intuitionist constructivism is not unrelated to such a representation. It takes a further step in that it no longer affirms the subordination of constructed truths to eternal truths, but only presupposes it: 'In fact all mathematicians and even intuitionists are convinced that in some sense mathematics bear upon

63   Cavaillès, *Sur la logique*, 17.

64   However, the *fact* of science is not sufficient for Kant: 'Such would be the case if we were to suppose as given facts the existence of mathematics and Physics as sciences, in order to then ask ourselves about their conditions of possibility. Such a method, which has been called regressive, is nothing other than the *apagogic* method, which Kant condemns, at least insofar as Philosophy must supply rigorous proofs for its affirmations, rather than settle for opinions' (Jules Vuillemin, *La Philosophie de l'algèbre* [Paris: PUF, 1962], 54).

65   Cavaillès, *Sur la logique*, 14.

eternal truths, but when trying to define precisely this sense, one gets entangled in a maze of metaphysical difficulties. The only way to avoid them is to banish them from mathematics.'[66] Being is thus no longer in the One, it is wholly in the construction: "'to exist" must be synonymous with "to be constructed".'[67]

HYPOTHESIS VIII (THE ONE IS NOT. THE OTHERS/THE ONE. THE RELATIVE ONE)

Axioms: *The One is not. The Others are different from it.*

Properties: *The Others are an infinite plurality and can receive only apparent properties which immediately vanish.*

If in the end we exclude even the merest reference to the One, we obtain an infinite multiplicity of qualities that cannot be attributed and an incoherent pluralism of the sciences. 'So anything there is, upon which you may fix your thought, must be frittered away in subdivision; anything we may take will always be a mass without a One' (165*b*).[68]

We rejoin Hypothesis III in this absolute dispersal. There is a small difference, however; we considered the third Hypothesis only in the place that it then occupied: culmination of the second Hypothesis, it had been obtained by the proliferation of the division of the One. The One was maintained as the ideal of science, and we distanced ourselves from it as we descended further in time, or lower in the space of division; in this way, the human sciences and their multiple branches were always connected in principle to an ideal of scientificity. But in the present case, we have not obtained the multiple by proliferation of the One. Instead, with the unity of science abolished (the One is not), and its participation in being reduced to nothing (the Mind as empty plasticity), we have turned to the so-called positive properties of particular objects; we are no longer attached to any ideal, the ideal is in the thing, and it is now only a matter of *doing* [*faire*]. Bricolage becomes the truth of science. **[69]** All combinations are possible and bear the name science. 'As with scene-paintings, to the distant spectator all will appear as one thing, and seem to have the same character and to be alike; but if you approach nearer, they seem many and different, and this simulacrum of difference will make them seem different in character and unlike one another' (165*c*).[69] Brunschvicgian epistemology continues to connect the historical realizations of science to Mind or Man and thus continues to rely on

---

66   Arend Heyting, *Intuitionism: An Introduction*, second edition (Amsterdam: North Holland, 1966), 3.

67   Ibid., 2.

68   TN: Cornford, *Plato and Parmenides*, 238.

69   [TN: citing Cornford, *Plato and Parmenides*, 239tm]. See Claude Lévi-Strauss' analysis of the collar painted by François Clouet, in his *La Pensée sauvage* (Paris: Plon, 1962), 33ff.

a supporting anthropology as the ideal of its epistemology (*homo faber, artifex, sapiens*).[70] With this term of reference annulled, combinatory or structuralist epistemology has no other space than that in which this pure multiplicity repeats; it identifies itself with its object. As identical to it as the epistemology of Hypothesis I (that of neo-positivism) was to its object, it differs from it in that there epistemology was the science of science. At present, in the absence of science, it is its object that identifies itself with its activity, that becomes pure activity. But this is no longer the activity of Mind or of Man, this is the activity of the structure.[71]

In Lacanian terms, since in this hypothesis science is excluded, though not its relation to that which it itself ordinarily excludes, it is here found sutured to the multiple discourse. Suture of a foreclosure, in other words quite simply a suture: the One is then the sutured subject and bears the name of Mind (Brunschvicg); the multiple discourse, deprived of the One (for if one thing is sutured to another, this other lacks from the former), has nearly carried out a foreclosure. Foreclosure, since it is only just [à peine] a subject that it has excluded. Nearly, because this discourse, losing, in its perpetual difference with itself ('It is therefore mutually that they are others; this is the sole resource that remains for them, at the risk of only being the others [of] nothing' [164c]),[72] the unity of this foreclosure, comes to re-establish a suture *in each* of its elements. We were at least hoping for psychosis; all we got was the dream – ὄναρ ἐν ὕπνῳ, says Plato (164d).

HYPOTHESIS VII (THE ONE IS NOT. THE ONE/
THE OTHERS. THE ABSOLUTE ONE.)

Axioms: *The One is not. It does not participate in being in any way.*

Properties, relations: *No property and no relation can be assigned to it. It is unknowable.*

We can at present thoroughly deny the unity of science, along with its participation in anything else whatsoever. We can even say that if the unity of science has no sense, then it is multiplicity that has a sense (return to Hypothesis VI): in fact this multiplicity in no way participates with this [70] One. It does not even have a name, or at least, in its lack without remainder, even its name is carried away. Nothing outside of it can bear the name of science. There is quite simply no

---

70   Léon Brunschvicg develops this anthropology in his work *De la connaissance de soi* (1931).

71   We refer on this point to the analysis of Pierre Macherey, *Pour une théorie de la production littéraire* (Paris: Maspéro, 1966), 165–173.

72   TN: Cornford has: 'They must, then, be other than each other; that is the only possibility left, if they are not to be other than nothing' (236).

longer any science at all, and no epistemology either:[73] 'science and opinion and sensation, definition or name, all that or anything else that might be, can it be referred to what is not? In no way' (164a-b). As Plato's commentators have explained, we reconnect with the first Hypothesis; but whereas before we had at our disposal, in the One absolutely One, a signifier of the unnameable, here we instead *indicate* the unnameable of the signifier. The neo-Platonists conceived the first as a transcendent being (here the ideal of science) and the second as the abyss of the nothing (the lack of science), foreclosure of all foreclosure. Does a place remain for anything else? For that, we need to introduce the ninth and last Hypothesis.

HYPOTHESIS IX (THE ONE IS NOT. THE OTHERS/ THE ONE. THE ABSOLUTE ONE.)

Axioms: *The One is not. The Others are, but they are neither one, nor several, having no relation with the one. No property and no relation can be assigned to the Others. They are unknowable.*

We must now posit that if neither science nor its unity are absolute, the inverse symmetry with respect to the first Hypothesis here implies a status for the *Others* than the One. They are in some way. But in their turn they, like the One of Hypothesis I, have no other status than that of a 'non-real thing in thought'. Things, rather, and things in an infinite number. We can indeed then confer upon them the name of epistemology, but we only obtain the shattered epistemology of a non-science. Even this name is illegitimate; rather it is the reign of ideologies without number and without predicates. The circulation of signifiers is indefinite; they are signifiers without signification: 'if the one is not, nothing is' (166c). Their circulation, moreover, strips them of that 'anteriority to the subject' for whom there would be signification.[74] Every signifier is thus sutured to every other. All that remains are sutures, everything comes to be lacking, even if it be from nothing.

This Hypothesis is thus symmetrical with the first, but in an inverted form; it was the One that played the role in the first that the Others play at present (a structure of the subject), and the Others of the first played the role of the One at present (they were foreclosed by the One, whereas now it is by them). But as the Others were not, and this One is not, we have in both cases simply foreclosed not *to* the exterior, but the exterior itself, and we thereby obtain a foreclosure of

---

73   See Étienne Gilson, *Les Tribulations de Sophie* (Paris: Vrin, 1967): one philosophy chases after another and every science does the same. Theology alone remains one and the same (which refers us back to the first Hypothesis and forecloses all the abominated others).

74   Miller, 'Suture', CpA 1.3:51.

foreclosure, namely the suture that we have just [71] indicated – suture of fore-closure there (Hypothesis I), proliferation of sutures here (Hypothesis IX).

If, deploying the third Hypothesis, we reduce to these nothings that they have become these Others than the One-nothing, we then obtain the Hypothesis symmetrical to Hypothesis I, that of the One reduced to nothing and inexistent others. In this way the structures of the two hypotheses (I and IX) are exactly identical, as are, at the beginning of Hegel's *Logic*, those of being and of noth-ingness (here the One as being absolutely, and the One as absolutely not being): being

> is pure indeterminateness and emptiness. – There is *nothing* to be intuited in it, if one can speak here of intuiting; or, it is only this pure empty intuiting itself. Just as little is anything to be thought in it, or, it is equally only this empty thinking. Being, the indeterminate immediate is in fact *nothing*, and neither more nor less than nothing. [. . .] *Pure being and pure nothing are therefore the same.* The truth is neither being nor nothing, but rather that being has passed over into nothing and nothing into being.[75]

No more hypotheses are possible, and the circle is thus complete. The exer-cise is finished.

It is not a question of concluding, since the matrix is self-sufficient; we will add nothing, then, except for some further turns of the screw.

1. The matrix can now be put to other uses. There is no need to believe that it was made for science. The most we could say, on condition of adopting the second Hypothesis (which made for each being its correlative one in the divi-sion of the One), is that it is Greek science that induced this metaphysics of the one and the multiple in Plato (in its logical rigour, and not in its mystical accep-tation, for mythologies about it were not lacking before the Greeks), and so it is not by chance that it functions as well as it possibly can when we reintroduce a dialectic of science into the matrix. *Verum index sui.*

2. On the other hand, we acknowledge that we have only considered science (and epistemology as the discourse on it) in terms of its kinds of unity, and of its existence, but not in terms of its nature, nor of its content, nor its functioning, nor its real history, etc. It's a matter of science reduced to the problem of its unity, but at least this matters, and we are prepared to affirm its fundamental character.

3. We said at the outset that there was an excess of the One-substance over the one-predicate, and that this is what partly prevented us from assimilating the One to science for example. Consequently such a substitution has not been

---

75   Hegel, *Science of Logic*, 21:69; cf. Hegel, *Encyclopedia of Philosophical Sciences*, §86–§88.

carried out; it has only resulted occasionally from the nature of certain Hypotheses.

The danger resided in the concept of unity, which, as a super-eminent essence, risked receiving properties due more to Platonist metaphysics' [72] valorization of essences than to their reduction to the simplest logical expression. We would thus have harvested, along with the wheat of the One, the One as pure formal term, the chaff of the One as value. This danger must be dissipated.

To be sure, each Hypothesis secreted several metaphysical excesses over the amount of logic that it contained, relative to those axioms that we used to frame the beginning of its formulation. But if we take account of the integral and circular character of the matrix, we can consider each excess as due only to the fact that in each Hypothesis, the One can retain or foretell the properties that it receives in another. Step by step, then, the axiomatic matrix as a whole will have reabsorbed the excesses of each particular axiomatic. At bottom, in a given Hypothesis, the One-substance only exceeds the one-predicate by the possible number of predicates it is capable of receiving in all the others. Oddly enough, the dialectical exercise in the *Parmenides* might reduce [*réduirait*] the essentialist metaphysics by making it circulate in the matrix (whereas in the dialogues without matrix, the ethical or political dialogues, Essence retains on the contrary the splendours and privileges of its solitary valorization).

The excess of sense is thereby referred to its true cause, the equivocity of the One due to its distribution across opposed Hypotheses. The One is only substance because it is the support common to all predicates, contradictory or not, that the matrix distributes across it.

We will add moreover that Plato mostly limits in each Hypothesis the risks of excess and limits his attention to the case in hand.

4. The result is that in order to manifest this distributive circulation we had to reduce the One to its signifier alone, i.e. to introduce the plane of language. This is to restate here with regard to the general dialectic what was verifiable in each Hypothesis wherever we introduced this plane (with the distinctions that it involves: language-metalanguage, and the ontology it implies: being and the existence of non-real objects), without which the game [*jeu*] of the Hypotheses would have been unplayable. The introduction of language is necessary in order *to save truth through the sacrifice of the thinkable*, which is the sole duty of the logician.

5. The consideration of these aspects or planes [*plans*] can resolve a last difficulty, one that might arise from interrogating the status of 'our own discourse'.

Our self-examination might proceed as follows: To use a matrix of epistemologies is already to prejudge epistemology itself. To which we would respond: no doubt, but in which place of the matrix is this presupposition located? One can refuse the question, and so on to infinity, but it is already useful to know that we can arrange the exercise of the matrix in any of its various cases by a process of *metonymization* that amounts to substituting, for the language used, the plane of its metalanguage – or again, to replace in the whole of the preceding discussion 'science' by 'epistemology', and 'epistemology' by the matrix exercise itself. And so whoever claims that to refer to a matrix of epistemologies is the mark of a flagrant scepticism will have done nothing more than reposition this exercise as part of Hypothesis VIII. [73]

We will thus obtain, by generalizing from this discussion, the following dialectics of epistemologies (we have grouped the Hypotheses in pairs):

Hyp. I–V	The absolute One	=	One sole epistemology is true, but which one? Impossible to know (absolute idealism).
Hyp. II–IV	The participated One	=	One sole epistemology is true, that which communicates to others by division (dogmatism of participation).
Hyp. VI–VIII	The participated Non-One	=	All epistemologies are true, none are privileged (relative scepticism).
Hyp. VII–IX	The absolute Non-One	=	None are true (absolute scepticism).

And finally Hypothesis III, the mediation of all the others, will be no more than the name of the matrix exercise itself.

One will thus choose one's place in the matrix and one will be quite glad (or surprised) to discover neighbours that perhaps one did not know – one's neighbours, which is often to say, one's destiny. But one cannot leave the table. The only bad players are to be found among those who have already been dealt their cards.

CHAPTER EIGHT

The Cercle d'Épistémologie
On the Archaeology of the Sciences: Questions for Michel Foucault[1]

Editors' Note: The following is an English translation of the questions the Cercle d'Épistémologie presented to Michel Foucault in preparation for volume nine of the Cahiers *(CpA 9.1) as well as the 'New Questions' (CpA 9.3) the Cercle put to Foucault once they received his reply. In the context of volume nine of the journal, Foucault's 'Response to the* Cercle d'Épistémologie' *appears between the two sets of questions; Foucault's text would soon serve as a template for the introduction to his* Archaeology of Knowledge, *published in 1969. Here, the Cercle's initial questions are presented in their entirety, and the 'New Questions' are presented in English translation for the first time.[2]*

[5] Our sole intention in posing these questions to the author of *History of Madness*, *The Birth of the Clinic*, and *The Order of Things*[3] is to ask him to set forth some of the critical propositions that ground the possibility of his theory and the implications of his method. Given the Cercle's interests, we asked him to specify his answers with regard to the status of science, its history, and its concept.

ON THE EPISTEME AND THE EPISTEMOLOGICAL RUPTURE

Since the work of Gaston Bachelard, the notion of epistemological rupture has served to name the discontinuity that the philosophy and history of the sciences believes it can identify between the birth of every science and the 'tissue of tenacious, interrelated, positive errors' that is retrospectively recognized as

---

1   TN: First published as Le Cercle d'Épistémologie, 'Sur l'archéologie des sciences. À Michel Foucault', CpA 9.1 (summer 1968): 5–8. Translated by Christian Kerslake, revised by Knox Peden.

2   TN: In the reproductions of this 'Response' following its initial publication in the *Cahiers*, the Cercle's initial questions to Foucault have appeared in a truncated form, with the middle two pages of their four-page set of questions omitted. These reproductions include both the multi-volume *Dits et Ecrits*, first published by Gallimard in four volumes in 1994 and reproduced in a two-volume edition in 2001, as well as the English translation of the text collected in the volume *Aesthetics, Method, and Epistemology*, ed. James Faubion (New York: The New Press, 1998), 297–333, which was based on a translation that first appeared in *Theoretical Practice* 3–4 (1971).

3   TN: Page references to the English translation of *Les Mots et les choses*, *The Order of Things* (London: Tavistock, 1970) and the English edition of *History of Madness*, ed. Jean Khalfa, trans. Jonathan Murphy and Jean Khalfa (London: Routledge, 2006) are given after the French.

preceding it. The familiar examples of Galileo, Newton, and Lavoisier, but also those of Einstein and Mendeleev, serve to illustrate the horizontal perpetuation of this rupture.

The author of *The Order of Things*, by contrast, identifies a vertical discontinuity between the epistemic configuration of one epoch and the next.

We ask him: what relations obtain between this horizontality and this verticality?[4]

Archaeological periodization breaks up the [historical] continuum into synchronic sets, grouping together knowledges in the shape of unitary systems. [6] By the same token, it effaces the difference that, in Bachelard's view, separates scientific discourse at each moment from other kinds of discourse, and, by assigning each a specific temporality, makes of their simultaneity and solidarity a surface effect.

We would like to know whether the archaeologist seeks or requires [*veut*] this effacement, or if he intends here to distinguish two registers, hierarchical or not?

If it is true that an epistemic configuration is obtained by articulating the relevant selected traits in a set of statements, then we ask:

- What governs the selection, and justifies, for example, the following phrase: 'Only those who cannot read will be surprised that I have learned such a thing more clearly from Cuvier, Bopp, and Ricardo, than from Kant and Hegel' (*The Order of Things*, 318/307).
- What validates the configuration obtained in this way?
- Does it make sense to ask what defines an *episteme* in general?

Further, we ask: does archaeology recognize a concept of science in the singular? A concept of science that is not exhausted by the diversity of its historical figures?

---

4   In this question we aim to take up the thread of the following passage from Georges Canguilhem's article on Foucault's book (*Critique* 242 [July 1967], 612–613): 'Where theoretical *knowledge* is concerned, can that knowledge be elaborated in the specificity of its concept without reference to some norm? Among the theoretical discourses produced in conformity with the epistemic system of the seventeenth and eighteenth centuries, certain ones, such as that of natural history, were rejected by the nineteenth-century *episteme*, but others were integrated. Even though it served as a model for the eighteenth century physiologists in animal economy, Newton's physics did not go down with them. Buffon is refuted by Darwin, if not by Étienne Geoffroy Saint-Hilaire. But Newton is no more refuted by Einstein than by Maxwell. Darwin is not refuted by Mendel or Morgan. The succession from Galileo to Newton to Einstein does not present ruptures similar to those that can be identified in the succession from Tournefort to Linnaeus to Engler in systematic botany' (Canguilhem, 'The Death of Man, or the Exhaustion of the Cogito', trans. C. Porter in *The Cambridge Companion to Foucault* [Cambridge: Cambridge University Press, 2003], 87–88).

ON READING

What use of *the letter* does archaeology presuppose? This is to say: what *operations* does it apply to a statement in order to decipher, throughout what it says, its conditions of possibility, and to guarantee that we reach the non-thought which – outside it, in it – incites it and systematizes it?

Does leading a discourse back to its unthought render fruitless any attempt to identify its internal structures, and to reconstruct their autonomous functioning? What relation can be constructed between these two concurrent systematizations? Is there an 'archaeology of philosophical doctrines' to be set against the technology of philosophical systems, such as that practised by Martial Gueroult?

The example provided by your reading of Descartes might help make this distinction (*History of Madness*, 54–57/44–47).

ON DOXOLOGY

How do we specify the relation that connects the epistemic configuration with the conflicting matters of opinion that play out across its surface?

Does the level of opinion only have negative properties: disorder, separation, dependence?

Might not the system of opinions that characterizes an author obey its own law, such that one could establish the rules in an [7] *episteme* that govern the range of doxological systems, with the presence of one opinion implying or excluding another from within the same system?

Why should the relation among the systems of opinions *always* take a conflictual form?

ON THE FORMS OF TRANSITION

With regard to the forms of transition that assure the passage from one large configuration to another, Chapter 6, part III of *The Order of Things* explains that if, in the case of natural history and general grammar, 'the mutation came about abruptly ... the mode of being for money and wealth, on the other hand, because it was linked to an entire *praxis*, to a whole institutional complex, had a much higher degree of historic viscosity' (192/180; cf. also 218/205).

The question is: what is the theory for which the general possibility of such a viscosity can be the object?

In what way, and according to what relations (causality, correspondence, etc.) can a form of transition be determined by such a viscosity?

In principle, are the discontinuities established between the configurations that succeed one another all of the same type?

What is the *motor* that transforms one configuration into another? Is it the principle of archaeology to attempt the reduction of this question?

OF HISTORICITY AND FINITUDE

We ask the author of *History of Madness, The Birth of the Clinic*, and *The Order of Things* how he would define the point [of leverage] from which he might raise the epistemic earth. When he declares that in order to speak of madness a 'language without support was necessary' (*Madness*, x/xxxv) that in the clinic something is beginning to change *today*, or simply that 'the end of man draws near', what status would he confer on this declaration itself?

Today, can he bring his own configuration to light?

If one were to call an author's historicity his belonging to the episteme of his epoch and 'finitude' the name that an epoch – notably our own – might give to its own limits, what relations or non-relations, according to Foucault, might be obtained between this historicity and this finitude? [8]

Would he be willing to consider an alternative between a radical historicism (whereby archaeology would be able to predict its own reinscription into a new discourse) and a sort of absolute knowledge (of which some authors might have had a presentiment, independently of epistemic constraints)?

Le Cercle d'Épistémologie

New Questions[5]

[41] It is not up to us to determine what, after Michel Foucault's 'Response', remains unresolved in the questions that we posed. For the movement whereby it exceeds the epistemological dimension to which we had confined ourselves is so forceful [*impérieux*] that it enables us now to forget the elisions that allow it.

Let there be no mistake: the text that one has just read [i.e. CpA 9.2], thanks to the systematic way its author articulates for the first time the necessary relations that obtain between *History of Madness, The Birth of the Clinic*, and *The Order of Things*, provides a renewed foundation to the archaeology of the sciences, and re-centres the theory of discourse that supports it, to the point of undoing its method of reading, as established in the introduction to *The Birth of the Clinic*.

This is why there are better things to do than repeat ourselves. The task presents itself of taking a new departure from this new text, and inserting ourselves, as Michel Foucault authorizes us to do, into the proceedings

---

5   TN: First published as Le Cercle d'Épistémologie, 'Nouvelles questions', CpA 9.3 (summer 1968): 41–44.

[*procès*] of a work whose greatest merit is that it is once again, and truly, *in progress.*

ON THE CIRCLE OF METHOD

Our first words must concern the circle of method.

In fact, the critique of continuity, which is so corrosive that it can accuse both Martial Gueroult and Heidegger of 'anthropologism', insofar as they both study totalities assembled under *proper names*, inevitably leads Foucault into a circle once he attempts to circumscribe his own objects. At the fundamental level he distinguishes as 'the referential', the set of statements to be studied has no other unity than that of the very law that regulates the dispersion of the 'different objects or referents' that this set 'puts in play', which means: the law defines what defines it.

We should acknowledge that this circle is in all likelihood [42] taken on board [*assumé*], since *discontinuity entails it*, in that it is both the 'object and instrument of research', and delimits 'the field of an analysis of which it is the effect'.

But a theory of this effect is surely necessary.

If, by virtue of its circularity, the method is obliged to set out from a provisional demarcation [*découpage*], how does this differ from the 'spontaneous syntheses' that Foucault's text puts on trial? This is what sets in motion a process of interminable, progressive-regressive correction. Will the circle of the archaeology of the sciences amount to the hermeneutic circle?

If, on the contrary, the first demarcation is definitive, then it is arbitrary.

What is there room for, between the interminable and the arbitrary?

ON THE RULE OF FORMATION

In order to resolve the problem of the unity of objects, the 'Response' proposes a novel concept, the 'rule of formation'.

This concept is put into play at the four levels which exhaust the aspects of discourses, and its effects are stated four times in identical terms. However, is the rule anything other than the name given to the relation (which is unspecifiable) of a variety to a unity, since its own singularity is opposed *without mediation* to the dispersion of objects that it is supposed to *form*?

If, for Michel Foucault, this rule is from the outset already capable of being articulated, we must then ask him, what are the properties that set it apart from other types of rules, and which distinguish it in particular from *structuralist rules*?

The 'Response' tells us that the system of a set of statements must be capable of forming solely the statements that are actually produced, and no others in addition, or in their stead. But is it not necessary to reconstitute a system of formation capable of indefinite productivity, *before* imposing upon it the limitation of only producing the finite number of statements that have taken place? Is Gueroult wrong, when he answers *in Descartes' place* to questions that the latter did not encounter, to consolidate in this way the power of the Cartesian system?

OF DISCOURSE, THE STATEMENT, AND THE EVENT

We must return now to the concept of discourse, whose value we note is not determined in the 'Response'. It seems that three senses of the term can be distinguished, which we might order in terms of the following process [*processus*].

1. In a first sense, discourse is a given grouping of given statements, where the statement figures as nothing more than the indeterminate entity of the *type* that is immediately subordinate to or beneath [*inférieur à*] discourse; it is in this sense that one speaks of the 'surface of discourses'. [43]
2. In another sense, discourse is the concept of that which draws its unity from the four criteria; it is in this sense that one speaks of the 'aspects of discourse'.
3. Finally, discourse as discursive formation is what results from the processing [*traitement*] of (1) by (2), that is, from among the possible groupings, the grouping that actually falls under the concept defined in (2). It is from this point of view that one can say that the discursive formation 'groups together a whole population of enunciative events'.

This whole process hangs upon the missing definition of the statement [*l'énoncé*], which enters into the concept of discourse in sense (1), and which discourse in senses (2) and (3) presupposes.

With regard to the statement, we might ask whether its definition as simply the smallest unit endowed with meaning is enough to specify it. And what are the criteria of individualisation [*individualization*] for such a statement, once the latter is deemed unanalysable? Do these criteria include that of *place*? And are they not all reducible to place alone? In that case, what would it mean to say that a statement *is repeated*?

There is more: place is a double determination, since the statement is conceived as an *element* in a system and as an *event* of enunciation. In fact, the 'Response' explicates the principle of reading the statement as element (grasped from laws of non-coincidence, splitting and dispersion, referring back to the rules of formation) all the while leaving us to understand that a principle of the statement as event also exists (grasped from the conditions governing the appearance of statements as events, across their articulation upon other events of a non-discursive nature).

However, are there actually *two* principles of reading? And what would be the second's articulation upon the first? In fact, the event, since it is always inscribed in a configuration, and related to the system of its conditions, seems to be nothing but an element.

But, here again, are not all the characterizations that one can possibly give to the *singularity* of the event reducible to the singularity of a *presence*? And does this latter have any aim other than to allow for the *dissolution* of units of all kinds secreted, so to speak, by this something that has no more precise a name than 'culture'?

Nevertheless, Michel Foucault can recognize, in the dispersion of events, 'a play of relations', 'a set of rules', which are themselves presented as founded in the *unicity* of a system defining the set of historical conditions of possibility for these events.

It appears to us that this sequence, (1) Units or Unities, (2) Singularity, (3) Unicity, (or terms that are equivalent), now forms a system, carries out a procedure (2 processes 1 in order to produce 3), and allows the following postulates to be presented as theses: [44]

1. Event and statement belong together, with every event appearing as a statement in 'the space of discourse'.
2. In the set of statements, which is finite in principle, every statement is irreplaceable.

If these postulates were made explicit, the question would still remain of knowing what permits the four 'rules of formation' to belong together, or to correspond to 'discursive formations' and to 'positivities'. Is it not the case that a principle of coherence is presupposed here, one that reduces the event in its pure emergence to the status of an element in the 'unconscious of the thing said'? Must we use the term '*Epoch*' to designate the system that allows us to make diverse events relevant, whether or not they are recorded?

Taking this one step further, would the abandonment of the principle of coherence entail as a consequence the genuine independence of the 'non-discursive event'? And do we not have to suppose that each time an event is taken up again as a statement and serves as an element in the set of knowledge, there is an irreducible remainder that limits the claims of a 'pure description of the facts of discourse', and which necessarily implies an articulation of knowledge upon that which it cannot integrate?

ON THE UNTHOUGHT

Finally, we will conclude with what seems to us to be the major discrepancy [*écart*] in the 'Response' with regard to what we had understood of Foucault's thought.

Since his axiom here is that *there is no unthought except that of rules*, he bars himself from speaking of the unthought of a statement or of a discourse: such an unthought will only ever be *another* statement, *another* discourse.

Must then the critique of continuity (of the book, of the work, of history as a whole, or of a formation that covers it, as metaphysics does for Heidegger) henceforth exclude the possibility that a statement might be produced *in order* to take the place of another? That is to say: in order to prevent it from appearing, in order to *repress it*?

And yet, recognition that a discourse can come to the surface in order to repress another one beneath it strikes us as the definitive achievement of psychoanalysis.

After the 'Response to the C   le d'Épistémologie', the question arises: *where* does Foucault stand now, in relation to Freud, and to Nietzsche?

Le Cercle d'Épistémologie

Michel Foucault has once again agreed to give a response to these questions. It will appear in a subsequent issue of the *Cahiers pour l'Analyse*.[6]

---

6   TN: The following issue of the *Cahiers*, no. 10, 'On Formalization', was the final issue of the journal and Foucault's response did not number among its contents.

CHAPTER NINE

Alain Badiou
Mark and Lack: On Zero[1]

[150] Epistemology breaks away from ideological recapture [*reprise*], in which every science comes to mime its own reflection, insofar as it excludes that recapture's institutional operator, the notion of Truth, and proceeds instead according to the concept of a mechanism of production, whose effects, by contrast, one seeks to explain through the theory of its structure.

What of an epistemology of logic?

The representation of this discipline within the network of ideological designators presents it as something foreign to the real, as a discourse that presupposes the positing [*position*] of Truth rather than the construction of an object. This is what Frege abruptly declares when he likens a proposition to a proper name whose reference, or denotation, is the True, or the False. It follows from this that logic incessantly coordinates as many linked inscriptions as necessary in order for it to pass from one invariable name-of-the-True to another: thus logic here becomes *the scriptural indefiniteness of truth's civil status* [*l'indéfini scriptural d'un état civil de la vérité*].[2]

On the basis of all this one can in fact demonstrate – as Jacques Lacan and Jacques-Alain Miller undertake to do – that, as something which can be known under several names, the True falls beneath its names, while nonetheless preserving its civil status through the iteration that, at its perpetual birth, has us ceaselessly registering its new anonymous names. The nominal movement, the repetitive compulsion that, in the chain of propositions, unravels our disbelief in the True's common patronym, marks nothing but the lack over which this movement glides without resistance or success.[3]

To this twofold process (preservation of the True; convocation and marking of lack), we will oppose the stratification of the scientific signifier.

---

1   TN: First published as Alain Badiou, 'Marque et manque: à propos de zéro', CpA 10.8 (winter 1969): 150–173. Translated by Zachary Luke Fraser with Ray Brassier.

2   Cf. Gottlob Frege, 'On Sense and Nominatum', in *Readings in Philosophical Analysis*, ed. Herbert Feigl and Wilfrid Sellars (New York: Appleton-Century-Crofts, 1949), 85–102. 'Every declarative sentence, in which what matters are the nominata of the words, is therefore to be considered as a proper name; and its nominatum, if there is any, is either the True or the False' (91). '[A]ll true sentences have the same nominatum, and likewise all false ones' (92).

3   TN: The French reads: '*Le mouvement nominal, la compulsion répétitive où se déploie l'impuissance à croire tenir jamais le patronyme usuel du Vrai, c'est la marque même, dans la séquence liée des propositions, de ce qui n'est qu'un manque sur quoi elle glisse sans résistance ni succès.*'

In our view, *both* Frege's ideological representation of his own enterprise *and* the recapture of this representation in the lexicon of Signifier, lack and the place-of-lack, mask the pure productive essence, the [151] positional process through which logic, as machine, lacks nothing it does not produce elsewhere.

The logic of the Signifier[4] is a metaphysics: a representation of representation, an intra-ideological process and progression.

I TRIPLE ARTICULATION OF THE LOGICAL PROCESS

The theory of logic pertains to the modes of production of a division in linear writing or inscription: the dichotomy of a structured set of statements which have been 'introduced' into the final mechanism as an (already processed) raw material.

The immediate consequence of this is that the sole requirement that the functioning of the mechanism must satisfy is that ultimately something must be *cut* in an effective fashion: the inscriptions [*écritures*] must be mechanically separated into two disjoint [*disjointes*] classes, which, by allusion to the mechanism most frequently employed, are called the class of derivable statements and the class of non-derivable statements respectively.

The classical definition of the *absolute consistency* of a system, according to which at least one well-formed expression not be derivable within it, designates precisely this minimal requirement. Its infraction would be tantamount to considering a mechanism that produces nothing at all – production in this instance being just the effective division of those materials on which one is operating.

On closer inspection, it becomes clear that this final division implies the successive operation of three intricated mechanisms: before they can be allocated [to the class of derivable or non-derivable statements], the syntagms must be *formed*, then *sorted*, since no derivational system is capable of submitting all of them to its principle of division. (This just means that every specialized machine has an input [*entrée*] into which only specific and previously processed materials can be introduced).

We must therefore distinguish the mechanisms of *concatenation*, *formation*, and *derivation*.

Any occlusion of the autonomy of the second mechanism – relative to the third – entails losing the very essence, i.e. the productive function, of the logical

---

4   By 'logic of the Signifier', we mean here the system of concepts through which the articulation of the subject is conceived: Lack, Place, Placeholder, Suture, Foreclosure, Splitting. These concepts have been produced by Jacques Lacan and we acknowledge a definitive debt to him even as we engage in the process that circumscribes their use: this is the critical procedure.

The thesis we are defending here aims only at delineating the impossibility of a logic of the Signifier that would envelop the scientific order and in which the erasure of the epistemological break would be articulated.

process.[5] And nothing is more important than to traverse the machineries of logic in their proper order.

(a) Concatenation: The absolutely primary raw material of the logical process [152] is supplied by a particular sphere of technical production: writing. This consists of a stock of graphic marks, separable and indecomposable, forming a finite (or at most, denumerable) set, a set we will call the 'alphabet'.

The first mechanism 'receives' these marks, from which it composes *finite sequences* (linear juxtapositions which may include repetitions). It is set up to produce all the finite sequences of this sort, and so it is these that we find in the output of this mechanism. Let S be this product.

(b) Formation: The second mechanism operates on S, so as to effect, step by step, a *perfect dichotomy*, one that separates without remainder those sequences the machine 'accepts' from those that it rejects. We will call those sequences accepted by the machine 'well-formed expressions', and the others 'ill-formed'.[6]

The operators (the 'components') of this mechanism are *the rules of formation*, which prescribe certain configurations as acceptable concatenations: thus, for example, the machine known as 'the predicate calculus with equality' will accept the sequences *I(x, x)* and *not-I(x, x)*, but will reject the sequence *x(I, x)*.

Through a dangerous semantic laxity, the rejected statements are often called 'non-sense'.

The set of rules of formation constitutes the syntax.

Let us note straightaway that if, as Gödel's celebrated theorem indicates, the final dichotomy (that of the third mechanism) cannot, for a 'strong' machine, be effectuated without remainder[7] – since there are always *undecidable* state-

---

5   The privileged operator of this occlusion is the concept of meaning or sense [*sens*], to which both the origination of the True (derivability) and the rejection of non-sense (syntax-formation) refer back.

6   That the division be without remainder means that given any inscription whatsoever (i.e. a finite sequence of signs of the alphabet), there exists an actual procedure that permits one to determine *unambiguously* whether the expression does or does not conform to the rules of the syntax.

For classical logics, this syntactic property can be made the object of a recursive demonstration over the number of parentheses in the expression. Cf. Stephen Cole Kleene, *Introduction to Metamathematics* (Amsterdam: North Holland Publishing Co., 1964), 72 and *passim*.

7   A strong machine is one capable of partitioning the inscriptions of recursive arithmetic.

Note that there exists a weak but *perfect* logical mechanism: the Propositional Calculus. This system is indeed:

– Consistent in every sense of the term;

– Decidable (for every well-formed expression, it can be mechanically known whether or not it is derivable);

– Complete (every well-formed expression is either derivable or such that to add it to the axioms would render the calculus inconsistent);

– Categorical (all of its models are isomorphic).

The mere existence of this Calculus presents several problems for the logic of the Signifier, since it contains nothing – not even an empty place – that would attest to a lack. In all rigour, this

ments – the very possibility of this result *presupposes the existence of a dichotomic mechanism that leaves no remainder*: the one which supplies the demonstrative mechanism with its raw material, the well-formed expressions. Only on the condition of a perfect syntax can we summon derivation's aporiae.

The split signifying order, marked by what it lacks, can be exhibited [153] only in its difference from an autonomous order that is indeed closed, which is to say, entirely decidable (the order of the formation of syntagms). In this sense, we cannot maintain that scission or compulsive iteration is the inevitable price of closure. What must be said, instead, is that the existence of an infallible closed mechanism conditions the existence of a mechanism that can be said to be unclosable, and therefore internally limited.

The exhibition of a suture presupposes the existence of a foreclosure.

Now, theoretical anticipations aside, what needs to be remembered at this point is that what we find in the output of the syntactic mechanism is the set of well-formed expressions, which we will call E.

(c) Derivation: The third mechanism operates on E and, in general, is set up to produce:

1. A perfect dichotomy between Theses (or derivable statements) and non-Theses (non-derivable statements).
2. A certain type of functional relation between these two divided halves.

This second condition is crucial. If dichotomy was the only requirement then the classical logical mechanisms (the formalization of arithmetic, for example) would be flawless, since all of these mechanisms do indeed separate well-formed expressions without remainder into the derivable and the non-derivable, i.e. into theses (T) and non-theses (NT).[8]

An undecidable statement, such as the one constructed by Gödel, is obviously not a statement that would be neither provable [*démontrable*] nor

---

system lacks nothing; nor does it mark the nothing of which it is already too much to say that it is even lacking.

One could say that the perfection of the Propositional Calculus provides the intra-logical, differential referent for the relative 'imperfection' of other systems.

8   It is an entirely *different* question to determine whether or not there exists for every well-formed expression a mechanical (effective) procedure that would allow us to know 'in advance' (i.e. without having to carry out the derivation) whether or not it is derivable.

The existence of such a procedure defines the *decidability* of a system. We know (Church, Kleene) that sufficiently strong logical mechanisms are generally undecidable.

We should not confuse *the decidability of a system* with the existence or non-existence of a statement such that neither it nor its negation are derivable. The problem of the existence of an undecidable statement is not a problem of decidability, but a problem of *completeness*.

A system may be decidable and yet incomplete: there then exist in it (undecidable) statements concerning which it is possible to 'decide' in advance, through an actual procedure, that they are neither derivable nor refutable. The converse, however, is not true: an important meta-mathematical theorem ties the undecidability results (Church) to the incompleteness results (Gödel). If a (sufficiently strong) formal system is undecidable, then it is either inconsistent or incomplete.

unprovable (which would be meaningless). On the contrary, the heart of Gödel's proof consists in the demonstration that such a statement *is not* provable. It is therefore clearly assigned to one of the two halves.

An undecidable statement is not the remainder of a cut, but a statement which is such that neither it nor its negation is derivable. Such a statement is certainly *irrefutable* (refutation = proof of the negation). But it is explicitly unprovable. There is indeed a division without remainder between derivable and non-derivable statements – but both Gödel's statement and its negation end up in *the same division*.

Everything depends here upon a special syntactic operator and the structure which it governs: the operator of negation. [**154**]

We cannot therefore take Gödel's theorem to mean that every dichotomy leaves a remainder, or that every duality implies a disjoint third term, one that would be de-centred relative to the rule that internally orders each term of the pair. This (common) reading of the theorem is a metaphysical import. In reality, the problem pertains to the particular structural conditions imposed on the third logical mechanism, over and above its separative function – this is summed up above in our condition 2.

What is required is as follows: in the alphabet, there needs to be an operator (it can be negation [symbolized as ~] or any other: the intuitive meaning of negation is an obstacle here) such that if a statement belongs to one division ($t \in$ T or $t \in$ NT), then the statement obtained by applying to it the operator (i.e. ~)[9] will be in the other division (~$t \in$ NT or ~$t \in$ T).

What is originally at issue here is not the cut as such, but a function relating the separated halves. The Gödelian limit does not bear on the dichotomy as such. Rather, it concerns the unity-of-correspondence of the disjoint parts.

Gödel's statement signifies: let there be a functional relation that sends each statement to its negation ($t \ldots$ ~t). There is no effective dichotomy that cuts through *all* of those relations.

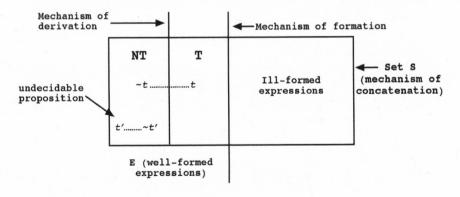

---

9   In conformity with common usage, we will use the symbol ~ to denote the function of negation throughout the remainder of this exposition.

One might hope to expel *from T* (the set of derivable statements) all the relations *t* . . . *~t*; otherwise, the system would be inconsistent. But one can then go on to show that some of these relations will always remain in NT: precisely those which concern undecidable statements.

What we are faced with here is a tearing of structure rather than a dichotomy. The key to the limitation [*limitation*] follows paradoxically from the fact that the separating mechanism is forced *not to be* perfect, and thus forced to preserve the concept of a reversible *relation* between the two halves. As a result, this limitation, far from attesting that the space produced by the division bears the trace of the tear that caused it, shows rather that one cannot indefinitely produce the sign of the latter within it; that in certain places the trace is effaced; that a strong mechanism [155] necessitates a complete division in rejection it effects, in each of its parts, of certain marks of the old Whole [*Tout*].

The undecidable is not the suturation of lack but *the foreclosure of what is lacking* through the failure to produce, within what is derivable, the whole of the non-derivable as negated.

The limitation means: that there exists at some point, between the parts T and NT, a *distance without concept*: one that delineates, in the space of non-theses, a statement whose negation cannot be inscribed within the space of theses, and which is therefore unrelated to this space. Gödel's theorem is not the site of separation's failure, but of its greatest efficacy.[10]

If, therefore, the theorems of 'limitation' result from the conditions of imperfection assigned to the dichotomic mechanism, we must reconfigure [*remanier*] the concept of the latter so as to incorporate those conditions. We will then say:

Logic is a triply articulated system (concatenation, syntax, derivation) that produces a terminal division in linear inscription such that, given a suitable syntagm, we should be able:

1. To allocate it to one of the two halves (T or NT);
2. To construct a syntagm obtained mechanically from the first by the addition of a functor (generally called negation), such that if the first is in one division, the second will be in the other.

Condition (1) is ideally[11] satisfied by classical mechanisms (set theory or the formalization of arithmetic). The second is satisfied only by weak mechanisms: a strong mechanism cuts *all too well.*

---

10   We will abstain from any attempt to decipher the status of the hiatus between intuitionism and formalism in Gödel's theorem. On this point, see our appendix on Smullyan's demonstration, and our critique of the concept of limitation.

11   'Ideally' because although it is true that every well-formed expression is either in T or NT, the existence of an 'effective' (recursive, algorithmic) procedure that would allow us to determine into which of these two classes it falls is shown to be impossible in many instances. This is the problem of the decidability *of the system* (cf. note 8).

II NULLITY OF THE THING – IDENTITY OF MARKS

This description of the logical mechanism allows us to question the construction of the concept of suture in this domain, and allows us to precisely determine the meta-theoretic function of the zero.

Let us declare our theses at the outset:

1. The concept of identity holds only for marks. Logic never has recourse to any self-identical *thing*, even when 'thing' is understood in the sense of the object of scientific discourse.

2. The concept of truth is an ideological designator, both recapitulating and concealing the scientific concepts of selection and division. It designates globally what is, itself, a differentiated mechanism.

3. The zero is not *the mark of lack* in a system, but the sign [156] that abbreviates the *lack of a mark*. Or rather: it is the indication, within a signifying order, that there is an inscription present in the rejected division of another order.

4. The logico-mathematical signifier is sutured only to itself. It is indefinitely *stratified*.

5. In logic, a lack that *is* not a signifier *has* no signifier: it is foreclosed.

6. The signifier in general is not articulated to lack through the concept of suture, whose purchase demands that the signifier satisfy a certain condition. And the construction of that condition is not the task of psychoanalysis but of historical materialism: only the *ideological* signifier is sutured.

Like Lacan's accounts of Gödel's theorem and the semantics of implication, Jacques-Alain Miller's discussions of Frege[12] and Boole are ambiguous in that they combine, simultaneously and indistinctly, what pertains to the effective construction of a logical mechanism with what pertains to the (ideological) discourse through which logicians represent their constructions to themselves.

Consequently, we should be wary of comprehending *within* the logical process itself any translation of the signs' connective agency back into the lexicon of subsumption. This notion, enclosed in the (specular) referential relation, like the related notion of denotation, masks the strictly functional essence of the mappings [*renvois*] at work inside logical mechanism.

Nothing here warrants the title of '*object*'. Here the thing is null: no inscription can objectify it.

Within this mechanical space, one finds nothing but reversible *functions* from system to system, from mark to mark – nothing but the mechanical dependencies of mechanisms. Semantics itself enters into logic only insofar as it operates between two logico-mathematical signifying orders, and on condi-

---

12   Cf. Jacques-Alain Miller, 'Suture', CpA 1.3.

tion that the functions of correspondence between these two orders are themselves logico-mathematical.[13]

Neither thing nor object have the slightest chance here of acceding to any existence beyond their exclusion without trace.

It follows that the Leibnizian requirement of self-identity, which is necessary in order to preserve truth, is intra-logical (theoretical) only insofar as it pertains to the identity of marks. It postulates, on the basis of an inaugural confidence in the permanence of graphemes [*graphies*], that there exists an 'identical' application of the signifying order to itself, one that preserves its structure. [157]

Moreover, it is science as a whole that takes self-identity to be a predicate of marks rather than of the object. This rule certainly holds for those *facts of writing* proper to Mathematics. But it also holds for those *inscriptions of energy* proper to physics. As Bachelard has admirably demonstrated, the only properly physical rule of substitution concerns artificial operators: 'The principle of the identity of instruments is the true principle of identity in every experimental science.'[14] It is the technical invariance of traces and instruments that subtracts all ambiguity from the substitution of terms.

Thus determined, the rule of self-identity allows of no exceptions and tolerates no evocation of what evades it, not even in the form of rejection. What is not substitutable-for-itself is something radically unthought, of which the logical mechanism *bears no trace*. It is impossible to turn it into an evanescence, a shimmering oscillation, as Frege does when he phantasmatically (ideologically) convokes then revokes the thing that is not self-identical in order to summon the zero. What is not substitutable-for-itself is foreclosed without appeal or mark.

Yet a homonymous predicate can indeed be constructed within logical systems: there exist 'calculi of identity' in which non-identity is marked.

In order to avoid the slippages of language, let us agree to give the name 'equality' to such a homonymous predicate, which we will denote by $I(x,y)$ (ordinarily, this would be read as: x is identical to y).

---

13   We believe Alonzo Church is right to identify Semantics with Syntax in the last instance (cf. his *Introduction to Mathematical Logic* [Princeton: Princeton University Press, 1956], 65: 'These assignments of denotations and values to the well-formed formulas may be made as abstract correspondences, so that their treatment belongs to theoretical syntax').

Semantics becomes *logical* (scientific) only when it is *the syntax of the difference between syntaxes*.

TN: For a more extended treatment of the relation between syntax and semantics, see Alain Badiou, *The Concept of Model* [1969], ed. Zachary Luke Fraser and Tzuchien Tho, trans. Zachary Luke Fraser (Melbourne: re.press, 2007).

14   Gaston Bachelard, *L'Activité rationaliste de la physique contemporaine* (Paris: PUF, 1951), 5.

We are going to show that the customary homonymy dissimulates a relation of presupposition that exhibits, again, the priority of the foreclosed [*du forclos*].

Consider for example a first-order calculus (one in which it is impossible to quantify over predicates): the predicative *constant* of equality I is implicitly defined by way of two axioms:[15]

I(x,x) (Total reflexivity)
I(x,y) $\supset$ [A(x) $\supset$ A(y)]

It might be thought that the axiom of reflexivity formulates within the inscriptions of the calculus (in the output of the syntactic mechanism) the fundamental self-identity of any letter at all. But this is not the case: what we have agreed to call the self-equality of a variable *is not* the self-identity of every mark. The best proof of this is that this equality allows for the construction of its negation: ~I(x,x) is a well-formed expression of the system, a legible expression.

Yet it would be wrong to imagine that ~I(x,x) (which should be read as: x is not equal – or identical – to itself) *marks* within the system, or positions within the mechanism, the unthinkable non-self-identity of the sign, and that such a (well-formed) expression organizes the suturing of the unthinkable to the calculus. On the contrary, far from marking the unthought, the [**158**] signifying existence of ~I(x,x) presupposes its functioning *without a mark*: it is necessary that one be *unable* to conceive that x, qua mark, is 'other' than x – the same mark placed elsewhere – in order for this statement to be logically produced. The mere convocation-revocation of x's non-self-identity, the shimmering of its self-differing, would suffice to annihilate the scriptural existence of the entire calculus, and particularly of expressions such as ~I(x,x), in which x occurs twice.

The production of the logical concepts of equality and self-inequality presupposes the foreclosure of what is scripturally non-self-identical. The lack of the equal is built upon the *absolute* absence of the non-identical.

No doubt the structure of a calculus of identity generally implies the derivation of the thesis ~~I(x,x):[16] it is false that x should not be equal to x.

---

15   In a second order calculus, in which one can quantify over predicates, equality would be defined explicitly, in conformity with the Leibnizian doctrine of indiscernibles, which is restricted here to the order of signs: two individual variables falling without exception under all the same predicates can be substituted everywhere, since there is nothing to mark their difference. In classical notation:

I(x,y) $=_{df}$ ($\forall a$)[$a(x) \supset a(y)$].

16   TN: The *Cahiers* text has '~I(x,x)' rather than '~~I(x,x)', but it is clear from the context that this is a misprint. As Badiou remarks, it is *false* that x should be unequal to x. The negation in the formula should therefore be double.

But as far as lack is concerned, this 'negation' marks nothing but the rejection of (or presence in) the other division (that of non-theses) of the statement ~I(x,x), which has been produced identically by the syntactic mechanism. No absence is convoked here that would be anything but the allocation to one class rather than to its complement – according to the positive rules of a mechanism – of what this mechanism receives from the productions of another.

This allows us to relate, without ideological infiltration, the concept of identity to the concept of truth.

Nothing transpires here of the thing or its concept.

But the statement 'truth is',[17] a purely expedient designation of an operational complex, signifies, so far as identity and equality are concerned:[18]

Identity: The relation that logic bears towards writing is such that it receives from the latter only those marks that have been certified by the signifying chain as capable of being substituted for themselves everywhere. In truth, this means any mark whatsoever, whose invariable recognition is rooted in the (external) technique of graphemes.

Equality: There exists a signifying order (a mechanism of derivation), whose selective constraints are such that the statements I(x,x) and ~I(x,x) are sent to two different divisions.

If, from a perspective that is more strictly that of mathematical logic, one wishes to consider the product of mechanism-3 as the set of derivable theses, one can say: the mechanism is set up in such a way that it produces I(x,x) and rejects ~I(x,x).

But these two inscriptions have already been produced in *the same division* (that of well-formed expressions) by a mechanism-2 (a syntax). Only on this basis is it possible to give any sense to the rejection of one of the two by the mechanism of derivation.

What is not equal-to-itself is only excluded here on condition of having to be placed within an autonomous signifying order, sedimentarily organized 'beneath' the one which no longer has a place for it.

To maintain at all costs, in this point, the correlation between the equal-to-itself and the true would be to say: truth is the system of constraints [159] which differentiate the mechanism-3, producing the single statement I(x,x) from mechanism-2, which produces I(x,x) and ~I(x,x) simultaneously.

The equal-to-itself as salvation of truth comes down to no more than a difference, thanks to a withdrawn effect [*par effet retiré*], between syntax and

---

17   TN: This is a reference to the article 'Suture', where Miller writes, after Leibniz: 'Truth is. Each thing is identical to itself' (CpA 1.3:43).

18   TN: The French reads '*Mais "la vérité est", pure désignation commode d'un complexe opératoire, signifie, s'il faut y pointer l'identité et l'égalité:*'.

derivation, between raw material and product. More precisely: a difference between two selection mechanisms, where the second is finer than the first.

III MARK OF LACK OR LACKING MARK?

We can now hazard the Zero.

To introduce it by way of a definition, the symbol zero is an abbreviator, standing for an inscription produced by a mechanism-2.[19] It is an *abstraction* (the construction of a one-place predicate) over a relation.

Let us provisionally adopt Frege's 'set-theoretical' language.

Given any relation between individual variables, say $R(x,y)$, it is possible to construct the class of all x satisfying $R(x,x)$, and to consider membership in this class as a property or predicate: the predicate 'to be linked to itself by the relation R'. One has thereby carried out *the abstraction of reflexivity over the relation R*.

Let us denote this new predicate $Ar \cdot R$. $Ar \cdot R(x)$ 'signifies': x has the property of being linked to itself by the relation R.

These considerations, which rest on an 'intuitive' concept of class, must now be abandoned, since they are foreign to the logical mechanism: they pertain only to the ideological pedagogy of the system.

In truth, all we have is a syntactic rule immanent to M_2, which allows us to:

(a) Construct, on the basis of a *two*-place predicate (R), the accepted inscription $Ar \cdot R$.

(b) To treat this inscription exactly like any other *one*-place predicate (which, for example, allows us to write $Ar \cdot R(x)$, etc.).

Abstraction here is therefore a rule that allows the mechanical formation of a one-place predicate from a two-place predicate.

Naturally, this abstraction can be carried out on the relation $I(x,y)$, which we have called the relation of identity. Since $I(x,x)$ is precisely one of the axioms of the calculus of identity, the M_3 of this calculus will trivially derive the statement $(\forall x)(Ar \cdot I(x))$, i.e.: every x is linked to itself by the relation I.

But the abstraction of reflexivity can just as well be carried out over the relation of inequality, $\sim I(x,y)$, since this inscription is produced by M_2.

We thereby obtain *one* of the possible definitions of the *zero predicate*:

$$0 = Ar \cdot \sim I$$

[160] $0(x)$ could then be read as: x is a zero, it has the property of not being equal to itself.

---

19   We will henceforth designate as M_1 M_2 and M_3 the mechanisms of concatenation, of syntax (of the predicate calculus), and of derivation (idem) respectively.

Satisfying $0(x)$ – being a zero – will in no way prevent the sign x, or the sign 0, from being everywhere substitutable for themselves: they remain identical, even where they support or name non-equality (or non-identity) to self.[20]

To say that the zero, so defined, 'aims at' ['*vise*'] a non-self identical object, or that it is the predicate of the void, convokes a metaphysical reading of Being and its Plenitude precisely at that point where only substitutions of inscriptions obtain.

For the inscription $\sim I(x,x)$ does not occupy the place of anything else; nor does it mark the place of a nothing.

As for the zero, it occurs at every place occupied by that to which scriptural convention has declared it equivalent: $Ar \cdot \sim I$. It is positively constructed by M_2.

We will call mechanism-4 the logical system that adds to M_3 the predicative *constant* (the proper name) 0, as it has been defined above. Of what lack could this addition be the mark, in the signifying order thus designated?

M_3, as we have seen, *rejects* the inscription $\sim I(x,x)$, and *derives* the inscription $I(x,x)$. Must we not consider that the predicate zero *marks* within the non-rejected division of M_4 what has been rejected in M_3? Is it not the predicate satisfied by 'no' term?

In truth, such descriptions are foreign to logical theory. The zero is simply an inscription accepted by M_2 and introduced, along with certain directions for use, in M_4.

If one nevertheless wants to think the zero's link to the non-figuration of $\sim I(x,x)$ in the derivation of M_3, a somewhat allegorical use of concepts is necessary. But it is acceptable to say: The zero marks in M_4 (in predicative form) not the *lack of a term* satisfying a relation but rather a *relation lacking* in M_3, the relation $\sim I(x,x)$. We must nevertheless add: if the relation can be lacking in M_3, it is *only insofar as it figures in M_2*.

Play of appearances and disappearances between successive signifying orders; never exposed to the convocation of a lack, whether in the object or the thing.

---

20   Some might find it surprising that we have here constructed the zero not as a term but as a *predicate*.

But it is Jacques-Alain Miller whom we must question about his reiteration of Frege's failure to distinguish between individual and predicative variables. For Frege, certainly, a predicate is a term. But this position is untenable, for it gives rise to Russell's paradox, which would eventually ruin Frege's formal arithmetic.

Miller's text, however, does not integrate the *theoretical inconsistency* of Frege's construction of number into its own *metatheoretical employment* of the latter. There results an epistemological equivocation, dissipated only if one distinguishes the level of functioning proper to each *mention* of Frege's (confused) text. Namely:

(a) A theoretical attempt to construct the finite cardinals.

(b) The theoretical errors in this attempt (the non-stratification of variables).

(c) The ideological re-presentation of the theoretical [*du théorique*] (denotation, concept, number of concept, etc.).

(d) The ideological re-presentation of these theoretical errors (theory of the zero).

System of differences between systems, ruled by substitutions, [161] equivalences, and withdrawals: *lacking mark, never mark of lack.*[21]

It is not a blank space whose place the zero names, but *the erasure of a trace*: it leaves visible beneath its mark (A$r \cdot \sim$I) *the other* mark ($\sim$I(x,x)), as rejected by derivation.

The zero is the mark (in M_4) of a mark (in M_2) that is lacking (in M_3).

On this side of the signifying chain, if the latter is scientific, there are nothing but other chains. If the signifier is sutured, it is only to itself. It is only itself that it lacks at each of its levels: it regulates its lacks without taking leave of itself. The scientific signifier is neither sutured nor split, but stratified.[22] And stratification repeals the axiom by which Miller, in another text,[23] characterized foreclosure: the lack of a lack is also a lack. No, not if that which comes to be lacking was always already marked: then the productive difference of strata suffices to name the interstice. The *halting points* are always prescribed.

IV THE TORMENT OF PHILOSOPHY

Must we therefore renounce [*annuler*] the concept of suture? It is, on the contrary, a matter of prescribing its function by assigning to it its proper domain.

From the fact that there exists a signifying order, namely science (stratified in such a way that no lack is marked in it that does not refer to another mark in a subjacent order differentiated from the first), an exception results. Science does not fall under the concept of the logic of the signifier. In truth, it is the fact that it does not fall under this logic that constitutes it: the epistemological break must be thought under the un-representable auspices of de-suturation.

Accordingly, *there is no subject of science*. Infinitely stratified, regulating its passages, science is pure space [*l'espace pure*], without inverse or mark or place of that which it excludes.

---

21   TN: '*marque manquante, jamais marque du manque*'.

22   Ramified calculi (the various instances of the theory of types) attempt to reduce stratification to a single stratum, via the construction of a *logic of stratification* that would 'express' the *stratification of logic*.

The inevitable axiom of *reducibility* indicates a certain failure of this endeavour (see for example, Wilfred Quine, 'On the Axiom of Reducibility', *Mind* 45 [1936], 498–500).

Hao Wang's 'expansive' system, Σ, is rather a *constructive traversal* of stratification. It is no less exposed to considerable difficulties concerning the construction of the ordinals. Cf. for example Wang, *A Survey of Mathematical Logic* (Peking: Science Press, 1964), 559ff., especially 643.

For our part, we are convinced that the stratified multiplicity of the scientific signifier, which is inherent to the process of scientific production, is irreducible to any of its orders. The space of marks does not allow itself to be projected onto a plane. And this is a resistance (or limitation) only from the viewpoint of a *metaphysical* want [*vouloir*]. Science wants the transformation-traversal of a stratified space, not its reduction [*rabattement*].

23   Miller, 'L'Action de la structure', CpA 9:6.

Foreclosure, but of nothing, science may be called the psychosis of no subject, and hence of all: universal by right, shared delirium, one has only to maintain oneself within it in order to [162] be no-one, anonymously dispersed in the hierarchy of orders.

Science is the Outside witho   a blind-spot.[24]

Conversely, the signifying structure defined by suturation can be designated in its particularity (as that which places lack), primarily as non-science. Thus the concept of suture is not a concept of the signifier in general, but rather the characteristic property of the signifying order wherein the subject comes to be barred – namely, *ideology*.

There is always a subject of ideology, for this is the very mark by which we recognize the latter. Place of lack, splitting of the closed: these are the concepts on whose basis we can elaborate the law governing the functioning of ideological discourse.

We should take the measure of what is at stake here, the possibility of articulating Historical Materialism and Psychoanalysis: the former producing the Schema [*Topique*] of particular signifying orders (ideologies), the latter producing the structures of their efficacy, the laws of entry [*entrée*] and connection through which the places allocated by ideology are ultimately occupied.

When Historical Materialism claims to be able to elucidate subjective enslavement to ideologies on its own, or when psychoanalysis effaces the specificity of the place where it must uncover the mark of lack in the generality of a logic of the signifier, then these disciplines are collapsed and reduced to one another. They become un-stratified: un-scientific.

We need to insist, then, that psychoanalysis has *nothing to say* about science, even if it can teach us a great deal about the scientists who serve it. Through this silence, psychoanalysis negatively determines the signifier of which it speaks, and in which it articulates Desire. Historical materialism provides a positive redoubling of this determination by producing the structural configuration in which ideological agency takes place.

Accordingly, to claim that the science/ideology difference could be effaced through a logic of oscillating iteration, and to nominate [*nommer*] a subject of

---

24   If one wants to exhibit writing as such, and to excise its author; if one wants to follow Mallarmé in enjoining the written work to occur with neither subject nor Subject, there is a way of doing this that is radical, secular, and exclusive of every other: by entering into the writings of science, whose law consists precisely in this.

But when literary writing, delectable no doubt but obviously freighted with the marks of everything it denies, presents itself to us as something standing on its own in the scriptural Outside, we *know* in advance (this is a decidable problem . . .) that it merely sports the *ideology* of difference, rather than exhibiting its real process.

Those writers who balk at the prospect of taking up mathematics should limit their agendas to the honourable principle of their own productions: to be *ideology exposed*, and thereby irreducibly sutured, even if autonomous.

science, is to preclude the possibility of conjoining, though their very disjunction, Marx and Freud.

To deploy the concept of suture in the very place where it is inadequate (mathematics), and to conclude that this concept enjoys a universal legitimacy over discourses by exploiting scientists' conflation of their own activity (science) with its (ideological) re-presentation, is to reflect science in ideology: it is to de-stratify it so as to prescribe to it its lack. [163]

We will call 'philosophy' the ideological region specializing in science, the one charged with *effacing* the break by *displaying* the scientific signifier as a regional paradigm of the signifier-in-itself: this is Plato's relation to Eudoxus, Leibniz's relation to Leibniz, Kant's relation to Newton, Husserl's relation to Bolzano and Frege, and perhaps Lacan's relation to Mathematical Logic.

Science, as we have shown, is that which relates only to itself, the multiple outside. No signifying order can envelop the strata of its discourse.

Whence the recurrent impossibility of philosophy, whose polymorphous historicity attests to the fact that the law of ideology is well and truly operative in it: philosophy transmits and insists the mark of its lack.[25]

And what does it lack? The effacement of the break presupposes the intra-philosophical construction of a concept of science. Philosophy is compelled to mark, within its own order, the scientific signifier as a *total* space. But science, indefinitely stratified, multiple foreclosure, difference of differences, cannot receive this mark. The multiplicity of its orders is irreducible:[26] that which, in philosophy, declares itself science, is invariably *the lack* of science. That which philosophy lacks, and that to which it is sutured, is its very object (science), which is nevertheless marked within the former by the place it will never come to occupy.

We can claim in all rigour that *science is the Subject of philosophy*, and this precisely because there is no Subject of science.

Taking up our invocation of Leibniz once more, this means that in order for ideology to be saved (i.e. the dominant class), the unclosable opening which science tears within it must be *placed* in it. Philosophy consummates itself in this placement.

This is why science and the practice of science will always torment philosophy. Summoning the multiple to its self-sufficiency, the game of science delights us with the lesson of its non-presence (unless it be as a symptom of its own lack)

---

25   TN: '*la philosophie véhicule et insiste la marque de son manque.*'

26   This is obviously not to say that regional 'syntheses', transferences [*transferts*], or intrications, are impossible. The history of the sciences thinks the *local connectivity* of strata, and the stratification of this connectivity.

Auguste Comte's greatness resides in his having seen that the multiplicity and hierarchy in the signifying order, whatever displacements and intersections might be engendered in it, were properties inherent to the concept of scientificity.

in philosophical discourse. Through science we learn that *there is* something un-sutured; something foreclosed, in which even lack is not lacking, and that by trying to show us the contrary, in the figure of Being gnawing at itself, haunted by the mark of non-being, philosophy exhausts itself trying to keep alive its supreme and specific product: God or Man, depending on the case.

Spinoza said so categorically.[27] Lautréamont too, [**164**] eulogizing mathematics with a sort of sacred delight:

O austere mathematics, I have not forgotten you, since your wise lessons, sweeter than honey, filtered into my heart like a refreshing wave (*Maldoror*, Book II).

And Lautréamont, divulging the key to his enthusiasm, adds splendidly: 'Without you in my struggle against man, I might have been defeated.'

In mathematics, there is indeed nothing lacking that is not already signifying [*signifiant*]: marks indefinitely substituted for one another in the complication of their entangled errancy.

Science is the veritable archi-theatre of writing: traces, erased traces, traces of traces; the movement where we never risk encountering this detestable figure of Man: the sign of nothing.

January, 1967

APPENDIX   GÖDEL'S THEOREM AND THE
ALTERNATING CHAIN OF SCIENCE-IDEOLOGY

With regard to which undertakings can Gödel's theorem be described as a *limitation*? There are, essentially, two:

(I) The (metaphysical) project which, following Hilbert, enjoins every formal system to seal itself around the internal statement of its own consistency.

Once subjected to this injunction, mathematics would no longer expose knowledge to the indefinite abyss in which it stacks its signifying orders: under the aegis of what Husserl called a 'nomological system', it would provide the constitutive charms [*maléfices constituants*] of philosophy with a language that is closed, unique, and self-norming; one which, itself immobile, would efface the wound which was historically opened within the weave of ideology by the *fact* of science.

To force the scientific signifier willingly to occupy the place where it is occluded – this is a nice trick, but one with which this signifier refuses to comply. We will see why.

27   In a famous text: Spinoza, *Ethics*, Book I, appendix. Man would never have ventured beyond illusion had it not been for this surprising *fact*: mathematics.

(II) The project which, by means of the completely controlled reconstruction of a logistical system, claims to exhaust what otherwise presents itself according to the opacity that results from a history: let us call this 'intuitive' arithmetic.

We have already indicated how the first requirement should be regarded. It admirably illustrates *philosophy's* failure to prescribe to mathematical inscriptions even the unity of a space of existence. It experiences stratification's resistance to the schemes of closure that philosophy has sought to impose upon the former for the sake of its own salvation. [**165**]

So it was for the Pythagoreans, those metaphysical architects of Number, in whose time the diagonal of the square represented a limitation: a limitation correlative to an *expectation* ordained by the position of the integer within the operational unlimitedness [*l'illimité*] of a Principle. It was this unlimitedness of principle whose extra-mathematical – i.e. ideological – significance was evinced by the warping of the irrational, which determined the difference of another stratum.

An occasion to insist that there are no, and that there cannot be, crises *in* science, since science is the pure affirmation of difference.

But that a crisis in the (ideological) *representation* of science can induce a (positive) reconfiguration of science itself should not surprise us, given that the material of science is, *in the last instance*, ideology, and that an 'a priori' science by definition deals only with those aspects of ideology which represent it in the latter: a science continually breaking with its own designation in representational space.

It remains for us to address the 'hiatus' that allegedly separates Formalism from Intuition, the former failing to derive all the truth of the latter.

Let us begin by noting that the sense of 'intuitive' at issue here should be defined as the historical state of a science, both in the received, familiar intricacy of its density, and the binding, lawful circulation of its inscriptions.

Thus the problem relates an entirely coded scriptural artifice to the immanence of a historico-institutional discourse living off the abbreviations, equivocations, and univocal smoothing of an inoffensive mass of 'normal' signifiers legitimated by custom and practice.

Let us also note that the paradox of which Gödel makes implicit use occurs in ordinary language in the ancient lesson of the Liar: a statement that exhausts itself in stating its own falsity.

Thus, 'limitation' here comes down to the possibility of constructing a *predicate of non-derivability* (call it ~D) in a formal language and applying this predicate to a *representative* of the statement formed by this very application. Call this ~D(n), where n 'represents' ~D(n) in a sense that demonstrates the proof.[28]

---

28   TN: 'Soit ~ D(n) où n, en un sens qui fait la preuve, "représente" ~ D(n).'

Gödel's theorem does not then express a hiatus so much as a *reprise*, within the system's architectonic transparency, of certain ambiguities produced in language by the (ideological) concept of Truth. If one tries to make the Derivable subsume the True, then like the latter the former operates as a snare at the ungraspable juncture between science and its outside.

Gödel's theorem is thus one of formalism's *fidelity* to the stratifications and connectivities at work in the history of the sciences, insofar as they *expel* from the latter every employment of the True as (unlimited) principle.

But we have to engage with it if we are to understand it. To this end, we are going to give a largely intuitive but nevertheless complete and rigorous demonstration of the essential core of a limitation theorem.

This demonstration is taken from Raymond M. Smullyan's *Theory of Formal Systems* (Princeton, 1961).

Our exposition is governed by pedagogical considerations: in principle, this proof requires *no* particular mathematical knowledge – but this does not mean that it can be read inattentively.

The exposition proper will be accompanied by parenthetical commentaries [in italics], which reduplicate its meaning, in a way that is often dangerously ideological. Their function is didactic. [**166**]

The handful of further remarks prefaced by a !! are not necessary for an understanding of the deduction, but serve to suture it to the discourse of those readers who, knowing a minimum of mathematics, might be justifiably tempted to move faster than I will here.

The structure of the demonstration is as follows:

I) *Description of the System*
   1. mechanism-2;
   2. numbering of the inscriptions produced by M_2 (*g* function);
   3. function of representation (φ function);
   4. mechanism-3;
   5. consistency.
II) *Diagonalization Lemma*
   1. diagonalization and W^* classes;
   2. Gödel statements;
   3. representation of a class of numbers by a predicate;
   4. diagonalization lemma.
III) *Condition for the Existence of an Undecidable Statement.*

(In what follows, results will be annotated according to this table: if, for example, the condition of consistency is evoked, it will be noted: (I,5)).

I DESCRIPTION OF THE SYSTEM

1) *Mechanism-2*

Let E designate the production of a mechanism-2 (a syntax), i.e. the set of well-formed expressions of a logical system.

We will suppose that the following inscriptions [*écritures*], among others, figure in this production:

Predicates *p*, the set of which we will call P.

Closed statements, the set of which we will call S.

(Let us note right away that these designations pertain to this demonstration's semantic legibility. But purely set-theoretical data would suffice here: E, P ⊂ E, S ⊂ E.)

2) *Numbering the expressions*

We are now going to give ourselves the set of integers, N, in its 'intuitive' sense, i.e. one that is recognizable to anyone familiar with the arithmetical tradition: 1, 2, 3, and so on.

And we are going to suppose that we have numbered all of the expressions in E. In other words, to every inscription $e \in$ E there corresponds an integer, noted $g(e)$; in addition, we will suppose that, reciprocally, every integer corresponds to one, and only one, expression in E.

!! We therefore posit the existence of a bi-univocal mapping *g* of E onto N.

(This step is essential; it inscribes the inscriptions of M_2 *as a denumerable infinity. If, moreover, our system 'formalizes' arithmetic, then it will be able to 'talk' about its own inscriptions, by 'talking' about the numbers which correspond to those inscriptions through the numbering function.)* [**167**]

3) *Function of Representation*

(We now want to make sense of the idea that our system is a strong one, i.e. that it operates on the inscriptions of arithmetic.

Intuitively – and vaguely – this could be taken to mean that the inscription formed by an expression and a number is a new expression, internal to the system. Or, if one prefers: that in applying or 'mapping' an expression onto a number, one obtains an inscription within the system, which thereby 'talks' about numbers.)

We are going to assume that there exists a function φ, which we will call 'the representation function', which associates the pair formed by an expression and an integer with another expression. Thus:

$$\varphi(e, n) = e'$$

(with $e \in E$, $n \in N$, $e' \in E$).

!! φ is therefore a mapping of $E \times N$ into E. We have:

$$(E \times N) \underset{\varphi}{\to} E \underset{g}{\to} N$$

(*The most interesting case is one where the expression e is a predicate: to put it intuitively, $\varphi(p,n)$ can 'express' the mapping from the 'property' p to the number n. And we should then be able to ask, without ambiguity, whether or not the expression $\varphi(p,n)$ is true; whether or not the number n has that property. It should therefore be possible to consider the expression $\varphi(p,n)$ as complete, i.e. as producing a univocally justifiable meaning for an evaluation.*)

We will posit that every expression $\varphi(p,n)$ is a *closed statement* (belongs to S; see I.1): $\varphi(p,n) \in S$.

4) Mechanism-3

That a mechanism-3 (of derivation or demonstration) operates upon the closed statements means:

– That there exists in S a set of expressions which we will call *provable*. Let D be this set ($D \subset S$).
  (S – D) therefore represents the set of unprovable statements.
– That there also exists in S a set R of *refutable* expressions. (R is thus the set of the expressions whose negation is provable.) ($R \subset S$)

(*We have revealed the two conditions that characterize a mechanism-3: dichotomy (derivable and non-derivable, D and S – D), and correspondence via negation, which gathers together the expressions whose negations can be derived (R).*

Gödel's problem, accordingly, consists in knowing whether every unprovable (closed) statement is refutable. Is it always the case that (S – D) = R ?

Our task is to establish the structural conditions that render this equation impossible.) [**168**]

5) Consistency

We want there to be no encroachment of the provable upon the refutable, which would amount to a contradiction. No expression should, therefore, simultaneously belong to both D and R: the system will be said to be *consistent* if the intersection of these two sets is void, i.e. if $D \cap S = \emptyset$.

!! At the level of generality at which we are operating, it is clearly possible to abstain from all interpretation, and say that we assume the following:

– E, P ⊂ E, S ⊂ E, R ⊂ S, D ⊂ S.
– R ∩ D = ∅.
– N, E $\underset{g}{\rightarrow}$ N (where g is bi-univocal onto).

– (E × N) $\underset{\varphi}{\rightarrow}$ E, with $(\forall p)(\forall n)[(p \in P, n \in N) \rightarrow \varphi(p,n) \in S]$.

II DIAGONALIZATION LEMMA

1) Diagonalization and W* Classes

Among expressions of the form $\varphi(e,n)$, there are some which are particularly interesting: those in which the number n is precisely the number $g(e)$ that 'numbers' [*numérote*] (see I.2) the expression e.

The expression $\varphi(e, g(e))$ is called the *diagonalization of e*.

(*This is the core of the proof: we 'map' the expression to the number that 'represents' it.*)

Let us now consider a set of expressions of E, any set whatsoever: call it W (so that we simply have W ⊂ E).

We will suppose that there are within W diagonal expressions of the form $\varphi(e, g(e))$. We are going to associate the class of *numbers* W* to the set *of expressions* W; this class W* will encompass all the numbers that number expressions whose diagonalization is in W.

For any number n, to belong to W* means that there exists an expression e, such that:

(a) $g(e) = n$ (n 'represents' e);
(b) $\varphi(e, g(e)) \in$ W (the diagonalization of e is in W).

Or again, using the classic symbol ↔ for equivalence:

$n \in$ W* ↔ $[n = g(e)]$ and $[\varphi(e, g(e)) \in$ W$]$

Naturally, if W contains no diagonal expressions, then W* is the empty class.

[169] We therefore have the following situation:

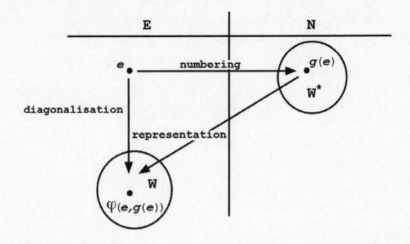

!! Let φ_d be the diagonal-function over E defined by: $\varphi_d(e) = \varphi(e, g(e))$. We then have: $W^* = g°\varphi_d{}^{-1}(W)$.

2) Gödel Statement for a Set of Expressions

The guiding idea is now to associate a set W of expressions with a (closed) *statement* which is such that its 'truth' depends on its position with respect to W – a statement, in other words, that is provable *if and only if it belongs to* W.

Such a statement (belonging to S, see I.1), call it G, therefore satisfies (recall that D is the set of provable statements) the statement:

$$G \in D \leftrightarrow G \in W$$

It is called a *Gödel statement for* W.

(A Gödel statement for the set of expressions W, if it exists, is therefore a statement whose demonstrability is 'expressible' in terms of belonging to W. We have here a rough equivalent to what Gödel demonstrates – laboriously – in his system: the possibility of constructing in the latter the predicate 'provable in the system'.)

(3) Representation of a Class of Numbers in the System

We will say that a *predicate* $p \in P$ (see I.1) represents a class of integers $A \subset N$, if we have:

$$\varphi(p, n) \in D \leftrightarrow n \in A$$

(The 'mapping' [application] of p onto the number n yields a provable statement if and only if this number belongs to the class A. This is a very formal

elaboration of the following intuitive idea: the property p belongs only to numbers of the class A. Or: the class A is the extension of the concept p.) [170]

(4) Diagonalization Lemma

We are going to demonstrate the following proposition: *If a class of integers* W* *is representable in the system by a predicate, then there exists a Gödel statement for the set of expressions* W.

Let *p* be the predicate which represents W*. By definition (from the preceding paragraph):

$$\varphi(p, n) \in D \leftrightarrow n \in W^*$$

In particular, for *n = g(p)*

(i) $\varphi(p, g(p)) \in D \leftrightarrow g(p) \in W^*$

(*The* diagonalization *of the predicate p is* provable *if and only if the* numbering *of p belongs to* W*.)

But (see II.1), the very definition of the class W* is:

(ii) $g(p) \in W^* \leftrightarrow \varphi(p, g(p)) \in W$

By *juxtaposing the equivalences* (i) *and* (ii), we obtain (by substitution of a term equivalent to the one on the right in (i), or, if one prefers, by applying the transitivity of equivalence):

$$\varphi(p, g(p)) \in D \leftrightarrow \varphi(p, g(p)) \in W$$

Here we recognize (see II.2) the definition of a Gödel statement for W: $\varphi(p, g(p))$ is this *statement* (and it is indeed a closed statement since – (see I.3) – we have postulated that when *p* is a *predicate*, the expression $\varphi(p, n)$ always belongs to S).

(*What have we demonstrated? That if a class* W* *(of numbers) is represented by a predicate in the system, then the* diagonalization *of that predicate is a Gödel statement for the set of expressions* W.

Let us take one more step in the (ideological) description of this result.

Let W *be any set of expressions whatsoever. Suppose that* W *contains diagonal expressions (expressions 'mapped' onto the number that represents them in the numbering of expressions). Consider then the set of numbers that number these diagonal expressions. This set is* W* *(see the schema in II.1).*

To say that W is represented in the system is to say that there exists a predicate whose 'meaning' is: 'to be a number that represents a diagonal expression contained in W'.*

We now diagonalize this predicate ('mapping' it to its own numerical representation). We then obtain a statement, *the meaning of which would be something like: 'The number that represents the predicate, "to-be-a-number-that-represents-a-diagonal-expression-contained-in-W", is itself a number that represents a diagonal expression contained in W.'*

It is this statement that is not provable unless it belongs to W; *it is therefore a Gödel statement for* W.

Here one will recognize the underlying structure of the diagonal processes that, ever since Cantor, have provided 'foundational' mathematics with its principal instrument: the construction of a statement that affirms its own belonging to a group of expressions which this statement also represents or designates.)
[171]

III CONDITION FOR THE EXISTENCE OF AN UNDECIDABLE STATEMENT

The guiding idea for the completion of the argument is very simple: we are going to apply the diagonalization lemma to the class R of *refutable* statements. And we will thereby quite easily obtain *Gödel's theorem: if R* is representable (in the sense of* II.3*), then there exists a statement that is neither provable nor refutable (one which belongs to neither D nor R).*

If R* is representable, then there exists a Gödel statement for R (in keeping with the diagonalization lemma). Let G be this statement. By definition (II.2):

$$G \in D \leftrightarrow G \in R$$

(i.e. G is provable if and only if it is refutable . . .)

But $D \cap R = \emptyset$ (i.e. D and R have no elements in common: hypothesis of consistency, I.5).

Consequently G belongs to *neither* D *nor* R: it is an *undecidable statement.*

(What does the initial hypothesis signify: 'R is representable'? It signifies that there exists in the system a predicate whose 'meaning' would be: 'to be a number that represents a refutable diagonal expression'.*

As for the Gödel statement for R – the undecidable statement – we know, by the demonstration of the lemma, that it is none other than the diagonalization of the predicate that represents R. It is therefore a statement whose 'meaning' is something like:*

'The number that represents the predicate, "to-be-a-refutable-diagonal-expression," itself represents a refutable diagonal expression.'
Here one will recognize a kinship with the 'intuitive' argument of the Liar.)

This demonstration foregrounds the kernel of Gödel's discovery: if one can construct a predicate of refutability in a system, its 'mapping' to diagonal expressions results in the undecidability of a certain class of statements.

This demonstration also sheds light on the zigzagging movement that the proof co-ordinates 'between' the formal system and the 'intuitive' theory of integers: it is the representation (the numbering) of expressions that makes the diagonalization possible. Inversely, it is the construction of the W* classes in N that, predicatively 'reprised' in the system, renders possible the crucial demonstration of the lemma. In our vocabulary, we will say that this proof operates upon the connectivities between strata, which authorize trajectories and correspondences.

The scrupulous complexity of Gödel's demonstration, as compared to Smullyan's, has to do with the fact that the former has to establish the representability of R* for a *determinate* system (basically that of Russell and Whitehead's *Principia Mathematica*).

But the very general point of view adopted by Smullyan clearly draws out the structural and positive character of Gödel's discovery. As so often happens in mathematics, the latter deploys a network of conditional *constraints*: by prescribing for our system both consistency ($D \cap R = \emptyset$) *and* a 'strong' representative capacity [172] (the class of numbers R* is 'designated' by an expression in E), we can construct a 'remainder' in the set of statements, thereby showing that the disconnected sets D and R do not *overlap* with S.

We should bear in mind that the concepts of representability, consistency, disconnectedness, numbering, etc., have been given a mathematical assignation here, and retain none of their empirical or philosophical connotations. The concept of 'representative', in particular, is one that we have used in a figurative sense only instead and in place of that which it covers: *functions* (g and φ), defined in a perfectly classical way.

Thus, Gödel's result is peculiar and dramatic only with respect to a semantic saturation which *imposes upon* the discourse of science an *ideological expectation*.

Whoever poses to logic questions that are not problems runs the risk of registering as *resistance* what is in fact simply the deployment of those regional constraints through which this science's artificial object *occurs*.

In this way we re-encounter the articulated dialectic of science and ideology. In terms of the problem that concerns us here, its stages are the following:

I) The existence of a historical mathematics (namely 'intuitive' arithmetic), one that is open in principle (indefinitely stratified signifier).

II *a*) The ideological re-presentation of this existence as the trans-mathematical norm of thoroughly controllable rationality (ideological destratification of the mathematical signifier).

II *b*) The posing of a question to mathematics about their conformity to this ideological norm, in the form of the axiomatic and formalist *intention*, whose goal is to display a *well-founded transparency* (ideological motivations of Frege and Russell).

III) Break: the mathematical treatment of this ideological re-presentation of mathematics via the actual *construction* of formal systems that 'represent' historical arithmetic (*Principia Mathematica*).

IV *a*) The ideological re-presentation of this break: formal systems conceived as trans-mathematical norms of rational closure. The *idea* of a nomological system (Husserl).

IV *b*) The posing of a question to mathematics about their absolute conformity to the ideological norm of closure: this is the meta-mathematical *intention*, relative to the *internal* demonstration of a system's consistency (Hilbert).

V) Break: the mathematical treatment of ideological re-presentation via the actual *construction* of a mathematical metamathematics (arithmetization of syntax).

Gödel's theorem: the structural stratification of the mathematical signifier does not answer the 'question' of closure.

VI) Ideological re-presentation of this break: Gödel's theorem is experienced [*vécu*] as a *limitation* relative to the normative expectation.

Ideological exegesis of this 'limitation' as:
– openness of speech and concealment of being (Ladrière);
– finitude;
– splitting, suture;
– . . .

VII) Break: the general theory of the limitation-effect, positively conceived as a structural dimension [*instance*] of certain mathematical objects (Smullyan's epistemological truth). [**173**]

The epistemological upshot of this convoluted adventure reminds us that mathematics *operates upon its own existence as it is designated in ideology*, but that this operation, conforming to the specific constraints of a science, takes the form of a *break*, such that the (ideological) questions which make up the *material* upon which mathematics carries out its working reprise [*reprise oeuvrante*] find *no answer* in the latter.

By coming to figure in the space of mathematics' problematic, the ideological image of this science can henceforth only be *misrecognized* by whoever proffered it. In the shift from material to product, mathematics obeys rules of existence that *nothing* in the material could have indicated.

This makes it quite clear that science is science of ideology, and is even science of the ideology of the science of ideology, and so on, as far as you like. But ideology never finds itself in it.

Such is the law of the alternating chain in which what is known as 'the progress of science' consists: it is not because it is 'open' that science has cause to deploy itself (although openness governs the *possibility* of this deployment); it is because ideology is incapable of being satisfied with this openness. Forging the impracticable image of a closed discourse and enjoining science to submit to it, ideology sees its own order returned to it in the unrecognizable form of the new concept; the reconfiguration through which science, treating its ideological interpellation as material, ceaselessly displaces the breach that it opens in it.

Let us take stock here – this time in close proximity to Lacan – of the ridiculousness of the claim that progress is motivated by the 'intention' of discovery.

With regard to Gödel's theorem, and the limitative connotation that (in the wake of the irrational, the negative, and the imaginary numbers) heralded it, we should remember that science advances *precisely* through those who, putting to it the question of its obstruction [*arrêt*], are engaged in desperately ordering the place where it may be recognized that this question, however much it may be *reprised*, is not even understood.

January, 1967

CHAPTER TEN

Alain Badiou
Infinitesimal Subversion[1]

[118] I SUPPORT AND INOCCUPATION

The finite – which Hegel describes as the iterative transgression of its own limit – is essentially that which allows, and thereby demands, a supplementary inscription. Thus, what is constitutive for it is the empty place where that inscription which it lacks is possible. A number x_n is that which determines 'to its right' the place of its successor: $(x_nS) \rightarrow (x_nSx_{n+1})$. To be inscribed at one of the places distributed by S is to assign to the other place [*l'autre place*] the constraining exclusivity of the blank space. The numerical effect exhausts itself in the incessant shunting along of the empty place: number is the displacement of the place where it is lacking [*où il manque*].

However, this operation presupposes a (unique) space of exercise, that is to say, an out-of-place blank [*blanc*] where the place is displaced in the retroaction of the inscribed – this is what Mallarmé characterized as the initial or solitary or more profoundly as the 'gratuitous' blankness or whiteness, since it is what is written that bestows upon it its status as place of the writing that takes place.[2]

This is why the 'potential' infinite, the indefiniteness of progression, testifies retroactively to the 'actual' infinity of its *support*.

It is possible to demonstrate this by objectifying the concept of effective procedure, or algorithm, as a mechanical procedure. The Turing machine, which accomplishes this programme, is realizable as a material assemblage, but only if – and this is the only thing that distinguishes it from a legible inscription on physical paper – one assumes that the tape which provides the support for its successive marks is infinite. Everything that is mathematically ideal about the Turing machine, everything in it that pertains to rational universality, is encapsulated in this postulation. It is the fact that the concept of 'algorithm' cannot be entirely articulated within odological space that defines, in keeping with this very impossibility, the reality of the infinity-support.

---

1   TN: First published as Alain Badiou, 'La Subversion infinitésimale', CpA 9.8 (summer 1968): 118–137. Translated by Robin Mackay with Ray Brassier.

2   '*Quand s'aligna, dans un brisure, le moindre, disséminée, le hasard vaincu mot par mot, indéfectiblement le blanc revient, tout à l'heure gratuit, certain maintenant.*' TN: '[A]nd when in the lines chance appeared conquered word by word in a scattered minimum rupture, indefectibly the white [blank] returns, gratuitous before, now certain' (Stéphane Mallarmé, 'Le Mystère dans les lettres', in *Mallarmé*, ed. and trans. Anthony Hartley [London: Penguin, 1965], 204).

For an algorithmic sequence, the infinity-support is the non-markable unity of its space of inscription.

Let us now consider a domain of mathematical objects definable according to the construction procedures which their axioms prescribe. For [119] example, and as evoked above, the natural numbers defined through the logic of the 'successor' operation.

Let us suppose that these procedures allow us to designate a place such that none of the objects that are constructible within this domain can, on pain of contradiction, be marked within it. We will call 'infinity-point of the domain' the *supplementary* mark that conforms to the following conditions:

(a) It occupies the unoccupiable empty place.
(b) Apart from this occupation, it is governed by all the initial procedures.

Here, the infinite is the designation of a beyond proper to the algorithms of the domain: the marking of a point that is inaccessible[3] according to the algorithms themselves, but which supports their reiteration.

This infinite [*cet infini*] has a twofold relation to the procedures of construction, since only the latter allow us to determine the unoccupiable place which the former will come to occupy, while the former enables the efficacy of the latter to recommence. But the infinite is also exterior to the domain in which those procedures are exercised – this is its supplementarity – since it marks within this domain that which is averred in it only as void. We see then that the infinite closes off a domain by occluding the voids determined within it; but also that it opens up a higher domain as the first point of a second space in which the initial procedures can be exercised. This pulsation of closure and opening defines the infinity-point: it is the zero of a higher stratum.

Take for example the relation of order over the whole natural numbers. It allows us to construct the concept of a place which no number can occupy: the place of a number which would be larger than all others. This *place* is perfectly constructible, since the statement 'for all x, $x < y$' is a well-formed statement of the system, referring to a defined relation. Now, in this statement, the *variable* 'y' marks the place in question. However, no *constant* of the system, no *proper name* of a number, can occupy this place – i.e. can be substituted for the variable 'y' – without a contradiction ensuing. Although this place can be defined in terms of the procedures governing the numerical domain, it is nevertheless trans-numeric. *Every number is lacking in this place.*

---

3   In set theory, an inaccessible cardinal is precisely an infinity-point, relative to cardinals smaller than it, for certain expansive algorithms: (*a*) passage to the set of parts, (*b*) passage to the union-set, or set of elements of all sets which are elements of the initial set.

Suppose now that I augment the system's alphabet with a constant, call it *i* (which is not the symbol of any number), whose usage I define in terms of the occupation of this transnumeric place, positing that, for *every* number *n*, $n < i$.

In terms of the 'normal' models of the system, it is clear that *i is not* a [120] whole number. However, if I can operate on *i* (i.e. calculate with *i*) without contradiction, in conformity with the initial procedures governing the domain – if, for example, I can define the successor of *i*, that is $i + 1$, or the sum $i + i$, and so on – then I can say that *i* is an *infinite whole number*. By which should be understood: an infinity-point relative to the structure of order over the domain of natural whole numbers.

Thus the infinity-point is the marking of something inaccessible for the domain; a marking completed by a *forcing* [*forçage*] of procedures, one that obliges them to apply to precisely that which they had excluded. Of course, this forcing entails a modification of the way in which the domain is set out, since the constructible objects in the higher domain are able to occupy places which those of the domain itself 'unoccupy'. The new space in which the procedures can be exercised is disconnected from that which preceded it. The models of the system are stratified. We will call these effects of the marking of constructible empty places a *recasting* [*refonte*].[4]

The infinity-point of a domain is a recasting-inscription.

Note that while the infinity-support is required by the recurrent *possibility* of inscribing a mark in the empty place assigned by the primitive relation of the domain, conversely, it is the *impossibility* of a certain mark within that domain that gives rise to the infinity-point. While the former supports the rules of construction, the latter, which is inaccessible, recasts and relaunches them, thereby determining a new space of inscription, a difference in the support: *the infinity-point is the differential of the infinity-support.*

II VARIABLE SIGNATURE OF A REAL

We will now examine the following paradox: defining a concept of the infinite in terms of the inoccupation of a place, we have nonetheless conceded that in a

---

4   We have taken the concept of *recasting* [*refonte*] from François Regnault. He uses it to designate those great modifications whereby a science, returning to what was un-thought in its preceding epoch, carries out a global transformation of its system of concepts – *e.g.* relativistic mechanics after classical mechanics.

TN: *Refonte* can be translated as reconfiguration or overhaul, but its primary meaning – of recasting or reforging – is more evocative of the processes at work here. Regnault appears to have adapted the term from Bachelard. 'Crises in the development of thought imply a total recasting [*refonte*] of the system of knowledge. The mindset [*la tête*] must at such a time be remade. It changes species [. . .]. By the spiritual revolutions required by a scientific invention, man becomes a mutable species, or better, a species that needs to mutate, one that suffers from failing to change' (Gaston Bachelard, *La Formation de l'esprit scientifique* [1938] [Paris: Vrin, 2004], 18; *The Formation of the Scientific Mind*, trans. Mary McAllester Jones [Manchester: Clinamen, 2002], 26tm).

certain sense this place was always already marked. How then are we to recognize it, if it dissipates itself in the retrospective indistinction of the infinity-support? Being obliged to write that the place is unoccupiable, no doubt I must inscribe what will attest that it is *this* place, and no other. To differentiate the unoccupiable place requires the occupation constituted by the mark of this difference.

And in fact we have consented to write, without claiming to have gone beyond what is permitted by the laws of the domain, 'for all x, $x < y$'. What about this 'y', which we call a variable, which occupies the place in which no constant can be inscribed [**121**], and where the supplementary symbol will only come to be inscribed by forcing the recasting of the entire domain? And if the infinity-point is only what is substituted for a variable, must we not attribute to the latter the power, internal to the domain, of occupying the empty place, such that the true concept of the infinite would already be enveloped in the mobile inscription of x's and y's?

This is indeed what many epistemologies declare, Hegel's included. The literal inscriptions of algebra, such as a/b, are, relative to a given quantitative domain, 'general signs' (*allgemeine Zeichen*).[5] This means: substitutive infinities, whose finitude in inscription holds and gathers the scattered virtuality of inscription of all those quanta of the domain whereby one can, in calculating, substitute for a or b. Letters here are 'indeterminate possibilities of every determinate value,'[6] with the indetermination of quantitative possibility [*du possible quantitatif*] finding its fixed qualitative closure in the formal invariance of the mark – in Hegel's example, the *relation a/b* the bar /.

What Hegel thinks in this text is the *logical* concept of the variable, because he rightly rejects the notion of a 'variable magnitude', which he considers vague and improper.[7] Indeed, the idea of the variability of a magnitude confuses functional considerations (variations of a function) with algebraic considerations (literal or undetermined symbols); it conceals *substitution* under *correlation*. Hegel prefers instead the concept of that which, although related to a quantity (to number) is not a quantum. Letters (*die Buchstaben*)[8] are variables by virtue of the proper difference which assigns them to quanta, just as in logic one distinguishes between two lists of symbols of individuals: constants, i.e. proper names for which, once inscribed, nothing can be substituted; and variables, for which under certain circumstances constants can be substituted. Because of this

5   Georg W.F. Hegel, *Science of Logic*, trans. George di Giovanni (Cambridge: Cambridge University Press, 2010), 21:243. TN: The pagination here refers to the German *Gesammelte Werke*. (There appear to be some inconsistencies in Badiou's own listing of page numbers in the French version of this article).

6   Hegel, *Science of Logic*, 21:243tm.

7   Ibid., 21:249.

8   Ibid., 21:243.

capacity to disappear to make space for the fixity of marks, variables participate in true infinity: the dialectical sublation of the infinity of iteration.[9]

And it is true that the variable appears to be a crossroads of infinities. We have just seen in what sense it harboured anticipatively the powers of the infinity-point. But insofar as it can be replaced with a constant, and is exhausted in supporting virtual substitutions, the variable seems to mark *all* the places of the domain under consideration that can be occupied by constants. Thus, the variable could index [*indexer*] the infinity-support. This is indeed how Quine understands it when he quips: 'to be is to be the value of a variable',[10] if the being in question is the materiality of the mark and the ontological site is the space of its inscription.

However, this is not at all the case. As an effective inscription, the variable presupposes the infinity-support as the site of places. Placed there where a constant can come, it belongs to the same order of markings as that constant, rather than designating its type.

No doubt the variable marks a *constructible*, albeit not necessarily [122] *occupiable*, place of the domain. But this marking is entwined with the domain's own law, with its algorithmic finitude. Even if I inscribe a variable in an unoccupiable place, I do not for all that infinitize the domain; I do not transgress its rule, having thereby merely afforded myself the means of *writing the impossibility of the impossible*.

Take for example, in the domain of whole naturals, the equation:

$$4 - x = x$$

This is a possible equation, unlike, for example, $4 - 7 = 7$, which is not merely false but is, within the domain, strictly illegible, the term $(4 - 7)$ not being well-formed.

The general (indeterminate) possibility of writing $4 - x = x$, and, let us say, $x > 4$, allows me to *state* the impossibility of their conjoint inscription, in the form of the statement [*écriture*]:

---

9   TN: Badiou specifies here that he has taken from Jacques Derrida the French translation of Hegel's *Aufhebung* as *relève*; we have used the now-conventional English term 'sublation'.

10   TN: 'Whatever we say with help of names can be said in a language which shuns names altogether. To be is, purely and simply, to be the value of a variable. In terms of the categories of traditional grammar, this amounts roughly to saying that to be is to be in the range of reference of a pronoun. Pronouns are the basic media of reference; nouns might better have been named pro-pronouns. The variables of quantification, "something", "nothing", "everything", range over our whole ontology, whatever it may be; and we are convicted of a particular ontological presupposition if, and only if, the alleged presuppositum has to be reckoned among the entities over which our variables range in order to render one of our affirmations true' (Willard V. Quine, 'On What There Is', *The Review of Metaphysics* 2:5 [September 1948], 32; cf. Quine, 'Notes on Existence and Necessity', *Journal of Philosophy* 11 [1943], 113–127).

not-$(4 - x = x$ and $x > 4)$

This is a statement in which *no* constant can take the place marked by the variable x yet which, at the same time, writes this very impossibility. Here the variable enables the *explicit* marking of the unoccupiability of a constructible place.

Let us say that a variable ensures that impossible equations are sufficiently legible to read their impossibility.

Now, following a proposition of Lacan's, the real for a domain of fixed proofs is defined as what is impossible. It is by excluding certain statements, and by the impossibility for any constant of occupying certain constructible places, that an axiomatic system can operate as *this* system, and can allow itself to be thought differentially as the discourse of a real.

If every statement is derivable, the system is inconsistent; if every constructible place is occupiable, the system, marking neither differences nor regions, becomes an opaque body, a deregulated grammar, a discourse dense with nothingness. The variable, as inscription which disjoins the constructible from the occupiable – governing which constants belong to the former but not to the latter – testifies to the intra-systemic trace of the system's reality. The operator of the real for a domain, it in fact authorizes within that domain the writing of the impossible proper to it. The existent has as its category a being-able-not-to-be the value of a variable at the place it marks.

In this regard, the variable is the exact inverse of the infinity-point, whose inscription it prepares.

For it is in this place of the impossible, which the variable occupies *in order to designate its impossibility*, that the infinity-point will come to inscribe itself as a constant. The infinity-point once again occupies the unoccupiable place, it substitutes itself for the variable, but according to the writing *of the possibility of the impossible*. There is now a constant where the variable traced the prescribed lack of every constant. The infinity-point is the becoming-constant of a variable in the impossible place whose impossibility it indexes. [123]

The variable *realises* the difference of a system as the pure wake or trace [*sillage*] left by the disappearance of a mark – of a constant – whose lack-in-its-place the variable names. The infinity-point, through which this mark makes its return into the system, *irrealises* the latter: this is something mathematicians already knew, since they successively named 'irrational' and 'imaginary' those infinity-points for the domain of relations of whole numbers, and for the domain which, in the retrospection of its recasting, was constituted as 'real'.

Lacan would call this the hallucinatory position of the infinity-point, whose variable, far from enveloping its coming-forth, has instead marked its prosaic exclusion.

Thus the infinity-point, however much it may proliferate after the recasting, is axiomatically one, or a closed list [*liste close*]; whereas the variable is, one might say, as numerous as the constants: to write $x < y$ is another thing altogether than writing $x < x$, since the impossibility must be evaluated for *each* place, rather than the infinity-point relative to an algorithm being linked to *an* unoccupiable place, and the infinity-support, originally, to *every* place.

In a logical calculus, the list of variables is open. Far from folding the differences of the domain back into the unity of a mark, the variable, as instrument of the real of places, only redoubles them, distributing as many proper impossibilities as there are constants capable of entering or not entering into any given relation [*relation quelconque*].

The variable as mark is unable to figure the Infinity of marks of a domain, since it is coextensive with their reality.

III TO MARK THE ALMOST-NOTHING?

We are now going to deal with a particular class of marks, which, after some initial successes, were long held to be inadmissible: infinitesimal marks, in which the impossible and the infinite, the variable and the point, are distributed in the now unravelled history of a repression.

The intrinsic absurdity of an infinitely small number was indeed the dogmatic result of a very long journey punctuated, in its speculative origins, by Zeno's paradoxes. It is no exaggeration to say that an entire mathematico-philosophical tradition is bound up in it, a secular tradition whose unity is the result of a rejection – rejection of the minimal differential element which would seem to be inscribed as such in the fabric of continuity. The very opposition between indivisible atoms and the infinite divisibility of the continuum is maintained in the unitary space of this exclusion, since the *real* indivisibility of the atom assigns it a (very small) unit of dimension, rather than a punctuality; whereas the infinite un-interruptedness of divisibility is precisely what rules out the notion of an actual infinitesimal stopping-point. [**124**]

Whence the fact that Hegel can simultaneously approve of the 'atomistic principle', even the atomistic mathematics apparently delineated by Bonaventura Cavalieri's *indivisibles*, and the infinite divisibility of the continuum: he perceives with acuity their dialectical correlation, whose signature is the annulment of the infinitely small as such.

With regard to Cavalieri, Hegel shows how, for example, although hampered by an inadequate language, what the Italian mathematician envisages is not a *composition* of the spatial continuum by discrete elements, but the principle of a *relation* of magnitude. The primacy of the discrete is in no way restored here. No doubt 'the image of an *aggregate* of lines is incompatible with the continuity of the figure.'[11] But Cavalieri knows this perfectly well. His conception is not

---

11   Hegel, *Science of Logic*, 21:305.

set-theoretical, the continua [*les continus*] are not collections of indivisibles: 'continuous figures follow only the *proportion* of the indivisibles.'[12] We must understand that the atomism of indivisible elements serves only for the comparative ciphering of figures, leaving their continuous-being entirely untouched. 'The lines do not in fact constitute the whole content of the figure as *continuous*, but only the content insofar as it is to be arithmetically *determined*.'[13] In short: geometrical continuity is the void wherein indivisible atoms come to inscribe relations of magnitude. And this inscription does not breach the *infinite* divisibility of the continuous, a pure possibility left open by a relation of indivisibles which do not denote the former's quantitative *being*, but its figuration in the formal (qualitative) structure of this relation.[14]

The divisibility of the continuous in turn delivers no proper indivisible element. The decomposition of the continuum cannot reach an indivisible element, or even the reality of an 'infinitely small' part, any more than indivisible elements are able to compose the continuum. The division of the continuum is undone as soon it is posited, thereby restoring the adherence, the inseparable connectivity of the whole: 'Divisibility itself is only a possibility, and not a *concrete existence of parts*; multiplicity in general is only posited in continuity as a moment, immediately suppressed [or sublated].'[15]

Neither progression nor regression. In classical epistemology, we find a complicity of the atomistic and the continuous.

For as Hegel remarks,[16] the atom is never an infinitesimal of the continuum. The atom is the (arithmetical) One whose *combinatorial* proliferation produces not the continuum but the thing against the *backdrop* of the continuum. The veritable non-composable principle of the continuum and of movement remains the *void*, the unique [125] space of the inscription of Ones, the infinity-support wherein atomistic discreteness is marked. Hegel has no difficulty recognizing, in the retroactive continuity of the void, the cause of the mobile combination of atoms, the continuous restlessness of the negative, which obliges the discrete to determine itself as numeral [*numéral*], as a thing made of atoms.

Thus it appears that the couplet atoms/void, the physical objectivation of the couplet discrete/continuous, is constituted by excluding every infinitesimal composition of the continuum itself: there may be atoms *in* the void, but there are no atoms *of* the void.

---

12   Ibid., 21:306.

13   Ibid., 21:305.

14   On this point Alexandre Koyré takes up Hegel's argument, without explicitly mentioning it, in his 'Bonaventura Cavaliéri et la géométrie des continus', an article of 1954, reprinted in Koyré's *Études d'histoire de la pensée scientifique* (Paris: Gallimard, 1973), 334–361.

15   Hegel, *Science of Logic*, 21:188tm.

16   Ibid., 21:153ff.

Conversely, the Euclidean definition of the magnitude of a given type prohibits any foreclosure of the process of increase-decrease whose permanent possibility *is* the very concept of magnitude: 'We say that magnitudes (μεγέθη) have a relation (λόγος) between them when one of them can, when multiplied, surpass the other.'[17] From this Hegel concludes, in an accurate interpretation of the intentions of Greek mathematics, that a supposedly infinite *element* which, whether multiplied or divided, can never equal any finite magnitude whatsoever, has no relation at all with such a magnitude: 'Given that the infinitely large and the infinitely small cannot be respectively increased or diminished, neither one nor the other are, in fact, quanta'.[18] To attempt to think infinities as such, to *mark* them as numbers, amounts to establishing oneself strictly within the ἄλογος, the radical non-relation. One cannot therefore write an infinitesimal mark, for example dx, except in the composition of an *already given* relation [with dy], and remembering all the while 'that outside of this relation, it [the dx] is null'[19] – a nullity whose force is absolute, excluding any separate mention of dx. The dx is nothing, not even an acceptable symbol, outside the place assigned to it by the bar $/$.[20] The dx as mark is *adherent* to a determined blank space: it is the pre-existent bar of that relation alone that renders its inscription possible. For Hegel, it is precisely this anteriority of the bar that constitutes the quality of the differential, and thus its infinity.

Whence the obvious conclusion that in the expression 'infinitely small', 'small' means nothing, since outside the (qualitative) form of the relation, one cannot evaluate the magnitude of that which is nothing but a null mark, dx. Note that the same thing holds in contemporary analysis: if the separate mention of the differential is the rule there, this is not on account of its being any more of a *quantum*, but rather precisely because it is held to be an *operator*: it would thus be absurd to evaluate its magnitude.

Thus, historically, the mathematical project set about dispensing with any mention of the quantified infinite. Joseph Louis Lagrange, Hegel's principal scientific source, announces this expressly in the very title of his canonical work: *Theory of Analytical Functions, Containing the Principles of* [126] *Differential Calculus, Disengaged from all Consideration of Infinitely Small, Vanishing Quantities, Limits and Fluxions, and Reduced to the Algebraic Analysis of Finite Quantities* (1797).

The gesture of rejection is constitutive: the *impurity* of the origin of differential calculus was the isolated marking, the trace of the infinitely small. Thus the story of this calculus is also that of the effacement of this trace.

---

17   Euclid's *Elements*, Book 5, definition 4.

18   Hegel, *Science of Logic*, 21:239tm.

19   Ibid., 21:241tm

20   TN: 'Outside their relation they are pure nullities; but they are to be taken only as moments of the relation, as determinations of the differential coefficient dx/dy' (ibid., 21:251).

Remarkably, these conclusions were to survive, essentially intact, the Cantorian recasting, which as we know completely revolutionized the concept of the infinitely *large*. Georg Cantor displayed a truly Greek intransigence in his refusal of the infinitely *small*. As late as 1928, Abraham Fraenkel, faithfully echoing the master, writes:

> Put to the test, the infinitely small failed utterly.
>
> The diverse types of infinitely small considered up to the present time, some meticulously founded, have proved totally useless for getting to the bottom of the simplest and most fundamental problems of the infinitesimal calculus [. . .] and there is no reason to expect any change within this domain. No doubt it is *conceivable* (although one might justifiably judge it unlikely and consign it to a distant future) that a second Cantor should one day give an incontestable arithmetic foundation to new infinitely small numbers, which would then prove themselves of some use in mathematics, and which might perhaps open a simple way to infinitesimal calculus.
>
> But as long as no such thing exists [. . .] we must hold to the idea that one cannot, in any manner, speak of the mathematical – and thus logical – existence of infinitely small numbers, in an identical or analogous sense to that which has been given to the infinitely large.[21]

The strange violence of this text, in spite of the caveats, is symptomatic of an emergent ideological dimension [*est le symptôme d'un affleurement idéologique*]; the history of mathematical analysis is partly entwined with another history, incessantly counteracting it: that of the *repression* [*refoulement*] of infinitesimals. Here Hegel is, to take up an Althusserian expression, merely the philosophical *exploiter* of a remarkably long-lived conjuncture.[22]

At the beginning of the eighteenth century, in his essay *The Analyst*, Berkeley had instituted the merciless prosecution of the foundations of the new calculus, by attacking the weakest link of the theory: the extrapolation of operations, defined for finite magnitudes, to the supposedly 'infinitely small'. We know that Leibniz elided this embarrassing question through recourse, as dubious as it is extravagant, to the metaphysical postulate of pre-established Harmony:

> [. . .] it will be found that the rules of the finite succeed in the infinite [. . .] and that [127] *vice versa* the rules of the infinite succeed in the finite [. . .]: this is because all

---

21   Abraham H. Fraenkel, *Einleitung in die Mengenlehre*, in *Grundlehren der mathematischen Wissenschaften*, vol. 9 (Berlin: Springer, 1928).

22   In his *Philosophie de l'algèbre* (Paris: PUF, 1962), Jules Vuillemin also denounces any recourse to indivisibles as an intellectual regression: '[. . .] if one understands by differentials magnitudes at once smaller than our assignable magnitude and nevertheless different from zero, one returns to the precritical epoch of calculus' (523).

are governed by reason, and since otherwise there could be neither science nor rule, which would not conform with the nature of the sovereign principle.[23]

It is not difficult to understand why this 'it will be found' no longer satisfied anyone in the eighteenth century. All the more so given that, as Berkeley remarked, different rules applied for actual calculations: infinitesimals did indeed have peculiar operational codes. There was no shame in eventually 'neglecting' the dx on the way, when convenient, and the Marquis de l'Hôpital even innocently turns this into a *requirement* [*demande*], right from the beginning of his famous treatise, the first manual of differential calculus: '[we require] that a quantity that is neither increased nor diminished except by another infinitely smaller than it, can be considered as remaining the same.'[24]

But is it possible to maintain that these 'negligences' are 'rules of the finite'? And what is the meaning of this mark dx, which both counts and yet doesn't count? How can there be a circumstantial legitimacy to the effacement of an inscription, which one continues to consider as a separable constant?

Take the calculation of the 'difference', as was said at the time, of the product xy, where we already know the difference dx of x, and dy of y, that is to say, the infinitesimals 'associated' with each of these finite magnitudes. I expand $(x + dx)$ $(y + dy)$ yielding: $xy + y\,dx + x\,dy + dx\,dy$. In relation to xy, I thereby have a calculated difference, an 'increase' equal to $y\,dx + x\,dy + dx\,dy$. In order to obtain the classical formula $d(xy) = x\,dy + y\,dx$, I am required to 'neglect' the product $dx\,dy$ of the two infinitesimals. But why now, and not at the very beginning of the calculation? If, in fact, as l'Hôpital says, $dx\,dy$ is 'nothing' in relation to $x\,dy$ because

$$\frac{dx\,dy}{x\,dy} = \frac{dx}{x}$$

and dx, the infinitesimal proper to x, is nothing in relation to it, then this is all the more reason why the sum $(x + dx)$ must be, *from the start*, identified with x, such that the calculation no longer makes any sense. For Berkeley, the consecution of the operations *does not hold*, because in the course of the process I change the very principles of this consecution, invoking the rule of negligence only when it happens to suit me.

These objections seem so strong that in truth no attempt was ever made to rebut them, and, as we know, the use of infinitesimals progressively gave way to the 'finitist' notion of the *limit*.

---

23   Leibniz, *Mémoire de 1701 sur le calcul différentiel*, cited in Abraham Robinson, *Non-Standard Analysis* (Amsterdam: North Holland Publishing Company, 1966), 262–263.

24   Guillaume de l'Hôpital, *Analyse des infiniment petits pour l'intelligence des lignes courbes* (1696), cited in Robinson, *Non-Standard Analysis*, 264. De l'Hôpital's book essentially reproduces the ideas of Johann Bernoulli.

But more essentially, the epistemological nature of the obstacle becomes clearer when one notices that the exclusion of the infinitely small bears on *an infinity-point* relative to the structure of the ordered field [*corps*] of 'magnitudes'. Attempting to think the infinity of the differential, Hegel and all the mathematicians of his day took care above all not to punctualize it: it was this punctualization which classical reason found repugnant.

For an infinitesimal *element* (a 'point') d*x* would then indeed come to occupy the [128] unoccupiable place of the number smaller than all others; the place marked by a variable as site of the impossible. But *there is no* real number that is smaller (or larger) than all others: this is what the theory of continuous positive magnitudes proposes.

However, we will formulate the following *epistemological thesis*: in the history of mathematics, the marking of an infinity-point constitutes the transformation wherein those (ideological) *obstacles* most difficult to reduce are knotted together.

We have seen how, for example, irrational numbers and complex numbers were historically presented as marking an infinity-point ('inexistent' square roots, 'impossible' equations). We know something about the resistance provoked by introduction of the former in Plato's time (the end of the *Theaetetus* is an elaborate discussion of the concept of the minimal element), and by the latter in the period between the Italian algebraists of the sixteenth century and the clarifications proposed by Cauchy.

And as a matter of fact, since it is linked to the forcing of the empty spaces proper to a domain, the introduction of an infinity-point is a modification which must of necessity seem irrational, since in any given theoretical conjuncture rationality is defined precisely by the respect accorded these blank spaces, as the sole guarantors, variably indexed, of *real* difference for the domain. A mathematician like Evariste Galois, whose work is precisely linked to the algebraic theory of infinity-points – the theory of extensions of a basic field [*un corps de base*] – clearly understood that by establishing oneself in the constitutive silence, in the unsaid of a domainial conjuncture, one maintains the chance of producing a decisive reconfiguration. 'It often seems that the same ideas appear at once to many people as a revelation: if one looks for the cause, it is easy to find it in the works of those which preceded, where *these ideas were prescribed unknowingly by their authors*.'[25]

In science as in politics, it is the unperceived or overlooked [*l'inaperçu*] which puts revolution on the agenda.

But the risk taken had to be paid for, in Galois' case, by the uncomprehending ignorance of the academicians. For recasting is a theoretical violence, a subversion.

---

25   Évariste Galois, *Écrits et mémoires* (Paris: Gauthier-Villars, 1962), my emphasis.

Lacan's formula, according to which whatever is excluded from the symbolic reappears in the real, can be interpreted here as follows: in certain conditions, the excluded proper to an *already produced* mathematical structure reappears as the instigating mark of a real (historical) process of *production* of a different structure. If we spoke of the hallucinatory form of the infinity-point, as the foreclosed mark which comes back, this is because, arriving at that point where a variable, under the effect of a placed negation, sanctioned the real, the infinity-point declared by a mathematician often provokes accusations of obscurity at best and of madness at worst – and this primarily, as in the case of Galois, from established colleagues, such as Siméon Poisson.

One begins to understand why a mathematics which had *undertaken* the [129] laborious expulsion of infinitesimals subsequently took over, with the interested support of philosophers, the guardianship of the real which this expulsion – baptism of a finally rigorously-founded Analysis – forced it to assume at the beginning of the nineteenth century, under the attentive direction of Baron Cauchy.

It is all the more understandable given that the problems raised by Berkeley were truly serious. In their general form, they amounted to the following: What does our definition of the infinity-point imply concerning the extension of algorithms to that impossible term which determines the unoccupiable place where it holds? The surprising inventiveness of the Greeks and the Italian algebraists lay in showing that one can *calculate* with irrationals or imaginary numbers. But in the end the recasting cannot conserve everything. If one closes the real numbers algebraically, no doubt one obtains a macro-field [*surcorps*] (complex numbers) which constitutes their punctual infinitization. But this macro-field is no longer ordered: the structure of order is not valid for the recast domain. If one compactifies the normal topology of these same real numbers by adding a 'point at infinity', the algebraic structure of the field is lost, and so on. Most often, a recasting through the marking of an infinity-point, bound as it is by definition to the possibility of extending *the specific structure of which it is the infinity*, guarantees nothing as to the other procedures defined in the domain, which play no role in the construction of the empty place where the supplementary mark comes.

We know for example that the field of real numbers is *Archimedean*: given two positive numbers a and b, where $a < b$, there always exists another whole number n such that $b < na$.

Now this essential property would not survive the introduction of an infinitely small element dx, defined as the infinity-point of the place that has the property of 'being smaller than all the others'. In fact, for every real positive *finite* number ε, the infinite smallness of dx demands that $dx < \varepsilon$. In particular, for *every* whole number n, $dx < \varepsilon/n$, since ε/n is also a real *finite* number. Consequently, given any positive finite ε and any whole n, for an infinitesimal dx, n dx < ε. One cannot hope to surpass a given finite ε by multiplying the infinitesimal dx by a whole number, however large: the domain of real numbers, recast by the marking of an infinitely small number, is *non-Archimedean*.

Is this an isolated loss? Is it not natural to suspect that the explicit intro- duction of infinitesimals would wreak such havoc amidst those interleaved structures which constitute the field of real numbers as to leave Analysis paralyzed? This much is clear: in refusing to assign any markable actuality to dx, Lagrange following d'Alembert and Hegel following Berkeley *comply with the obstacle*.[26] An epistemological prudence serves here to shore up the repression of a punctual imperceptible [*un imperceptible ponctuel*]. Until just a few years ago, the question appeared to have been resolved: the nearly- nothing, the infinitely-small, has no mark of its own. The infinitesimal *is not a number*. [130]

IV THE INNUMERABLE NUMBERED

But the infinitesimal *is* a number: a statement which subverts Analysis in the exclusion from which it ended up being born, and which restores, on a new foundation, the inventive innocence of the pioneers of the 'new calculus'.

From a broader perspective, this subversion displaces the uninterrupted effect exerted by Zeno's aporias of continuity and divisibility across several epochs of the concept [*à travers plusieurs époques du concept*]; it rearranges the field of rationality which these aporiae governed through the (often mute) imperative that commanded us not to expose ourselves to them.

In the last ten years, the work of Abraham Robinson[27] has established that we can entirely reconstruct classical analysis by 'immersing' the field of real numbers in a non-Archimedean field, by an inaugural marking of an infinity- point – an infinitely large number – and a correlative free recourse to infinitesi- mal elements.

Aside from finally relieving the secular repression of these concepts, Robinson's discovery administers a convincing proof of the productive capacity of formal thought. In fact, Robinson secures the coherent marking of a large class of infinity-points by exclusive recourse to the theory of formal systems.

Consider the general form of the problem which history bequeathed to us

---

26   TN: 'Lagrange après d'Alembert, Hegel après Berkeley, sont, dans le rejet de toute actu- alité marquable pour le dx, *selon l'obstacle*.'

27   See the fundamental text, to which we will make constant reference: Abraham Robinson, *Non-Standard Analysis* (Amsterdam: North Holland Publishing Company, 1966). Robinson's discovery is dated autumn 1960. The first publications came in 1961. But the basic idea figured implicitly in Thoralf Skolem's work on non-standard models of arithmetic, work which dates back to 1930–35.

in the form of a refusal: no number exists that is larger than *all* others. That is to say: no number larger than the terms of every strictly increasing *infinite* series. On the other hand, given a *finite* set of numbers, it is very clear that one can always find a number larger than all those in that set. This is even the principle of the *indefiniteness* of the numerical domain, itself subtended by the infinity-support: every finite series can be surpassed. The relation of order transgresses finitude.

Formally, such indefiniteness of a relation (here, that of order) can be expressed as follows: take a formal system S comprising of an infinite set of constants, denoted a_i, (in our example, the marks of numbers), and a binary relation $R(x, y)$ where the variables x and y denote the reality of the places to which R distributes the constants (in our example, $R(x, y)$ says that $x < y$). Let us suppose that for every finite set of constants $\{a_1, a_2, \ldots, a_n\}$, it is *coherent* with the axioms of the formal system S to affirm that a constant b exists which maintains, with $a_1, a_2, \ldots, a_n$, the relation R. [131]

In other words, suppose that for *all finite* sets of constants, the statement:

$$(\exists y) \, [R(a_1, y) \cdot \text{and} \cdot R(a_2, y) \cdot \text{and} \ldots \cdot \text{and} \cdot R(a_n, y)]$$

is coherent with system S.

In this case, relation R structures an indefiniteness over the constants: every finite series $a_1, a_2, \ldots, a_n$ makes space for the marking of a 'continuation-point ["*point-de-suite*"]' according to R (a majorant or upper bound, in the case where R is the relation of order). To emphasize that the indefiniteness is attached to this marking, we will say that a relation that obeys this condition is transgressive-within-the-finite, or, more simply: *transgressive*.[28]

Now let us consider $R_1, R_2, \ldots, R_n \ldots$, the series of transgressive relations that our system S allows (and for simplicity's sake we will suppose that this set is denumerable). We will associate with each of these relations a *supplementary mark*, which does not figure amongst the constants a_1 of the system in its initial form. For the mark associated with R_n we will write ρ_n. We then *adjoin* as new axioms *all* statements of the type $R_n(a_i, \rho_n)$ – that is, all statements affirming that the relation R_n holds between a constant a_i and ρ_n. R_n traverses all the transgressive relations in the series, while a_i successively adopts all possible values among the constants of the system S.

In the case of the relation of order over the whole natural numbers, this amounts to associating with < (which is obviously transgressive-within-the-finite) a supplementary mark i (which is not the name of a number), and to positing as axioms *all* statements $n < i$, where n is a numerical constant. We

---

28   In the English text, Robinson uses the adjective 'concurrent' to characterize such relations.

recognize in i an *infinity-point* for the structure of order of the whole natural numbers.

Generally speaking, the new system obtained by the above procedure is *the formal theory of infinity-points for the transgressive-within-the-finite relations of a given system.*

It is important to note that it is a question of a simple *extension* of S: all we have done is to *add* a constant and some statements. All the rules and axioms of the initial system remain unchanged, all the theorems of that system are *also* theorems of the theory of infinity-points. In particular, the universally-quantified theorems remain valid, and are thus extended to the 'case' of the supplementary constant (see the appendix to this text).

So, in the formal system of whole numbers, the universal assertion assigning to *every* number n a successor $n + 1$ remains true, with the result that to the supplementary constant i is assigned a successor $i + 1$. More generally, if we have a theorem of the initial system of the form 'every x has the property P', elementary logical rules allow us to prove $P(a_i)$ for every constant. In particular, we would then have: 'ρ_n has property P'. We have indeed arrived at the conditions in which we can relaunch those algorithms [132] that founded the infinity-point.[29] The *structure* of the initial domain is in certain regards conserved in the recast domain. We will thus call the new system the *transgressive extension* of the initial system.[30]

The key question is evidently that of knowing whether the transgressive extension is a *coherent* system; whether, logically speaking, we have the right to introduce the supplementary axioms required. Will not the addition of *all* the statements of the form $R_n(a_i, \rho_n)$ end up contradicting the fact that the relations R_n are only transgressive within the finite? Because in the system of natural whole numbers it is *false*, for example, that one number can be larger than all the others. Does *infinite* transgression not exceed the logical powers of the formal language adopted?

Pure logic gives us the answer, in the form of a very general theorem, which underlies the whole construction:

If a system is coherent, its transgressive extension is also coherent.[31]

We are thereby authorized in marking an infinity-point for every relation that is transgressive-within-the-finite: this marking conserves the formal coherence

---

29   TN: '*Nous sommes bien dans les conditions de relance des algorithmes, qui fondent l'infini-point.*'

30   Robinson uses the word 'enlargement'.

31   This theorem depends upon another, which is fundamental in the theory of formal systems: the theorem of compactness [*compacité*]. This theorem guarantees that a system whose number of axioms is infinite is coherent if all its finite sub-systems (whose number of axioms are finite) are coherent.

and defines a 'non-standard' extension of the structure which is the 'standard' (ordinary) model of the system.

Once this has been established, everything runs smoothly. Given the usual theory of real numbers (as a base system), let R denote its domain (the 'objects' marked by the constants). The relation of order is obviously transgressive. Take α, the infinity-point relative to this relation: α is 'larger' than every element of R: it is *infinitely large*.

Since the universal statements of the initial theory are also valid for α ('return' of algorithms on the infinity-point), and since a sum and its product exist for *every* pair of numbers in R, we can define, for example, $\alpha + 1$, $\alpha + \alpha$, or α^n, etc., *all* of which will be infinitely large (larger than every constant of R).

We should note, by the way, that the infinity-point α, the *scriptural* instrument of the recasting, retains no particular privilege within the recast domain – a good illustration of the *effacement of the cause* in the apparatus of a structure. In particular, even if α is formally *inscribed* as a unique constant of transgression, it is no more the smallest infinite number than it is the largest – as we have just seen. Thus the number $\alpha - r$, where r is any positive number *from the initial domain*, is evidently smaller than α. It nonetheless remains an infinite number. If in fact it were not infinite, it would have to be because it is smaller than a finite number, say t. But $\alpha - r < t$ implies that $\alpha < t + r$, [**133**] which is absurd, α being infinite, and $t + r$, the sum of two finite numbers, being finite. There is in reality an indefinite number of infinite numbers smaller (or larger) than α: the recasting distributes the infinitely large numbers in an open space, both towards the 'bottom' and towards the 'top'. It is in this space that the mark α denotes no assignable, particular position: its operation dissipates it.

Nevertheless, it is clear that every complete *writing* of an infinite number, every trace *effectively* constructed to designate it on the basis of the graphical material of the extension, carries with it at least a mention of α: every writing which combines *only* the constants of the initial system denotes a number of the initial domain, a finite number. The *causality* of the mark α is here, in the domainial effacement of that which it designates, the omnipresence marked for every occupation of a place where only the 'new' infinite numbers can come. The marking of an infinity-point is an operation of the *signifier* as such.

Similarly, the infinitely small is introduced by way of a scriptural combination on the basis of α. We can thereby define $1/\alpha$, since R is a field [*corps*], and therefore the statement 'every element has an inverse' is an axiom for R. The theorem of the coherence of the extension guarantees the existence of this inverse for the infinitely large element α. Now, this inverse is *infinitesimal* (i.e. infinitely small relative to the constants of R).

To illustrate the point, take a real positive *finite* number a, as small as you like (a constant of the initial system). It is *always* the case that $a < \alpha$, since α is infinitely large. By dividing the two members of the inequality by the product

$a\alpha$ – which is an infinitely large number – we obtain $1/\alpha < 1/a$ for every finite positive a, and therefore $1/\alpha < a$, since $1/a$ is obviously finite if a is finite, i.e. $1 / \alpha < a$. Consequently, *whatever* positive finite number a we take, $1/a$ is smaller than a.

And in turn, this infinitesimal $1/\alpha$ or α^{-1} gives us, by way of an extension of the algorithms, an infinite family of infinitesimals. Specifically, if β is infinitesimal, however large a whole finite number n is, $n\beta$ is still infinitesimal. In fact, $\beta < a$ for *every* finite a (since β is infinitesimal and a finite), and consequently $\beta < a/n$ (a/n remaining finite), and so $n\beta < a$.

In this way we verify that the domain of the extension is non-Archimedean.

Finally, let $R[\alpha]$ be the macro-domain [*surdomaine*] of R or R recast according to the marking of an infinity-point for the relation of order. It contains, apart from the isomorphic field of real numbers (R, denoted by the constants of the initial system), an infinity of infinitely large elements, and of infinitely small elements. [134]

More precisely, let us call *standard* [*conformes*] numbers those marks of $R[\alpha]$ which belong to R, and which are the constants 'from before the recasting'. We can distinguish, amongst the positive numbers of $R[\alpha]$:

- *finite numbers*: numbers included between two standard positive non-null numbers. Naturally, every standard number is finite. But there are other kinds of finite numbers too: for example the sum of a standard number and an infinitesimal is a finite non-standard number.
- *infinite numbers*: numbers larger than every standard number.
- *infinitesimal numbers*: numbers smaller than every standard number (and following convention, we will take zero to be an infinitesimal).

Within this framework, it is possible to provide a very simple definition of something that remained a vague idea during the heroic period of differential calculus: infinite proximity. A number a is infinitely close to a number b if the difference $a - b$ is an infinitesimal number.

It is on this basis that Robinson reconstructs all the fundamental concepts of analysis in a language which, while often reminiscent of that of the Marquis de l'Hôpital, is nevertheless now assured of its systematicity.

Let us remark first of all that in $R[\alpha]$ there exist *whole infinite numbers*: in fact, the transgressive extension of R is *also* an extension of N, the set of whole natural numbers, which is a sub-set of R. Now take a series $s_1, s_2, s_3, \ldots, s_n, \ldots$ of standard numbers. We will say that the standard number l is the *limit* of the series s_n if for every *infinitely large* whole number n, $l - s_n$ is *infinitely small*; the verb 'is' can be substituted for the classical 'tends towards', because to be infinitely large (or small) means: to be an infinite (or infinitesimal) *number*. The concept of convergence is no longer constructed according to the attribution of vanishingness, or tendential properties, but by recourse to *elements* of the defined subsets of $R[\alpha]$.

Thus we find that the principal objection of Hegel – and of Lagrange – to the idea of the limit is subverted by the punctualization of its definition, even as the idea of limit loses its foundational function. For we know that following the decline of infinitely small numbers (a decline marked by d'Alembert's initial clarification of their status), Cauchy, Bolzano and Weierstrass would establish a definitive foundation for differential calculus in the concept of limit: in their eyes, this procedure had the inestimable merit of accepting, thanks to the rationalizing sanction of repression, *only finite marks* in the text. When I say: 'the series s_n has as its limit the number l if, for any positive number ε, there is a whole number M such that $n > M$ entails $|l - s_n| < \varepsilon$', the only numerical constants mentioned (ε, n, M) are all finite. The concept of limit therefore effects a rejection of every infinitesimal mark, and this is precisely why, in the *Encyclopédie*, d'Alembert salutes its positivity:

> It is not at all a question, as one ordinarily says, of infinitely small quantities in *differential* calculus: it is a question only of the limits of finite quantities. Thus the metaphysics of infinite and of infinitely small [135] quantities larger or smaller than each other is totally useless to *differential* calculus. The term *infinitely small* is only used as an abbreviation, to shorten the expression.[32]

Conversely, this positivity, which Hegel also recognized, is for him a failure to express (genuine) infinity. The underlying idea that dx marks a proximity, that x 'tends towards' a value x_0, has no speculative meaning for him: 'Approximation or approach [*rapprochement*] is a category that says nothing and renders nothing conceivable: dx already has its approach behind it: it is neither nearer, nor further away, and the infinitely near is equivalent to the negation of proximity and of approximation.'[33]

In non-standard analysis, this negation is converted into the numerical *existence* of an infinitesimal, which marks the infinitely small difference. As for the positive ruse of a detour via finite marks, it becomes redundant, for infinite proximity is *numberable* [*chiffrable*]. Both partisans and adversaries of the concept of limit are dismissed, the common terrain of their opposition being defined by their refusal of such a numbering [*chiffrage*].

Similarly, the continuity of a function to the real (standard) point x_0 gives way to statements such as: $f(x)$ is continuous at point x_0, where $a < x < b$, if and only if, for every x infinitely close to x_0 (that is, where $x - x_0$ is infinitesimal), $f(x)$ is infinitely close to $f(x_0)$, which is to say: where $f(x) - f(x_0)$ is infinitesimal.

32   Jean d'Alembert, 'Différentiel', *Encyclopédie*, vol. 4 (1754), 985–989.
33   Hegel, *Science of Logic*, 21:269tm.

To define Cauchy's integral, we will divide the interval $[a, b]$ into *infinitely numerous* slices (the series x_n of these slices will be indexed on the whole numbers of $R[\alpha]$, which includes infinite whole numbers, so that 'infinitely numerous' has a strict numerical meaning); we will ask that each slice be *infinitely small* (in other words that $x_{n+1} - x_n$ be an infinitesimal number), and so on.

Analysis is indeed shown to be *the site of denumerable infinities*.

Retrospectively, the classical and Hegelian case against infinitesimal quanta is thereby entirely defeated.

No doubt Hegel, or Berkeley, were merely engaging in the spontaneous epistemology of the mathematics of their time. They did not *contradict* these mathematics. But if Berkeley established the fundamental obscurity of Analysis only so as to secure by comparison religion's right to mystery, Hegel in his turn validated the rejection of the infinity-point only in order to run to the aid of a mathematics in search of a foundation so as to bestow upon it the poisoned chalice of 'qualitative' relation. The debasement of multiplicity, the refusal to think the concepts of Analysis according to a logic of marks, however much they may have been fuelled by a confused scientific actuality, are nonetheless *enslaved* to speculative objectives. It is these objectives alone that require the supremacy [**136**] of quality, and the relative discrediting of algorithmic or *inscribed* thinking: i.e. of structural thinking.

That this retroactive effect has been prepared, throughout the history of philosophy, by a secret and permanent supremacy of the continuous over the discrete, is unequivocally declared by Hegel: 'the variation of variable magnitudes is determined qualitatively and is, consequently, continuous'.[34] Quality and continuity are mutually implicating – an implication which has weighed upon the very history of the theoretical concepts of differential Calculus, and which has in part governed the censuring of infinitesimals.

Quality, continuity, temporality and negation: the oppressive categories of ideological objectives.

Number, discreteness, space and affirmation: or, better, Mark, Punctuation, Blank Space [*Blanc*] and Cause: the categories of scientific processes.

These are the formal indices of the two 'tendencies' that have been in struggle, according to Lenin, since the beginnings of philosophy. They have been in struggle *within* the discourses themselves, and formative for science's historical choices. A struggle between the materiality of the signifier and the ideality of the Whole.

Within mathematics, infinitesimal traces have been the victims of this struggle: not because they contravened some supposedly formal atemporality, but because a ramified history supported the Reason of an epoch in excluding them, and in not linking [*enchaîner*] the infinite through them.

---

34   Ibid., 21:278.

That the act and the effect of the infinite should be a question of gaps [*écarts*] and of written supplements, is indeed what no one wanted to hear, as Cantor's experience showed, two centuries after the founders of the 'new calculus'.[35]

The unforeseen return of infinitesimals, received in a state of renewed astonishment [*stupeur*],[36] even if it arrives too late for Analysis (which is certainly no longer in search of its fundaments or foundations), has the inestimable value of *disintricating* by means of a science that which, in the orchestrated complacency of their rejection, owed less to the necessities of the concept than to those constraining illusions whose salvation required an ideal guarantee. [137]

APPENDIX

Some may be surprised to see us assert that the axioms of a formal system are 'conserved' for its transgressive extension, whereas, for example, $R[\alpha]$ is non-Archimedean while R is Archimedean. But this perfectly exemplifies the *formal* character of the procedure.

In the initial system, the Archimedeanism is expressed with a *statement* of the type: 'for two numbers a and b such that $a < b$, there always exists a whole number n such that $b < na$'.

We might formalize this statement as follows:

$$(\forall x)\,(\forall y)\,[x < y \rightarrow (\exists n)\,(y < nx)]$$

We say: this formalized statement *is indeed a theorem of* $R[\alpha]$. But of course, the quantified variable 'n' takes its values *from among the whole numbers of* $R[\alpha]$, which includes, as we know, *infinite* whole numbers.

$R[\alpha]$ is not Archimedean, in the sense that for an infinitesimal, there does not exist a *finite* n such that the infinitesimal multiplied by n might surpass a given finite number.

But *the formal statement* of Archimedeanism remains valid, because in multiplying an infinitesimal by a suitable whole *infinite* number, one can indeed surpass every given finite number.

---

35   And as is shown even today, in 1968, by the incredible and grotesque popular success of Georges Antoniadès Métrios' widely-publicized book, *Cantor a tort* [*Cantor is Wrong*] (Puteaux: Sival Presse, 1968) – a risible symptom of the reactionary obstinacy which characterizes the paramathematical ideologies of the infinite.

36   Cf. the painful retraction to which Fraenkel very honestly admits in the third edition of his *Abstract Set Theory*, just after a passage devoted to the sterility of the infinitely small: 'Recently, an unexpected use of infinitely small quantities, and particularly a method to found Analysis (calculus) on infinitesimals, have been rendered possible on the basis of a properly non-Archimedean and non-standard extension of the field of real numbers. For this surprising development, the reader . . . etc.' (*Abstract Set Theory* [Amsterdam: North-Holland, 1966], 125).

CHAPTER ELEVEN

Alain Grosrichard
An Eighteenth-Century Psychological Experiment[1]

[101] The text we have decided to present is an extract from the last of eight Essays published by Jean-Bernard Mérian between 1770 and 1780 in the *Nouveaux Mémoires de l'Académie royale des Sciences et Belles Lettres de Berlin*. In it, Mérian devotes himself to writing the history of the responses to a problem that the Irish surveyor William Molyneux once proposed to John Locke, whose *Essay on Human Understanding* he had just read:

> Suppose a Man born blind, and now adult, and taught by his touch to distinguish between a Cube, and a Sphere of the same metal, and nighly of the same bigness, so as to tell, when he felt one and t'other, which is the Cube, which the Sphere. Suppose then the Cube and Sphere placed on a Table, and the Blind Man to be made to see. Quaere, Whether by his sight, before he touch'd them, he could now distinguish, and tell, which is the Globe, which the Cube.[2]

Noting the disagreement among the multiple responses put forth over the course of 80 years – by Locke, Leibniz, Berkeley, Condillac, and Diderot, among others – Mérian proposed his own response, or rather a *solution*, that is, identification of the conditions required if the proposed response was to make the problem disappear: these conditions were those of the realization of an *experiment*.[3]

My task here is to examine these eighty years that separate the statement of

---

1   This text is excerpted from a *diplôme d'études supérieures*, written under the direction of Georges Canguilhem. TN: First published as Alain Grosrichard, 'Une Expérience psychologique au dix-huitième siècle', CpA 2.3 (March 1966): 101–113. Translated by Knox Peden and Peter Hallward.

2   TN: John Locke cites Molyneux's letter in his *Essay concerning Human Understanding* (book 2, chapter 9, §8, online at gutenberg.org). After this summary of the problem, Locke continues: 'To which the acute and judicious proposer answers, "Not. For, though he has obtained the experience of how a globe, how a cube affects his touch, yet he has not yet obtained the experience, that what affects his touch so or so, must affect his sight so or so; or that a protuberant angle in the cube, that pressed his hand unequally, shall appear to his eye as it does in the cube." – I agree with this thinking gentleman, whom I am proud to call my friend, in his answer to this problem; and am of the opinion that the blind man, at first sight, would not be able with certainty to say which was the globe, which the cube, whilst he only saw them; though he could unerringly name them by his touch, and certainly distinguish them by the difference of their figures felt.'

3   TN: The French word *expérience* can mean either experiment or experience; here the primary meaning is generally 'experiment', but our translation varies with the context, and readers should keep both meanings in mind throughout.

a problem that was apparently fully ready to be converted into an experiment, and the actual proposal for this experiment, which Mérian presents as necessary. Why did it not occur to people earlier, to complement the theoretical hypotheses with an experimental verification? I do not intend to participate in the condescending astonishment of the psychologist, who is so confident today that his method is well-founded. On the contrary, I would like to show that what became necessary so much later was not the experiment considered as the verification of speculative hypotheses, but rather a *new kind of experiment*, which I will call an experiment of prescientific psychology invented by the philosopher in order to replace another kind of experiment, an experiment or experience of philosophy – [102] one invented *by empiricist and sensualist philosophy* so as to maintain the coherence of its discourse.

I THE PHILOSOPHICAL EXPERIMENT, OR THE
BLIND MAN AT THE PILLARS OF HERCULES

'The dominion of man, in this little world of his understanding [is] much what the same it is in the great world of physical things . . .'4 I would like to read Locke's *Essay* as if it was written in the way that a landowner might tour the fields of his understanding, making an inventory of the properties he has rightfully come to acquire. In constructing his physics, Descartes made man the master and owner of the universe. On one condition, however – that of distinguishing properly between a subject of objectivity on the one hand and a subject of sensible qualities on the other, on pain of losing all right to the certainty of his knowledge. Among the ideas arising from sense, none are exemplary: they can only inform me about myself [*moi*] considered as a composite substance and not about the world such as it is in reality. They have *truth value* – they allow us to construct a science of the external world – only when referred by the subject of objectivity to the eternal truths created by a God, truths recognized as truthful and deposited in the soul like seeds, Descartes says. Or as Locke will read them: 'primitive *notions*, imprinted and engraved so to speak in our soul, which receives them from the first moments of its existence.'5 Thus man is only the subject of knowledge, he can only play the role of the *owner* of the world, because he is the *depository* of the truths of an Other.

The *Essay* seeks to establish this: all these ideas – claimed to be innate, deposited by an Other – are *mine*, and mine as a man. In the *Second Treatise on*

---

4   John Locke, *Essay Concerning Human Understanding*, book 2, chapter 2, §2.
5   TN: This translates the French version of Locke that Grosrichard appears to rely on here (*Oeuvres de Locke et Leibnitz*, ed. and trans. François Thurot [Paris : F. Didot Frères, 1839]), of the opening lines of Locke's *Essay*, book 1, chapter 1, §1. Locke's original reads: 'primary notions, characters, as it were stamped upon the mind of man; which the soul receives in its very first being, and brings into the world with it.'

Civil Government,[6] Locke founded the ownership of land on labour. It is the same in the *Essay on Human Understanding*: on the basis of a natural given or datum delivered by perception, the understanding can, through the labour of reflection, produce all of its ideas, right up to ideas of infinity and of God. [103]

Over the course of an ideal genesis of the psychological subject's ideas in which the two Cartesian subjects are intermingled, the *Essay* produces everything, while declaring that it presupposes nothing. In truth, we can find hidden there the duality of at least two Cartesian functions, if not subjects. The supposedly natural genesis of a psychological subject's knowledge is in fact always finalized [*finalisée*] by a philosophical understanding, in this case that of the *Essay*'s author. The philosopher, purporting to describe the true genesis of knowledge – that is, as soon as he gets serious and *writes* – decrees the genesis of true knowledge. The philosopher is this silent other who pretends to describe [rather than decree] – as when, for instance, he goes out into the world and transforms himself into an educator, and furtively presents his student with a carefully chosen nature.[7] It remains the case that from the frontiers of perception, from what is for a Cartesian most obscure and confused, the discourse of the *Essay* covers little by little, without rupture or leap, the entire domain of Cartesian knowledge, ultimately rejoining the other frontier, that which, facing the divine infinite, limited the domain of Cartesian understanding. Everything is acquired, from what used to be merely on loan. Everything, except the truth value of this everything.

For this genesis remains ideal precisely insofar as it bases itself on a subject unsullied by experience, a subject through which appear the simple ideas of perception. How will the reader understand this discourse *as true*? How could it be anything other than an opinion for him? The answer is: if he makes it his own. And yet, in order to make it his own, to understand it, he must place himself beneath its words and grasp that for which they are the signs, i.e. ideas: he must return to this *place*, of which the philosopher speaks, and put himself *in the place* of the originary psychological subject. 'All that I can say in favour of the truth of what I propose,' writes Locke (in the same terms that Berkeley, Condillac, and others will later use), 'is that I call upon each to observe and experience it in himself.'[8] This pinnacle [*comble*] of subjectivity is the pinnacle

---

6   Locke, *Second Treatise on Civil Government*, chapter 5, 'On Property.'

7   Condillac will write in his *Cours d'études*: 'I needed to bring myself close to my student and to put myself totally in his place; I needed to be a child rather than a tutor. I would thus let him play and would play with him, but I would point out to him everything he was doing.'

8   TN: Grosrichard's citation appears to combine two passages from Locke's *Essay*, taken from *Oeuvres de Locke et Leibnitz*, ed. Thurot, 40. In the original, the first passage (*Essay*, book 1, chapter 3, §25) reads: 'All that I shall say for the principles I proceed on is, that I can only appeal to men's own unprejudiced experience and observation whether they be true or not'; and the second (*Essay*, book 2, chapter 1, §1) reads: '[. . .] for which I shall appeal to every one's own observation and experience.'

of objectivity. We have here a repetition, in wholly different conditions, of the Cartesian invitation to undertake at least once in one's life the experiment of the *Cogito*.

We were brought up in the domain of opinion, and according to chance: against this inevitably contingent experience that has always been our imposed lot, it is necessary to institute an experience that is my own. This exemplary experience requires a genuine experimentation of myself by myself. [104] The natural within me is only given if I search for it. It is not easy to attain a transparency to myself that would not be a mirage, or to touch a firm ground that would not be a basis for prejudice.

And yet, prejudice, the primary mirage, is situated at the very level of this perception that one considers a natural given. It is here that Molyneux's *problem* arises, not really for the philosopher, but for the common man who alone hesitates over the response [to the problem] because he does not see that the unity of his perception is constituted by a judgment. This is a problem, then, with a didactic value. The error of the non-philosopher is unavoidable. If I say 'I see a globe' (whereas I ought to say 'I judge that the coloured surface that I see indicates a globe that I could touch'), it is because my awareness of this judgment disappears beneath a habit whose unlimited power to deceive me has been rendered necessary by the demands of survival. In a world governed by the principles of mechanism, the only objective knowledge is knowledge by *touch*; touch alone immediately provides me with access to the 'primary qualities' of things. But if in order to *know* objectively it is necessary to enter into contact with bodies, this contact may be fatal to my body: the demand for objectivity is at the same time the threat of death. Here the veracity of touch, the sense of succession and contact, finds its limit here from the point of view of life. What compensates for this limit is *sight*, in itself the least objective sense, but the one that grasps the whole [*atteint l'ensemble*] and that can 'touch bodies at a distance.' All my knowledge of the world is elaborated on a ground that is already *constructed*. To go beyond this, in search of the simple elements constitutive of my perception, is thus to break with the judgment that allows me to survive, and to shatter the unity of my self [*moi*]. However, I must undertake this transgression if I want to know, and move forward in a domain wherein I can always say *I* [*Je*] without any longer having to say *me* [*moi*].[9]

This is a necessary enterprise if I want to own my knowledge and be responsible for my experience from its origins. But is it possible? Yes, in principle: it is possible to reach this extreme frontier in myself, this thin line where the impact of more or less tiny solid entities that come from the outside to strike my senses gives rise to a sensation and a simple idea, *because the soul is one*, a unity that is

---

9   TN: the French reads: '*Pourtant, je dois entreprendre cette transgression si Je veux connaître, et m'avancer dans un domaine où Je peux toujours dire Je sans pouvoir plus dire* moi.'

at once sensitive and reasonable. As a result, the subject is in principle responsible for all of his knowledge. And this is why the coordination of sensations coming from five sources that have nothing in common and provide five series of heterogeneous ideas is the doing of a judgment. The unity of perception is thought as a system of signs, not grounded in nature as it seems, but instituted.

If this transgression is possible, with a physiological-philosophical theory justifying it in principle, how might it be realizable? It can be realized by a kind of experimentation that, this time, is specifically scientific – and it is here that we find the real [105] function of Molyneux's problem.[10] I say a scientific kind of experiment because Molyneux proposes an *instrument* of experimentation or experience [*d'expérience*], one constructed according to theoretical criteria: the blind man; a *laboratory* – the understanding – in which everything is eliminated or neutralized that is not pertinent to the object of research, the pure sensations of sight; a qualified *experimenter*, the philosopher.

'Suppose a man born blind!' – this is a strange statement, whereby the author imposes an empty form in which a place is marked for the subject to seek his origin, to which an imperative summons him. Put yourself in the place of the man born blind, who regains sight and rediscovers what you see truly [*en vérité*]. Molyneux's born-blind man is not a concept from pathological physiology, for the very reason that physiology did not have its own concepts back then. For the surgeon who operates on cataracts, the only theoretical reference at his disposal to help him reflect on his practice was Locke's empiricism: the born-blind adult is an adult whose understanding is perfectly developed, but incomplete, marked by obscure blotches. The operation [that removes a cataract] is the opening of a window. By the same token, the philosophy of knowledge does not need any confirmation in 'real' experiences or experiments. On the contrary, to take at face value the declarations of a blind person and the observations of the surgeon would amount to a lack of rigour. The real blind person does not know what he should see, and what is more what he will see will be immediately obscured since he will have to transmit it in the terms of common language to an observer, who quite often is not a philosopher. Not to mention that to wait for a surgeon to provide a subject for the experiment would condemn us to wait for the opportunity to arise, one that is relatively rare and difficult to repeat.

Why select from the world a subject already overrun by prejudices, when we can build one in ourselves, in the ideal space of the understanding? That way we can retain only what is essential, and eliminate the contingent. The born-blind man regaining sight is an instrument constructed in light of an experiment of the philosophy of knowledge, and, as in chemistry when we

---

10   As Mérian will write, the man who is born blind and regains his sight stands at the Pillars of Hercules of sensation.

produce a body that only exists in nature in a composite state, this instrument is destined to *produce* a pure sensation, which is to say the other side [*l'envers*] of a simple idea. The results of this experiment in the understanding do not have to be communicated in language since they apply in the domain that is beneath language. Here more than at any other moment of analysis, everyone must advance *alone* within oneself in the quest for truth: 'It would be useless to multiply the testimonies [. . .]. It's up to the philosopher to descend within himself, and to draw the truth from the bottom of the pit.'[11] [106]

There is no place in Locke's empiricism for an experimental psychology in the sense that we usually understand it, even prescientifically. If so many years passed before Molyneux's proposal could demand an experimental realization, this is because it was posited within the space of a philosophy of experience [*expérience*], in all senses of the word. The understanding must have the same authority [*empire*] over its ideas that man has over the external world in experimental physics: this is why, within its world, the understanding constructs its techniques and instruments from experience.

I would like to note here that such a situation is only possible due to an essential equivocation, which bears on the concept of *sense* [*sens*]. For Locke's empiricism, a sense is nothing but the fine grate against which the external world strikes, in the form of bits, grains, dust, and mist.[12] Struck, this grate transmits the impression to the soul where it becomes sensation and is combined with others via judgment. A sense is never thought of as an organ of the senses, as inserted in an indivisible organic totality that makes normal perception possible, because to think the unity of perception as organic perception, it is necessary to think of a power other than the reasonable soul that unifies by judging: the power of life. Faced with a text from the surgeon William Cheselden[13] in which the reactions of born-blind patient to his cataract removal are related in detail, contemporaries did not *read*, in the panic of the patient, a perception that restructures itself with the scarring of the wounded *eye*, but only the astonishment of an *understanding*, and the long time it takes to acquire the habit of governing a territory newly annexed to its empire. This blind man did not surprise his contemporaries; he was, after all, only the crude realization of the pure blind man posited by Molyneux. [107]

---

11   Mérian, paraphrasing Berkeley.

12   This theory of *sense* (e.g., the retina) will endure, right up to a period in which, alongside it and without contradicting it, a new theory of the *organ* of sense (the eye) will be developed: see for example Louis de Jaucourt's articles in the *Encyclopédie*.

13   William Cheselden, *Philosophical Transactions*, number 402 (1728).

II THE SOUL OF THE BEAST AND THE SOUL OF
MAN, OR THE IMPOSSIBLE EXPERIMENT

Undertaking an analysis of the understanding beyond perception, empiricist philosophy justifies itself on the basis of a philosophical psychophysiology, one that is complicit with this philosophy insofar as it has no domain of its own: its domain is the underside [*l'envers*] of philosophy's, and it contents itself with saying *the same thing* in different terms. For reason, what is beneath the self is not opaque. Perception is a mirror that reflects back to the non-philosophical subject the image of a constituted self, which he believes to be originarily *one* – it is a mirror that the philosopher must go through, however. The soul is responsible [for all that it perceives], right up to the place where it opens up, through the machinery of the body, to the external world.

In 1728, the same year of Cheselden's account, David Boullier,[14] making use of the structural analogy between the human body and that of animals, declared that animals have a soul, and added: 'What man is in certain respects animals are in their entirety.' He thereby demarcated, by making the animal a *level* of man, a domain in which the reflexive analysis of the understanding could no longer reach: that of the 'sensitive' soul, separate from the reasonable soul that is given to man alone.[15] Around 1670 Thomas Willis had distinguished between the sensitive and the reasonable soul, but it remained a matter of two functions of one and the same soul. The introduction, so to speak, of the animal into man establishes, we believe, the very possibility of psychology itself. Although it does not yet have its name, psychology now has its object, at least, a phenomenon in the sense that Newton understands it, and one that can serve as a basis for a psychophysiology of perception. It is precisely because the animal is only a certain level of man within man that one can, by coming back through reflexive analysis within man to the natural level of perception, make a psychology of the animal. And, in return, by anatomizing the animal and experimenting on it (which is not possible with man), one can develop a psychophysiology of perception that would not simply be the underside of a philosophy of the reasonable soul, but that would nevertheless be applicable to man: man and animal [now] mutually hold the truth of each other [*l'homme et l'animal sont vérité mutuellement l'un de l'autre*].[16] [**108**]

Full experimentation confined to the interior of the understanding thus loses its justification. The theory of the sensitive soul leads, with Charles Bonnet

---

14   David Boullier, *Essai sur l'âme des bêtes* (1728).

15   Here of course one thinks of Leibniz's phrase: 'we are empirical in three quarters of our actions.'

16   Condillac will write in the *Traité des animaux* [*Treatise on Animals*, 1755]: 'If animals feel, they feel as we do', and: 'It would not be very interesting to know what animals are, if this were not means to know better what we are.'

for example, to a fibrillary theory of sensation, which ought to allow us to account physiologically for the harmony of a perception independent of judgment. From now on, I *see a globe*, and it is not by a forgotten judgment, but by a certain arrangement of fibres in my brain at the very outset of my life, and a resonance among these fibres, through which they acquire a permanent constitution. How then might we come to know the pure sensation of each sense? Psychology and physiology complement one another here in a surprising way. Bonnet writes: 'We do not know what the Soul itself is: but we do know that ideas are attached to the play of certain fibres: we can therefore *reason* about fibres because we *see* these fibres.'[17] In this way reflexive psychological analysis gives physiology its bearings in an undifferentiated fibrillary substance; and in return physiology, because it uses the microscope to compose these groups of fibres that correspond to the degrees of elaboration and differentiation of ideas, enables us to *see* the fibres that must correspond to pure sensation, i.e. to the simplest forms of sensation: it is the *microscope* that becomes the instrument of experimental psychology. From now on it is no longer reflexive analysis that provides physiology with something simple to explain: instead physiology provides the simple element to psychology. On the basis of what the physiology of fibres provides for it, psychology can extrapolate and lead analysis beyond a perception that is always already constituted for it.

Setting out from the pure sensations of each sense, at the level from which all judgment is excluded, the genesis of knowledge can thus only be the transformation of sensations by themselves. In declaring that Locke is unfaithful to his own principles since he implicitly admits an innateness of the faculties of understanding and an unconscious judgment that unifies perception, Condillac aims to treat these faculties themselves as a degree of transformation of sensation: the whole genesis of the understanding is conducted on the basis of a primary matter that is sensation, and by means of a motor principle which is that of pleasure and pain. The coordinated perception of a world – for the animal as for the human – is the result of a *natural education*: *natural* since it is a matter of a natural given, naturally transformed by natural operations; but *education*, in which touch is the educator of the other senses (and not the *instructor*, as it is for Locke or even Berkeley), in making a multiplicity of *I* refer back to the same *self* [*moi*]. [**109**]

In this way, an opacity henceforth prohibits the understanding, as it experiments within itself on its origins, from pushing the analysis all the way down to the level of the simple. For to dissect the understanding in order to satisfy the requirements of founding knowledge and mastering its authority or empire would no longer suggest the (necessary but reversible) undoing of a judgment, but rather the denial of oneself as living.

17   Bonnet, *Essai de Psychologie*, 1754.

III THE NECESSARY AND REDISCOVERED EXPERIMENT

Faced with this opacity that threatens the understanding's authority over itself, philosophy invents a technique that allows it to obtain the equivalent of Molyneux's experiment, with the conditions that accompany it: the determination and limitation of variables, and theoretical knowledge of the instrument.

Two paths are thus presented. The first option is to produce an experimental model of the origin, knowing full well that it is now a matter of fiction, but one by means of which we can speak of what lies beneath [*l'en-deçà*] language: this is a fiction because the philosopher can no longer content himself with a genesis of knowledge within the space of a reasonable soul, because his genesis must produce not only an understanding, but a knowing *man*. A motionless block of marble in human form is substituted for Locke's blank slate.

By according touch[18] to his statue, by finally transforming the marble into skin that can touch itself, Condillac also gives it both life and consciousness of itself. Thus begins this education that transforms the diversity of sensations into the unity of perception, the senses into sense organs: the retina into an *eye* that can turn, whose lens can swell, whose lid can close. Yet it is remarkable that when Condillac, criticizing Cheselden, proposes a philosophically experimental use of the cured blind man [*l'aveugle opéré*] in order to respond to Molyneux, he defines, in order to make the experiment convincing, conditions that tend to refer the cured blind man back to a model of the blind man that can be ideally situated in the development of the *Treatise on Sensations*. He does this by *imitating* the fictive through [110] tricks [*artifices*] that might be undertaken in the real: 'A sure means of making experiments capable of dissipating all doubts would be to enclose in a glass box a blind person who has just had his cataracts removed.' The tighter one makes this glass cage, the more one neutralizes the sense of touch. And yet, what is this glass cage that progressively entraps (and Condillac sets no limit on its tightening) the cured blind man, if not an attempt to rediscover the state of the statue at the moment when he is given sight? The glass has the rigidity of stone, but it is transparent. Motionless, covered over with skin of glass, the subject of the Condillacian experiment is reduced to a pure sensory retina, the place where the man who turns himself to stone intersects with the statue that we bring to life.

Diderot follows a different path. Instead of producing, like Condillac or Bonnet,[19] a fiction that opens what is beneath language to the language of the

---

18   Which, in an eighteenth century context, means inextricably both touch in the strict sense, and coenaesthesia.

19   His fibrillar theory forces Bonnet to invent an 'automaton', the sole model possible at the origin. 'Let us not even attempt to study Children [. . .]. Children are hardly born before their senses open at once to a large number of different impressions. There results a sequence of movements and a combination of ideas that it is impossible to follow and untangle.'

philosopher (and that, if an experiment is necessary, replaces the real blind man in the space of fiction), Diderot opts to question without experimental tricks those in whom nature obliterated a sense at birth, but that human effort has been able to restore. This is in part Diderot's enterprise in the *Letter on the Blind*. But this is to ask the subject to articulate in common language what is beneath its level, the level of the normal man's perception (the perception that remains the point of reference). It would then be necessary to ensure that the subject of the experiment, that the *blind man, be a philosopher* and to educate him accordingly, reversing Molyneux's imperative to philosophers: make yourselves blind! No longer capable of finding the born-blind man in himself, the philosopher, in order to neutralize the other subjectivity he needs, in order to see through it the visible in its purity, must make the blind man a philosopher, which is to say, thoroughly aware of the gaps in his experience and master of his language.

Inasmuch as the history of Molyneux's problem allows us to clarify its origins, experimental psychology is the set of techniques that philosophy invents to retain mastery of this space of the understanding, which became transparent solely on condition of undoing [*dénouer*] its judgments. In a sense, such an experimental psychology figures as an enterprise of philosophy against a scientific psychology that might seek to become independent [of philosophy]. The threat of psychology's separation from philosophy is experienced by [111] the latter as a tragedy.[20] Why? We still will not be able to answer this question, once we have discerned, in Mérian's project, those legitimate and honest satisfactions that the philosophy of the eighteenth century still dreamed of drawing from a knowledge of man's nature – but we will be able to imagine the tragedy in the form of an allegory: the tragedy of a philosophy that watches its child separate from it, and yield to the seductive discourse of the barbarians.

But let us return to its happy *discourse*, which organizes a world with so much confidence.

IV MÉRIAN'S SEMINAR

With Diderot, the question of experimentation on man was posited in technical terms: how might we reproduce, with a real subject provided by surgery, the ideal conditions of experimentation in the understanding? This is a question that can be asked another way: *how might we experiment on a living man [le vivant] without killing him*? In the case of Molyneux's problem, surgery procured for philosophy a subject who, duly prepared, could more or less satisfy Molyneux's ideal conditions.

But here an objection arises, one founded on the recent observations of physiologists and surgeons, one with which Diderot probably was not familiar

---

20   The expression is Georges Canguilhem's.

but that Mérian raises: no one who is born *absolutely* blind is *operable*. It follows then that surgery can no longer provide the subject of the experiment for philosophy. It is up to philosophy entirely to invent its experimentation, to *fabricate* its blind man. What we read in Mérian are the techniques of fabrication of this subject of the experiment. The technical problem then becomes a philosophical problem, that of the *right or legality* [*droit*] of this experiment: *How do we experiment on man without negating or denying him?* However, Mérian eloquently shows that, in positing the necessity of such an experimentation, sensualist philosophy provides its justification *at the same time*. [112]

To render children artificially – but provisionally – blind is not to negate man, it is merely to go against an idea of man born from a popular prejudice, a prejudice that makes of man an essence, and in that sense not perfectible.

On the contrary, man is perfectible: for sensualism, this alone distinguishes man from animal. But it is precisely because there is no rupture in man between animal and reason, between nature and the possibility of exceeding it, that the prejudice so easily takes hold – the prejudice that confuses in a single essence the imperfectability of the animal and the always possible progress of reason.

The progress of man is considered [*pensé*] in economic terms. Instead of passively receiving from nature what it wastefully provides, the art of men can, by experimenting on nature and knowing its laws, predict it, direct it, impose an order on it, and maximize what it yields. Advances in the techniques of production are not considered as a refusal of nature, but as the maximum utilization of nature, on the basis of our scientific knowledge of it.

Natural production, in man, concerns the ideas of a perception that is at one with the goals of life. And man perfects himself because he is the product of the rational utilization of what is in him by nature. He cannot change this nature, the five senses reunited in perception, or increase its capital. But he can increase the yield and at the same time the quality of the product. It is not a question then of perfecting each [individual] sense, but of adjusting or developing perception, of mastering it by knowing its laws, which is to say, of perfecting the use of each sense and of doing so in such a way that the development of one sense does not harm that of the others.[21] To do this, a particular and successive attention is necessary for each sense, with the others provisionally held in reserve.

The techniques for knowing Nature within man, which require and allow it to be dissected and de-composed, allow in return for it to be re-composed according to a constructed order, which is no longer that of chance and habit, but of a nature ordered by reason. Because reason is in man the product of a

---

21   Cf. Diderot: 'The help that each of our senses gives the others prevents them from perfecting themselves [. . .]. But it would be very different if we were to exercise them separately in occasions where the help of one sense alone would suffice.'

natural progression, the order imposed by reason will be the only genuine natural order. Man makes use of what nature gives him in order to perfect his nature. [113]

And so the techniques of experimentation for knowing [*connaître*] are also the techniques for the production of a man capable of knowing better: the advances of knowledge are thus necessarily and naturally linked to the advances of the one who allows us, as an object of experimentation, to know. To conduct experiments in the school of the artificially blind[22] is also to constitute for the subject of the experiment an experience that renders him as perfect as his nature entails.

Mérian's proposal, in which the philosopher is the director (delegated by the sovereign) of a laboratory – a laboratory that is also an establishment which offers care and assistance, a hospital, a school, a factory, and which culminates in an Academy of philosophers – is certainly the product of a psychology that still remains inseparable from its philosophy, and for which knowing how man feels, thinks, and knows is indistinguishable from knowing how *he should* feel, think, and know – so as to be a good citizen.

This study opened with a man who denied divine seeds. It closes by giving the floor to another, who built a school. *Who* today occupies the place of the philosopher who put himself in the place of God, and who is the tree?[23]

APPENDIX
Chevalier de Mérian
THE HISTORY OF MOLYNEUX'S PROBLEM[24]

[115]. . . We very much hope, then, for an increase in the number of observations that are authentic, and undertaken by philosophers. Then we could compare them, and perhaps find something in one that lacks in the others. Cheselden first lit the torch; in two pages of observations made almost at random he clarifies things that larger tomes had tangled up. Who knows what a series of comparable experiments might yield,

---

22   TN: this is a reference to Mérian's 'Séminaire d'aveugles artificiels' (CpA 2.4:119), as presented in the appendix to this chapter.

23   TN: This last paragraph reads: '*Cette étude s'ouvrait sur un homme qui niait les semences divines. Elle se clôt pour laisser la parole à un autre qui bâtit un séminaire. Qui, aujourd'hui est à la place du philosophe qui se mettait à la place de Dieu, qui est l'arbre?*' Given the references to and significance of marble in the text, *l'arbre* here may perhaps be a typo for *marbre*. In response to a question about this the author replied: 'after all, what is written is written, whether or not it's a slip of the pen' (letter from Alain Grosrichard, 12 February 2012).

24   This is an extract from Mérian's eighth essay, read before a public assembly of the Academy of Berlin, 4 June 1772, publis   in the *Mémoires de l'Académie*, Classe de Philosophie Spéculative, 1780.

TN: First published in the *Cahiers pour l'Analyse* as Chevalier de Mérian, 'Histoire du problème de Molyneux (Huitième mémoire)', CpA 2.4 (March 1966): 115–122.

experiments expressly directed toward this goal, with all necessary measures prepared in advance.

M. Abbé de Condillac anticipated me in this hope. He examines what must be done in order to draw the most from these kinds of experiments, how to prepare the blind man before giving him sight, the things he must be taught and those he should remain ignorant of, and the way he should be questioned and observed.

He thinks that, before the first bandages are removed, the blind man ought to be enclosed in a glass cage. This would certainly offer means for determining the influence of Touch on Sight. For if this man does not see beyond the cage, if the objects outside are only coloured glass for him, then we can imagine the consequences without my having to go into them. But this experiment, deftly handled, would teach us more than we can imagine, and as our blind man emerges from the shadows his experience will shed new light on an infinity of objects about which we talk endless nonsense.

The trouble is that such occasions are rare. We must wait for them to arrive by chance. Not all subjects are equally suitable; there is not enough time to prepare them; the circumstances may be unfavourable. [116]

If the occasions are rare, true observers are no less so, and it will be difficult to ensure they are on hand when needed. Philosophers are too indolent, and are not curious enough to seek out the means of learning more; they prefer arguing to seeing. For most, philosophy is a profession [métier] rather than a science. Instead of consulting Nature, they harp on with obscure words, dated systems, and banal demonstrations. Given this state of things, we should not be surprised that since Cheselden, which is to say for more than forty years, we've had no new experiments on such an important subject.

And finally, even Cheselden's experiment has a drawback, which it shares with all experiments that involve cataract operations on those born blind. Cataracts hardly produce a total blindness, and thus it is not a total blindness that is cured. Whence it follows that these blind people, since they have already combined, however imperfectly, tangible extension with the weak light they experience, would be unable to have pure, unalloyed visual perceptions once they do open their eyes. The colours and light that they see are already outside of them and spread out in space, or at least they are outside of their eyes. As a result, they would no longer be suited to satisfy us on questions of purely visible extension, nor on those which relate to it, nor perhaps on other matters that we cannot yet predict.

What would be the solution to all these problems? What might offer a sure way of having subjects prepared at length and at our leisure, who would fulfil all the requisite conditions for conducting our experiments with success? Let us here give free rein to our imagination.

In order to shed light on the origin of language and the different idioms that we speak, it has often been proposed to raise together, from a young age, two or three children separated from all interaction with other men,[25] and in places where no human sound would strike their ears, to see if they would manage to devise themselves a language, and what that language would be.

What I am imagining is perhaps just as daring. But in Philosophy we must examine everything, devise everything, pursue all conjectures, and fear nothing.

The plan would be to take infants from their cradles, and to raise them in profound darkness until they reach the age of reason. Supposing that we had a sufficient number of them, there is nothing that we could not undertake to do. Some would be left to mere nature, others would be more or less educated, and a few would even be given the most excellent education that their condition allows. We would teach the latter to read by touch [*lire en relief*]; we would teach them the Sciences, Physics [117], Philosophy, Geometry, and above all, Optics. Some would be raised in isolation, others in groups or societies, and at a certain age we would choose the most intelligent among them to form learned societies. It would be very entertaining to listen to them argue about the nature and properties of Light – this would be rather like certain disputes among certain scholars on certain subjects they understand about as clearly, and to whom one might ask: *quid rides? fabula de te narratur* [*Why do you laugh? The story is about you*].

In a word, since their minds would be in our hands, so to speak, since we would be able to mould them like a soft wax and to develop in them types of knowledge in whatever order we please, we would be able to take all precautions and vary the experiments in all imaginable ways.

Once acquainted with the ideas that they would have acquired in this state, and the order in which they have acquired them, it would be that much easier for us to interrogate them when the time comes to drop the veil from before their eyes, and to direct the interrogations in such a way to draw the greatest profit from their responses, compared with one another. What light could we not expect from this? It would surely go beyond anything we can anticipate, and would bear on a number of objects that we did not have directly in view.

I foresee two kinds of difficulties here, one physical, the other moral.

First of all, we might fear that these infants would completely lose their power of sight and thus become irremediably blind [*sérieusement aveugles*]. Were this so, it would certainly be necessary to renounce this enterprise, both out of a sense of justice and because this would be a waste of time and effort. I frankly do not see why we would have to fear such a dreadful turn of events, and I know of no fact that proves it. However I will leave the discussion of this question, which is beyond my competence, to those who make knowledge of the

---

25   TN: We have retained Mérian's use of gendered language throughout, translating '*hommes*' as 'men'.

human body their particular object of study. If this blindness turned out to be a matter of a simple cataract, our experiments could still proceed, though it might perhaps be inhuman to attempt them. But is it really demonstrated that the crystalline lens becomes tarnished in the darkness? If kept for several years in a place that the light of day does not penetrate, does glass lose its transparency, to the point that it can never be recovered?

Another objection, diametrically opposed to the preceding one, seems more well-founded to me. It will be said that light is everywhere, and that there is no darkness so thick that light cannot illuminate the eye once it becomes accustomed to it. The pupil dilates in obscurity, and seizes the faintest glimmers. This is how the cat and the [118] owl in the night discern objects, and probably the mole in his subterranean dwelling. Some prisoners, enclosed in the blackest dungeons, once glimpsed a faint light at the end of several weeks, and their sight strengthened from day to day; eventually they could even perceive the rats coming to gather their crumbs.

It is true that since these prisoners enjoyed sight before being plunged into darkness, one can doubt whether it would be the same for a child who will have never exercised the visual organ, who understands nothing of its use, who does not know how to move it, and in places in which a small portion of light would not suffice to irritate the fibres to the point of opening the pupil. But even in such circumstances, we would suffer no shortage of resources. We would make use of a blindfold whose most advantageous construction will have been overseen by experts. In the same way, I would leave to skilful scientists and doctors questions concerning the salubrity of the air, and the general health of our young students.

Finally, it will be objected – and this is the most serious objection – that nobody would want to sacrifice their children to experiments in Metaphysics, that it would be unjust to require it of them, and that this would be an act of cruelty toward these children.

I respond that my plan is addressed to philosophers inflamed with the love of Science, who know that one only aspires to great things by trampling on popular prejudices. What is more, the execution of this plan would surely not be my affair nor that of any particular agent, but rather that of a sovereign or of a magistrate invested with public authority. And I would ask, furthermore, a question of most of these tender-hearted mothers who might fear my proposition, and who might be inconsolable at the thought of keeping their children blind until a certain age: how do you yourselves spend this precious time with them? Alas, you do nothing more than spoil their hearts and blind their minds [*leur aveugler l'esprit*]!

But, without even referring to the resources we would offer these houses from which we would gather the children, who belonging to no one should belong to the public good, turn your eyes to the streets of a large city. Look at all of these objects of disgust and pity, these cursed and crippled children, who are indeed often rendered irreversibly blind by these monsters who call themselves their parents. Where would be the evil in snatching these tender victims from their torturers to have them serve our experiments and to put them in a position of one day becoming useful citizens, perhaps even illustrious citizens?

I am so far from believing that one might lose out in being raised in the manner I propose, that, on the contrary, I know of few educations that I would prefer to this one. [119]

If our senses, rather than deploying themselves all at once, were to be successively developed one by one, it is likely that we would be able to draw many more services from them. They are weakened by their simultaneous action, and one is only perfected at the expense of another. Not even a single one among them comes to the degree of perfection of which it is capable, because the soul, having but a limited force, is too divided, too distracted in the midst of this multitude of sensations that assail it from every direction. If it were able to devote itself entirely to each particular sense, and combine it with others only after carrying the impressions and ideas it provides to the highest degree of clarity, and after having it fortified it such that it can resist any attack – if, I say, this were done, then what precision and accuracy [*justesse*], what order in our thoughts and actions, what force of mind and character would not result from it! What men we would be!

Let us make no mistake. Everything depends on these first series of sensible impressions, and the secret of education turns solely on this. These are the rudiments of our reason and of all our knowledge. They determine our turn of mind, our morals, our inclinations, our conduct, and to a large extent, our destiny in the world. All his life, if his first impressions were poorly arranged in his brain, a man will be nothing but a false and dubious mind, a muddle-head of weak character. If the supposition we've just proposed could be carried out, we would become beings as perfect as our nature entails.

So great a happiness, no doubt, is not in store for man. However, either I am much mistaken, or one would obtain a portion of these advantages in our School of the artificially blind.

First of all, the most necessary of our senses, and the one that serves as the principal instrument of our knowledge, could be cultivated more or less the way we desire. The sense of Touch, once rid of sight (which causes it the most distractions), once free to operate on its own terms, would acquire the most exquisite finesse in our subjects. Their deft hands would become capable of handling the finest objects and distinguishing the subtlest nuances; their fingers would be like little microscopes. What a school for training mechanics, sculptors, and artists of any kind! But I also see others being trained as physicists, naturalists, and geometers of the first order, and above all as philosophers spared the thousand prejudices that we imbibe from infancy, that education serves only to deepen rather than destroy, that subsequently require so much effort to overcome, that despite all our efforts we never entirely surmount, and that most men take with them to the grave. [120]

There, in the shadows and the silence, one would study Nature, one would study oneself: one would learn to discern exactly the objects of each sense, and one would be wholly prepared to receive that of Sight, without transmitting with it the false judgments and errors that the habitual confusion with Touch leads us to. The soul circumscribed in a tighter sphere would exercise its faculties with a redoubled vigour. In the end, the Sages to whom the surveillance of this establishment would be entrusted would have the leisure and convenience to present objects and to generate ideas in the most natural order, or the one most in line with their goal, and to proportion their lessons to the different capacities of their students. What will ease their labours is the knowledge that, in the task to which they are devoted, there will be at least as much to gain for themselves as for their disciples.

I think I have proven that for the children raised this way there will be infinitely more to gain than to lose. At bottom, what do they lose? A possession of which they have no idea, and as a consequence no desire. We have always seen how indifferent those born blind are about this; they do not understand what advantage this new sense is supposed to bring. Saunderson had contempt for most of the men who enjoyed it; he considered their minds to be slow and heavy [*matériels*], and did not want to change places with them.

But even if we admit that being deprived of Sight for a certain period may be a real loss; will it not be richly compensated for? Does it count for nothing, this ineffable pleasure that you have long prepared them for? Imagine their transports of joy, the flood of delights that will inundate them, when we make them pass from night into day, from the darkness to the light, when a new universe, an altogether dazzling world unfolds before them as from the depths of Chaos! Can there be anything comparable to such an instant? And does not a whole life spent intoxicated with pleasure pale in comparison? For after all, almost all our pleasures are only repetitions. Novelty itself, which has so many charms for us, boils down to various arrangements of things that we already know; it is the same dough, tossed in different ways. Whereas here we have things that are genuinely new, of an absolute novelty, new in both substance and form, of which we have neither presentiment nor idea, and that can be tied to nothing that was previously known to us.

The wonders of nature are lost on most men. They grow accustomed to them by slow and imperceptible gradations, before they become capable of reflection, and far from judging them worthy of research they live and die without paying attention to them. These wonders would make a very different impression on those who appreciate the cost of such research, if presented to them for the first time [121] after they have attained the age of reason. Think of the pleasant surprise that would be in store for them! Think of the movements of curiosity they might excite in their souls!

Now all of these pleasures we thus prepare for our blind charges, we tear them away, so to speak, from Nature in order to offer them to them. It is true that Nature will maintain its rights, by granting them only by degrees the full enjoyment of light and the universe that is illuminated by it. But this very process will direct their desire for knowledge, and each step they make will be marked by discoveries.

I imagine them struck motionless with astonishment at the first impression of light, this magnificent being that a veil had thus far hidden from their gaze, and at the varied play of colours for which it is the inexhaustible source. Once they recover from their surprise, how often they will fall back into it, when, as they begin to move, as Sight is joined to Touch, they see this light and these colours projected into space, illuminating, painting, decorating the earth and the firmament, when little by little they come to sense, flowing out of them and as if created before their eyes, the greenery of the fields, the verdure of the prairies, the glowing empire of Flora, and in the distance, the woods and mountains whose pale shades limit their view and define the horizon. Raising their eyes, they perceive, extended around them like a glorious pavilion, this azure canopy in which shines in all its splendour this star to which they owe the new day that illuminates them. And then, in a beautiful night, quite different from the one they have just left behind, the moon and the stars will bathe them in their soft and vibrant light. What animated scenes, what enchanting forms will follow one another across this beautiful theatre, and will be for them, as for Cheselden's blind patient in his transports of delight upon the hills of Epsom, so many new ways of seeing, so many new subjects of ecstasy!

And ultimately to the attractions of natural beauty will be joined the attractions of science. Think of the discoveries to be made from this new sense, from its association with others and in particular with Touch! What an opportunity for Geometry, for Optics, for Natural History, and for Philosophy! Each of these sciences, in this new domain, will display its new charms to those among our students who will be initiated into them. As I pointed out above, we will be able to direct the course of their mind, to make their ideas grow and to develop them in a hundred different ways, by varying objects and sensations. We will be able to choose the points of view in which we want to place them, and the order in which we want to lead them. We will suggest to them combinations we would like to see them try: we will behold, so to speak, the production of their ideas. By doing so we will clarify for them the most difficult matters, and resolve the thorniest questions. They will make discoveries for us in discovering for themselves [122]: and it will turn out that in these dark places an excellent Academy of philosophers was formed.

Do you still think that they would hold it against you for having failed to care for them? I think that, on the contrary, they would be more disposed to appreciate what you have done for them, that they would thank you with tears of joy, and that comparing themselves with others, they would be glad their whole lives for the education you have given them. If I had received a similar education, I would think myself all the more worthy of being here: the essay I have just read to you would have been infinitely shorter, and infinitely better.

CHAPTER TWELVE

François Regnault
The Thought of the Prince

[23] PART ONE: MANIFEST DISCOURSE, OR, WHAT IS SAID

There is a politics [*une politique*] in Descartes.[1] Of course, there are few texts to be found by Descartes on politics, but it is not impossible to deduce a politics from the very principles of Cartesianism. Since he was a French gentleman who (for good reason) felt no guilt about his titles of nobility, and since he found the regimes under which he had lived here and there 'almost always easier to put up with than changing them [would have been]'[2], and since he was not one of those 'meddlesome and restless characters'[3] who wanted to reform everything, he never envisaged giving *his* own account of the possible forms of regime, or of the problem of the best kind of government. However, the facts show he was quite capable of pronouncing on such matters when the occasion arose. As evidence, consider the line that Princess Elisabeth of Bohemia threw to him over the course of a conversation that took place in the summer of 1646, during which she suggested that he should share with her his reflections on Machiavelli's *The Prince*, which

---

1   The main idea for this article – that Machiavelli's thought is the non-place and bad conscience of the classical theory of right [*droit*] – came from Louis Althusser and the course he gave on Machiavelli in 1961 or 1962. In the third part, I apply to Machiavelli the first section of Jacques Lacan's article, 'Function and Field of Speech and Language in Psychoanalysis' (*La Psychanalyse*, t. 1, pp. 93–110; now in *Écrits* [Paris: Seuil, 1966], 247–265). I owe a great debt to Michel Serres' article entitled 'Un modèle mathématique du cogito', which appeared in the second issue of the *Revue philosophique* (April–June 1965), as well as to the first appendix to the second volume of Martial Gueroult's *Descartes selon l'ordre des raisons* (Paris: Aubier-Montaigne, 1953; *Descartes' Philosophy Interpreted According to the Order of Reasons*, trans. Roger Ariew [Minneapolis: University of Minnesota Press, 1985]). Lastly, the texts by Machiavelli can be found in *The Prince* and the *Discourses on Levy*, and the letters of Descartes and Elisabeth on Machiavelli in *Oeuvres de Descartes*, ed. Charles Adam and Paul Tannery (Paris: Vrin, 1964–1983), vol. 4, 447, 449–452, 485, 493ff., 519, 528.
    TN: The letters are translated into English in *The Correspondence between Princess Elisabeth of Bohemia and René Descartes*, ed. and trans. Lisa Shapiro (Chicago: University of Chicago Press, 2007), 138–150. For the works of Descartes and for his letters to Princess Elisabeth, the page reference to the standard Adam and Tannery edition (AT) is given here, volume number followed by page number, since this pagination is reproduced in the cited English translations.
    This article was first published as François Regnault, 'La Pensée du Prince,' CpA 6.2 (January 1967): 23–52. Translated by Christian Kerslake, revised by Steven Corcoran.
2   TN: Descartes, *Discourse on Method*, in *The Philosophical Writings of Descartes*, vol. 1, trans. John Cottingham, Robert Stoothoff, and Dugald Murdoch (Cambridge: Cambridge University Press, 1985), AT 6: 14.
3   TN: Descartes, *Discourse on Method*, AT 6: 14.

she had read some six years previously.[4] 'By inviting him to read Machiavelli's *Prince*, [24] by submitting to him difficulties on the deployment of force, or the conditions of peace, she obliged him to clarify his sentiments on the subject of civil life, that necessary extension of moral life, even if experience plays a greater role here than reason amongst the generality of men.'[5] Thanks to this we have the following: a letter from Elisabeth dated July 1646 inviting him to come visit; Descartes' reply dated September 1646 after his reading of *The Prince*; Elisabeth's response of 10 October 1646; and Descartes' response of November 1646, which in some sense closes the chapter of Cartesian politics. What we learn is that this politics must be founded on reason and that, if there are cases where the use of violence is permitted, tolerating them in no way precludes the politician from being a good man, or from 'thinking that [since] a good man is he who does everything true reason tells him to, so the best thing is always to try to be one.'[6]

Cartesian politics versus Machiavellian politics. Two problematics, a sole drama. A rift. Morality and politics. The scholar or scientist [*savant*] and the politician. Two temperaments.

We have to set off again, from a better footing.

I   THE DAY OF THE SABBATH

1. *Letter of September 1646*: 'Instead, in order to instruct a good prince, however newly he has come to power, it seems to me one should propose to him

---

4   TN: In her edition of the *Correspondence*, Shapiro notes: 'Elisabeth seems to have made this specific request to comment on Machiavelli's *The Prince* in person, though it follows on her earlier effort to receive Descartes' thoughts on maxims for guiding civil life' (139). She refers to the letter of 25 April 1646 (not included in the 'Quatre lettres sur Machiavel' by Descartes and Elisabeth that follow Regnault's article in this issue of the *Cahiers*, as CpA 6.3), written by Elisabeth in response to an early draft of Descartes' treatise on *The Passions of the Soul* (1649). After making various specific objections, Elisabeth writes: 'I find it much less difficult to understand all that you say on the passions than to practice the remedies you prescribe for their excesses. For how is one to foresee all the accidents that can come upon one in life, as it is impossible to enumerate them? And how are we to prevent ourselves from desiring with ardour those things that necessarily tend to the conservation of man (such as health and the means to live), but that nevertheless do not depend on our free will? As for knowledge of the truth, the desire for it is so just that it exists naturally in all men. But it would be necessary to have infinite knowledge to know the true value of the goods and evils which customarily move us, as there are many more such things than a single person would know how to imagine. Thus, for this it would be necessary to know perfectly everything that is in the world.

Since you have already told me the principal maxims concerning private life, I will content myself with now hearing those concerning civil life, even though civil life often leaves one dependent on persons of so little reason that up to this point I have always found it better to avail myself of experience rather than reason, in matters that concern it' (*Correspondence*, AT 4: 405–6).

5   TN: the source for this quotation appears to be Jacques Chevalier's introduction to his edition of René Descartes, *Lettres sur la morale. Correspondance avec la princesse Elisabeth, Chanut et la reine Christine* (Paris: Boivin, 1935), xiv.

6   TN: Letter from Descartes to Elisabeth, September 1646; *Correspondence*, AT 4:490.

altogether contrary maxims, and it should be supposed that the means he used to establish himself in power were just, as in effect I believe they almost always are, when the princes who practice them think them to be. For, justice between sovereigns has different limits than that between individuals, and it seems that in these cases God gives the right to those to whom he gives force. But the most just actions become unjust when those who perform them think them so.'[7]

2. *Article 146 of Descartes' Treatise of the Passions.* 'Thus, for example, suppose we have business in some place to which we might travel by two different routes, one usually much safer than the other; [25] even if Providence were to decree that we will not escape robbery by following the route that is usually safer, and that we could have taken the other route without any danger, we should not for all that become indifferent about choosing one or the other, or rely upon the immutable fatality of this decree; reason insists that we choose the route which is usually the safer.'[8]

3. Lastly, the text that ends the whole sixth Meditation, and refutes objections to the goodness of the veracious God that could be extrapolated from the fact that our nature sometimes makes us find poisoned meat pleasant, or that those suffering from dropsy have an increased thirst the satisfaction of which would nevertheless be fatal, or that our brain can erroneously sense a pain in the foot that is merely conveyed to it by the nerve joining the foot to the brain.[9] Descartes' answer is that it is preferable that nature deceive us sometimes, rather than deceive us always;[10] it mostly happens that we eat healthy meats and we are thirsty for good reason, and the brain is 'far more often excited by a cause hurting the foot.'[11] *Ergo*, it is more reasonable that nature has decided to speak in general, rather than always to remain silent.

These three cases, drawn from works of different status, ultimately all have the same form: the mind finds itself in an *equivocal* situation. Is my King legitimate or not? Is the path that I am about to take dangerous or not? Is this meat poisoned or not? Has my foot been struck or not? In the first case, the King knows the answer and not I; in the two others, it is Providence that knows it, or has chosen it for all eternity. In other words, in principle there is no equivocal

---

7   TN: *Correspondence*, AT 4: 487, cited in CpA 6.3:55.

8   TN: Descartes, *The Passions of the Soul*, in *The Philosophical Writings of Descartes*, vol. 1, AT 11: 439–440tm.

9   TN: Descartes, 'Sixth Meditation', *Meditations on First Philosophy*, in *The Philosophical Writings of Descartes*, vol. 2, AT 7: 83–90.

10   TN: Descartes, 'Sixth Meditation', AT 7: 89: '[I]t is much better that it [nature] should mislead us on this occasion than that it should always mislead when the body is in good health.'

11   TN: Descartes, 'Sixth Meditation', AT 7: 89.

situation, either in nature or in society, which has not been solved from above. We know this, then, from considering the *ordinary* course of Providence, whose reassuring frequencies are denoted by expressions such as 'almost always', 'in these cases' (first text), 'even if' (second text), 'usually', 'in this encounter' (sixth Meditation). In all three cases the human mind – knowing, as a result of its indispensable reading of Descartes' metaphysics, that God cannot deceive us, and founding itself on this very metaphysics, not in order to settle the difficulties of real life situations, of that whole zone that one will henceforth call 'fortune' ['*la fortune*'], but so as not to allow these difficulties to create an aporia in being – must reproduce, or mime, the ways of Providence. The mind decides to lift the equivocal factor, which it knows can only cause difficulties or confusion, rather than a genuine *problem*. The ambiguous course of fortune must be submitted to the univocal divisions of the soul. Three decisive wagers follow from this: [26]

1. The subject *must* consider his prince as legitimate: '*it should be supposed* that the means he used to establish himself in power were just . . .', 'it *seems* that in these cases God gives the right . . .'[12]
2. The traveller must choose the path with the best reputation, even if this decision leads to no knowledge about the outcome of the journey. 'Nevertheless, we should not be indifferent as to which one we choose'.[13]
3. If I am hungry, I will eat. If I am thirsty, I will drink. The only taster who might check my foods for poisons is Providence itself; if the Pope has such a taster, man does not. If I have a pain in the foot, I will attend to it. Without suspicion.

In short, fortune presents me with situations that are reflexive:

xRx (the King is the King (for himself), and I must not judge him)

or symmetrical:

xRy implies yRx.

(1. if the unjust prince has his throne in the same way as does the just, then, alas! – the just and the unjust are alike.

2. if the poisoned meat tempts me like the healthy one does, then, alas! – healthy and poisoned food are alike).

---

12   TN: *Correspondence*, AT 4: 487; CpA 6.3:55.
13   TN: Descartes, *The Passions of the Soul*, AT 11: 439.

And my soul must act as if these situations were not reflexive or asymmetrical.[14] It is a matter, at any cost, of tipping the scales one way or another, scales whose equilibrium only ever indicates the degree of indifference, the lowest degree of freedom. Resolution has no other power.

On the other side of this structure, there is another aspect that consists in re-establishing a symmetry, an indifference, even at the point where Providence seems not to mince its words.

Thus, in the letter to Elisabeth of 6 October 1645, a ruse of reason is evoked in order to render political engagement a merely optional matter [27]:

I confess that it is difficult to measure exactly just to what degree reason ordains that we be interested in the public good. But also this is not a matter in which it is necessary to be very exact. It suffices to satisfy one's conscience, and one can in this matter give a lot to one's inclination. For God has so established the order of things and conjoined men together in so tight a society that even if each person related himself wholly to himself and had no charity for others, he would not ordinarily fail to work for them in everything that would be in his power, so long as he used prudence, and principally if he lived in a century when mores were not corrupted.[15]

A more precise text gives us the key to this invitation to indifference (the letter to Elisabeth of 15 September 1645):

After having thus recalled the goodness of God, the immortality of our souls and the greatness of the universe, there is also one more truth the knowledge of which seems to me quite useful. This is that, even though each of us is a person separate from others and, by consequence, with interests that are in some manner distinct from those of the rest of the world, one must, all the same, think that one does not know how to subsist alone and that one is, in effect, one part of the universe and, more particularly even one part of this earth, one part of this state, and this society, and this family, to which one is joined by his home, his oath, by his birth.[16]

'One must, all the same, think' just as, with regard to the prince, 'it must be supposed' –a litaneutical expression. But this text also allows us to see that there is only a single structure: *metaphysice*, nothing is reflexive or symmetrical, but

---

14   Let the unjust prince acknowledge that he is not a prince! Let the healthy meat show itself, and disavow the poisoned! Or at least let Providence, if not me, recognize its univocal paths!

15   TN: *Correspondence*, AT 4:316–17tm.

16   TN: *Correspondence*, AT 4:293.

rather unilateral and decisive. Faced with fortune, the soul must arrest reflexivity, displace symmetry, upset balance and equilibrium, but neither can man do anything about it, because at bottom there are no clear and distinct ideas of the collective. He has such ideas of God and of the soul, immediately; about the universe, he has them mediately; but of society, he has none (or only in the very long term, according to Descartes' initial moral theory). My interests are distinct from everybody else's, herein resides the principle: 'justice between sovereigns has different limits than that between individuals'.[17] But Providence has so conjoined me to the rest of the world that I cannot move my little finger without rendering some service. In its Holland cheese, there is no rat, however solitary and well-fed, that refuses to profit from the hand that feeds it.[18]

A method arises from this, one that is rationally correct and perfectly efficient, and not a word of which contradicts Cartesian metaphysics (for I object as much to those who talk of there being definite policies in Descartes [*de* la *politique chez Descartes*] as to those who would see in Machiavelli's work anticipated objections to Cartesianism; the question here is not one of prophetic [28] refutations, or of a retrospective papering over of the cracks, but rather of the relation between a place and *its* non-place) and one that Descartes is able to employ against Machiavelli, as follows:

FIRST RULE (OF OPTIMISM THROUGH LIFTING EQUIVOCATIONS):

Providence, in its metaphysical perfection, has created only asymmetrical truths (for nothingness, if it has no properties, cannot possess that of inverting being).

So, if fortune leads you to believe that xRy implies yRx, instead your soul should assume that the true relation is only either xRy or yRx.[19]

---

17   TN: *Correspondence*, AT 4:487; CpA 6.3:55.

18   TN: The French reads: '*Dans son fromage de Hollande, il n'est rat, si seul se croie-t-il, qui ne profite aux Levantins eux-mêmes.*' This is a reference to a poem from Jean de La Fontaine's *Fables*, 'Le Rat qui s'est retiré du monde', 'The Rat who withdrew from the World': 'The sage Levantines have a tale/About a rat that weary grew/Of all the cares which life assail/And to a Holland cheese withdrew . . .'

19   When it comes to the equivo   ons of fortune or of life, Descartes always proceeds in this way; without mentioning the second maxim of his provisional moral code (which cannot be evoked here because of its status), we might cite for example:
– The famous passage in the 4th Meditation on indifference, on the lowest degree of freedom.
– Article 170 of the *Treatise on the Passions*, against irresolution.
– The whole letter of 6 October 1645 to Elisabeth, notably this passage: 'But as one can have different but equally true considerations, of which some lead us to be content, and others on the contrary prevent us from being so, it seems to me that prudence demands that we dwell principally on those which give us satisfaction. Almost all the things in the world are such that we can regard them from a side which makes them appear good and from another which makes us notice defects. And I believe that if one must make use of one's skill in something, it is principally to know how to look at them from the angle which makes them appear most to our advantage, as long as this does not involve our deceiving ourselves' (*Correspondence*, AT 4: 306).

SECOND RULE (OF OPTIMISM THROUGH EQUIVOCATION ABOUT DANGEROUS UNIVOCITIES):

Providence, in its metaphysical perfection, has created only symmetrical truths.

So, if the urgencies of life or the blows of History present you with an unequal situation, one where xRy implies non-yRx (for example, the prince has taken power unjustly, and nobody can confuse him with a just prince), *let your individuality* (the union of your soul and body), by trusting its inclinations, and by not requiring you to measure too precisely 'just how far reason' commands you to take an interest in 'public affairs', *re-establish the ordinary symmetries of fortune.* Then you can by rights proceed to the application of rule number one.

It follows from these two (non-Cartesian) rules that the Prince simultaneously plays the role of a decisive Providence and responds to life's urgencies [29], and that one must be willing sometimes to attest to the legitimacy of his power (by invoking the ordinary metaphysics of decrees from above, founded on eternal reason) and sometimes to dissimulate his usurpations (by appealing to the benefit of doubt that accompanies the equivocations of fortune's hazards). Indeed, this could be the definition of divine right: that nobody knows whether what the King decides is due to inspiration or to calculation, whether he continues Creation by prolonging it in History, or breaks it by establishing something new.

The conjunction that I have made of these two rules is by no means some underhanded indictment of Descartes. It is enough to say that there are no clear and distinct ideas in politics, which itself changes nothing about our knowledge that Providence governs the world. One must therefore wager that the King who reigns is the good one; Cartesianism is shaken neither by the possibility nor by the necessity of making a wager. Divine veracity serves as the ultimate guarantee behind the lifting of sensory equivocations.[20] Simply, Cartesianism is not incompatible with absolute Monarchy (it neither requires it, nor banishes it). But that we should give this guarantee (to whom?) does not prevent us from drawing attention to the two procedures Descartes uses when faced with Machiavelli.

Reading Descartes' two letters on Machiavelli will convince us that there is scarcely a passage, or even a sentence, that does not obey these laws. The essential text is the one cited above[21], which confers the right to use force and legitimacy on the prince who thinks of himself as legitimate (I think myself just, therefore I am: the comparison with the Cogito is inevitable). Just as we might expect, this text obeys our two rules:

---

20   'The terms that awaken only sensible ideas are all equivocal', says Malebranche (*The Search for Truth*, VI, 2, 2).

21   TN: i.e. Descartes' letter to Elisabeth of September 1646, *Correspondence*, AT 4: 487.

1. The means the prince employs in order to establish himself seem equivocal to us. So, let us suppose that God, by right, etc . . .
2. But also: the means by which the prince establishes himself before our eyes appear to have the character of a usurpation. So we should re-establish the equivocation: no one can know what goes on in the thought of the prince. Machiavelli 'has not made sufficient *distinction*' between just princes and unjust princes, and this serves to subvert Justice. However, we must not attempt to distinguish whether such and such a prince is just, as this would overthrow the prince (and clarity in this domain is impossible). Indeed, by overly explicating the thought of the prince concerning his own legitimacy, one will end up rendering him obscure, just like the truth, as Descartes often reminds, whose very examination of what it is offends it.[22] [30]

Similarly, the Prince has to distinguish between his friends and his enemies, and if he can do anything he likes against the latter, he cannot against the former. What Machiavelli is talking about is situated beyond love and hate, and if Descartes retains Machiavellianism it is only against enemies, which nullifies its effect.

Take the following phrase by way of example: 'As for allies, a prince ought to keep his word to them exactly, even when this is disadvantageous to him. For the reputation of always doing what he promises *can never be more disadvantageous* than useful.'[23]

Such a phrase, in my view, is proof that Descartes' realism, whereby with respect to particulars he consents to almost everything Machiavelli says, nevertheless remains infallibly subordinated to a metaphysical decision; one must posit that breaking one's word will always serve the prince less than keeping it would. Now, it is obvious that there is no possible historical assurance for such a thing. All the refutations of the letter of September 1646 may thus be referred back to an assurance of this type, and they draw on our two rules. In the majority of cases, we must then apply the first rule and hope for the best, which is always possible – the end of the first letter on Machiavelli again attests to this: 'Since in all worldly affairs there are some reasons for and some against, one should consider principally those that make one approve of what happens'.[24]

The second rule is more difficult to apply, but it functions so long as the text of Machiavelli the adversary is *interpreted*. This is what happens in the following passage:

---

22 'It is a notion so transcendentally clear that it is impossible to ignore' (letter of 16 October 1639).
23 TN: *Correspondence*, AT 4: 488; CpA 6.3:55.
24 TN: *Correspondence*, AT 4: 492; CpA 6.3:57.

Thus I disapprove of the maxim of chapter 15 [of *The Prince*], which claims that, 'as the world is very corrupt, it is impossible that one will not ruin oneself if one always wants to be a good man, and that a prince, in order to maintain himself, must learn to be wicked when the occasion requires it'.[25] That is, unless perhaps by a good man he means a superstitious and simple man who does not dare to go to battle on the Sabbath, and whose conscience can be at rest only if he changes the religion of his people. But thinking that a good man is he who does everything true reason tells him to, it is certain that the best thing is always to try to be one.[26]

Of course, Descartes can content himself with disapproving of Machiavelli when he counsels evil, but the deontology he follows [31] also requires him to refute such counsel as soon as Machiavelli offers a reason for it. Now, they are in agreement with regard to the corruption of the world (that is, they agree to use this phrase that was current in the language of the day), but here Descartes goes further than he needs to: he goes so far as to admit that it is true that the good man will *always* be ruined, on condition that by 'good man' Machiavelli means 'the superstitious man'. And indeed, Machiavelli means nothing else: a good man, when all is said and done, is a man who would not dare to fight on the day of the Sabbath. So Descartes' 'unless' thus becomes 'rightly', the concession is made the cause, reticence becomes avowal, and the restriction is universalized. 'It impossible not to become ruined, if one always wants to be a good man' is not some disillusioned aphorism in Machiavelli, but (and obviously the whole of *The Prince* must be read to give value to this sentence) that which designates as such the hitherto unthinkable and unthought field of what must here be called politics. This is the new place that Machiavelli *institutes* (for if the Prince, the Medicis, or whoever, do not know how to establish a new principality in the Italy of the Renaissance, then Machiavelli, armed with examples and history, will fortify a new place for it in the domain of theory). It is relative to this place that it can rightly be said that 'every good man is merely superstitious'. But this is a phrase uttered by Descartes, as if reluctantly, as an intolerable paradox. And doubtless no Cartesian[27] would have gone so as far, moralizing more than his master, but doubtless the founder of the Cogito and modern philosophy possessed greater ability than his successors to venture to the limits of his own thought. Here he both does and does not cross this limit by stating, in a lightning-flash and in the exact form of a denegation, the truth of his apolitics [*son apolitique*].

For it must not be said that Descartes does not understand Machiavelli's realism. He knows and says that immoral means can be used in politics, and

---

25   TN: Machiavelli, *The Prince*, trans. George Bull [1961] (London: Penguin, 2003), 50tm.

26   TN: *Correspondence*, AT 4: 490; CpA 6.3:55.

27   There can be no question of Spinoza here, who made for Machiavelli the *place* that is well known.

when it comes to realism, there is always room for discussion. Descartes' deaf-ness [*surdité*] is more fundamental, and with him all classical politics is deaf. In Machiavelli he does not encounter an objector, and nor does he receive a lesson in realism in *The Prince*. He stumbles not on a contradiction, or on any obstacle. There is nothing he is trying to evade. Simply, he is entirely *unaware of* another place[28], a difference without identity. Or again, the unconscious instant of this lightning-flash that makes him say 'unless' opens up to him, in order for it to close again forever, the very place of history, and reveals to him, by way of a likely joke, the point at which his ahistoricism encounters and excludes the *vérità effetuale della cosa*.[29] [32]

And to cure this wound, which is all the more serious for being impercep-tible, he will read Machiavelli's *Discorsi*, so as to declare to Elisabeth in the letter of November 1646: 'I have since read his *Discourses*, in which I noticed nothing bad.'[30]

All the *Discorsi*, in order to overcome the one book that is the *Prince*, to re-establish disequilibrium after the equivocal oscillation, to save optimism; a heavy and innocent volume, measured by its weight of reassurance, like the metaphysical and blank restfulness of the Sabbath that balances out the work of the week.

ANNEX

To clarify what I have said about the unilaterality of the Cogito and the symmetries of Fortune, I ask for permission to add a column to the structural table drawn up by Michel Serres in an article, published in the *Revue Philosophique* (no. 2, April-June 1965), to which I owe a large debt. On the basis of a persuasive reading of a passage of Descartes' Rule III, Serres has brought to light an analogy of structure between very different levels of Cartesianism: an analogy that applies as much to the intra-intuitive order of the Cogito, subject to non-transitivity (to unilateral-ity), as to the discursive, transitive order that requires a displacement of thought. In this connection, one can recall that the pre-geometrical contents of the Cogito (which it is fully entitled to perceive), in other words the relations of necessity and sufficiency between the three dimensions [of space], do not fall under the juris-diction of the evil demon, which lies in wait for the soul as it moves around [*à ses déplacements*], rather than in its immobile apperceptions. The order of reasons as a discursive method is only guaranteed subsequently, and by God. I add to this that the relations, intransitive and transitive, which found two different orders,

---

28   TN: '*il méconnaît entièrement un lieu autre*'; *méconnaître* can mean to misjudge, to misunderstand or to be unaware of, but in keeping with the translation of Miller's articles in this volume, it could also be translated as to miscognize.

29   Machiavelli, *The Prince*, chapter 15 [Bull trans., 50].

30   TN: *Correspondence*, AT 4: 531; CpA 6.3:61.

have the effect of reducing the radical *disorder* of Fortune. This could be depicted at each level as follows: [33]

MICHEL SERRES' TABLE			Our addition: THE FIELD of FORTUNE, in other words, of morality and politics, which contains:
Method	Intuition	Deduction	equivocations to be dispelled
Mechanical model	Topography	Transmission	equilibria to be destroyed
Geometrical model	Spatial Intuition	Sequence of similarities	'difficulties encountered' to be resolved
General model	Figure	Movement	an immobility (a confusion of the mind) to ward off
Philosophy	Cogito, sum	Order of Reasons	an irresolution of the mind to be cured

REMARKS:

1) The line that separates our column from Serres' table represents the passage from fact to right or law [*droit*], from opinion to philosophy, etc.

2) Under the column of intuition one could also place *books*, and under that of deduction, *travels*. Books and travels (the book of life) are, in the leading [*conduite*] of life, the two privileged figures of learning (*Discourse on Method*, I), such that once they are fulfilled and experienced as two impasses, only philosophy is left to lead one to the truth.

II THE POINT OF SUPPORT AND THE POINT OF VIEW[31]

'History' and 'politics' were named as such above, with impunity. These terms are meant to signify the new field of historical materialism, which had to wait until Marx to find its place. This wait must be given its status here; or rather, this non-wait, since while waiting for the production of a science, those who exist wait for nothing. I mean that Descartes precisely did not [34] wait for Marx in the way that one leaves a field for a future pioneer to clear; he simply ignored the field and stitched up the land registry in another way. Nor was Machiavelli waiting for anything by declaring that such a field was arable and by making room for it in the ideological earth that was given to him. For Machiavelli, however, can that which has not yet been cleared even be called a field? Can one announce a *terra incognita* upon which one has only just begun to tread?

---

31   TN: '*Le point d'appui et le point de vue.*'

If we speak of history, we must recognize that Machiavelli at least did not invent what had been *given*. He found History as historical past, as a set of exploits and stories, already made, just as Descartes did; and like Descartes, like everyone, he was familiar with History in the sense of actions to accomplish, decisions to take, campaigns to lead and speeches to make, discussions to arrange and armies to muster. Descartes participated in many military campaigns, and Machiavelli was the organizer of a few others.

It is this History, which above we called the domain reserved to Fortune, that Machiavelli declared to be an eternal return:

> No one should be surprised if, in discussing states where both the prince and the constitution are new, I shall give the loftiest examples. Men nearly always follow the tracks made by others and proceed in their affairs by imitation, even though they cannot entirely keep to the tracks of others or emulate the virtue [*virtù*] of their models. So a prudent man should always follow in the footsteps of great men and imitate those who have been outstanding. If his own virtue fails to compare with theirs, at least it has an air of greatness about it.[32]

This is why 'the prince should read histories'.[33] More, there is history only to the extent that already-found solutions have been forgotten. So if it is history in the traditional sense one wants to speak of, then Machiavelli was a reader of the Ancients, of Livy first and foremost, and he was immersed more than anyone in the Ancients, we might dare to say more even than Bossuet himself, who subscribed to the idea of a general progress in history, or at least to that of the impossibility of leading [*reconduire*] what he called an 'epoch' back to another one.

But one point is essential: the idea (which only just qualifies as transcendental) that paths are always already blazed by others, supports the idea that examples to be followed should prevail over principles to be discovered. It is here that something changes radically: it cannot even be said that Machiavelli reasoned by *starting from* examples (as Leibniz did); rather he reasoned *by* examples. In *The Prince*, in the last (and often attained) instance, there is nothing but [35] examples. He says magnificently: 'In this world, there is nothing but vulgarity.'[34] With examples, he is always magnificent. As with Nietzsche[35], the eternal return goes hand-in-hand with a pluralism that has no other recourse than itself. And it was no coincidence that Elisabeth the dethroned Princess – the one who read *The Prince* with the ulterior motive of effecting a restoration, the one who had a real

---

32   *The Prince*, opening of chapter 6 [Bull trans., 19tm].
33   Ibid., end of chapter 14 [Bull trans., 49].
34   Ibid., end of chapter 18 [Bull trans., 58tm].
35   Here it is necessary to follow faithfully Gilles Deleuze's reading of Nietzsche in his *Nietzsche and Philosophy* [1962], trans. Hugh Tomlinson (Minneapolis: University of Minnesota Press, 1983).

interest in reading it,[36] the one who, being a princess with nothing more than 'the title',[37] should bring the grain of history (thrones and battles, injustices and derangements [*déraisons*]) to the Cartesian millstone – understood Machiavelli's design without needing it to be spelled out, and who, after having partially justified Cesare Borgia for authorizing prompt acts of violence instead of a 'long sequence of miseries', pulls herself up by saying: 'But if he is wrong to have made these general maxims from those cases which occur in practice on very few occasions, others do the same [. . .] and I believe that this comes from the pleasure they draw from putting forward paradoxes that they can later explain to their students.'[38] All that remained for Descartes was simply to accentuate the princess' concession, and to say 'it is true that it was his [Machiavelli's] plan to praise Cesare Borgia that led him to establish general maxims for justifying particular actions which could have been difficult to excuse.'[39] In Machiavelli's work, Descartes cannot but misunderstand [*méconnaître*] (not by any blunder, but because classical rationalism, and in particular the theory of legal right, defines itself as subsuming every example under a law, and not a law under an example) the status of examples, which are not examples of anything, but rather the very matter, if not the motor, of History, and which designate the forces which move it, the processes which command it; in short, the structures that historical materialism had to produce. For here, unless things are seen through to the end, to the point of the possibility of science, one can only consider the facts that Machiavelli cites as examples of something else, thus leaving no other choice than to compensate for the charge of empiricism (a great insult in the West) by pointing up the merits of realism (itself no great praise in the West).

But Elisabeth had understood the essential point: 'The author's maxims tend towards [the justification of] establishment [*tendent à l'établissement*].'[40] Now, the establishment of the prince is that innovation [*nouveauté*] that did not take place historically, but whose theoretical place Machiavelli discovered – and the theoretical innovation is what [36] has to guarantee that examples can be used without subsumption, that there is always an example to establish or institute [*instaurer*].[41] Example is opposed to model. In justice one sets or makes an

---

36   In 1640, the year in which she read it, a book had appeared on the legitimacy of re-establishing her House, which had been overthrown at Montagne-Blanche in 1620. Descartes, it is thought, was at, if not a participant in, this battle.

37   Letter from Elisabeth to Descartes, 10 October 1646, *Correspondence*, AT: 4:522; CpA 6.3:59.

38   TN: Ibid., AT 4:521, CpA 6.3:58.

39   TN: Letter from Descartes to Elisabeth, November 1646, *Correspondence*, AT 4: 531; CpA 6.3:61.

40   TN: Ibid., *Correspondence*, AT 4: 520; CpA 6.3:58.

41   TN: 'Or l'établissement du prince est cette nouveauté qui n'eut pas lieu historiquement, mais pour laquelle Machiavel trouve son lieu théorique, et la nouveauté théorique est ce qui [36] doit garantir que les exemples peuvent être employés sans subsomption, qu'il y a toujours à instaurer un exemple.'

example, precisely so that things do not start all over again. And it is this institution that imposes upon the symmetry of eternal return the unilaterality of the
new.

By way of a countercheck, one might now produce the following analogy
between Descartes and Machiavelli, whose formal criterion is the substitution
of asymmetry, 'xRy implies ~ (yRx)', for symmetry, 'xRy implies yRx'. The Prince
in Machiavelli would then play the role of the Cogito in Descartes, which indeed
institutes the unilateral, hypermathematical relation of the 'I think' to the 'I am'
(in the same way as the straight line implies the line, and not the reverse). The
site of unilateral relations would thus be metaphysics in Descartes, corresponding to the new politics in Machiavelli, while the symmetrical domain of Fortune
in Descartes would be the analogue of 'cyclical' history in Machiavelli:

	DESCARTES	MACHIAVELLI
SYMMETRY	Fortune, place of equivocations	The eternal return in history
ASYMMETRY	The decision of the Cogito	The establishing of the new Prince

However, if we take into account the fact that for Descartes the prince is the
author of his own legitimacy, we might also sketch another configuration that
would render analogous not formal relations but domains:

	DESCARTES	MACHIAVELLI
THE GIVEN	Fortune: one must support the just Prince	The establishing of the new Prince, finally decentering eternal return
METAPHYSICS	The Cogito: the unilaterality of Right	Transcendental History: eternal return

Now the very possibility of these two analogies and the impossibility of
preferring one over the other is enough to show that such a structure is not fruit-
ful and should be abandoned. Apparently the Prince [37] is like a Cogito, and the
Cogito like a Prince. But in fact they both belong to different fields. The fields
established by each of the authors (metaphysics, historical materialism) appear to
have the function of putting order into the ambiguous field of Fortune, but by
means of two radically different operations: in Descartes, metaphysics makes
possible in principle the subsumption of cases under the rule that encourages a
wager on the legitimacy of the prince. In Machiavelli, it is materialism which
makes impossible the subsumption of examples under any rule; it is this that
subverts the notion of the rule and historicizes it by exemplifying it. In sum, from
whichever side our analogies are approached, there is always one through which
the difference emerges. It is precisely because Machiavelli declares that there is no
law except of the object of which it can be the law (not the example of the law, but
the law of the example, just as there will be laws of *the* mode of

capitalist production in Marx), that there can be no recourse here to an analogism understood in the structural sense; insofar as the aim is to make an analogy between two objects, one of them in particular, *rather than either one indiscriminately*, will repel it. So we must leave open the break between Machiavelli and Descartes, without taking account of the difference between epochs, while admitting that Machiavelli himself barely advances beyond this break.

To summarize: to say that a difference cannot let itself be 'structuralized' is to denote the effect of a break; and to declare that the process of exemplification in Machiavelli is such that he cannot pass off the laws he states either as rationalist subsumptions or as empiricist generalizations, is enough to give the reason for this difference and to indicate this break. Machiavelli is neither a rationalist, nor an empiricist; nevertheless nor is he a scientist or scholar [*savant*], which would prevent us from naming his break as epistemological in a Bachelardian sense, were it not for the fact that that nobody is capable of inhabiting a break, not Descartes, not Machiavelli, not we, not I – one must be either before or after it, and it is by giving rise to a science that both the break and one's stepping over it are constituted. The only breaks, therefore, are epistemological. In order to assign to Machiavelli his own place, we might then take up the formula that Georges Canguilhem applies to Galileo: he was in the true, he did not say the true[42] – except that, in the true, Machiavelli does not say much, even if he hazards a few steps, as a lone rider.

Let us try to clarify so unstable a position:

    I.   Archimedes, according to Pappus: 'δός μοί πού στῶ καὶ κινῶ τὴν γῆν' [Give me a place to stand, and I will move the earth]. [38]

    II.   Descartes: 'Archimedes demanded just one firm and immovable point in order to shift the entire earth; so I too can hope for great things if I manage to find just one thing, however slight, that is certain and unshakeable.'[43]

    III.   Machiavelli: 'Nor I hope will it be considered presumptuous for a man of low and humble status to dare discuss and lay down the law about how princes should rule; because, just as men who are sketching the landscape put themselves down in the plain to study the nature of the mountains and the highlands, and to study the low-lying land they put themselves high on the mountains, so, to comprehend fully the nature of the people, one must be a prince, and to comprehend fully the nature of princes one must be an ordinary citizen.'[44]

---

42   Georges Canguilhem, 'La Signification de l'œuvre de Galilée et la leçon de l'homme', *Archives Internationales d'Histoire des Sciences* 17: 68–69 (July-December 1964), 218; reprinted in his *Études d'histoire et de philosophie des sciences* (Paris: Vrin, 1968).

43   Descartes, beginning of the second Meditation [Cottingham trans., 16].

44   *The Prince*, Dedication to Laurent de Medici [Bull trans., 3–4]. Cf. Maurice Merleau-

IV. Descartes: 'As for the rest, I am also not of the opinion of this author in
what he says in the preface: [the preceding text follows]. For the crayon
represents only those things that are seen at a distance, but the principal motives and actions of princes are often such particular circumstances that one can imagine them only if one is a prince oneself, or
perhaps if one has been party to their secrets for a very long time.'[45]

1) From the first proposition, the deduction is made that if it is always possible
to place oneself on Sirius in order to see Archimedes raise the Earth, then this
can only be done by virtue of image and illusion. In fact, the Archimedean point
is a point of knowledge; a good Archimedean, Platonist in his soul, can know
that experience is of no use, and that mechanics alone proves the possibility of
such a point of support, without one's occupying it. *Therefore only two possible
positions remain*: to be at [*sur*] the decentred point of science, or to remain on
the round face of that which is not science.

2) If we apply this deduction to the second proposition, the only point of support
that remains is that of the Cogito, since every historical or terrestrial point of
support wavers in equivocation. Thus the guarantee of the Cogito is God alone,
the counter-point of the Cogito: Lacan writes that 'Descartes' approach is, singu-
larly, one of safeguarding the *ego* from the deceitful God [39], and thereby safeguarding the *ego's* partner – going so far as to endow the latter with the exorbitant
privilege of guaranteeing eternal truths only insofar as he is their creator.'[46] The
fourth proposition confirms the second and denies that the point of support of
the Cogito can be a point of view upon History. Everyone, including the Prince,
only has his Cogito for himself, and even supposing that the Prince by divine
grace possessed some clear idea about the legitimacy of his taking of power that
was refused to us, it would nevertheless remain true that no subject would have
any more right to look over it than would one Cogito over another. Lacan again:
'"Cogito ergo sum", *ubi cogito sum* [. . .]. Of course, this limits me to being there in
my being only insofar as I think that I am in my thought; to what extent I really
think this concerns me alone and, if I say it, interests no one.'[47]

3) In Machiavelli, the thought of the Prince interests the thought of the subject.
That no doubt means that it is up to men to make, or at least to write, their own
history. But, if we apply the preceding deduction to this proposition III, it means
that there are only two points: the point of view of a science which, as it has

Ponty, *Signes* (Paris: Gallimard, 1960), 273.

45   In the letter of 10 October 1646 we come across Elisabeth's final return [*reprise*] to
Descartes' view on this issue.

46   Lacan, 'Science and Truth', *Ecrits*, 865/735 [reprinted in CpA 1.1:16].

47   Lacan, 'The Instance of the Letter in the Unconscious', *Ecrits*, 516/429.

recourse to historical exemplification, ceases to be Platonic and becomes exper-imental, and which therefore is simultaneously the point of support for estab-lishing the new in theory and the point of application where this establishment takes (its) place in history.

What we should retain from this confrontation of topics is that there is only ever one point from which one knows, and that in Archimedes and Machiavelli this point of knowledge can be assigned, and doubles itself with a point of appli-cation (the Earth, the matter of history), the difference being that when one is a Platonist it is not necessary to experiment, but when a Machiavellian it is.

In Descartes, there is only one point *of view*, that of philosophy or meta-physics, to which all others must be referred [*rapportés*].

Above all, we should retain that, beyond the above-designated points, there is no other point, and in particular no *tertium* [40] *punctum*, no Sirius from which to consider Descartes and Machiavelli, and the epistemological point at which we situate ourselves to designate the break is itself no doubt only a point of view; a non-Cartesian one, but just as philosophical. This is why it is neces-sary, on account of the impossibility of finding a structure without difference that governs both Descartes and Machiavelli (and also, on account of a finite and limited number of possible positions, a structure that might simultaneously integrate the sixteenth century and Machiavelli), to exclude all recourse to an archaeological configuration.[48]

A metaphysics without break cannot intersect or tally with a thinking that is thoroughly subject to the break that situates it,[49] on the basis of a field of empiricity that it has not yet shaken off as thoroughly as metaphysics, in a new field that it neither traverses nor dominates, but where it maintains itself. Were such an intersection tenable, then the Cartesian system would suffer just as much as would Machiavellian establishment [*instauration*].

This to-and-fro between the point of view and the point of support that is the Prince (I support you with my knowledge, support me with your weapons) and that bears experimental witness to historical science, cannot coincide with the Cartesian exclusion of fortune as a place of equivocations, with that univer-sal point of view which has need of all its most immobile obviousness in order to perceive its contents, and of divine veracity to authorize its displacements.

---

48 Michel Foucault allows us to understand precisely this with regard to politics in *Les Mots et les choses* (Paris: Gallimard, 1966), page 218 [*The Order of Things* [1970] (London: Routledge Classics, 2002), 223], by explaining that the adequation of the system of wealth to the configuration it implies does not come without the cost of a *transformation* from which natural history, for its part, is exempted, since it is already theoretical [*théorique*] by nature: 'Wealth is a system of signs that are created, multiplied, and modified by people; the theory of wealth is linked throughout to politics.'

49 TN: '*Une métaphysique sans coupure ne peut recouper une pensée qui subit de part en part la coupure qui la situe . . .*'

This is why extension itself is without any privileged point. Cartesianism is a quasi-Eleaticism and not a dialectic.

With regard to the place of the true that Machiavelli laid down while failing to say it – he still appeals to *virtù* to name the foundation – it is therefore left to Cartesian metaphysics not to fill or block it up, but rather to deny or repudiate it, and this is the function of the theory of clear ideas, which denies them to politics. We should avoid any geneticism: I say the function, not the goal. The Cogito is not the refusal of politics as a science, but the means for doing without it. So there can be no Cartesian politics. Or rather, yes there can: Cartesian politics is a politics like any other; not a science, but a strategy. [41]

III 'THE SCALES IN WHICH CONJECTURES ABOUT THE PAST MAKE PROMISES ABOUT THE FUTURE OSCILLATE'[50]

If materialism means abandoning the subsumption of examples under a rational law and adoption of the epistemological point of view according to which there can only be theory insofar as it is a theory *of* its objects, we will admit Machiavelli's materialist epistemology as an example of historical method. It's this materialism that we were trying to establish above. But in this way, all that is attained is a materialism in history, proving by example that there are only examples, and not the materialism *of* history; the latter remains something *encountered*, *given*, instead of being an object to be constructed. So, materialism itself will be an epistemological project, the faithful philosophy of a science yet to come, an owl that took flight too soon, a monster. Thus in order to show that what is at stake is something other than history as it is read or made, we would need to show that it's a matter of history as we construct it, or history as we understand it through theory. We will not claim that Machiavelli himself proceeded in this way, but merely that he indicated the intentions and the direction, and gave himself the minimum of means for doing so. The solution is the following: Machiavelli does not content himself with given history, nor does he manage to construct the theory of history; rather he remains between the two, which means something if we can say that he *undoes* the first kind of history. For this purpose the concepts of primary historicization and secondary historicization will now serve as our keys.

They will be introduced in the following propositions, which summarize a passage from the end of the first section of Jacques Lacan's Report on the Congress of Rome, where he picked out precisely the point that commands (and from above) all the sciences known as sciences of interpretation. It would do

---

50   TN: '*La balance ou les conjectures sur le passé font osciller les promesses du futur*'. The quotation is from Lacan; see the following note.

historians no harm to examine these propositions, since they continue to move back and forth between the empirical chain [*chaîne*] of detailed events to the idealist flesh [*chaire*] of risky resurrections, always leaving one of these two seats vacant.

I. 'For Freud [. . .] it is a question of remembering [*rémémoration*], that is, of history; he rests the scales – in which conjectures about the past make promises about the future oscillate – on the knife-edge of chronological certainties [*certitudes de date*] alone. Let's be categorical: in psychoanalytic anamnesis, what is at stake is not reality, but truth, because the effect of full speech is to reorder past contingencies by conferring on them the sense of necessities to come, such as they are constituted by the scant freedom through which the subject makes them present.'[51][42]

It follows from this that history has to acknowledge:

(a) the knife of chronological certainties, certainties of date; this is the intolerable point of reality that history (of the subject) cannot do without, and the only meaning that the word reality should henceforth receive: a kernel of the impossible, according to Lacan's expression, i.e. the empirical minimum, which, as it is the minimum, is itself not even empirical (that the head of Louis XVI was cut off is indeed a fact, a real, but to know what this willed and meant it is not the order of reality, but of truth).[52]

(b) that this dimensionless knife can assign no date unless the fact produced is already submitted to primary historicization: 'the events are engendered in a primal historicization – in other words, history is already being made on the stage where it will be played out once it has been written down, both in one's heart of hearts and outside.'[53]

(c) that the conjectures of a conscious discourse upon a past that is already by itself historical cannot but be the work of a secondary historicization, one that needs to constitute the first history retrospectively by undertaking, with what is left of it, the distortions that are necessary to maintain a discourse stitched up with lies or blank spaces.[54]

---

51   Lacan, 'The Function and Field of Speech and Language in Psychoanalysis' [1953], *Ecrits*, 256/213.
52   'History [. . .] constitutes the emergence of the truth in reality [*dans le réel*]' (Lacan, *Ecrits*, 257/214).
53   TN: Lacan, *Ecrits*, 261/216; Regnault's original French citation includes an error, replacing Lacan's 'the events' with 'the elements'.
54   Unless one wants to understand nothing of it, one should not consider our order of

II. Therapeutic and scientific work consist in unstitching the secondary distortions that have persisted under [psychic] censorship, and which are nourished negatively by it during the perfecting of the 'current historicization [*historisation actuelle*]', which consists in saying to the subject not 'your unconscious was in reality your history', but instead that '*your "history"* was, in truth, *the unconscious*'. In this sense, primary historicization finds its place after secondary historicization. We have thus taken advantage of the subject's modicum of freedom in order to make the knife vacillate, and to substitute, for the contorting historicization of conscious discourse, true history – the true history which, by leading this discourse back to its alleged origins, is the only one able to rid the stitched-up narrative of its distortions, hems and hitches, and to 'reorder past contingencies by giving them the sense of necessities to come.' [43]

III. It is necessary to apply the preceding [operation] to History. 'Apply' is a bad word, because the structure here is the same, and there is no reason that any agency [*instance*] should be inscribed in this play of historicizations and retrospections that might be pertinent enough to allow an individual aspect of this play to be distinguished from a collective one. The unconscious, as is well known, is no more collective for Freud than it is for Marx, and the categories of individual and society should be left here to the false questioning of romantic sociologists. Nevertheless, it is fully legitimate to invoke here the whole problematic of 'coming-to-consciousness' [*prise de conscience*] according to Marx who, in the Preface to the *Contribution to Political Economy*, lets it run its course, without guiding or swelling it, t   ,ugh the channels and dikes [*digues*] of the mode of production – as when i.. speaks about the 'ideological forms under which men assume consciousness' of the conflict between productive forces and the relations of production, and demands that we carefully distinguish these forms from the science of this conflict (and we might add: and also, from the science of these forms).[55]

IV. The preceding must be applied with all the more reason to politics, which, as action, presupposes a freedom and an end, and which more than anything else makes the truth emerge in the real.

Now these considerations of ends and tasks to be accomplished receive their theoretical status when we say that secondary historicization has first of all

---

exposition as itself historical. [It's a matter of] the time, if you like, of knowing. [*Temps, si l'on veut, du savoir*].

55   One could connect Marx's phrase 'Mankind always sets itself only such tasks as it can solve' to Lacan's phrase, cited above, concerning the freedom of the subject between past contingencies and necessities to come. This in-betweenness [*entre-deux*] of the subject is the place that remains to it for becoming conscious of a task, with the help of science.

the function *in actu* [*en acte*] of an *ideal* (and following Kant one could say: of an imperative, for this is what defines political action as 'practical'). This is the role, as Lacan says, played by the 'supposed laws of history' insofar as they are eminently progressivist and give to history the biological form of the development of a seed, for one does not escape this geneticism when representing history as task or ideal. To this project – for it is one – Bossuet and Comte equally conspire, as does the Marx of 'coming to consciousness', along with every politician *by necessity*, including Machiavelli himself. Witness this text from the *Discorsi*:

> I repeat therefore that, as an incontestable truth to which history as a whole bears witness, men may second their fortune, but cannot oppose it; may follow the weave of its thread, but not [44] break it. I do not believe for all that they should give up. Though they know not the end, and move towards it along obscure paths and deviations, there is always hope; and from this hope, they should draw the strength to never give up, no matter what the misfortune and misery in which they might find themselves.[56]

However, applying again the principles outlined above, we should add the following: secondary historicization is not science, and whoever has a science of history or a science of semblance [*d'un semblant*] must go further and lead the censored ideas (all the stronger for being censored) of subjects and peoples back to the primary historicization, so as to rub out [*biffer*] the primitive trauma and obtain cures in analysis and history. For whoever speaks only of progress, for whom progress applies as if to an embryo, wants neither to change nor to be cured.

We can then thus establish a principled difference between authors of secondary historicization and those of science (possible or real), that is, at bottom those of primary historicization, of history without censorship or distortion. To the side of the deceitful chatter that normally occupies the centre of our attention, there must be a place, an ambiguous and vacillating place, both for historians of the primary [historicization] and for scientists [*savants*], scientists capable of pushing as far as the complete undoing of the official pages [of history] and of demolishing the machines of consciousness. This co-incidence can only take place in history. In saying that Machiavelli is both beyond the break and yet only ventures a few steps, I do not mean to give him any other place than this one, which is unstable but leaves no seat vacant for the established historians.

---

56   TN: Machiavelli, *Discourses*, Book II: 29, trans. Leslie Walker, ed. Bernard Crick [1970] (London: Penguin, 2003), 372tm. 'Fortune blinds Men's Minds when she does not wish them to obstruct her Designs' (368).

A) The 'secondary' historians of classical times are those who have cast a cloud or veil over the prince's usurpation and who, concealing the fact that primitive traumas had already been historical events (and not origins without tears), sketch out a continuous and progressive history. This genre of history perhaps began when Polybius (who Machiavelli had read) said in the Preface of the first book [of his *Histories*]:

> Just as Fortune made almost all the affairs of the world incline in one direction, and forced them to converge upon one and the same point; so it is my task as a historian to put before my readers a single point of view of the means by which she has brought about the execution of her design. It was this peculiarity which originally determined me on undertaking this work. Another reason was that I had seen that nobody of our time had taken up the task of writing a universal history [. . .]. No one as far as I knew, who by assembling all the facts and setting out their order, had gone to the trouble of making us see the beginning, the motifs, and their conclusion.[57] [45]

This genre continues when Bossuet divides into epochs a Universal History monarchized to the core. Historians of progress, of the ideal, and of hopes and expectations [*espérance*].

> *One day all will be well, this is our hope*
> *All is well today, that is the illusion,*

says Voltaire,[58] another progressivist historian, failing to see that [*méconnaissant que*] he says in two lines the same thing twice, for if 'one day . . ', why not 'today'?

Machiavelli also sometimes has recourse to this genre of history when he wants to encourage, reassure and, simultaneously, deceive. The unessential side of Machiavelli.

We can now, by differentiating them, deduce the principal respective discordances in this concert between Descartes and Machiavelli.

B) Descartes, one will recall, remains within the limits of classicism, but sometimes ventures right up to them. Consequently, he rarely proceeds to secondary historicizations other than negatively, in the form of a denegation. To put it another way, he declares two things:

---

57   TN: *The Histories of Polybius*, vol. 1, trans. E.S. Shuckburgh (London: Macmillan, 1889), 4.

58   Voltaire, 'Poème sur le désastre de Lisbonne, ou examen de cet axiome "Tout est bien"', online at http://www.voltaire-integral.com/Html/09/13_Lisbonne.html.

– the prince himself is the author of the legitimacy of his taking power, which properly designates the primary historicization that cannot but define every event – as Lacan says, any assumed instinctual stage is before all else a historical stigmata:[59] 'a page of shame that one forgets or undoes, or a page of glory that obliges'. This applies to the prince, who is immediately his own historian.

– consequently nobody can gossip about the prince, which serves right away to veil his primary historicization under a cloak of illegibility, to which one cannot even impute any dissimulation: the King is naked, but nobody sees it, and nobody sees the cloak either. A Bossuet weaves more ample ornaments around the actions of princes. He turns them into epochs. For Descartes, there is therefore no History, as what is primary is the affair of princes, who are better placed than us, and as what is secondary is whatever suffices to wreath what is primary in smoke. This absence of history is due to the fact that the truth cannot be explained in words: what is evident [*l'évidence*] evades historicization. [**46**]

C) As for Machiavelli, he spent his time reading Livy, i.e. reviewing the origins before they were sewn up (and little matter that here Rome serves as the figure of the origin). Machiavelli is the one who bears [*qui porte*] the efficacy of the unconscious as much with respect to seizures of power in the past as to the powers to be seized one day – to be seized soon. He is to be counted among the historians who perform a renewal or a 'leading back' [*reconduction*], a role which is similar to that of the analyst. He is on both the side of the ideal and of progress. 'On both sides', as two texts attest:

1. The first chapter of Book III of the *Discorsi*[60] is entitled: 'In order that a religious institution or a state should long survive, it is essential that it should frequently be restored to its original principles'. Machiavelli explains therein that the function of this return to origins is to re-consolidate a power: 'it is desirable that there ought to elapse at most ten years between these great actions [*grand coups*] [that suddenly recall one back to the origins], because by this time men begin to the change their habits and break the law [*user les lois*]'.[61] Such is the progress of secondary historicization. It is therefore necessary to undo it and return to the origins, either because events oblige it, or because one decides it for oneself: this decision can then take the symbolic form of a 'recapture [*rattrapage*] of the State':

---

59   Lacan, 'Function and Field', *Ecrits*, 261/217.
60   Louis Althusser was able to extract this chapter from the constraints of its Livian context.
61   TN: Machiavelli, *Discourses*, III:1 [Crick ed.: 388].

The magistrates who governed Florence from 1434 to 1494 used to say that it was necessary to 'reconstitute power' every five years; otherwise it was difficult to maintain it. Now, by 'reconstituting power' they meant re-instilling men with that terror and that fear which they had instilled when they first assumed power, and chastising those who, according to their principles, had behaved as bad citizens. But as the remembrance of this chastisement disappears, men are emboldened to try something fresh and to talk sedition. Hence provision has of necessity to be made against this by restoring that government to what it was at its origins.[62]

(When Machiavelli himself, prince of science, undertakes this procession back towards the origins, it is not by chance that he celebrates it with some adornment:

When evening comes [47] I return home and go into my study, and at the door I take off my daytime dress covered in mud and dirt, and put on royal and curial robes; and then decently attired I enter the courts of the ancients. Affectionately greeted by them, I partake of that food which is mine par excellence and for which I was born. There, where I am not ashamed to talk with them and inquire the reasons of their actions; and they out of their human kindness answer me. And, for the duration of four hours I feel no worry of any kind, I forget all my troubles, I stop dreading poverty, and death itself ceases to frighten me.[63] And because Dante says that it is not science unless one retains what one has understood, I noted down from these conversations what I believed was essential, and composed a short work *De principatibus*, where I excavate to the best of my power the problems posed by such a subject: what is sovereignty, how many species of it are there, how one acquires it, how one keeps it, how one loses it.[64]

This is a letter that locates secondary historicization (the stripping away of mud and dirt), the return to primary historicization (the dialogue with the dead), and the moment of science, with its 'time for comprehending' and its 'moment for concluding').[65]

2. But one can also carry out this return to principles in a fashion other than symbolic, by having recourse to the *virtù* of the single citizen. And then it is no

---

62   TN: *Discourses*, III:1 [Crick ed.: 388].

63   TN: The standard English translation has 'I give myself up entirely to them' here; cf. Crick, 'Introduction', *Discourses*, Crick ed., 71. See following note.

64   Machiavelli, Letter to Francesco Vettori, [10 December] 1513. TN: What is presented here is a translation that stays close to Regnault's French citation (of a text originally in Italian); for an alternative English translation of the letter, see Roberto Ridolfi, *Life of Niccolò Machiavelli*, trans. Cecil Grayson (London: Routledge and Kegan Paul, 1963), 151–152, cited in Crick's introduction to Machiavelli, *Discourses*, 71.

65   TN: For Lacan's distinction between the 'time for comprehending' and the 'moment of concluding', see his 'Logical Time and the Assertion of Anticipated Certainty', *Ecrits*, 209/171.

longer about leading back, but about establishing or instituting. This is what is foreseen in the chapter cited above, but also by the entire conclusion to *The Prince*, which calls upon Laurent de Medici, or any X, to introduce into the matter of history a form that is proper to it, and to lift the curtain on novelty. Novelty being marked as follows: 'Besides this, we now see here extraordinary, unprecedented signs brought about by God: the sea has opened up; a cloud has shown you the path; the rock has poured water forth; here manna has rained; everything has converged for your greatness. The rest you must do yourself.'[66] The rest – let us understand historical experimental science, which Laurent will hasten to miss, and whose banner Machiavelli alone brandishes. The scales that made the exile of San Casciano into a solitary victor, and the Prince of the Medicis [48] into the representative of all the setbacks[67] suffered by an Italy that was about to be tamed by the European powers, rests on nothing but the double-edged blade of the return to origins. For if to return to them is to shore up one's power, then victory will go to whoever returns first. But whoever returns has perhaps already been back several times before. Thus, in its great regular Orders, and in the conversion it performs on itself with Saint Francis and Saint Dominic, Machiavelli explains, the Church shores up an old power, one that operates through the confessional, wherein the word is spread that those who govern are good. So the rest that is still to be done is clear: it involves making someone who never passed through the origins to go back to them – a process that will require that this person undo all that has covered them over. *The Prince* has the precise function of developing this second possibility of the return to principles, now confided to the sole *virtù* of the innovator.

Further on in the chapter of the *Discorsi* on origins we read: 'it is as the physicians say, when talking of the human body: *Quod quotidie aggregatur aliquid,*

---

66   *The Prince*, chapter XXVI [Bull trans., 83].

67   In this sense Georges Mounin is right to call Machiavelli an 'unarmed prophet' (Mounin, *Machiavel* [Paris: Seuil, 1958], 202). Mounin's *Machiavelli* does a good job of cleaning-up and leading us back to Machiavelli. Unfortunately, Mounin's thesis that, since he is ignorant of economics (which is true), Machiavelli is neither a precursor nor a founder of Marx's science, seems to us insufficient to contest Machiavelli's materialism when it comes to history, which we have tried to establish. This is because Mounin holds that 'both before and after Machiavelli, there have always been two solutions, equally metaphysical and eternal', namely the compatibility or incompatibility of morality and politics. I think that Machiavelli is *beyond* the debate between these two terms, terms which, if separated, are reconciled, and if reconciled, break apart. The relation between morality and politics is precisely a non-problem for Machiavelli and no doubt a non-problem *tout court*. All the 'baggage' that is dragged along by the name of Machiavellianism is nothing more than the reinscription, within public discourse, of an innovation that has nothing to do with it. Elsewhere, Mounin adds (cf. 224–225) that this opposition, before being philosophical, is to be found first of all in the facts. This is to adopt the realism of 'the thing before the word', of 'the thing without words'. An eternal mirror! One day, some Archimedes of language will write, rather forcefully: 'show me a death without words [*une mort sans phrase*], and I will believe in reality.' But this Archimedes has already come.

quod quandoque indiget curatione [Every day it absorbs something which from time to time needs treatment].'[68]

The body – whether that of a patient or of the corpus of history – is thus the historicized thing from which, in order to treat it, one must remove what it has secreted, and add whatever will revive it. [49]

Where Descartes' medicine is content (less and less towards the end, it's true) with nature and its mechanical exercise, Machiavelli already perceived origins and retrospection.

If it is a nature, it is no longer an origin, and if it is an origin, it is a historicization. In nature, the one which Grace visits, and in the name of which Descartes proclaims 'let the prince do what he wants, let him pass', Machiavelli already saw the throne of usurpation; there is no throne that is not already usurped, and no nature whose chatter does not seek to justify it and itself.

Off to the side of Descartes and Machiavelli, and off to the side of the question, there are historians of the ideal and of germination. Between Descartes and Machiavelli, there is this misunderstanding: the former's suspension of judgment makes him misunderstand the Discourses that the latter puts forward on the proper names past and present that are inscribed or repeated in the contorted book [*le livre distordu*]. These exemplary proper names[69] make clear the refusal of subsumptions, which I have termed materialism, and surround themselves with justifications, and it belongs to one of them, 'Machiavelli', inscribed in the margin, to lead them back to their original inscription, who thereby risks reinforcing the trace of the name as much as he risks crossing it out forever. It is a work of dehistoricization, which clears a place for historical science, but remains on its threshold.

For, of a science, there is no historicization but rather a historicity.[70] [50]

PART TWO: LATENT DISCOURSE[71]

Let us now move the reader out of the way of the mild delirium that looms before us. In what way will he understand the fact that, while all that can be expected of Descartes is a strategy, nevertheless those who attribute to him a politics '*indigent curatione*' [are needing treatment], i.e. are in need of cure and leading back [*reconduction*]? A cure is what Elisabeth requested from Descartes:

---

68   TN: Machiavelli, *Discourses*, III:1 [Crick ed.: 386].

69   We should refer back to the start of the *Eighteenth Brumaire of Louis Bonaparte*, where Marx begins his calculations on classes on the basis of substitutions of proper names operated by the revolutions of Cromwell, 1789 and 1848 (Marx, *Eighteenth Brumaire* [1852], chapter 1). This is how one writes History.

70   The concept of which is to be constructed. Cf. Althusser, *Lire le Capital*, vol. 2 (Paris: Maspéro, 1965), 58ff.

71   First read the four letters that follow [i.e. the letters of Descartes and Elisabeth published as CpA 6.3].

'They promise me that in Germany I will have enough leisure to study it (your method), and I will not bring there any greater treasure, from which I hope to take more satisfaction, than your writings. I hope you will permit me to take the work on the *passions*, even though it was not able to calm those that the last piece of misfortune has excited. It must be that your presence brought the cure to them, since neither your maxims nor my reasoning had been able to' (letter of July 1646).[72] Cure in the sense that one might take the waters; but what is this 'last piece of misfortune'?

In 1680 Elisabeth died, shrouded in devotion, as an Abbess at the Lutheran monastery of Herford: shrouded from every clear idea, and filled [*assombrie*] with gloom by an 'entourage of people whose melancholic devotion she suffered as a martyrdom'. Had she forgotten the mechanics on the basis of which the man who had left her thirty years previously, had for her dismantled this melancholy?

For *then* [*ensuite*], in 1650, he died, far from her, close to a reigning Queen, and because she was an early-rising Queen [*une Reine matinale*[73]]: he to whom she had said, 'it must be that your presence brought the cure, since neither your maxims nor my reasoning had been able to.' Her transference onto him of all that the caresses of those who surrounded her, by dint of proliferating, had deprived her – for thirty years, 'keeping all these things in her heart', she would have to apply this transference to her own reason, the only possession [*bien*] which, being the best distributed,[74] was left to her of a dead man.

For *then*, returning to that year of 1646 when she would come to miss without recourse this presence, did she not hand [**51**] her cure over to those miraculous fountains he had told her about at The Hague? They would be, these fountains, so many figures, ciphers, landmarks or rings, which would recall her to the past order of reasons, but without being able to take their place, in the philosopher's absence.[75]

This is why, in that letter of 10 December 1646, which is an abridged account of her whole life, the Princess will proceed by leaps and gaps, and by jumping from one subject to another: the whole of her life of exile and her resentment over her usurped throne she would condense in the figure of Machiavelli, and the role of Doctor of Princes she would displace onto Descartes, the philosopher: 'I find that the rule you observe in his preface is false because

---

72   TN: *Correspondence*, AT 4: 449; CpA 6.3:52.

73   TN: This is a reference to the suggestion that Descartes' death of pneumonia, in Stockholm in February 1650, might have been brought on by his obligation to teach his employer Queen Christina early in the morning.

74   TN: an echo of the famous opening of Descartes' *Discourse on Method*: '*Le bon sens est la chose du monde la mieux partagée*'.

75   TN: '*Ce seraient, ces fontaines, comme autant de chiffres, de jalons, d'anneaux qui la rappelleraient à l'ordre des raisons passé, mais n'en pourraient tenir lieu, le philosophe vacant.*'

the author has never known a person who sees clearly all that he sets about doing, as you do, and who by consequence, in private and retired from the confusion of the world, would nevertheless be capable of teaching princes how they should govern, as seems to be the case from what you have written.'[76] And with this reiterated epistolary transference, she moves on to the fountain at The Hague, which, in the remainder of the letter (of 10 October 1646) causes her reason to wobble, despite appearances: this clear and distinct water is reputed for its purgative properties, but it is also a white water, mixed with milk, 'said to be refreshing', which will triumph over her on her last day. What weight would tip the scales to the side of clarity? How to settle the equivocation? Everything here, even the cipher or coded message [*chiffre*] she evokes at the end, attests to her need to know more about he history.[77]

And now here he is, who was to meet her arbitrary message with an arbitrary response, and who, subjecting her demands to secondary historicization, takes up her own weapon against Machiavelli, to accuse him of improperly generalizing from examples (Cesare Borgia). Then, reinforcing in his response the hiatus of a sudden change of subject with an 'also' that lays it bare ('Your Highness has also noted very well the secret of the miraculous fountain' [November 1646]), he will take up the said Fountain and invent, regarding it, a rapid and mechanical alchemy. The strangest thing about this letter is that he rivals her credulity, since he produces on this occasion a text so out of the ordinary that Martial Gueroult could not resist citing it in a brief biography of Descartes: 'I even dare to think that interior joy has some secret power to make Fortune more favourable.'[78]

Does this invitation to make do without him, all reason drained [*toute raison bue*], and to take her chances at the roulette of Fortune, not resolve a more secret drama? Definitely – [it resolves] the misunderstanding between Descartes and Machiavelli, through Elisabeth's [52] intervention, wheeling around the *Discourses* of the two Others. Even more definitely, [it refers to] the crime that was the occasion for her inviting Descartes to read Machiavelli, and which she calls 'our last piece of misfortune' in the July letter. As Baillet tells us, 'at the time a rumour spread that a very dark act had been perpetrated on the advice of Princess Elisabeth.' This dark act was the murder by Philippe, her brother, of [François] de l'Espinay for having 'cajoled' their sister Louise:

---

76   TN: *Correspondence*, 10 October 1646, 146.

77   TN: '*Il n'est pas jusqu'à ce chiffre allégué dans la fin qui ne marque sa demande à en savoir plus long sur son histoire.*' This may be an echo of the reference to a secret code or cipher in Elisabeth's letter of 10 October 1646, AT 4: 542; CpA 6.3:59.

78   Descartes, letter of November 1646, cited by Martial Gueroult in the *Dictionnaire des auteurs* (Laffont: Bompiani, 1964); the rest of the letter, on the play of chance, should also be read. TN: Regnault writes 'joie extérieur' instead of 'joie intérieure', as the letter itself has it; the passage is printed correctly at CpA 6.3:60.

'Princess Elisabeth, her elder sister, who is a virtuous girl, who is so well educated and who is more shapely than her sister, cannot endure the fact that the Queen her mother sees in a good light a man (l'Espinay) who had made such a great affront to their house. She incited her brothers against him; [. . .] the youngest of them, named Philippe, harboured the deepest resentment of this injury, and one evening, near the place in The Hague where one went out for a walk, he attacked Espinay.'[79] Another day, Louise's lover was killed in Philippe's presence. Elisabeth and Philippe were then driven away from Holland by their mother.

Now, if a repressed Machiavelli returns to Elisabeth at this moment, was this not so that she could reread in him the authorization to get rid of scoundrels, and to put in her brother's hands the task of avenging less their sister's liaison than the flippancy of the Queen of Bohemia (who was well pleased, so the story goes, that her daughter Louise had been enjoying herself), their mother, who was undeserving of the throne, and so to make of her brother a new Prince, an Orestes who might exorcise [conjurât] the crucial image of her dethroned Father?

But the fountains of science were not to flow again for her Highness, who could do no more than bequeath her House to speculative philosophy, and her Oedipus to the cloister. The pot of history would have to simmer some more, cooked by Freud with his cure, and Marx with his mandrake.[80]

---

79   Tallement des Réaux, Historiettes, and AT 4: 450.

80   TN: 'Il faudrait qu'il en cuisît encore à l'Histoire, Freud de sa cure, Marx de sa mandragore.' This may be a reference to Machiavelli's play La Mandragola [The Mandrake], published in 1524.

Appendix: The *Cahiers pour l'Analyse* (1966–69), Tables of Contents

Article 2   **André Green:** L'Objet (a) de Jacques Lacan, sa logique et la théorie freudienne

Article 3   **Luce Irigaray:** Communications linguistique et spéculaire (Modèles génétiques et modèles pathologiques)

Article 4   **Xavier Audouard:** Le Simulacre

Article 5   **Jean-Claude Milner:** Le Point du signifiant

Article 6   **Serge Leclaire:** Compter avec la psychanalyse (Séminaire de l'ENS, 1965–66)

VOLUME 4: *LÉVI-STRAUSS DANS LE DIX-HUITIÈME SIÈCLE*
PUBLISHED SEPTEMBER–OCTOBER 1966.

Introduction   **Jacques Derrida:** Avertissement

Article 1   **Jacques Derrida:** Nature, Culture, Ecriture (de Lévi-Strauss à Rousseau)

Article 2   **Jean Mosconi:** Sur la théorie du devenir de l'entendement

VOLUME 5: *PONCTUATION DE FREUD*
PUBLISHED NOVEMBER–DECEMBER 1966.

Introduction   **Jacques-Alain Miller:** Avertissement: Concept de la ponctuation

Article 1   **Serge Leclaire:** Les Éléments en jeu dans une psychanalyse (à propos de l'Homme aux loups)

Article 2   **Michel Tort:** Le Concept freudien de 'Représentant'

Article 3   **Daniel Paul Schreber:** *Mémoires d'un névropathe* [1903; extract translated by Paul Duquenne].

VOLUME 6: *LA POLITIQUE DES PHILOSOPHES*
PUBLISHED JANUARY–FEBRUARY 1967.

Introduction   **François Regnault:** Avertissement: Politique de la lecture

Article 1   **Martial Gueroult:** Nature humaine et état de nature chez Rousseau, Kant et Fichte

Article 2   **François Regnault:** La Pensée du prince (Descartes et Machiavel)

Article 3   **Descartes et Elisabeth:** Quatre lettres sur Machiavel

Article 4   **Machiavel:** Le Retour aux origines (Pour qu'une religion et un état obtiennent une longue existence, ils doivent souvent être ramenés à leur principe; *Discorsi*, III, 1)

Article 5   **Bernard Pautrat:** Du Sujet politique et de ses intérêts: Note sur la théorie humienne de l'autorité

Article 3   **Cercle d'Épistémologie:** Nouvelles questions
Article 4   **François Regnault:** Dialectique d'épistémologies
Article 5   **Thomas Herbert:** Pour une théorie générale des idéologies
Article 6   **Jacques-Alain Miller:** Action de la structure
Article 7   **Antoine Culioli:** La Formalisation en linguistique
Article 8   **Alain Badiou:** La Subversion infinitésimale
Article 9   **Judith Miller:** Métaphysique de la physique de Galilée
Article 10   **Jacques Nassif:** Freud et la science
Article 11   [Unsigned]: Chimie de la Raison: Préambule
Article 12   **Antoine Lavoisier:** 'Discours préliminaire' au *Traité élémentaire de Chimie*
Article 13   **François Dagognet:** Sur Lavoisier
Article 14   **Dmitri Mendéléeff:** Similitude des éléments et loi périodique
Article 15   **Gaston Bachelard:** La Classification des éléments d'après Mendéléeff
Article 16   **Jean le Rond d'Alembert:** Éléments des sciences
Article 17   **Georges Cuvier:**   ɔgrès des sciences

VOLUME 10: *LA FORMALISATION*
PUBLISHED WINTER 1969.

Article 1   **Jacques Brunschwig:** La Proposition particulière chez Aristote
Article 2   **George Boole:** L'Analyse mathématique de la logique
Article 3   **Georg Cantor:** Fondements d'une théorie générale des ensembles
Article 4   **Bertrand Russell:** La Théorie des types logiques
Article 5   **Kurt Gödel:** La Logique mathématique de Russell
Article 6   **Jean Ladrière:** Le Théorème de Löwenheim-Skolem
Article 7   **Robert Blanché:** Sur le système des connecteurs interpropositionnels
Article 8   **Alain Badiou:** Marque et manque: à propos du zéro
Article 9   **Jacques Bouveresse:** Philosophie des mathématiques et thérapeutique d'une maladie philosophique: Wittgenstein et la critique de l'apparence 'ontologique' dans les mathématiques